The Church and Her Scriptures

The Church and Her Scriptures

—— *Essays in Honor of Patrick J. Hartin* ——

EDITED BY

Catherine Brown Tkacz
AND Douglas Kries

PICKWICK *Publications* · Eugene, Oregon

THE CHURCH AND HER SCRIPTURES
Essays in Honor of Patrick J. Hartin

Pickwick Publications
An Imprint of Wipf and Stock Publishers
199 W. 8th Ave., Suite 3
Eugene, OR 97401

www.wipfandstock.com

PAPERBACK ISBN: 978-1-6667-1282-7
HARDCOVER ISBN: 978-1-6667-1283-4
EBOOK ISBN: 978-1-6667-1284-1

Cataloguing-in-Publication data:

Names: Tkacz, Catherine Brown, editor. | Kries, Douglas, editor.

Title: The Church and her Scriptures : essays in honor of Patrick J. Hartin / edited by Catherine Brown Tkacz and Douglas Kries

Description: Eugene, OR: Pickwick Publications, 2022 | Includes bibliographical references.

Identifiers: ISBN 978-1-6667-1282-7 (paperback) | ISBN 978-1-6667-1283-4 (hardcover) | ISBN 978-1-6667-1284-1 (ebook)

Subjects: LCSH: Bible—Study and teaching. | Bible—Theology. | Hartin, P. J. (Patrick J.)

Classification: BS476 C487 2022 (print) | BS476 (ebook)

03/16/22

Contents

Contributors

Sebastian P. Brock, the foremost scholar in Syriac language today, is a Fellow of the British Academy, Emeritus Reader in Syriac Studies at Oxford University, and Emeritus Fellow at Wolfson College, Oxford. Initially an expert in Septuagint textual studies, he moved into wide-ranging projects in Syriac, editing several unpublished texts and analyzing Syriac dialogic poems, for instance. His numerous books include *The Luminous Eye: The Spiritual World Vision of St. Ephrem* (1992), *Fire from Heaven: Studies in Syriac Theology and Liturgy* (2006), and *Treasure-house of Mysteries: Explorations of the Sacred Text through Poetry in the Syriac Tradition* (2012). The prestigious École Pratique des Hautes Études in Paris bestowed on him the PhD *honoris causa*; the British Academy awarded him the Leverhulme Medal and Prize (2009).

Sr. Sara Butler, STL, PhD, is a member of the Missionaries of Service of the Most Blessed Trinity and Professor Emerita of Dogmatic Theology at the University of St. Mary of the Lake, Mundelein, Illinois. Her scholarly interests center on the place of women in the Church and the doctrine of Holy Orders. Her publications include *The Catholic Priesthood and Women: A Guide to the Church's Teaching* and essays on deaconesses, women's religious life, Mariology, and ecclesiology. She has served on the International Anglican-Roman Catholic Commission, the International Theological Commission, the U.S. Bishops' Committee on Doctrine (as consultant), and as President of the Academy of Catholic Theology.

Michael Cameron earned the PhD from the University of Chicago and is Professor of Historical Theology at the University of Portland. He is the author of *Christ Meets Me Everywhere: Augustine's Early Figurative Exegesis* (Oxford, 2012), *The Essential Expositions of the Psalms by Saint Augustine*

(New City Press, 2015), *Unfolding Sacred Scripture: How Catholics Read the Bible* (Archdiocese of Chicago: Liturgy Training Publications, 2015), and many essays on Augustine's use of the Bible. He was Latin Patristics editor for the first sixteen volumes of *The Encyclopedia of the Bible and Its Reception* (De Gruyter, 2009–). Currently he serves on the editorial boards of *Augustinian Studies* and the *Augustinus-Lexikon*.

Patrick J. Hartin is the honoree of this volume. He holds two doctorates in biblical studies and ethics and has been tenured at three universities—one in the United States and two in his native South Africa. Fr. Hartin's work is discussed in the introduction of this volume and his many books and essays are listed in a bibliography at the end of the book. He is an expert on many subjects, but especially on the Letter of James.

Douglas Kries received his doctorate in theology from Boston College and is now Professor of Philosophy at Gonzaga University, where he has been a colleague of Fr. Hartin for many years. His research is in the area of medieval political philosophy generally and he publishes especially on the political thought of St. Augustine. Among his works are *The Problem of Natural Law* and (with Ernest L. Fortin and Michael W. Tkacz) *Augustine: Political Writings*. Currently he is at work on a monograph on Robert Bellarmine. He has previously collaborated with Catherine Brown Tkacz as co-editor of *Nova Doctrina Vetusque: Essays on Early Christianity in Honor of Fredric W. Schlatter, S.J.*

Richard J. Ounsworth, OP, joined the Order of Preachers in 1995 and was ordained priest in 2001. He then studied theology at Oxford and served as University chaplain in Leicester. He returned to Oxford in 2005, completing his doctorate on the Letter to the Hebrews. Since 2003, he has been tutor and lector in Biblical Studies and New Testament Greek at Blackfriars, Oxford. He is the author of *Joshua Typology in the New Testament* and co-author of *When the Son of Man Didn't Come*. He is also co-editor and translator of *A Perfect Priest: Studies in the Letter to the Hebrews*.

Patrick Henry Reardon, an Orthodox priest in Chicago, is a Senior Editor of *Touchstone: A Journal of Mere Christianity*. His sermons are a weekly feature on Ancient Faith Radio, and he is the author of *Christ in the Psalms*, *Reclaiming the Atonement*, *The Jesus We Missed*, *Christ in His Saints*, and commentaries on Genesis, Numbers, Chronicles, Job, Sirach, Romans, and Revelation. His articles have appeared in such journals as *The Scottish Journal of Theology*, *The Catholic Biblical Quarterly*, *Pro Ecclesia*, and *St. Vladimir's Theological Quarterly*.

Jeanne-Nicole Mellon Saint-Laurent is Associate Professor of Historical Theology and Syriac Patristics at Marquette University. She studied with Fr. Patrick Hartin at Gonzaga University as an undergraduate and then took advanced degrees from the University of Notre Dame and from Brown. Her publications include *Missionary Stories and the Formation of the Syriac Churches* and *History of Mar Behnam and Sarah: Martyrdom and Monasticism in Medieval Iraq*.

Anna M. Silvas, of University of New England in Armidale, New South Wales, Australia, has invested much of her scholarship in St. Basil the Great and St. Gregory of Nyssa, culminating in *The Questions of the Brothers,* the first edition of the Syriac translation of Basil's *Small Asketikon.* The influential sister of those saints Silvas has also treated in *Macrina the Younger: Philosopher of God*; related is her essay "Kassia the Melodist (ca. 810–ca. 865) and Her Use of the Scriptures" in *The Early Middle Ages* (edited by Consolino and Herrin). More recently she has published the fruit of her years lecturing at the John Paul II Institute in Melbourne: *The Mystery of Christian Marriage: The Scriptures and the First Thousand Years.*

Catherine Brown Tkacz was the first woman to earn the PhD in Medieval Studies at the University of Notre Dame. After managing the *Oxford Dictionary of Byzantium* project at Dumbarton Oaks and working for the National Endowment for the Humanities, she focused on biblical studies and theology. She has lectured at Oxford and Mannheim and, is, on a recurring basis, Visiting Research Professor of Theology at the Ukrainian Catholic University in L'viv. Among her over 130 publications are several on the history of deaconesses and a forthcoming book, her fourth: *Women as Types of Christ, East and West.* Bishop Thomas Daly appointed her external faculty at Bishop White Seminary in 2015. Pope Francis has appointed her to his new commission for the study of women and the diaconate.

Thomas G. Weinandy, OFM Cap, was born in Delphos, Ohio, and entered the Franciscan Capuchin Order in 1968, receiving ordination in 1972. He earned his Doctorate in Historical Theology at King's College, University of London, and has since taught in a number of Catholic universities in the United States. For twelve years he was the Warden of Greyfriars, Oxford, teaching history and doctrine within the Faculty of Theology at the University of Oxford. He has written or edited twenty books and published numerous articles in academic journals and edited books of essays. His latest book is *Jesus Becoming Jesus: A Theological Interpretation of the Synoptic Gospels.* He is a former member of the Vatican's International Theological Commission. Pope Francis conferred upon him the Pro Ecclesia et Pontifice Award in 2012.

Introduction

THE TITLE FOR THIS book has been chosen with care. Had we simply called it *The Church and the Scriptures*, we would have had a title for a book discussing entity A and entity B and, presumably, the nature of the relationship between the two. For readers already interested in that rather abstract question, such a title might have been suitable, but we dare think it would have been decidedly uninteresting and, more importantly, unintriguing to contemporary Catholic readers. It would not have provoked many questions.

But "her" is the proper adjective here, so that our title is *The Church and Her Scriptures*. With the word "her," we are intending to make claims and provoke reflections about the relationship between entity A and entity B. These claims are not especially novel in the history of the Catholic Church, but they are rarely emphasized in our time. By returning to earlier reflections of the Church, we are not interested in embarking upon the well-trod trope of the unhelpful effects of the rise of modern historical-critical methods for reading the Bible. Indeed, the contributors to this volume all, to one degree or another, make use of the fruits of the historical-critical approach and even practice its techniques. We do, however, think that it is crucial to raise again a set of questions that have faded into the background for many Catholics, and perhaps for almost all contemporary Christians.

What are we suggesting, then, by using one three-letter word instead of another? The singular feminine possessive adjective makes three assertions, which we will consider in reverse order. The first in order of explanation is that the Church somehow "possesses" the Scriptures, so that the Bible is not an independent, free-standing entity all by itself. How can this be? One possible implication of the term "possession" is something that one owns and that one can sell or give away or alienate from oneself. The automobiles we own are possessed in this way. If we get tired of our automobile, or if it begins to wear out, we can "trade it in" for a different one or just sell it outright. We can walk or drive away from the cars we own and never have to worry about them again. Obviously, this is *not* the sense in which the Church would possess the Bible. Another sense of possession, however, is "belonging," and this sense more accurately describes our claim: The Scriptures belong to the Church, a point our honoree discusses in his essay.[1] But the original sense of belonging was something like "being suitable for"; this sense is preserved in our expression "a sense of belonging." Thus, the Bible is suited for the Church, and in this way it belongs to the Church. When we say that we "belong" in a place or a job or a vocation, we mean that we are especially suited for the town we reside in, or the job we hold, or the family or religious order to which we belong. We are "at home" there, as it were. How is it, we will therefore need to consider, that the Bible is "at home" in the Church? How do the Scriptures "belong" there? How is the Bible the Church's "belonging" or "possession"?

The word "her" in our title is also feminine. What assertion are we making here? The practice of the Church in referring to herself as feminine is an ancient one[2] that is rooted especially in the Church's typological reading of the Song of Songs. She understands herself as "the bride of Christ" based on this manner of reading or interpreting the Bible—especially the Old Testament. But the bride of Christ has a sort of authority by means of which she may interpret the Scriptures. Particularly in the Catholic understanding of the doctrine of inspiration, it is (and was from the beginning) the Church that first receives inspiration. The Church is empowered to declare the boundaries of the canon of the Bible, of what should be deemed to be the authentic testimony that constitutes the Scriptures. It was not the case that Jesus wrote some fine books and that those books defined and instituted the Church; rather, Jesus founded or "married" a Church, the Catholics say, and the Church then produced and defined and "instituted" the Bible. The Bible thus belongs to the Church in the sense that the Bible's deepest meaning is what the Church understands and proclaims it to be. The Church is the authoritative and most profound interpreter of the Bible. St. Augustine stated this point famously in writing against

---

1. Hartin, "The Gift of *Dei Verbum*," below, esp. at the section "Both the Old and New Testaments Emerge from the Church and Belong to the Church," 30–32.

2. The Congregation for Divine Worship and the Discipline of the Sacraments explicitly affirmed this practice in *Liturgiam Authenticam*, esp. 30 and 31.d: "Insofar as possible in a given vernacular language, the use of the feminine pronoun, rather than the neuter, is to be maintained in referring to the Church."

the Manicheans: "I would not believe the gospel if the authority of the Catholic Church did not move me."[3]

Finally, the little word "her" is also singular rather than plural. The first two assertions we have written about give rise to some rather obvious potential objections about unity or singularity, for we have been speaking rather glibly of "the Church" as a unity; indeed, we have been speaking about a plural—the "Scriptures"—as a unity when we also refer to "them" as "the Bible." Despite the whole panoply of differences within the Church and within the Bible at all moments of history, the Church has always understood herself as somehow "one" and "catholic"; and it has always understood the many different books of the Scriptures, written in different genres and different languages and different times and places and even addressed to different local churches as a single "Bible." How are these many different things "one"? How can they form a unity, so that we may use a singular pronoun?

If we begin to think, then, about *The Church and Her Scriptures*, a whole set of questions—most of them first raised even as the Christian Scriptures were emerging within the Church—suddenly become urgent again. Our collection of essays all strive to show how the early Church read her Scriptures with these questions in mind. The most successful theoretical account of how to do this was probably Augustine's *De doctrina christiana*, and Augustine's attempts to understand the Bible are considered in some of the essays that follow. Our goal, however, is also to cast light on how the early Christians—those actually constituting the early Church—lived in light of their Scriptures and how they practiced the Christian faith in light of their Bible. To this end, some of the essays included here reflect on those more practical and pastoral approaches as well.

In our time, one who has practiced reading the Bible in communion with the Catholic Church most intentionally, earnestly, and generously—both in his native South Africa and in the United States—has been Fr. Patrick J. Hartin, whom we seek to honor with this volume of essays. While he has always understood the Bible as an essential unity, Fr. Hartin has been especially devoted to the study of the Letter of James. Indeed, the climax of the extensive writing part of his living the Bible is surely his *James*, published by The Liturgical Press as part of its Sacra Pagina series.[4] Although he is extremely well-versed in all of the current methods of reading the Bible, and especially the New Testament, he also advocates for the study of the

---

3. Augustine, *Answer to the Letter of Mani*, 1.5.6 (p. 236).

4. Hartin, *James*. A complete bibliography of the academic writings of Fr. Patrick J. Hartin appears below as the final section of the present volume.

Bible in the manner of the early Church, and especially for Augustine's approach to the New Testament.

Most of all, Fr. Hartin has always taken to heart James's exhortation, "Be doers of the word, and not hearers only" (Jas 1:22), and he has always accepted James's assertion—echoing Proverbs—that "God opposes the proud, but gives grace to the humble" (Jas 4:6). A native of South Africa, Fr. Hartin recalls that he was extremely pleased as a twelve-year old boy to be Catholic because of the Church's resistance to the apartheid regime. He was ordained a priest in Johannesburg in 1971 and, after studying in Italy, he taught languages and eventually became headmaster of St. Benedict's College high school. After earning two doctorates from the University of South Africa (in Ethics and in the New Testament), he taught at two of South Africa's finest universities, the University of Witwatersrand and the aforementioned University of South Africa, earning tenure at both institutions. He served the Catholic Church in South Africa not only as a teacher and scholar, but as a very successful author of religious education textbooks as well as columns and short articles aimed at adult faith formation. The opportunity to study and serve as Catholic Chaplain at Claremont McKenna College brought Fr. Hartin to the United States originally; from there he soon went to Gonzaga University where he was tenured for the third time and served for the final twenty-one years of his forty-three-year career. There he taught and wrote especially on the New Testament, but also in that University's Classical Civilizations program. During those years, he also published ten of his eighteen books. Although he retired from Gonzaga in 2016, he still teaches at St. Patrick's Seminary in Menlo Park, California, and his scholarship continues apace. He has said that what has motivated his productive academic career has been his students, his teaching, and his scholarship—in that order. He has also been active in contributing to seminaries and has ministered to several parishes within the Diocese of Spokane. With the publication of *The Church and Her Scriptures*, the Most Reverend Thomas Daly, Bishop of Spokane, and the Faith and Reason Institute at Gonzaga University extend their thanks and congratulations to Fr. Hartin for the enormous service he has rendered to the Catholic Church in Spokane.

On February 16, 2016, Fr. Hartin delivered his final public lecture as professor at Gonzaga. Sponsored by the Gonzaga Faith and Reason Institute and the Gonzaga Socratic Club, the talk addressed the principles that motivated and animated his entire career in biblical studies. He credited those principles as arising not directly from himself, however, but from Vatican II's statement on biblical interpretation, *Verbum Dei*. As a result, his lecture was devoted to commenting on that document of the Church.

This final, magisterial lecture constitutes the featured essay of *The Church and Her Scriptures*.

Inspired by Fr. Hartin's remarks, the Gonzaga Faith and Reason Institute sponsored panels of public talks devoted to the question of how the Church had read the Bible throughout its history, and especially in the period of the early Church. Scholars from Europe, North America, and Australia participated. Many of the essays in this collection originated in that cycle of lectures, which were held over a three-year period. Additional contributions to our collection have been invited from scholars of the Bible who work along the same lines as Fr. Hartin. Together, the collected essays are intended to limn and extend the "Hartinian" approach to reading the Bible with the Church, which approach has its roots in *Verbum Dei*.

As noted, in Fr. Hartin's view, reading the Bible with the Church includes paying attention to the Patristic period of biblical interpretation. Our collection begins with an examination of the rich encounter of the Syriac Church with the sacred texts. Professor Sebastian P. Brock, like Fr. Hartin, finds analogy between the multi-layered meanings of Scripture and the Incarnation of the Word of God, in which both humanity and divinity are discerned. Using a wealth of texts, including 160 sermons newly edited (2017), Brock sets forth how St. Ephrem, St. Jacob of Serugh, and St. Isaac sought to engage in transformative contemplation the symbols, mysteries, and types conveyed through the Bible, and to make this accessible to the faithful.

The deepness of the multivalent readings of the Syriac church is also the theme of our second essay, which is focused on Ephrem alone, and in particular on his writings about Mary. This essay, composed by Jeanne-Nicole Mellon Saint-Laurent, builds on Professor Block's essay, as both explore the use of symbols and icons within the exegesis of the Syrians. We are particularly pleased to include this contribution by Professor Saint-Laurent in our collection, as Fr. Hartin taught the New Testament to her in her undergraduate years at Gonzaga.

A contemporary of St. Ephrem in the fourth century was St. Macrina the Younger, who encountered the Scriptures within the Greek-speaking Church of Asia Minor. She was the older sister of Basil the Great and Gregory of Nyssa, and much of what we know of her comes through the writing of the latter. Professor Anna D. Silvas explores what is said of Macrina's experience with the Scriptures in a contribution titled "St. Macrina the Younger, the Spirit of Holiness, and the 'God-Breathed Scriptures.'" Silvas also emphasizes the richness of the interpretative approach of the early Church and its layers of meaning.

St. Macrina died in 379; six years earlier St. Augustine had read Cicero's *Hortensius*—a work which propelled him to make "some study of the Sacred

Scriptures and find what kind of books they were."[5] With the fourth and fifth essays in our collection, we turn from the Syriac and Greek churches to the Latin church and to its famous African bishop and Bible scholar. Professor Michael Cameron initiates this analysis by considering Augustine's own recounting of his early experiences of the Scriptures in the *Confessions*, which is a favorite book of Fr. Hartin precisely because of its grappling with the Bible. In his final lecture at Gonzaga, Fr. Hartin had also recommended that biblical scholars consider the work on hermeneutics of the twentieth century scholar Paul Ricoeur. Professor Cameron takes up this suggestion and attempts to show how Ricoeur's work helps to illuminate Augustine's engagement with the Bible.

Our second essay on Augustine treats the Latin exegete's first work on the New Testament, *The Lord's Sermon on the Mount*. In his commentary on James, Fr. Hartin had pointed out that the Letter of James has many connections to the Gospel of Matthew and may even contain some echoes of the Sermon on the Mount.[6] Douglas Kries's contribution to our collection takes up Augustine's treatment of the Sermon and especially Augustine's reading of the Sermon in light of the problem of warfare.

With the contribution of Richard J. Ounsworth, OP, *The Church and Her Scriptures* focuses on an important subject evident in several essays: typology, traditionally a key method for the Church's understanding of the Old Testament. Indeed, typology, or the figurative sense, enables the Church to knit the Old Testament with the New to form a single Bible. Ounsworth's treatment is comprehensive, considering even evidence from the period before the composition of the New Testament. He considers three examples in particular from the New Testament, namely the "Son of Man," Jonah, and the bronze serpent. He argues that typology, so important for Christian exegesis in the early days of the Church, remains essential in our time.

From Ounsworth's general exposition of the problem of typology or the figurative sense of Scripture, our collection turns to specific use of typology in the Gospel of Matthew. In a move that Fr. Hartin strongly approves, Catherine Brown Tkacz, a colleague of his at Bishop White Seminary, sets traditional typological interpretation in counterpoint with a close textual study of the Gospel of Matthew. Susanna's history in the Greek Book of Daniel, Tkacz shows, was the narrative template for Matthew's passion narrative, while at the same time Christ transformed Daniel's vision of the "Son of Man" into a prophetic thread running through the gospel. Thus a woman's ordeal and a

---

5. Augustine, *Confessions*, 3.5.9.

6. Hartin, *James*, esp. 67, 89, 96, 113, 119, 137, 169, and 260–61.

man's vision are complementary indications of Jesus as the Christ, a dynamic affirmation of the spiritual equality of the sexes.

Whereas the woman Susanna is focal as a prefiguration of Christ in Tkacz's scholarship, the subsequent essay in our collection concerns itself with the "women of Galilee," a group mentioned in several places in the Gospels and referring to the women who followed and ministered to Jesus and the disciples. The topic is one Fr. Hartin treated briefly in 1993.[7] The leader of these women is usually identified as Mary Magdalene. Sr. Sara Butler, MSBT, analyzes the history of the retrieval of these women, including the modern correction of longstanding misreadings in the West of the biblical texts concerning the women of Galilee and in particular of the Magdalene. Critically, she addresses the implications of the ministry of these women and the significance of recovering their example for the Church in our time.

The Church and Her Scriptures concludes with two essays on hymns. The first of these is on the Psalms, which are thought to have originally been hymns that were chanted or sung during Temple worship. In Luke 24:44, the risen Christ says that the psalms—along with the law and the prophets—are written about himself, and thus Fr. Patrick Henry Reardon titles his offering to our collection "The Christian Psalter." He notes that the book of Psalms is the mostly frequently cited Old Testament biblical book in the New Testament. He also explores the interesting ways in which the Christians understood the psalms to contain various, multiple voices attesting to Christ.

Germane to contemporary discussion of religious pluralism is the final essay, by Thomas Weinandy, OFM Cap. The Christology expressed in three hymns found in the writings of St. Paul presents the uniqueness of Jesus as universal savior and definitive Lord. Building upon the document *Dominus Iesus*, Fr. Weinandy shows that the Pauline hymns of Colossians 1:15-20, Ephesians 1:3-14, and Philippians 2:5-11 affirm that Jesus alone established a new salvific order, "for only in communion with him is one united to his Father through the indwelling of the Holy Spirit." Neatly the last two of our essays with their focus on the hymns of the Psalter and of St. Paul bring us back to the first essay after Fr. Hartin's, for Sebastian Brock draws on the hymns of the Syriac Fathers, and all these lyrics, from Old and New Testament and the Church fathers, laud the nature and generosity of God.

Consistently the essays in this festschrift express a distinctively Catholic interpretation of the Bible. This is true of those studies that concern Christians of the past, Greek, Latin, and Syriac, whose analysis and lived experience of the Scriptures informed their lives, and it is likewise true of those essays that seek now to advance such analysis "for the sake of our

---

7. Hartin, "Women Disciples in Mark's Narrative."

salvation" (*Dei Verbum* 11b). This is the hallmark of the teaching, preaching, and scholarship of Fr. Patrick Hartin, whose life has been devoted to the Church and her Scriptures.

Feast of Saint Mary Magdalene,
Apostle to the Apostles
July 22, 2021

Bibliography

Augustine, St. *Answer to the Letter of Mani Known as* The Foundation. In *The Manichean Debate*, translated by Roland Teske. The Works of Saint Augustine I/19. Hyde Park, NY: New City, 2006.

———. *Confessions*. Edited by Michael P. Foley, translated by F. J. Sheed. Indianapolis: Hackett, 2006.

Congregation for Divine Worship and the Discipline of the Sacraments. Fifth Instruction. "*Liturgiam Authenticam*: On the use of vernacular languages in the publication of the books of the Roman Liturgy." March 28, 2001. https://www.vatican.va/roman_curia/congregations/ccdds/documents/rc_con_ccdds_doc_20010507_liturgiam-authenticam_en.html.

Hartin, Patrick J. "The Gift of *Dei Verbum*." In the present volume.

———. *James*. Edited by Daniel J. Harrington. Sacra Pagina 14. Collegeville, MN: Liturgical, 2003; 2nd edition revised and expanded, 2009.

———. "The Role of the Women Disciples in Mark's Narrative." *Theologia Evangelica* 26 (1993) 91–102.

1

The Gift of *Dei Verbum*

Patrick J. Hartin

Gonzaga University / Diocese of Spokane

Personal Framework

IN THIS MY FINAL lecture at Gonzaga University, I shall reflect on an issue that has preoccupied me over the past forty years as a Catholic biblical theologian: the distinctiveness and nature of a Catholic interpretation of the Scriptures. When I commenced my academic career teaching Scripture (more specifically the New Testament) in South Africa, I was the sole Catholic—the other Scripture scholars belonged mainly to the Reformed Tradition. I learned a lot from my colleagues who provided me with invaluable insights and experiences. At the same time, they gave me a context where I could wrestle with this question of the nature of a Catholic approach to interpreting Scripture as well as the contribution it can offer to the wider Christian world.

Before coming to Gonzaga in 1995, I consulted with my Bishop, Reginald Orsmond of the Archdiocese of Johannesburg, South Africa. I would like to take the opportunity of acknowledging this evening that he has been one of the greatest influences in my life and in my faith and I would not be here tonight if it were not for him. He asked me, "Why do you want to teach at Gonzaga?" My answer was simple: "Because it is a Catholic college and we have no Catholic colleges in South Africa. I should like to have the opportunity of teaching in a Catholic environment."

Shortly after my coming to Gonzaga, Fr. Jim Dallen, Chair of the Department of Religious Studies at the time, asked me during a conversation, "What would you identify as specific to the nature of a Catholic interpretation of Scripture? What is central to the way in which a Catholic scholar approaches and interprets the Scriptures?"

Lest my intention be misunderstood, I need to address a prior question: *"Why is it important to identify a Catholic interpretation of the Scriptures?"* In raising this question, in no way do I intend to be polemical and to set up barriers between Catholics and Protestants, barriers that have been wonderfully broken down by Vatican II. My life has been enriched by the ecumenical movement in so many ways. Following the Second Vatican Council's lead, Catholic scholars were encouraged to embrace a deeper study of the Scriptures by using methods and tools already pioneered by Protestant scholarship in interpreting the Bible. This led to a deeper understanding of the origins, sources, and historical growth of the Scriptures, as well as a deeper collaboration between Catholic and Protestant scholarship. However, in the euphoria for these new paths of interpretation, something got lost. The distinctive wealth of insights into understanding the Scriptures that have always been at the heart of a Catholic interpretation of the Scriptures, beginning with the Fathers of the Church, has been eclipsed, at times forgotten, often ignored, and even ridiculed. The Church in the new millennium needs to reengage and appropriate this lost heritage of our tradition.

Reflections on Some Significant Insights into *Dei Verbum*

One of the most significant documents of Vatican II is *Dei Verbum*, or as it is known in English, *The Constitution on Divine Revelation*. Fifty-five years ago, on November 18, 1965, in the fourth and final official session of the Council, this document, *Dei Verbum* [hereafter, in citations, DV], was promulgated with impressive near-unanimity.[1] The text, solemnly proclaimed by Pope Paul VI on that day, demonstrates the traces of its long four-year journey through the Council and is naturally the result of many compromises. Yet, the final document presents a true synthesis of enormous significance. The text brings together the heritage of Church tradition with the wealth of a developing critical biblical scientific scholarship that, true to the spirit of the Council, opens the foundational documents of the faith to the world of today. What is of unique significance is that *Dei Verbum* does not treat the past as a fossil to be preserved as if in a museum, but knows rather that the upholding of tradition only occurs through its appropriation within new contexts and experiences. As Jesus' teaching, addressed within

---

1. The final vote by the Council Fathers was as follows: out of a total of 2,350 votes, 2,344 were *placet*, while only 6 were *non placet*!

the context of an Israelite and Semitic milieu, was appropriated by Paul and the other Apostles within the context of the Greco-Roman world, in like manner the Fathers of the Council endeavored to appropriate the foundational documents of the faith in the context of today's world. In this sense, *Dei Verbum* hands on the Scriptural teachings of the Councils of Trent and Vatican I through a process of ongoing vital appropriation.

At the heart of the Catholic tradition is an approach to life that harmonizes opposites. Rather than separating life into binary opposites of either/or, the Catholic ethos has always operated with a unifying embrace of both/and. For example, the Catholic Tradition celebrates the unity of Scripture *and* tradition, faith *and* reason, divine *and* human, nature *and* culture. So too in the study of Scripture there is need to embrace past traditions of interpretations emanating from patristic times and the worship life of the church *and* a scientific historical-critical understanding of the Scriptures.

Highlighting some major insights from this document provides a clearer framework for identifying what is central to a Catholic interpretation of the Scriptures. For this, the first three chapters of *Dei Verbum* are focal: Chapter I: "Revelation Itself"; Chapter II: "Handing on Divine Revelation"; and Chapter III: "Sacred Scripture, Its Inspiration and Divine Interpretation." These chapters provide insights into the nature of a Catholic approach to understanding the Scriptures that remains true to its traditions while at the same time opens the Scriptures to the great insights that have emerged over the course of the last century. Further, returning to the document of *Dei Verbum* some fifty-five years later sheds light on some forgotten treasures that have either been overlooked, misunderstood, or even misinterpreted. I still remember vividly studying this document at the Gregorian University in Rome in 1970, some five years after its publication—the liberating freshness and beauty of this document remain with me to this day.

The Relationship between Revelation, Scripture, and Tradition

Prior to Vatican II, seminary training depended on a manualist theology that presented revelation as God's disclosure of unattainable truths that comprised the "deposit of faith."[2] In contrast to this approach, *Dei Verbum* opens by presenting revelation as primarily the personal self-revelation of the triune God in Christ, who invites human beings to enter freely into a dialogue of love:

---

2. See theological manuals such as Tanquerey, *Manual of Dogmatic Theology.*

> In His goodness and wisdom God chose to reveal Himself and to make known to us the hidden purpose of His will (see Eph. 1:9) by which through Christ, the Word made flesh, man might in the Holy Spirit have access to the Father and come to share in the divine nature (see Eph. 2:18; 2 Peter 1:4). Through this revelation, therefore, the invisible God (see Col. 1:15, 1 Tim. 1:17) out of the abundance of His love speaks to men as friends (see Ex. 33:11; John 15:14–15) and lives among them (see Bar. 3:38), so that He may invite and take them into fellowship with Himself. (DV 2)

In place of presenting revelation in the form of abstract truths, revelation is now approached in terms of an encounter between persons that seeks a response of faith. A personal commitment is made through the grace of the Holy Spirit: "To make this act of faith, the grace of God and the interior help of the Holy Spirit must precede and assist, moving the heart and turning it to God, opening the eyes of the mind and giving 'joy and ease to everyone in assenting to the truth and believing it'" (DV 5). This commitment of the person of faith goes beyond mere intellectual acceptance of truths to an encounter with the invisible God in an intimate way as that of friends.

By speaking of God "manifesting" and "communicating" himself (Articles 3–6), Vatican II introduced into official Catholic teaching the language of divine "self-communication." The high point of this divine self-communication was the death and resurrection of Christ, together with the outpouring of the Holy Spirit (Article 4). *Dei Verbum* sees revelation to be a past, present, and future reality. While revelation is essentially completed in the past with Christ and the apostolic church ("the treasure of revelation, entrusted to the church" [Article 26]), revelation is repeatedly actualized in the event of human faith until its consummation in the face-to-face encounter with God at the end. Since faith is an encounter "now" with God in Christ, so too revelation is an actual, present, self-disclosure of God who invites such faith. As reciprocal realities, faith and revelation go together.

The Debate between Scripture and Tradition

The Council of Trent (1546) had declared "the gospel" to be the "source of all salvation and conduct," adding that "this truth and rule of conduct are contained in the written books [of the Bible] and the unwritten [apostolic] traditions" (DS 1501).[3] Despite Trent's language about the gospel (namely,

---

3. DS is the standard abbreviation for the compilation of documents called the *Enchiridion Symbolorum.*

revelation) being "the source" (in the singular), there emerged in Catholic theology a "two-source" theory of revelation according to which Scripture and tradition were regarded as two distinct sources for revealed truths. It was argued that tradition could and does supply some truths that are not found in Scripture. This view supported the model of revelation as a communication of truths that would otherwise have remained hidden in God. Although *Dei Verbum* did not explicitly rule out this "two-source theory," this view is difficult to maintain given Vatican II's understanding of revelation as primarily God's self-revelation and the stress placed on the unity between Scripture and tradition.

> Hence there exists a close connection and communication between sacred tradition and Sacred Scripture. For both of them, flowing from the same divine wellspring, in a certain way merge into a unity and tend toward the same end. For Sacred Scripture is the word of God inasmuch as it is consigned to writing under the inspiration of the divine Spirit, while sacred tradition takes the word of God entrusted by Christ the Lord and the Holy Spirit to the Apostles, and hands it on to their successors in its full purity, so that led by the light of the Spirit of truth, they may in proclaiming it preserve this word of God faithfully, explain it, and make it more widely known. (DV 9)

Joseph Ratzinger, in his *Commentary on Chapter II of Dei Verbum* published shortly after the Council, offers a significant understanding about the relationship between Scripture and tradition.[4] His study provides the death-knell to any notion that there are two equal sources of revelation: Scripture and tradition. He explains their relationship beautifully: "It is important to note that only Scripture is defined in terms of what it *is:* it is stated that Scripture *is* the word of God consigned to writing. Tradition, however, is described only functionally, in terms of what it *does*: it hands on the word of God, but *is* not the word of God."[5]

The Holy Spirit preserves this unity of Scripture and tradition. The Spirit's inspiration ensures that the word of God communicated by Christ to

---

4. See Ratzinger, "Divine Revelation," "Preface," "Chapter 1," "Chapter II," and "Chapter VI." Translated from the original edition: Vorgrimler, *Zweite Vatikanische Konzil, Kommentare.* Ratzinger makes an important caution in regard to how tradition is considered: "[N]ot every tradition that arises in the Church is a true celebration and keeping present of the mystery of Christ. There is a distorting, as well as a legitimate, tradition. . . . Consequently, tradition must not be considered only affirmatively, but also critically; we have Scripture as a criterion for this indispensable criticism of tradition, and tradition must therefore always be related back to it and measured by it" (185).

5. Ratzinger, "Divine Revelation," 194.

the Apostles and consigned to writing *is* the word of God. This same Spirit ensures that this word of God continues to be handed on faithfully to all successive generations, as Jesus promised in the Gospel of John: "These things I have spoken to you while I am still with you. But the Helper, the Holy Spirit, whom the Father will send in my name, he will teach you all things and bring to your remembrance all that I have said to you" (John 14:25–26).[6] Under the guidance of the Spirit, the handing on of the word of God (tradition) enables future generations to gain a deeper insight into and understanding of the word of God in new contexts and new ages: in this way tradition continues to "hand on the word of God, but *is* not the word of God."[7]

In his commentary, Ratzinger contends further that the Council remains attentive to its ecumenical concerns. He argues that there is nothing in this understanding of the relationship of Scripture and tradition that would pose a concern to any Christian. On the one hand, "no one is seriously able to maintain that there is a proof in Scripture for every Catholic doctrine."[8] On the other hand, Ratzinger quotes a Protestant scholar, Heinrich Ott who said: "Moreover, it is also surely true for a Protestant who has not forgotten the basis of the Reformation that we do not acquire certainty about God's revelation only from Scripture, but also through preaching and the inner testimony of the Holy Spirit."[9]

In describing the relationship between Scripture and tradition, the Council emphasized the Holy Spirit's role as foundational for ensuring the preservation of the word of God: "For Sacred Scripture *is* the word of God inasmuch as it is consigned to writing *under the inspiration of the divine Spirit*, while sacred tradition takes the word of God entrusted by Christ the Lord and the Holy Spirit to the Apostles, and *hands it on* to their successors in its full purity, so that led *by the light of the Spirit of truth*, they may in proclaiming it preserve this word of God faithfully, explain it, and make it more widely known" (DV 9).[10]

6. All the English translations of the Scriptures are taken from The English Standard Version (ESV) unless otherwise noted.

7. Ratzinger, "Divine Revelation," 194.

8. Ratzinger, "Divine Revelation," 195.

9. Ratzinger, "Divine Revelation."

10. Emphasis added. It is revealing to note that Pope Benedict reinforced his insights expressed in his commentary on *Dei Verbum* about the relationship between Sacred Scripture and tradition in his Post-Synodal Apostolic Exhortation, *Verbum Domini*: "The living Tradition is essential for enabling the Church to grow through time in the understanding of the truth revealed in the Scriptures; indeed, 'by means of the same tradition, the full canon of the sacred books is known to the Church and the holy Scriptures themselves are more thoroughly understood and constantly made effective in the Church' (DV, 7). Ultimately, it is the living Tradition of the Church which makes

The Role of the Magisterium (the Teaching Office)

Dei Verbum offers a noteworthy clarification of the vital role that the magisterium (the teaching office of the Church) plays in the relationship between Scripture and tradition. Contrary to the way in which the magisterium's role had been presented especially in the manuals, *Dei Verbum*'s significant insight presented the magisterium as the servant of God's word, rather than its master: "But the task of authentically interpreting the Word of God, whether written or handed on, has been entrusted exclusively to the living teaching office of the Church, whose authority is exercised in the name of Jesus Christ. *This teaching office [magisterium] is not above the Word of God, but serves it*" (DV 10b; emphasis added).

The servant role of the teaching office of the Church ensures that the understanding of the Word of God is authentically handed on and interpreted. Just as the task of tradition is to hand on the Word of God, so the role of the magisterium is to hand on an authentic understanding of the Word of God as well as how it has been understood throughout tradition. The true function of the magisterium lies in its role as servant of the community. This corresponds to the role Jesus assigned to Peter after his resurrection: "'Simon, son of John, do you love me?' . . . 'Feed my sheep'" (John 21:15–17). Thus Peter and his successors are placed at the service of God's people. The most important aspect of this service is to give an authentic understanding of the word of God to God's people. In this light, the magisterium is at the service of God's word, not above it. Ratzinger stresses this role of the magisterium as a servant of God's word:

> For the first time a text of the teaching office expressly points out the subordination of the teaching office to the word, i.e. its function as a servant. . . . One can hardly deny that the point which sees only Scripture as what is unclear, but the teaching office as what is clear, is a very limited one and that to reduce the task of theology to the proof of the presence of the statements of the teaching office in the sources is to threaten the primacy of the sources which . . . would ultimately destroy the serving character of the teaching office.[11]

The image of "servant of the word" contains a richness and beauty that also poses a challenge to the role of the teaching office of the Church.

---

us adequately understand sacred Scripture as the word of God. Although the word of God precedes and exceeds sacred Scripture, nonetheless Scripture, as inspired by God, contains the divine word (cf. 2 Tim 3:16) 'in an altogether singular way' (cf. *Propositio* 3)." Benedict XVI, *Verbum Domini*, par. 17, pp. 37–38.

11. Ratzinger, "Divine Revelation," 197.

Before giving an authentic understanding of God's word, the teaching office is called to approach the Scriptures as a listener. A servant needs to listen in order to carry out a task. When instead the Scriptures are approached in order to find texts to prove or support magisterial teachings, the relationship between the magisterium and the Scriptures is distorted. The magisterium is not above the Scriptures but at its service. As a servant, the teaching office approaches the Word of God with an openness that allows God's Word to speak, rather than approaching the Scriptures with preconceived conclusions. Ratzinger expresses this approach eloquently:

> The explicit emphasis on the ministerial function of the teaching office must be welcomed as warmly as the statement that its primary service is to listen . . . as a faithful servant who wards off attempts at foreign domination and defends the dominion of the word of God both against modernism and against traditionalism. At the same time the contrast between the "listening" and the "teaching" Church is thus reduced to its true measure: in the last analysis the whole Church listens, and, vice versa, the whole Church shares in the upholding of true teaching.[12]

The Inspiration and Interpretation of Sacred Scripture

Chapter III of Dei Verbum, "Sacred Scripture, Its Inspiration and Divine Interpretation," examines the nature of inspiration and the way the Sacred Scriptures are read and interpreted in the context of the Catholic Church. Understanding the growth and development of this chapter over the four sessions of the Council is vital to discovering the intent of the Fathers of the Council and the significant contribution of the teaching that emerges from the final text of Dei Verbum, Articles 11, 12, 13.[13] In 1967 (two years after the end of the Council), Alois Grillmeier wrote an outstanding study of "the growth of the text and the theological statement of Chapter III of the Constitution Dei Verbum." He produced what is undoubtedly a foundational and authoritative commentary for understanding Chapter III of Dei Verbum and all scholarship needs to take its presentation seriously.[14] Three

12. Ratzinger, "Divine Revelation," 197.

13. Some recent scholarship has tended to overlook the intent of the Council Fathers in this regard through other concerns and presuppositions. For an overview see Miller, "For Our Salvation"; and also volume 6 of Letter and Spirit: A Journal of Catholic Biblical Theology (2010), edited by Scott W. Hahn.

14. Grillmeier, "Inspiration and Interpretation of Scripture." For the original German see Vorgrimler, Zweite Vatikanische Konzil, 405–701.

aspects of the teaching of *Dei Verbum* are particularly significant here, and they are spelled out in Chapter III (Articles 11, 12, 13).

The Inspiration of Sacred Scripture (DV 11a)

Those divinely revealed realities which are contained and presented in Sacred Scripture have been committed to writing under the inspiration of the Holy Spirit. For holy mother Church, relying on the belief of the Apostles (see John 20:31; 2 Tim. 3:16; 2 Peter 1:19–20; 3:15–16), holds that the books of both the Old and New Testaments in their entirety, with all their parts, are sacred and canonical because written under the inspiration of the Holy Spirit, they have God as their author and have been handed on as such to the Church herself. (1) In composing the sacred books, God chose men and while employed by Him (2) they made use of their powers and abilities, so that with Him acting in them and through them, (3) they, as true authors, consigned to writing everything and only those things which He wanted. (4) (DV 11a)

The text concisely summarizes the traditional teaching of the Church, as can be seen from the biblical references and the endnotes.[15] Significantly, it upholds two foundational principles regarding the nature of the Sacred Scriptures. Through the inspiration of the Holy Spirit, these writings have been recognized as having *God as their author* as they have been handed on in the context of the Church. At the same time, *the human authors* retain all their faculties and abilities in composing their writings. God's inspiration works in a unique way. The human writers compile their writings, as any human author does, by using their own abilities in selecting freely their material and arranging their document with their own methods, skills, styles, and language. Nevertheless, the inspiration of the Holy Spirit ensures that the message they communicated and "consigned to writing [consisted of] everything and only those things which [God] wanted."

15. Endnotes to Article 11a: [Note 1:] "cf. First Vatican Council, Dogmatic Constitution on the Catholic Faith, Chap. 2 'On Revelation': Heinrich Denzinger, *Enchiridion symbolorum et definitionum* (hereafter Denzinger), 1787 (3006); Biblical Commission, Decree of June 18, 1915: Denzinger 2180 (3629): Enchiridion Bible (hereafter EB) 420; Holy Office, Epistle of Dec. 22, 1923: EB 499. [Note 2:] cf. Pius XII, encyclical 'Divino Afflante Spiritu,' Sept. 30, 1943: A.A.S. 35 (1943) p. 314; EB 556. [Note 3]: 'In' and 'for' man: cf. Heb. 1, and 4, 7; ('in'): 2 Sm. 23,2; Matt.1:22 and various places; ('for'): First Vatican Council, Schema on Catholic Doctrine, note 9: Coll. Lac. VII, 522. [Note 4]: Leo XIII, encyclical *Providentissimus Deus*, Nov. 18, 1893: Denzinger 1952 (3293); EB 125."

In interpreting the Scriptures, these two dimensions, the divine and the human, must be maintained. In these Sacred writings we encounter God communicating with / to us through human writers. To experience God's Word more effectively, we need to understand the human words within the context of their own time, their historical context, and cultural worlds. A careful and clear understanding of the human words enables a deeper encounter with the Word of God. The analogy of the Incarnation of the Word of God is helpful in this regard. Because the Word of God took on human flesh, becoming human in every way that we are except sin, we encounter God through the humanity of Jesus Christ. In like manner, God's Word takes on flesh in the words of the Scriptures. Through those human words we encounter the Divine Word and come to an understanding of the Divine Word. God accommodates himself to the human person's way of expression while at the same time ensuring that the message of salvation emerges through this human communication.

In examining the development of the text of Article 11a, one notices that the teaching on inspiration has been transformed from purely "mechanistic ideas" to a more personalistic understanding.[16] No longer is the human author spoken of as "a living instrument," or is God referred to as "the principal author." The scriptural authors are referred to as "true authors" who use all their capacities and abilities in composing their writings. Each writing displays a unique style and method of presentation as well as each author's limitations. Despite their humanity and inadequacies, God achieves his purpose in communicating his saving message. God and man do not act independently. While the human author maintains his freedom, God's inspiration guides him in communicating what God intends.

A Foundational Insight: The Centrality of Biblical Truth
is "Truth for the Sake of Our Salvation" (DV 11b)

Therefore, since everything asserted by the inspired authors or sacred writers must be held to be asserted by the Holy Spirit, it follows that the books of Scripture must be acknowledged as teaching solidly, faithfully and without error that truth which God wanted put into sacred writings (5) *for the sake of our salvation.* Therefore "all Scripture is divinely inspired and has its use for teaching the truth and refuting error, for reformation of manners and discipline in right living, so that the man who

---

16. Grillmeier, "Inspiration and Interpretation of Scripture," 229.

belongs to God may be efficient and equipped for good work of every kind" (2 Tim. 3:16–17, Greek text). (DV 11b)[17]

An examination of this text within the context of the whole document demonstrates that the Council Fathers emphasized the truth of Scripture within the context of a theology of salvation. The first two chapters of the document, as we have noted, stressed the personal encounter with the Word of God *for the purpose of our salvation.* The aim of inspiration and of the divine communication in the Scriptures was not focused on a communication of individual intellectual propositions, but rather on the communication of a message of salvation.

The significance of this insight and teaching cannot be overstated. The intent of the Council Fathers emerges clearly from a study of the document from its genesis on, as it underwent numerous clarifications and iterations. An earlier draft of this text from 1962 that was rejected stated that, "It is completely forbidden to admit that the sacred authors could have erred, since divine inspiration of its very nature precludes and rejects all error in everything, both religious and profane."[18]

A comparison of that initial draft with the final text promulgated in 1965 demonstrates that the commission rejected a notion of the inerrancy of scripture extending to all religious and profane matters within the Scriptures. Throughout the Council, attention was drawn to numerous examples of undoubtable human errors in the books of Sacred Scripture. The intervention of Cardinal König on 2 October 1964 drew attention to Oriental studies that had elucidated how Scriptural historical information diverges from the truth of scientific information.[19] Cardinal König offered as an ex-

---

17. Emphasis added. The endnote (5) in the text refers to St. Augustine, *De Genesi ad Litteram* 2, 9, 20 (Patrologia Latina 34:270–71); Epistle 82, 3 (Patrologia Latina 33:277, Corpus Scriptorum Ecclesiasticorum Latinorum 34.2:354); St. Thomas, "On Truth," Q. 12, A. 2, C. Council of Trent, session IV, Scriptural Canons: Denzinger 783 (1501). Leo XIII, encyclical, *Providentissimus Deus*: EB 121, 124, 126–27; and Pius XII, encyclical, *Divino Afflante Spiritu*: EB 539.

18. The full Latin text reads: "Ex hac divinae Inspirationis extensione ad omnia, directe et necessario sequitur immunitas absoluta ab errore totius Sacrae Scripturae. Antiqua enim et constanti Ecclesiae fide edocemur nefas omnino esse concedere sacrum ipsum errasse scriptorem, cum divina Inspiratio per se ipsam tam necessario excludat et respuat errorem omnem in qualibet re religiosa vel profana, quam necessarium est Deum summam Veritatem, nullius omnino erroris auctorem esse." See Grillmeier, "Inspiration and Interpretation of Scripture," 200.

19. "laudata scientia rerum orientalium insuper demonstrat in Bibliis Sacris notitias historicas et notitias scientiae naturalis a veritate quandoque deficere." Grillmeier, "Inspiration and Interpretation of Scripture," 205.

ample, Mark 2:26[20] that states that David "entered the house of God, in the time of Abiathar the high priest, and ate the bread of the Presence, which it is not lawful for any but the priests to eat, and also gave it to those who were with him." However, 1 Samuel 21:1–9 attests that this event happened under the priest Ahimelech, the predecessor of Abiathar!

Another interesting discrepancy occurs in the opening verses of the Gospel of Mark where Mark writes:

> *As it is written in Isaiah the prophet,*
>
> Behold I send my messenger before your face,
> who will prepare your way,
> the voice of the one crying in the wilderness:
> "Prepare the way of the Lord,
> make his paths straight." (Mark 1:2–3; emphasis added)

Despite Mark's attribution, this quotation is not derived exclusively from the Prophet Isaiah. Two texts are amalgamated from two different prophets: The first part comes from the prophet Malachi 3:1, "Behold, I send my messenger, and he will prepare the way before me." The second part, "The voice of one crying in the wilderness," comes from Isaiah 40:3. The writer Mark fuses the two texts and identifies them as originating solely from the prophet Isaiah, "As it is written in Isaiah the prophet." Probably, Mark is relying on memory and simply conflates the two texts. Examples like these show that the human authors are mistaken in a number of instances.

Reflecting on such inconsistences as these, the Council Fathers realized that a statement such as "divine inspiration of its very nature precludes and rejects all error in everything, both religious and profane" is simply untenable. This called the Fathers to search for a more precise and subtler understanding of inspiration and inerrancy that went beyond the previous encyclicals of *Providentissimus Deus* and *Spiritus Paraclitus*.[21] The declaration in the final text is an unambiguous witness that the Council Fathers wished to present a clear formulation on the truth of Scripture that took account of the results of critical research both scientific and literary. As Grillmeier assesses this development, "At the same time, however, it has made possible a fuller picture of the historical and human conditionedness of Scripture. A purely *a priori* and 'absolute' doctrine of inerrancy, as the text of 1962 sought to present, is scarcely compatible with the facts."[22]

---

20. Grillmeier, "Inspiration and Interpretation of Scripture," 205.
21. Grillmeier, "Inspiration and Interpretation of Scripture," 207.
22. Grillmeier, "Inspiration and Interpretation of Scripture," 231.

Article 11b reaches its climax with this statement: "It follows that the books of Scripture must be acknowledged as teaching solidly, faithfully and without error *that truth* which God wanted put into sacred writings *for the sake of (our) salvation.*"[23] This teaching had been anticipated and prepared throughout the Constitution.[24] It is not a matter of dividing Scripture into those parts that are inspired and those that are not. Rather, the focus is that God's inspiration works with human persons to ensure that the communication of God's saving truth is handed on "solidly, faithfully, and without error."

Pierre Grelot, who played a significant role in the renewal of the studies in Sacred Scripture and taught at L'Institut Catholique de Paris from 1961 to 1983, offered an insightful explanation of the intent and meaning of these words:

> Rather than starting . . . from the psychology of the sacred author, we are going back, in two different respects, to the definition of Scripture as the *word of God addressed to men through the intermediation of the inspired writers.* God speaks to men only to give them his revelation: thus, the truth of Scripture is of the same order as that of this revelation. God does not speak to men except by other men: in Scripture his teaching passes through that of the sacred writers in order to reach us. To clarify the present problem it is necessary to reflect on two points: the *truth* of the divine revelation and the *teaching* of the sacred authors.[25]

The entirety of Scripture is under the influence of the inspiration of the Holy Spirit. In communicating to us the truth of our salvation, God accommodates himself to the human person. His gift of inspiration ensures that the message of salvation is communicated "solidly, faithfully, and without error." Contrary to those who argue that this is a new development beyond

---

23. The Latin text of Article 11b reads: "Cum ergo omne id, quod auctores inspirati seu hagiographi asserunt, retineri debeat assertum a Spiritu Sancto, *inde Scripturae libri veritatem, quam Deus nostrae salutis causa* Litteris Sacris consignari voluit, firmiter, fideliter et sine errore docere profitendi sunt." Note that the English translation has omitted to translate "nostrae" ("our"). Emphasis added.

24. See DV, Article 7: "nuntiam salutis scriptis mandaverunt"; Article 8: "praedicatio apostolica, quae in inspiratis libris speciali modo exprimitur"; Article 10: "igitur Sacram Traditionem, Sacram Scripturam et Ecclesiae Magisterium, iuxta sapientissimum Dei consilium, ita inter se connecti et consociari, ut unum sine aliis non consistat, omniaque simul, singula suo modo sub actione unius Spiritus Sancti, *ad animarum salutem efficaciter conferant*"; see also Chapter VI: "Sacred Scripture in the Life of the Church," Articles 21–26. Emphasis added.

25. Grelot, *La Bible*, 103. Quoted and translated by Grillmeier, "Inspiration and Interpretation of Scripture," 231. Emphasis added.

the traditional teaching of the Catholic Church, a look back at Leo XIII's document *Providentissimus Deus* is very instructive. Pope Leo addresses the relationship between the natural sciences and the Scriptures. His clarity and pastoral insight warrant a lengthy quotation, and his words are as applicable today to every Professor of Sacred Scripture as they were in 1893:

> We have to contend against those who, making an evil use of physical science, minutely scrutinize the Sacred Book in order to detect the writers in a mistake, and to take occasion to vilify its contents. Attacks of this kind, bearing as they do on matters of sensible experience, are peculiarly dangerous to the masses, and also to the young who are beginning their literary studies; for the young, if they lose their reverence for the Holy Scripture on one or more points, are easily led to give up believing in it altogether. It need not be pointed out how the nature of science, just as it is so admirably adapted to show forth the glory of the Great Creator, provided it be taught as it should be, so if it be perversely imparted to the youthful intelligence, it may prove most fatal in destroying the principles of true philosophy and in the corruption of morality. *Hence to the Professor of Sacred Scripture a knowledge of natural science will be of very great assistance in detecting such attacks on the Sacred Books, and in refuting them. There can never, indeed, be any real discrepancy between the theologian and the physicist, as long as each confines himself within his own lines, and both are careful, as St. Augustine warns us, "not to make rash assertions, or to assert what is not known as known."*(51) If dissension should arise between them, here is the rule also laid down by St. Augustine, for the theologian: "Whatever they can really demonstrate to be true of physical nature, we must show to be capable of reconciliation with our Scriptures; and whatever they assert in their treatises which is contrary to these Scriptures of ours, that is to Catholic faith, we must either prove it as well as we can to be entirely false, or at all events we must, without the smallest hesitation, believe it to be so."(52) To understand how just is the rule here formulated we must remember, first, that the sacred writers, or to speak more accurately, the Holy Ghost "Who spoke by them, did not intend to teach men these things (that is to say, the essential nature of the things of the visible universe), things in no way profitable unto salvation."(53) Hence they did not seek to penetrate the secrets of nature, but rather described and dealt with things in more or less figurative language, or in terms which were commonly used at the time, and which in many instances are in daily use at this day, even by the most

eminent men of science. Ordinary speech primarily and properly describes what comes under the senses; and somewhat in
the same way the sacred writers—as the Angelic Doctor also reminds us—"went by what sensibly appeared"(54) or put down
what God, speaking to men, signified, in the way men could
understand and were accustomed to.[26]

The foundation for what is explicitly stated in *Dei Verbum* 11 is laid
in what Pope Leo says here, especially in quoting St. Augustine: "[*the Holy
Ghost*] *who spoke by them, did not intend to teach men these things (that is
to say, the essential nature of the things of the visible universe), things in no
way profitable unto salvation*."[27] God communicates the truth of the message of salvation for us through the human author. Scientific, historical, and
other matters belong to the realm of the context and the time of the communities and authors behind these documents. A clear distinction needs
to be observed between the *message* of salvation and the *way* in which that
message is being communicated *"for the sake of our salvation."* To ignore
this principle or distinction is to deviate from the tradition as articulated by
Pope Leo, going as far back as St. Augustine, and reaffirmed by *Dei Verbum*
11 in articulating *"the truth . . . for the sake of our salvation."* Moreover,
disregarding this teaching degenerates into fundamentalism.

Scriptural Hermeneutics (DV 12)

How, then, ought one to understand the Bible? This is addressed in *Dei
Verbum* 12. First, Article 12a presents the foundation on which the ways of
interpreting the Scriptures should be based:

> [S]ince God speaks in Sacred Scripture through men in hu-
> man fashion, the interpreter of Sacred Scripture, in order to see
> clearly what God wanted to communicate to us, should carefully
> investigate what meaning the sacred writers really intended, and
> what God wanted to manifest by means of their words. (DV 12)

Of significance is the description of the relationship and unity between God and the human author that restates what had been developed
in the previous Article. The starting point for the interpreter of Sacred

26. The English translation of the text of Pope Leo XIII, *Providentissimus Deus*, par.
18, where he quotes St. Augustine (n51): *In Gen. op. imperf.* ix., 30; (n52): *De Gen. ad
litt.* i. 21, 41; and (n53): *De Gen. ad litt.* ii., 9, 20; and St. Thomas Aquinas (n54): *Summa
theol.* p. I, q. lxx., a. I, ad 3. Emphasis added.

27. Quoting Augustine, *De Gen. ad litt.* 2.9.20.

Scripture is to investigate the meaning that the sacred authors wanted to convey. Through the inspiration of the Spirit this meaning will reflect "what God wanted to manifest by means of their words." What God intends to communicate to us is to be found first and foremost in understanding what the human authors intend to communicate. Through the power of God's inspiration, the truth of salvation that the human authors intend to communicate is identical to the truth of salvation that God intends to communicate. In an analogous way to the Incarnation, an understanding of the words and person of Christ leads to an understanding of what God is communicating through his Son Jesus.

Next, Article 12b and c offer hermeneutical rules for appreciating the truth of salvation that emerges from the intention of the sacred writers. Two important dimensions are stressed, one building upon the other. The first is the literary analysis of the Scriptures, aided by critical biblical scholarship, and the second, with the text thus clarified, is the spiritual and theological meaning of sacred Scripture.

CRITICAL BIBLICAL SCHOLARSHIP

> To search out the intention of the sacred writers, attention should be given, among other things (*inter alia etiam*), to "literary forms." For truth is set forth and expressed differently in texts which are variously historical, prophetic, poetic, or of other forms of discourse. The interpreter must investigate what meaning the sacred writer intended to express and actually expressed in particular circumstances by using contemporary literary forms in accordance with the situation of his own time and culture. For the correct understanding of what the sacred author wanted to assert, due attention must be paid to the customary and characteristic styles of feeling, speaking and narrating which prevailed at the time of the sacred writer, and to the patterns men normally employed at that period in their everyday dealings with one another. (DV 12b)

This clear and unambiguous statement about the use of historical, critical, and scientific methods for the interpretation of Scripture brought to a culmination what had in fact started in the Catholic Church much earlier. The earliest and most significant Catholic scholar to employ methods of critical biblical scholarship in the interpretation of Scripture was undoubtedly Marie-Joseph Lagrange, OP, founder of L'École Biblique (School of Biblical

Studies) in 1890.[28] In the first part of the twentieth century, however, the Catholic Church was reluctant to adopt the methods that Protestant scholarship had adopted over the course of the previous century. The hesitation was largely due to the philosophical underpinnings of these methods that had led to undermining central Christian beliefs. Then, under the pontificate of Pius XII (1939–58), the true patron of Catholic Biblical Studies, a remarkable regeneration of Catholic scriptural studies occurred.[29] Notably in 1943 he promulgated *Divino Afflante Spiritu*, announcing that the time for fear was over and that Catholic scholars should use modern tools in their exegesis. He encouraged the use of the principle of literary forms to solve historical problems.[30] After his death attempts were made to turn things back: attacks were made on some outstanding scholars at the *Biblicum* (Luis Alonso Schökel, Stanislaus Lyonnet, and Max Zerwick). The latter two were removed from their positions at the *Biblicum*. Thus there was an atmosphere of fear and foreboding as the Second Vatican Council was called into being. Happily that was dispelled, and Pius XII's endeavors and accomplishments in the realms of biblical scholarship came to fruition in *Dei Verbum*. Here Catholics were encouraged to adopt and use those methods of interpretation that had been flourishing for a long time among Protestant scholars.

Dei Verbum 12b identifies the use of literary forms (genres) as the starting point for understanding the intention of the sacred authors. The Council Fathers endorsed the critical investigation of all types of literature that are found within the Scriptures as well as other forms of communication (*inter alia etiam*). This embraces what is referred to as the historical critical method.[31]

---

28. Lagrange joined the Dominican Order in 1879 and was ordained in 1883. After teaching church history at Toulouse (1884–88), he studied Oriental languages at the University of Vienna. In 1890 he went to Jerusalem and established the École Biblique (School of Biblical Studies). A prolific scholar, he founding in 1892 a journal, the *Revue Biblique* (*Biblical Review*) and in 1903 he started a series of scholarly commentaries on the Bible, the *Études bibliques*, to which he contributed three volumes: on the historical method of Old Testament criticism, on the Book of Judges, and on the Semitic religions.

29. First, in 1941 the Pontifical Biblical Commission condemned an overly conservative distrust of modern biblical research. In *Divino Afflante Spiritu* (1943) Pius XII also encouraged the making of new translations of the Bible from the original languages rather than from the Vulgate.

30. Building upon this, in 1955 the Pontifical Biblical Commission declared that Catholic scholars had complete freedom *(plena libertas)* regarding the earlier Commission decrees of 1905–15 except where they concerned issues of faith and morals (very few actually did). Catholics were now free to adopt modern positions on authorship and dating.

31. This significance of the historical critical method as holding pride of place in the interpretation of the Scriptures was again reaffirmed by the Pontifical Biblical

The Council has gone farther than previous magisterial documents in situating these methods within the whole context of the message of salvation. The use of these methods of historical criticism (such as literary criticism, the criticism of history of forms, tradition criticism, source criticism, redaction criticism) provides the starting point in the search for understanding the intention of the author. After this investigation, the intention of the author needs to be placed within the framework of *Dei Verbum*'s aim of discovering the message of salvation. The intention and message presented by the human author provides the starting point for discovering the divine message of salvation.

SPIRITUAL OR THEOLOGICAL MEANING
OF SACRED SCRIPTURE

> But since Holy Scripture must be read and interpreted in the sacred Spirit in which it was written (*sed, cum Sacra Scriptura eodem Spiritu quo scripta est etiam leganda et interpretanda sit*), no less serious attention must be given to the content and unity of the whole of Scripture if the meaning of the sacred texts is to be correctly worked out. The living tradition of the whole Church must be taken into account along with the harmony which exists between elements of faith. It is the task of exegetes to work according to these rules toward a better understanding and explanation of the meaning of Sacred Scripture, so that through preparatory study the judgment of the Church may mature. For all of what has been said about the way of interpreting Scripture is subject finally to the judgment of the Church, which carries out the divine commission and ministry of guarding and interpreting the word of God. (DV 12c)

Further insights into the interpretation of the Scriptures is provided from *its theological context*. Since all Scripture is inspired by the one Spirit, it must be read and interpreted *as a unity*. The Letter of James and the Letters of Paul are prime examples. They are part of the same one body of Sacred Scripture. As such their teaching on the relationship between faith and works must be read not in opposition to each other, but so that each illuminates the other through their different perspectives. On a further level, the living tradition of the whole Church must continue to help in the understanding and interpretation of texts. For example, the text of Isaiah 7:14 cannot be read

---

Commission in 1993 in its lengthy document on "The Interpretation of the Bible in the Church" (April 15, 1993).

in isolation from the tradition of the way it was interpreted in the Greek translation and its acceptance by Matthew 1:23 as well as in the ongoing interpretation of the Church's tradition.

Since the individual author is limited by his historical and cultural context, he may have only an incomplete knowledge and awareness of the meaning and implications of his message within the wider context of the history of salvation. For this reason, the understanding of the scriptural text must go beyond the limitations of the human, historical author. Contrary to what is often stated, Christianity is not a religion of the book. Christianity is a religion of a person, the Christ! Everything in Sacred Scripture leads to and reflects upon Christ. The interpretation of Sacred Scripture must give attention to the entirety of revelation within the unity of all Scripture as well as how this unity of Scripture has been handed on and interpreted in the tradition of the Church under the guidance of the Spirit. As the Council Fathers continued to stress, the Apostolic Fathers and the way in which they re-read the Scriptures in the light of the Christ event is a powerful and authoritative witness to the true interpretation of Sacred Scripture.

Indeed, the key to the revitalization of Christian thought and life lay in a critical appropriation of the great sources of Catholic life and thought—the liturgy, the Sacred Scriptures, the writings of the early Church Fathers. Henri de Lubac expounded this in a small book called *Catholicism* (1938), which had an enormous influence and launched an important theological movement, Ressourcement Theology. The biblical dimension of Ressourcement Theology culminated in the final chapter of *Dei Verbum*: "*Sacred Scripture in the Life of the Church*" (Articles 21–26). Here the Council dreamed of the whole Church being nourished by the Bible at every level of its existence. A prayerful knowledge of the Scriptures would foster among all the baptized a living union with Christ and a life centered on him and blessed by the Holy Spirit.

For the interpretation of Scripture is always an ongoing mutual process. Historical-critical exegesis holds its rightful place as a starting point and as a corrective. However, it remains just that: a starting point. The living tradition and faith of the Church always leads to a deeper awareness and understanding of the Sacred Scriptures. As the Fathers of the Church have shown, a re-reading of the Scriptures leads the church to a fuller insight into the meaning (*sensus plenior*) of Sacred Scripture. Grillmeier summarizes this understanding: "Thus the Council recommends a combination of technical exegetical hermeneutics and total theological method with a living Church understanding of faith, which leaves everyone with their necessary individuality, but points the common goal to all: the ever fuller understanding and assimilation of the reality of salvation."[32]

Article 13 concludes Chapter III with reference to an analogy of faith in the Incarnation of the Word made Flesh. By quoting St. John Chrysostom, the Council affirms that the Word of God, the Wisdom of God, has adapted itself to the limitations of our human nature: "the marvelous 'condescension' of eternal wisdom is clearly shown, 'that we may learn the gentle kindness of God, which words cannot express, and how far He has gone in adapting His language with thoughtful concern for our weak human nature.'"[33] The humanity of God's word in the word of Scripture is analogous to the mystery of the Incarnation of the Word of God in the humanity of Jesus Christ. This analogy is of vital significance. The Council Fathers offer a way of understanding God's working with us humans in the communication of his message of salvation. God works through man. The genius is once again evident in the Catholic dictum "both . . . and" as in "both God and man" as opposed to the dichotomy of "either . . . or" as in "either all God (fundamentalism) or all man (secular historicism)." The fears that trapped a Catholic understanding of the Scriptures in the century leading up to *Dei Verbum* have now been laid to rest. *Dei Verbum* liberated the Scriptures from a century-long tendency to embrace a fundamentalism regarding the Scriptures out of fear of succumbing to a secular humanistic worldview. God speaks through the human word and true respect must be given to each: one discovers the divine word through the human word.

As stressed previously, a true understanding of the intent of *Dei Verbum* can only be understood from an examination of the long path the document underwent over the four years of the Council. Failure to pay attention to this development and growth results in not understanding the clear teaching of the Council. The point is pellucid in Grillmeier's insightful conclusion to his commentary on *Dei Verbum*, Chapter III:

> The Constitution brings home to us in this very Chapter the way in which the Church must concern itself with Scripture. By pointing the way to a clearer understanding of the co-operation of God with men in the inspiration of Scripture, it also frees us from false attitudes in the search for the truth in Scripture. We are not to devote our energies to the defence of positions that were set up against an enemy that has long since departed, but rather to the discovery of the fullness of truth that God caused

32. Grillmeier, "Inspiration and Interpretation of Scripture," 245.

33. DV 13, quoting St. John Chrysostom, *In Genesis* 3.8 = Homily 17.1 (Patrologia Graeca 53:134). The key term rendered "adapting" here is, in Latin *attemperatio*, in English "suitable adjustment," in Greek *synkatabasēs*.

to be written down for the sake of our salvation. In declaring the purpose of all hermeneutics to be the discovery of the *sensus divinus* in the *sensu humano* and the purpose of the inspiration of Scripture the sure, faithful and the infallible making known to us of the truth of salvation, the Constitution is presenting the word of Scripture as the medium of a constant spiritual dialogue of God with men. To contemplate "the living word of God"—the theme of the Constitution from beginning to end—leads to a deepening understanding of inspiration, to a positive understanding of the doctrine of inerrancy, and at the same time to its humanization and to a comprehensive concern with Scripture. *The age of anxiety in relationship to Scripture is to be regarded as over—a new life with it is to start.*[34]

A Foundational Framework for a Catholic Interpretation of the Scriptures

I opened with a reference to my own personal framework. I return to consider the wider framework that arises from the document *Dei Verbum*. These reflections offer essential elements for pursuing an authentic Catholic interpretation of the Scripture. Practically speaking, from this document, we discover a foundational framework upon which a Catholic interpretation of the Bible rests.[35] Four factors are essential for providing this framework for a Catholic interpretation of the Scriptures. These four factors are not exclusive, but foundational. They also show how a Catholic interpretation of the Scriptures differs from a fundamentalist reading of the Scriptures as well as from a purely modernistic and secular, scientific-historical reading of the same texts.

---

34. Grillmeier, "Inspiration and Interpretation of Scripture," 246. Emphasis added.

35. Our lives are lived out within the context of certain frameworks that give them significance and meaning. A framework helps us to make sense of our actions and to understand them from a moral perspective. As the Canadian philosopher Charles Taylor has articulated: "That is, when we try to spell out what it is that we presuppose when we judge that a certain form of life is truly worthwhile, or place our dignity in a certain achievement or status, or define our moral obligations in a certain manner, we find ourselves articulating inter alia what I have been calling here '*frameworks*.'" See Taylor's foundational work, *Sources of the Self*, 260. In 1999 Taylor delivered the Gifford lectures, "Living in a Secular Age?" and has published a number of works in this connection, such as *Varieties of Religion Today* and his major work on secularization, *A Secular Age*.

The Origin and Unity of the Scriptures Begin in the Liturgy:
Both the Old and New Testaments Emerge from the Church
and Belong to the Church.

For the interpretation of any text or document, context is all embracing. The same is true for the interpretation of the Scriptures. The Scriptures are, first and foremost, an ecclesial document—they belong to the Church. The Scriptures arose within the setting of the Church at worship. Paul's letters show unambiguously that they were written specifically for churches and were read when the church gathered for worship. In the context of the liturgy, Paul, the earliest writer of the Christian Church, set forth his teaching and insight into the Gospel message and the way of life the members of the community were to lead. The Letter to the Colossians illustrates this point dramatically, "And when this letter has been read among you, have it also read in the church of the Laodiceans; and see that you also read the letter from Laodicea" (Col 4:16). Peter himself attests that the same authority was given to the writings of Paul as to the Old Testament: "Just as our beloved brother Paul also wrote to you according to the wisdom given him, as he does in all his letters when he speaks in them of these matters. There are some things in them that are hard to understand, which the ignorant and unstable twist to their own destruction, as they do the *other Scriptures*" (2 Pet 3:15–16; emphasis added).

Writing a hundred years later, Justin Martyr, expresses this idea very clearly:

> On the Day which is called Sunday we have a common assembly of all who live in the cities or in the outlying districts, and the memoirs of the Apostles or the writings of the Prophets are read, as long as there is time. Then, when the reader has finished, the president of the assembly verbally admonishes and invites all to imitate such examples of virtue. Then we all stand up together and offer up our prayers, and, as we said before, after we finish our prayers, bread and wine and water are presented. He who presides likewise offers up prayers and thanksgivings, to the best of his ability, and the people express their approval by saying "Amen." The Eucharistic elements are distributed and consumed by those present, and to those who are absent they are sent through the deacons. . . . Sunday indeed, is the day on which we all hold our common assembly because it is the first day on which God, transforming the darkness and [prime] matter, created the world; and our Savior Jesus Christ arose from the dead on the same day. For they crucified Him on the day before that

of Saturn, and on the day after, which is Sunday, He appeared to His Apostles and disciples and taught them the things which we have passed on to you also for consideration.[36]

The people of Israel preserved their Sacred Scriptures in their synagogue liturgy. The early Christians continued to embrace these Scriptures in their own liturgy, using the pre-Christian Greek translation, the Septuagint, as their authentic text.[37] As Justin Martyr demonstrated above, the early church used the writings of the apostles together with the sacred writings of Israel as they gathered in worship. This acceptance of the writings of Israel together with the writings of the apostles within the liturgy led the church to see the essential unity of both the Old and the New Testaments. This clearly demonstrates that the Scriptures arose out of the liturgy. A famous Catholic dictum says, *Lex orandi, lex credendi* ("Our prayer life reflects our beliefs"). For this very reason, Catholic scholars need to honor this framework and bring together the experience of worship with the experience of their scholarship.

The experience of the framework of the liturgy illustrated and strengthened the belief in the unity of the Old and New Testaments as founded upon a single divine authorship and centered on Christ. Given this framework, the early Christians drew upon the Old Testament to understand the meaning of the events that they had experienced. For them the Old Testament explained the death of Jesus and pointed to it. Christ was the unity that bound these two testaments together. The Old Testament pointed the way to Christ and in turn Christ explained and elucidated the Old Testament.

The richness of the heritage of Christianity that all Christians share together needs to be honored and valued. As Catholics, we are indebted to the importance that Protestant Christianity has preserved, celebrated, and treasured in the Sacred Scriptures over the past five centuries. The rift in the sixteenth century resulted tragically in Catholicism losing sight of the place that Sacred Scripture should hold and does hold in their tradition. The great beauty of Vatican II was to honor Pope John XXIII's instructions to take ecumenism seriously. In doing so, Catholic scholars were able to appropriate legitimately this scholarship undertaken by Protestant scholars over the course of two centuries leading up to Vatican II. Catholicism was able to restore the Scriptures to their rightful place within our liturgy and our faith.[38]

36. Justin Martyr, "The First Apology" in *Writings of Justin Martyr*, 106–7.

37. See *Dei Verbum*, Chapter VI, Article 22. See also my discussion in the next section, "The Authority of the Septuagint as the Christian Old Testament."

38. See *Dei Verbum*, Article 21: "The Church has always venerated the divine Scriptures just as she venerates the body of the Lord, since, especially in the sacred liturgy,

However, Catholic biblical scholarship also recognizes that the framework of the Catholic faith and liturgy does differ from that of other Christians. All biblical scholarship needs to be appropriated within a framework that also remains true to the Catholic faith and liturgy. As the Word of God is God's self-communication to us, the focus of the Scriptures is to speak not only to the past but also to the present and future. The goal in reading and studying these sacred writings is for the transformation of the individual in holiness and the edification of the Church as the body of Christ in love.

The above discussion identifies how different this approach is to that of those who study Scriptures today in a different framework, especially those within the university academy who see these writings as merely ancient literary documents to be treated as archaeological artifacts. Catholic academic biblical scholars are also challenged to move beyond the limited embrace of a secular, scientific historical criticism and work within the framework of the Scriptures, the Old and New Testaments, as emerging from a liturgical context whose home is within the Church.

The Authority of the Septuagint as the Christian Old Testament

The Septuagint is the most important ancient translation of the Old Testament. It was made into Greek from Hebrew by Jews living in Alexandria, Egypt, during the third century BC. According to the legend, seventy Hebrew scholars each translated the Scriptures into Greek only to find that they had each created the exact same translation. For this reason, it is called in Greek *septuaginta* ("[the translation of the] seventy"), hence the name Septuagint (or LXX) in English. The Septuagint is more inclusive than the canon received by rabbinical Judaism after the time of Christ. The Catholic Old Testament is based upon the Septuagint and contains seven more books than those contained in the Hebrew Bible.[39] The New Testament authors, when referring to the Old Testament, quoted almost exclusively from the Greek Septuagint text rather than the Hebrew proto-Masoretic Text of the rabbis. Consequently, the Apostles themselves have given an added authority to the Septuagint since it is their text. For these reasons the Septuagint

---

she unceasingly receives and offers to the faithful the bread of life from the table both of God's word and of Christ's body."

39. Books of Wisdom, Sirach, Baruch, 1 and 2 Maccabees, Judith, Tobith, and the so-called additions to Daniel and Esther. These books are referred to as the "Deutero-Canonical Books" in order to identify that they come from this "Second Canon of Alexandria."

became the official version of the Old Testament for Catholics. *Verbum Dei*, Article 22, reflects these arguments when it states:

> The Church from the very beginning accepted as her own (*ut suam suscepit*) that very ancient Greek translation of the Old Testament which is called the Septuagint (LXX); and she has always given a place of honor to other Eastern translations and Latin ones especially the Latin translation known as the Vulgate. (DV 22)

This declaration that "from the very beginning the Church accepted [the Septuagint] as her very own" translation is highly significant. Not even the Latin Vulgate receives this distinction! The Latin Vulgate and other translations such as the Syriac are acknowledged as holding places of honor, but they are not accorded the same status as the Greek Septuagint as the Church's "very own."[40] The significance and importance of upholding the authority of the Septuagint, as it is defined in *Dei Verbum*, needs to be taken seriously.

A major dispute between Saints Augustine and Jerome highlights what is at stake and the role that the Septuagint should play, especially in translations. Augustine strongly took issue with Jerome over a new translation of the Old Testament into Latin that Jerome had made directly from the Hebrew with no reference at all to the Septuagint. Augustine had valued Jerome's earlier translation of the Old Testament into Latin from the Greek Septuagint. However, translating directly from the Hebrew into Latin without any reference to the Greek Septuagint concerned Augustine, for he saw this as a deviation from the tradition of the Church. Augustine held a clear insight into the authority of the Septuagint in church tradition and gave attention to the significance of the apostolic authority conferred upon the Septuagint as the Church's own translation.[41] As the Church's translation, the Septuagint

---

40. I would like to refer to an exceptional study on the authority of the Septuagint in relation to that of the Hebrew Bible by my colleague Professor Catherine Brown Tkacz entitled *Alētheia Hellēnikē*.

41. Augustine also accepted the divine inspiration of the Septuagint itself. He believed that in the translation from the Hebrew text (centuries after the Hebrew was written), God had guided the translation and gave the Septuagint a greater authority because it brought a deeper insight and meaning to the Hebrew text. As Augustine wrote: "But the Church has received the Septuagint as if it were the only translation, and it is the one that the Greek Christians use, most of them without knowing that there is any other. From the Septuagint a translation into Latin has been made, to which the Latin churches adhere, and this remains true even though we now have the presbyter Jerome, a most learned man, an expert in all three languages, who translated these same scriptures into Latin not from the Greek but directly from the Hebrew. . . . The churches of Christ still maintain that no single translation is to be preferred to the authority of such a large group of men. . . . But since such a great mark of divinity did appear in

forms the basis for the Church's claims to the fulfillment of prophecy. By
way of illustration, take the specific instance of Isaiah 7:14, in light of Augustine's insights.[42] In that verse, the Greek Septuagint uses the word *parthenos*
(virgin): "Therefore the Lord himself will give you a sign. Behold, the virgin
(*parthenos*) shall conceive and bear a son, and shall call his name Immanuel."
When Matthew narrates the birth of Jesus, he understands Jesus' birth as a
literal fulfillment of this prophecy of Isaiah and uses the Septuagint text in
quoting the prophet: "Behold, the virgin (*parthenos*) shall conceive and bear
a son, and they shall call his name Immanuel which means, God with us"
(Matt 1:23). However, in the Hebrew text of Isaiah 7:14, the Hebrew word
is *'almah* (which can mean "a young girl of marriageable age" or "virgin").
While in the Hebrew text, the meaning is vague, the Jewish translators of the
Septuagint understood this Hebrew word *'almah* to refer clearly to a virgin
by translating it as *parthenos*, the technical term for a virgin, as is seen in the
Greek reference to the statue of the virgin goddess *Athena Parthenos*. Mat-
thew unmistakably uses the Septuagint text and thus gives a clear example
of how within the apostolic tradition (containing the Greek Septuagint and
Greek New Testament), both Testaments refer to each other and form the
basis for the apostolic tradition of the virgin birth. As noted earlier, the Old
Testament points to the future and the New Testament looks back to the
Old Testament. In doing so they both point to the birth of Christ from the
Virgin Mary. Based solely on the Hebrew Bible one could not uphold this
firm authentic tradition of the unity of the Scriptures.

Augustine's thoughts find clear expression in the text of *Dei Verbum*,
Article 22: "The Church from the very beginning accepted as her own that
very ancient Greek translation of the Old Testament which is called the Septuagint." The apostles and the early Church Fathers received the Bible in the
form that it took among the people of Israel in Alexandria and the Church
accepted it as her own ("*ut suam suscepit*"). The consequence for Catholics of
this understanding of the Old Testament is enormous. The Septuagint is the
authoritative Bible for Catholics, not the Hebrew Bible.

Surprisingly, an examination of the *New American Bible (Revised Edition)*, the approved translation of the United States Catholic Bishops Conference, shows that it fails to honor this teaching of *Dei Verbum*, Article 22. In
translating Isaiah 7:14, instead of giving preeminence to the Septuagint over
the Hebrew text, the translators do the opposite. They render the Hebrew

---

them, any other reliable translator of these Scriptures from the Hebrew into any other
language . . . agrees with the translators of the Septuagint." Augustine, *The City of God*,
18.43, on pp. 326–27.

42. This example was in fact noted two and a half centuries before Augustine in
Justin's *Dialogue with Trypho* (Dial. 66–67) in *Writings of Justin Martyr*, 253–56.

text but relegate to a footnote the text of the Septuagint.[43] Moreover, in the first edition of the New American Bible the original translators did translate the Septuagint text as "virgin" while providing the Hebrew text in a footnote. Without explanation, a different set of translators later reversed this in the New American Bible (Revised Edition). By doing do, they overturned the long-standing tradition of the Catholic Church as well as the teaching of *Dei Verbum* 22. Clearly this is not what the Council Fathers intended!

The Bible as the Word of God is Authoritative.

Dei Verbum at its very beginning demonstrated that "the Word of God" contains the language of divine "self-communication." The climax of this divine self-communication came with the death and resurrection of Christ, together with the outpouring of the Holy Spirit. Since Scripture contains the self-communication of God to humans, the texts must be read within this framework. Scripture as God's word communicated to humans is the authority for humans.

In comparison, since the Enlightenment everything has changed. Human reason constructed within a rationalistic worldview has become the measure of all things. Scripture is required to answer at the court of human reason so constructed. The idea of a Divine Authorship is anathema. Modern exegetes approach the text as needing to obey their cultural standards of objectivity. Modern readers begin with unbelief and select what they wish from the Scriptures as dictated by the confines of their own cultural constructs. By way of contrast, early Christians started with the belief that the meaning of Scripture must become our own!

---

43. Isaiah 7:14: "Therefore the Lord himself will give you a sign;[a] *the young woman*, pregnant and about to bear a son, shall name him Emmanuel." Footnote [a]: "7:14 Isaiah's sign seeks to reassure Ahaz that he need not fear the invading armies of Syria and Israel in the light of God's promise to David (2 Sm 7:12–16). The oracle follows a traditional announcement formula by which the birth and sometimes naming of a child is promised to particular individuals (Gn 16:11; Jgs 13:3). *The young woman: Hebrew 'almah designates a young woman of marriageable age without specific reference to virginity. The Septuagint translated the Hebrew term as parthenos, which normally does mean virgin, and this translation underlies Mt 1:23.* Emmanuel: the name means 'with us is God.' Since for the Christian the incarnation is the ultimate expression of God's willingness to 'be with us,' it is understandable that this text was interpreted to refer to the birth of Christ." Emphasis added.

Scripture Is Inspired and Speaks in Many Ways and at Many Levels (Senses of Scripture).

Dei Verbum 12b,c drew attention to the twofold dimensions of interpretation: critical biblical scholarship and the spiritual or theological meaning of Sacred Scripture. This captures the essence of a Catholic interpretation and understanding of the Scriptures. Since Vatican II, however, especially in Catholic academic circles, attention has focused almost exclusively on critical biblical scholarship, while the search for the spiritual or theological meaning of the Scriptures has often languished. This results in the Scriptures being approached solely as a human word without giving due attention to the framework of the Scriptures as the Divine Word expressed in human words. Catholic scholarship needs to see these writings also within the framework of God's communication with humans. For this reason, Article 12c offers the true guide for moving deeper into the text rather than simply remaining on the human level of interpretation.

For all Christians, the inspiration of the Scriptures remains the overarching framework for their interpretation. The Spirit is not only at work in the author, but the Spirit is also at work in the Church in guiding human reason into the wisdom of God. The early interpreters followed the methods used by the writers of Scripture themselves. These methods authorized patristic interpreters to seek deeper levels of meaning in all the texts of Scripture.

Origen (185–253 CE), the Alexandrian Master, lies at the beginning of the whole tradition of the spiritual interpretation of the Scriptures. Without doubt, Origen is the greatest ancient interpreter of the Scriptures. Henri de Lubac, one of the great *Ressourcement* theologians prior to Vatican II, in an outstanding study on Origen, accomplished much in rehabilitating Origen's scriptural thought and insights: "The wells once dug by Origen have long been covered over with sand. But the same deep layer of water is still there, which he can help us find once again in order to quench the same thirst."[44]

Origen based his principles on the inspiration of Scripture. He saw the Bible as the word of the Spirit and as the place or sphere of the presence of the Spirit. Scripture contains a deeper meaning than the obvious one, and this deeper meaning is the one intended by the Holy Spirit—the spiritual meaning. In fact, Origen drew attention to three senses of Scriptures: their *historical or literal sense* or meaning, their *moral sense* and their *mystical sense*. As Origen states in a homily on Leviticus: "The divine Scriptures have three senses: historical, moral, and mystical; so we say that they have a

---

44. Lubac, *History and Spirit*, 174. French original: *Histoire et esprit*.

body, a soul, and a spirit."[45] The historical sense refers to the literal description of events; the moral sense (or spiritual sense) draws out the meaning for any and every person's soul; and the mystical sense sees the meaning in its future relationship to Christ, to the Church, or to the certainty of faith. Origen refers to the threefold ritual of sacrifices in Leviticus as a symbol of this threefold sense of Scripture: "The oven, in my opinion, because of its hollow form, signifies what is most profound in Sacred Scriptures; the pan indicates the passages that one ends in understanding by stirring them and turning them over; the griddle designates the things whose meaning the world uncovers at first glance."[46]

Origen's Alexandrian religious milieu was accustomed to interpreting the Scriptures in an allegorical or spiritual sense as is evident in the outstanding Jewish scholar, Philo. The writings of Clement of Alexandria, Origen's predecessor at the Alexandrian catechetical school, also show a strong predilection for interpreting the Scriptures in an allegorical way. However, the strongest influence on Origen in his interpretation of the Scriptures undoubtedly remains Jesus, Paul, and the Scriptures themselves and their methods of interpretation. As Henri de Lubac argues:

> Origen's great master in exegesis is thus not Philo. Rather, through an already firmly established tradition that found a particularly perceptible echo, with some risk of distortion, in the Alexandrian milieu, that master was far likelier to have been Jesus himself, who said: "Search the Scriptures. . . . It is they that bear witness to me; . . . it is Moses [and the prophets] who wrote of me." Origen also often quotes that other saying of the risen Jesus to his disciples of Emmaus: "O foolish men, and slow of heart to believe all that the prophets have spoken!" Exaggerating the importance of such declarations, but more by explaining their meaning in minute detail than by amplifying them, the Origenian work develops a rich meditation on the relation of the two Testaments whose seeds go back to the very earliest days of the Church. There is only one God, author of both Testaments, faithful to himself throughout both, and it is the same gesture of that God that is manifested by both, each in its own way; it is the same salvation that each announces. For every Christian, the first Testament already contains Christ in a mysterious way, but it is consequently only understood through him: "The divine Logos has the key of David, and since he has

---

45. Origen, *Homilies on Leviticus*, 5.5, quoted in Lubac, *History and Spirit*, 174.
46. Origen, *Homilies on Leviticus*, 5.5, quoted in Lubac, *History and Spirit*, 161.

come with this key, he opens the Scriptures, which were closed before his coming."[47]

The implications for the task of interpreting Scripture can immediately be seen. When faced with a biblical text, the interpreter realizes that it has not only an historical or literal meaning, but also a deeper, hidden meaning—a spiritual and a mystical sense—that is intended by the Spirit. For Origen, the true understanding of the Scriptures requires an openness of mind and heart, and therefore of faith. The truth of the texts, their deep meaning, their spiritual significance, is always discovered within what is written. Origen's vast writings and insights were to have an enormous influence on patristic and medieval interpreters who continued to seek out different levels or senses.

While Origen discerned a threefold set of meanings in Scripture, many of the Fathers spoke of a fourfold sense of Scripture that they found evident within the New Testament and which they classified in different ways. One could generally list them in this way:

> (1) *The Literal Sense of Scripture:* The meaning conveyed by the words of Scripture and discovered by exegesis.
>
> (2) *The Spiritual Sense of Scripture:*
>
>> (a) *The allegorical sense:* A deeper and more profound understanding of events by recognizing their significance in Christ. Thus St. Paul finds in the story of Hagar and Sarah an allegory of the Old and New Testaments (Gal 4:21–31). The allegorical also includes *typology:* The Old Testament presents types that are fulfilled in the New Testament. Thus Melchizedek is a type or prefiguration of Christ, the High Priest (Heb 7:1–28).
>>
>> (b) *The moral sense:* Events and instructions challenge believers to lead a virtuous life as part of the Body of Christ and created in God's image.
>>
>> (c) *The anagogical sense* (Greek: *anagōgē* [*ana+agein*] "leading upwards"): A mystical interpretation of a text that detects allusions to heaven or the afterlife. Scriptural events are viewed in terms of their eternal significance; for instance, the Church is seen as a sign of the heavenly Jerusalem.

A medieval couplet summarizes the senses in this way:

47. Lubac, *History and Spirit*, 190–91.

The Letter speaks of deeds; Allegory to faith;
The Moral how to act; Anagogy, our destiny.[48]

The widespread tradition expressed in the New Testament itself and by biblical commentators from the Fathers onwards was to interpret Scripture as richly meaningful, in this fourfold sense.

In contrast, the world of modern biblical scholarship acknowledges no deeper meanings, no mysteries to be revealed. Only the literal sense is admitted, and it is equated with the intention of the author. Not only are these views in striking contrast to the framework in which the Fathers of the Church worked and with which a Catholic interpretation of the Scriptures operates, it is also contrary to the work of one of the great twentieth-century scholars of hermeneutics, Paul Ricoeur[49] who defines what has to be appropriated from the reading of a text:

> Not the intention of the author, which is supposed to be hidden behind the text; not the historical situation common to the author and his original readers; not the expectations or feelings of these original readers; not even their understanding of themselves as historical and cultural phenomena. What has to be appropriated is *the meaning of the text itself, conceived in a dynamic way as the direction of thought opened up by the text.*[50]

Ricœur's thought helps to speak to the Catholic understanding of the inspiration of the Scriptures as well. As we have noted, the Spirit is not only at work in the author, but the Spirit is also at work in the Church, and in the lives of present readers guiding human reason into the wisdom of God. Thus we can appropriate Ricoeur's understanding of the interpretation of the text: it is the Spirit who enables the reader to appropriate the "meaning of the text itself, conceived in a dynamic way as the direction of thought opened up by the text." The Spirit is the guarantor that the "direction of thought opened up by the text" is not simply an arbitrary meaning, but one that is significant for the spiritual life of the believer who reads the text within the framework of the Catholic Church and its magisterium.

---

48. "Lettera gesta docet, quid credas allegoria, / Moralis quid agas, quo tendas anagogia." Attributed to Augustinus of Dacia (thirteenth century), *Rotulus pugillaris*, quoted in Latin in the *Catechism of the Catholic Church*, par. 118.

49. The French philosopher Paul Ricoeur (1913–2005) was best known for combining phenomenological description with hermeneutics. As such, his thought is within the same tradition as other major hermeneutic phenomenologists, Martin Heidegger and Hans-Georg Gadamer.

50. Ricoeur, *Interpretation Theory*, 92. Emphasis added.

In Conclusion

Dei Verbum has demonstrated a profoundly biblical orientation. It challenges the theologian to consider "the study of the sacred page, as it were, the soul of sacred theology" (Article 24). This recommendation, taken from Leo XIII's Encyclical *Providentissimus Deus*, drew on the theological method of the Church Fathers, both Eastern and Western. The prayerful study of the Bible, both Old and New Testaments, was "the very soul" of their teaching.

The above four factors or principles provide the framework needed to cultivate and re-appropriate for today a Catholic interpretation of the Scriptures in line with the rich heritage of the Catholic tradition. We do this not uncritically, but with the awareness that we are working within the context of the Catholic Church. It is significant and essential for all believing exegetes to take seriously the inspiration of the Scriptures and to interpret them accordingly. For the Fathers of the Church, this was the fundamental principle: because the Scriptures are inspired, the interpreter must seek the meaning intended by the Spirit, the spiritual sense of the Scriptures. John states as well that the presence and action of the Spirit of truth is indispensable (John 6:63; 16:7, 13). The framework of faith is needed to "understand" the meaning of the words of Sacred Scripture.

The gift of *Dei Verbum* is that it leads us to acknowledge both the divine and human authors of Scripture as we seek to understand the truth which is given through them "for the sake of our salvation." Thus, historical-critical analysis is to facilitate authentic engagement with the spiritual meanings of Old and New Testaments. In prayer, informed by active participation in the liturgy, this is meant to lead both the individual believer and the church into holy union with God. This is eloquently described by Joseph Ratzinger in his *Commentary on Chapter VI of Dei Verbum*, Article 25:

> The reading of Scripture . . . reaches its highest point when the Church listens to the word of God in common in the sacred liturgy and within this framework itself experiences the active presence of the Logos, the Word in the words. The private reading of Scripture points ultimately towards this reading of the Bible that is in the fullest sense "ecclesial," but this ecclesial reading would lose its soul, were it not constantly nourished by total personal immersion in the word of God. In the daily enthronement of the Gospel the Council gave to the liturgy of the word a particularly solemn quality and thus endeavoured to place itself, as the "listening Church" (which it wanted, and had, to be, precisely as the "teaching Church": cf. Article 10), entirely under the dominion of the Gospel. This dominion of the Gospel

should last beyond the Council and can do so only if the Church lets itself be increasingly penetrated by the word of Scripture.[51]

Bibliography

Augustine. *The City of God (De Civitate Dei), Books 11–22.* Translated by William Babcock. WSA I/7. Hyde Park, NY: New City, 2013.

Benedict XVI, Pope. *Verbum Domini: The Word of God in the Life and Mission of the Church.* Frederick, MD: The Word Among Us, 2010.

Catechism of the Catholic Church. https://www.vatican.va/archive/ENG0015/_INDEX. HTM.

Enchiridion Symbolorum: Definitionum et declarationum de rebus fidei et morum. Edited by Henricus Denziger, revised by Adolfus Schönmetzer. Freiburg: Herder, 1967.

Grelot, Pierre. *La Bible, parole de Dieu.* Paris: Desclée, 1965.

Grillmeier, Alois. "Chapter III: The Divine Inspiration and the Interpretation of Sacred Scripture." In *Commentary on Vatican II*, edited by Herbert Vorgrimler, translated by Lalit Adolphus et al., 3:199–246. New York: Herder & Herder, 1967–69.

Justin Martyr. *The Writings of Saint Justin Martyr.* Translated by Thomas B. Falls. The Fathers of the Church 6. Washington: Catholic University of America Press, 1965.

Leo XIII, Pope. *Providentissimus Deus.* https://www.vatican.va/content/leo-xiii/en/encyclicals/documents/hf_l-xiii_enc_18111893_providentissimus-deus.html.

Lubac, Henri de. *Histoire et esprit: L'Intelligence de l'Écriture d'après Origène.* Paris: Éditions Montaigne, 1950.

———. *History and Spirit: The Understanding of Scripture according to Origen.* Translated by Anne Englund Nash with Greek and Latin translation by Juvenal Merriell of the Oratory. San Francisco: Ignatius, 2007.

Miller, Robert. "'For the Sake of Our Salvation,' Interpreting *Dei Verbum*, Art. 11, Fifty Years Later." *Journal of Scriptural Reasoning*, 15.2 (2016). https://jsr.shanti.virginia.edu/back-issues/volume-15-number-2-november-2016/for-the-sake-of-our-salvation-interpreting-dei-verbum-art-11-fifty-years-later/.

Paul VI, Pope. *Dei Verbum.* www.vatican.va/archive/hist_councils/ii_vatican_council/documents/vat-ii_const_19651118_dei-verbum_lt.html. English translation: www.vatican.va/archive/hist_councils/ii_vatican_council/documents/vat-ii_const_19651118_dei-verbum_en.html.

Ratzinger, Joseph. "Dogmatic Constitution on Divine Revelation: Origin and Background," "Preface," "Chapter I," "Chapter II," and "Chapter VI." In *Commentary on Vatican II*, edited by Herbert Vorgrimler, translated by Lalit Adolphus et al., 3:155–98, 262–72. New York: Herder & Herder, 1967–69.

Ricoeur, Paul. *Interpretation Theory: Discourse and the Surplus of Meaning.* Fort Worth: Texas Christian University Press, 1976.

Tanquerey, Adolphe. *Manual of Dogmatic Theology.* Translated by John J. Byrnes. 2 vols. New York: Desclée, 1913.

Taylor, Charles. *A Secular Age.* Cambridge: Harvard University Press, 2007.

———. *Sources of the Self: The Making of the Modern Identity.* Cambridge: Harvard University Press, 1989.

51. Ratzinger, "Chapter VI: Sacred Scripture in the Life of the Church," 271.

————. *Varieties of Religion Today: William James Revisited.* Cambridge: Harvard University Press, 2002.

Tkacz, Catherine Brown. *Alētheia Hellēnikē: The Authority of the Greek Old Testament.* Etna, CA: St. Palamas Monastery, 2011.

Vorgrimler, Herbert, ed. *Commentary on the Documents of Vatican II.* Translated by Lalit Adolphus et al. 5 vols. New York: Herder & Herder, 1967–69.

————. *Das Zweite Vatikanische Konzil, Dokumente und Kommentare, Part II.* Freiburg im Breisgau: Herder, 1967.

2

Three Syriac Fathers on Reading the Bible[1]

SEBASTIAN P. BROCK

Wolfson College, Oxford University

Some Preliminary Considerations

THERE ARE OF COURSE innumerable ways of reading the Bible, but basically these can all be classified under one or other of two headings, depending on their starting point: one takes its starting-point from the standpoint of faith, the other does not. For convenience these two approaches may be simply designated as the religious and the secular. The secular will include both the academic and the purely literary approaches to the Bible, and it has no concern with any ideas of inspiration. By contrast, the former approach, which represents the tradition of reading Scripture within the Church, sees the Scriptures as in some way or other inspired, however this is understood–and there are a large number of ways of understanding what is meant by inspiration in this context. Basically what is involved here is a recognition of the activity of the Holy Spirit. This role of the Holy Spirit should not only be understood as being an active one with reference to the original authors, but also as being of importance in the course of the transmission of the biblical text,[2] and above all (as will become evident from the emphasis given to it

---

1. This contribution is a slightly expanded form of an article under the same title published in *Sobornost/Eastern Churches Review* 33 (2011) 6–21.

2. The late Dominique Barthélemy has an illuminating discussion concerning the differences between "authorial authenticity" and "scriptural authenticity," and the implications of this for the biblical text: only a single text can have authorial authenticity, whereas several different stages of the biblical text can have scriptural authenticity. Although Barthélemy is primarily talking about the developments in the history of the Hebrew text (now considerably clarified by the Qumran biblical manuscripts), what

by the Syriac Fathers) in the way that the Scriptures are read (or heard) by the individual reader, for the reader too needs to be open to the Holy Spirit in the same sort of way that the original authors were.

At the outset it is important to notice an essential difference between the two approaches: for the secular approach, there is going to be (at least in theory) only one correct interpretation to any given passage. It is a case of interpretations being either right or wrong: the Biblical text is univalent. For the religious approach the biblical text is, by contrast, multilayered, and so it is multivalent: there can be innumerable meanings to a single passage; all of them are potentially valid, provided they are meaningful in a particular context, and (supremely important) provided the reader is fully open to the Holy Spirit, and not consciously or unconsciously trying to impose his or her own ideology upon the text.

Many different analogies have been offered for the different levels of meaning in the biblical text, but for our present purposes the most helpful is the analogy of the humanity and divinity of Christ: the outward humanity of Christ is there for everyone to see, but it requires the interior eye of faith to perceive his hidden divinity. The secular approach sees just the outward body, as it were, of the biblical text, but for the religious approach there is a completely different spiritual dimension as well. Another illuminating analogy is provided by George Herbert ("The Elixer"):

> A man that looks on glass
>
> on it may stay his eye,
>
> or, if he pleaseth, through it pass
>
> and then the heaven espy.

It is also important to emphasize that the two approaches, secular and religious, are not rivals: it is *not* a case of either/or. Rather, they need to be seen as complementary: both are perfectly valid approaches, but they operate on completely different planes. It is also very possible for the one to be illuminating to the other. It is only when one or other approach tries to claim that it is the *only* correct approach that they come into conflict.

With these preliminary remarks, it is time to turn to our immediate topic, the contribution to the subject of a third tradition of Christianity, alongside the Latin West and the Greek East, that of the Syriac Orient.[3]

---

he says about scriptural authenticity is equally applicable to the ancient versions (as he points out with reference to the Septuagint–but one can equally include the other ancient versions, as well). See Barthélemy, *Critique textuelle de l'Ancien Testament*, 58*–63*, 77*, 109*–111*.

3. For the wider significance of this, see my "Syriac Orient."

To serve as representatives of this tradition I shall take three writers, St. Ephrem, the theologian and poet who died in 373, St. Jacob of Serugh, another poet, who died in 521, and St. Isaac the Syrian (Isaac of Nineveh), the great writer on the spiritual life, who belongs to the late seventh century. The first two were living in the eastern provinces of the Late Roman Empire, while the third author lived further East, in what is now Iraq and western Iran, during the first century of Arab rule.

St. Ephrem

In many ways it is Ephrem who presents us with the most carefully thought-out understanding of the nature of Scripture and of the way in which it ought to be read.[4] Ephrem sees a pattern consisting of two stages, the first being that of divine initiative, and the second being that of human response.

Divine Initiative

Throughout his works Ephrem lays stress on the "chasm" that lies between Creator and creation: the human intellect is totally incapable of crossing over this chasm, which means that the only way that humanity can have any knowledge of God is because God himself has crossed over this chasm:

> If God had not wished to interpret Himself to us
> there would not have been anything in creation
> capable of saying anything about Him at all.
> (Hymns on Faith, 44:7)

God's way of revealing himself is through the "symbols," or "mysteries," which are latent in both Scripture and Nature (Ephrem speaks of these as being God's two "witnesses"). The Syriac term used, *rāzē*, is not easy to translate in English: it corresponds fairly closely to Greek *mystēria*, and can also mean the "Sacraments" (above all, the Eucharist). In many passages of his poetry, however, it seems more meaningful to translate *rāzē* by "symbols," though it is essential to realise that "symbol" is here used in the strong sense, where the symbol is understood as having an ontological connection with what it symbolizes. This is the normal understanding of the term "symbol" in all the Church Fathers, and it is only in modern usage that its meaning

---

4. On Ephrem, see especially Biesen, *Simple and Bold*; see also my *Luminous Eye*. Many of the passages quoted below will also be found in my rather longer discussion in "St. Ephrem the Syrian on Reading Scripture."

has been weakened, with the result that symbol is usually understood as essentially different from what it symbolizes.

These "mysteries" are, as it were, pointers to a divine reality, and they are omnipresent:

> These are the witnesses which reach everywhere,
>
> they are found at all times,
>
> they are present at every moment,
>
> rebuking the unbeliever who denies the Creator. (*Hymns on Paradise*, 5:2)

They are not, however, visible to the physical eye, but lie hidden, awaiting to be discovered:

> Lord, Your symbols are everywhere,
>
> yet You are hidden from everywhere.

This aspect of hiddenness is very important for Ephrem, who lays great emphasis on human free-will: God does not use compulsion, and he does not impose knowledge of himself on humanity. Ephrem explains the reason for this:

> Any kind of adornment that is the result of compulsion
>
> is not genuine, for it is merely imposed.
>
> Herein lies the magnitude of God's gift,
>
> in that a person can adorn himself of his own accord,
>
> seeing that God has removed all compulsion.
>
> (Nisibene Hymns, 16:1)

Like St. John Chrysostom, St. Ephrem frequently speaks of God "coming down to our level," his "condescension" in the original sense of that word. In order to illustrate how this takes place he uses the everyday imagery of putting on and taking off one's clothes.[5] In the Old Testament God "put on metaphors" (literally "names"), allowing himself to be spoken of in human language and in human terms, even though they are totally inadequate:

> It was out of love that God put on metaphors that were defective.
>
> (Hymns on Faith, 29:3)

This condescension on God's part must not be misinterpreted, and the metaphors he "puts on" must not be taken literally:

---

5. For this characteristic feature, see further my "Robe of Glory" (the whole issue of *The Way* is devoted to the spirituality of clothing).

If someone concentrates his attention solely

on the metaphors used of God's majesty,

that person abuses and misrepresents His majesty

and thus goes astray

by means of those very metaphors

with which God had clothed Himself for that person's benefit,

and so he is ungrateful to that Grace

which stooped down low

to the level of his childishness.

Although she has nothing in common with him,

yet Grace clothed herself in his likeness

in order to bring him to the likeness of herself.

(*Hymns on Paradise*, 11:6)

To make his point, Ephrem humorously compares God's method of teaching human beings something about himself to a person teaching a parrot how to talk, using a mirror:

Someone who is teaching a parrot how to speak

hides behind a mirror and teaches it in this way:

when the bird turns in the direction of the voice which is speaking

it finds in front of its eyes its own resemblance reflected;

it imagines that it is another parrot, conversing with it.

The man places the bird's image in front of it

so that by this means it might learn how to speak.

This bird is a fellow creature with the man,

but although this relationship exists, the man beguiles and teaches

the parrot something alien to itself by means of itself;

in this way he speaks with it.

The Divine Being, who in all things is exalted above all,

in His love bent down from on high and acquired from us what we are used to:

He has laboured by every means so as to turn all to Himself.

(Hymns on Faith, 31:6–7)

Ephrem continues with his use of clothing imagery when he describes the next stage in God's self-revelation to human beings: at the Incarnation the Divine Word "put on the body." This is in fact the standard phrase used in early Syriac writers, corresponding to "he was enfleshed" (i.e., incarnate; Greek *esarkōthē*) in the Nicene Creed. A variety of different, but related, phrases can be found, such as "he put on humanity, our humanity, our body, Adam," etc.

Human Response

So far Ephrem has only told us how *not* to respond to language about God in the Old Testament. More important is his guidance on how to perceive the "mysteries" and "symbols" latent in Scripture and Nature. Here he employs the image of the eye: just as the physical eye perceives objects when (according to the optics of Ephrem's time) it is filled with light, so too the inner eye of the heart (that is, the spiritual centre of the human person) becomes enabled to perceive the symbols and mysteries only when it is filled with the light of faith–and the greater the faith, the more symbols and mysteries will become apparent. For this inner eye of faith to function properly there are a number of prerequisites: in the first place, a person needs to ensure that his or her inner eye is pure and unsullied; only then can the eye become luminous, that is, filled with the light of faith.

> The Scriptures are laid out like a mirror
> and the person whose eye is luminous
> sees therein the image of Divine Reality.
> (Hymns on Faith, 67:8)

Then, equally important, there is the need for the presence of "Love and Truth," where "Truth" for Ephrem means right faith: a skewed faith will only distort a person's vision.

> Truth and Love are wings that cannot be separated,
> for Truth without Love is not able to fly.
> So too, Love without Truth is unable to soar up,
> for their yoke is one of harmony.
> (Hymns on Faith, 20:12)

Ephrem is thus laying down the parameters within which one should approach reading the Scriptures: in the absence of an attitude of love, the biblical text will not disclose any of its pointers to Divine Reality:

> Your fountain, Lord, is hidden
> from the person who does not thirst for You.

Your treasury seems empty
to the person who rejects You.
Love is the treasurer
of Your heavenly treasure store.
(Hymns on Faith, 32:3)

A wrong approach will actually prove counter-productive:

A person who seeks after Truth with a grudging spirit
cannot gain knowledge, even if he actually encounters it,
for envy has clouded his mind,
and he does not get any the wiser, even if he grabs at that knowledge.
(Hymns on Faith, 17:1)

By contrast, a right approach can have unexpected consequences, as we learn from Ephrem's Hymns on Paradise, where he gives a striking description of an experience of his own on reading the opening of the Paradise narrative in Genesis:

I read the opening of this book
and was filled with joy
for its verses and lines
spread out their arms to welcome me;
the first rushed out and kissed me,
and led me on to its companion;
and when I reached that verse
wherein is written
the story of Paradise,
it lifted me up and transported me
from the bosom of the Book
to the very bosom of Paradise.

The eye and the mind
travelled over the lines,
as over a bridge, and entered together
the story of Paradise.
The eye, as it read,
transported the mind;

in return, the mind too
gave the eye rest
from its reading,
for when the Book had been read,
the eye had rest,
but the mind was engaged.

Both the bridge and the gate
of Paradise
did I find in this Book.
I crossed over and entered;
my eye indeed remained outside,
but my mind entered within.
I began to wander
amid things not described.
This is the luminous height,
clear, lofty and beauteous:
Scripture named it Eden,
the summit of all blessings.
(*Hymns on Paradise*, 5:3–5)

For Ephrem, as for the Church Fathers in general, it is Christ who serves as the hermeneutical key to the Scriptures. All symbols find their full meaning in him. In another particularly striking passage Ephrem described how it was through Christ's very side, pierced on the cross (John 19:34) that he was enabled to enter Paradise (he begins by addressing Christ directly):

> I ran to all Your limbs, and from them I have received every kind of gift. Through the side pierced with the sword I entered the Garden fenced in by the sword (Gen. 3:24). Let us enter in through that side which was pierced, since we were stripped naked by the counsel of the rib that was extracted. The fire that burnt in Adam burnt him in that rib of his; for this reason the side of the Second Adam has been pierced, and from it comes forth a flow of water to quench the fire of the first Adam.[6]

Elsewhere in this prose work Ephrem playfully makes the point that Scripture is not univalent:

---

6. Ephrem, *Commentary on the Diatessaron* (1963), 21:10.

If there only existed one single sense for the words of Scripture, then the first commentator to come along would discover it, and other hearers would experience neither the labour of searching, nor the joy of finding. Rather, each word of our Lord has its own form, and each form has its own members, and each member has its own character. Every individual understands it in accordance with his capacity, and interprets it as it is granted to him.[7]

St. Jacob of Serugh

Despite living during the times of bitter theological controversy that arose over the Council of Chalcedon's Definition of Faith (451), Jacob came to be regarded as a saint both by the Syrian Orthodox Church (which rejects the Council) and by the Maronite Church (which accepts it), no small achievement!

His justly high reputation rests on his imposing number of sermons, or homilies, often of great beauty, which he delivered in verse, and it seems that he must have had a gift of oral composition similar to that of oral poets, for his verse homilies make use of a large number of short "building blocks," consisting of recurring four-syllable units. The majority of these verse homilies are on biblical topics.[8]

Jacob is particularly fond of bridal imagery, and at one point he describes Old Testament prophecy as a bride-to-be, whose face may only be unveiled by the Bridegroom, in other words, Christ:

> Just as only the bridegroom may lift up the bride's veil, so too
> the face of Prophecy, who is betrothed to the Crucified One,
> was only revealed when Christ the Bridegroom was revealed.
> (Letters, 173)

Like Ephrem, Jacob is emphatic that Scripture needs to be approached with an attitude of love; without it, there is no point in reading it, since it will only provide the words, but not the inner meaning.

---

7. Ephrem, *Commentary on the Diatessaron* (1990), 7:22.

8. A fine introduction to Jacob is provided by Kollamparampil in his *Salvation according to Jacob* and a selection of translations will be found in his *Jacob of Serugh: Festal Homilies*. A listing of all available translations is given by Bedjan in *Homilies of Jacob of Serugh*, 6:400–406; a large number of further homilies were published in 2017 by Akhrass and Syriany in Jacob, *160 Unpublished Homilies*.

Approach Scripture with love–and you will see its beauty,

for if you don't approach it with love, it will not allow you
to see its face.

If you read it without love, you will not get any profit,

for love is the gate through which a person enters into
its true understanding.

Scripture demands of you, when you take hold of it,

that, if you do not love it more than yourself, you should not
read it.

It says to you, "If you read me reluctantly,

I too will be reluctant to reveal to you my meaning.

Either love me, then open me and read, and see my beauties,

or don't read me, for you won't get any benefit if you
don't love me.

To the person who shows love to me as he reads me,
I will show love,

and if he asks me, I will give over to him all my treasures."[9]

Similarly, in the course of a Homily on the Ark and the Philistines (1 Samuel 5–6), he writes:

With the hearing (of the Scriptures) let love run to receive them,

for without love the person who hears will not be helped.

Scripture is a treasure full of riches for the person who
approaches it,

and the guardian who is in charge of it is love:

love is the key which is able to open all doors;

without it there is no way of entering into God's presence.[10]

Jacob quite often likes to compare the Scriptures to an ocean, and to their spiritual meanings as pearls, for which one has to dive down in order to bring them up:

The Scriptures of the Son are like the ocean

and in this ocean there lies a pearl, hidden from merchants.

The person who expounds the text is like a diver who dives
down in search of the pearl;

---

9. Jacob, *Homilies of Mar Jacob*, 4:282.

10. Jacob, Homily 86, in *Unpublished Homilies*, 180–83.

he gropes around in the depths, and brings up the pearl
with him.

Once the pearl has come up, it is handed over to the merchants

and everyone can gain great benefit from it, once they
have acquired it.

The intellect goes down, like the diver, into the scriptural
reading

to bring up, with itself, the message of salvation, the pearl.

You who listen, receive this message, like merchants;

profit from it, all of you, and grow rich from it spiritually![11]

The same image occurs in another Homily, but here Jacob adds a further requisite, the grace to appreciate what the diver–here the intellect–has found:

In the depth of the seas there is a pearl for the person
who seeks for it;

In Scripture too, there is the Word of Life for the person
who loves it.

The divine Scriptures are like the pleasant sea:

the intellect descends like a diver into their depths:

it feels around for the pearl in the depth of prophecy,

one full of beauty, and it brings it up to the surface.

The intellect is in need of Grace, the Mistress of
the treasure store,

so that she may give to it the riches which it has discovered
in the readings.

As a result of the gift of the Godhead, the soul becomes
enlightened,

enabled to behold the beauties that exist in the Scriptures
and to take hold of them.[12]

Jacob indicates that, in order to gain, through grace, spiritual insight and profit from reading the biblical text, prayer is also necessary:

All the words in the Scriptures are full of light.

May I become illumined, Lord, so that I may tell of your story
with a sense of wonder.

Mysteries (*or* Symbols) are concealed within the Scriptures.

11. Jacob, *Homilies of Mar Jacob*, 1:328.
12. Jacob, Homily 88, in *Unpublished Homilies*, 25–29.

O Son of God, grant to the intellect the ability to bring up
great wealth that lies within the divine Scriptures.
Make me worthy, Lord, to gather in and partake of
their treasures.
The word of salvation is a pearl for someone who loves it.
Approach, O hearer, hang it on your ear for your adornment!
An ordinary pearl, brought at a price, will only adorn one ear,
but the word of salvation (or Life) is far better than such a pearl
since ten thousand ears can be equally adorned by it![13]

The Old Testament has quite a number of passages which pose problems for readers. One such passage is Genesis 38, where Tamar dresses up as a prostitute and seduces Judah, her father-in-law. Very few of the Fathers offer any lengthy treatment of this chapter; Jacob, however, is an exception for he devotes a whole verse homily to the passage.[14] As is often the case, he takes as his starting point a passing hint provided by Ephrem, who presents Tamar as herself saying "It is for what is hidden in the Hebrews that I thirst" (Commentary on Genesis XXXIV:3), and elsewhere he comments "Since the King (i.e., Christ) was hidden in Judah, Tamar stole him from his loins" (Hymns on the Nativity I:12). Ephrem and Jacob are in fact following Jewish exegetical tradition which held that it was for the seed of the Messiah that Tamar (a gentile) was yearning: having been cheated of the promise that she should marry Judah's son Shelah (see Gen 38:11 and 14), Tamar was reduced to resorting to this highly unconventional ruse.

How does Jacob deal with the chapter? As is often the case in his verse homilies he starts off with a long prayer, asking for guidance in explicating the biblical text. He then goes on to emphasize two points: firstly, that the reader needs to approach the text with the right attitude, that is, with faith and love, if she or he is going to perceive the true significance of the passage; and secondly, that the very fact that this problematic chapter features in the biblical text at all indicates that there must be some deeper meaning behind the episode:

In the case of all the Mystery-filled narratives of
the Only-Begotten
it is right to listen with great love, O discerning reader,
for if love does not open the gate of your ear
then there is no passage to your understanding for the words.

13. Jacob, *Homilies of Mar Jacob*, 2:197.
14. Edited, with English translation, in my "Jacob's Homily on Tamar."

In the case of the story of Tamar, unless a mind that has faith
listens to it, the discerning woman will seem worthy
of reproach,

whereas, if an intellect that loves to listen to the mysteries
should hear this tale, it will render back in return for it praise.

All the words that the Spirit of God has placed in Scripture
are filled with riches, like treasures, hidden in the different
books.

Moses the scribe set the story of Tamar
like a jewel in his book so that its beauty might shine
out among its lections.

Why would he have written of a woman who sat like
a prostitute

by the crossroads, had she not been filled with some mystery?

Why did Moses, who drove away all prostitutes from his
people,

extol this one who had adorned herself like a prostitute?

Her action would have been wrong had there not been
some mystery there,

and it would not have been successful had it been something
hateful to God.

Her action was indeed ugly, but her faith made it beautiful,

and it was resplendent and dear because of the Mystery
that was performed in her.[15]

Throughout his verse homilies on biblical subjects Jacob displays a
wonderful gift of bringing out the riches that lie hidden beneath the surface
of the biblical text.

St. Isaac of Nineveh

Neither Ephrem nor Jacob were monks (event though later tradition presented Ephrem as one),[16] so with Isaac we enter a different world: whereas
Ephrem and Jacob were writing for a wide audience, Isaac's treatises on the
spiritual life were intended for a monastic readership, and it is only in the

15. Brock, "Jacob's Homily on Tamar," lines 137–56.

16. For an account of this misleading presentation of St. Ephrem, often followed
in the iconographical tradition, see (for example) the Introduction to my *St. Ephrem:
Hymns on Paradise*.

last couple of centuries that his writings have reached, and come to be appreciated by, a non-monastic audience, as well.[17] Although Isaac does not explicitly quote the Bible very often, he is clearly very familiar with its contents, and stresses the importance of reading it:

> We should consider the labour of reading Scripture to be something extremely elevated, whose importance cannot be exaggerated. For it serves as the gate by which the intellect enters into the divine mysteries and takes strength for attaining luminosity in prayer: it bathes with enjoyment as it wanders over the acts of God's dispensation which have taken place for the benefit of humanity–acts which make us stand continually in wonder, and from which meditation too takes strength, this being the firstfruits of this mode of life about which we are talking: from these acts prayer is illumined and strengthened.[18]

Isaac is fully in harmony with Ephrem and Jacob in his emphasis on the need for prayer before embarking on reading the biblical text:

> Do not approach the words of the mysteries contained in the divine Scriptures without prayer and beseeching God for help. Say "Lord, grant me to perceive the power in them." Reckon prayer to be the key to the true understanding of the divine Scriptures.[19]

If the aim behind reading Scripture is to be attained, then perseverance is needed:

> Persevere in reading Scripture . . . so that your intellect may be drawn towards the wonder of God at all times.[20]

Like Jacob (and many other writers), Isaac compares the Scriptures to an ocean into which one needs to dive down in order to bring up something of its riches. But even just swimming on the surface can have some benefit:

17. A helpful introduction to St. Isaac is provided by Alfeyev, *Spiritual World of Isaac*. Three collections of his writings are now available (the second and third have only recently come to light). References to these and to available translations can be found in my *Wisdom of St. Isaac*, ix, and, updated, in my bilingual edition, Syriac-English, *Wisdom of St. Isaac of Nineveh*, xviii–xix.

18. II.21.13 in Brock, *Isaac of Nineveh*, 116–17.

19. Isaac, *Ascetical Homilies*, 233. Homily 48 in this translation (made from the ninth-century Greek version) corresponds to Homilies 45–46 in the Syriac original (edited by Paul Bedjan in Isaac, *Mar Isaacus Ninivita*, and translated by Wensinck in Isaac, *Mystic Treatises*). A concordance to the different numberings is given in *Ascetical Homilies*, cxiii–cxv (also in my *Isaac of Nineveh*, xli–xliv).

20. Isaac, *Ascetical Homilies*, 31.

If the mind (just) swims on the surface of the waters of the ocean of the divine Scriptures, and its perceptions cannot fathom the great depth, so as to be able to grasp all the treasures in its deep, yet even this, by the power of its love, will suffice to pinion its thoughts by a single thought of wonder.[21]

Just as prayer is needed before reading Scripture, so too the reading of Scripture gives birth to prayer. Isaac describes this reciprocal effect as follows:

The reading of Scripture manifestly is the fountainhead that gives birth to prayer–and by these two things (sc. reading and prayer) we are transported in the direction of the love of God whose sweetness is poured out continually in our hearts like honey or a honeycomb, and our souls exult at the taste which the hidden ministry of prayer and the reading of Scripture pour into our hearts.[22]

If a sense of weariness creeps in, then this should be seen as Scripture's way of rebuking the reader; moreover, there can be quite wrong motives behind reading the biblical text:

Weariness in reading in reality rebukes the person who reads . . . and it is something which belongs to the portion of the idle: it scares away from us any reflection on God, and converse with it (sc. weariness) makes our intellect sprout out with the distraction of the world, with human illusions, with controversy, and the rest. Or it may be that those who read just for the sake of recitation do so in order to receive from the Scriptures material for human glory, or a sharpening of the mind.[23]

Isaac then contrasts these wrong approaches with the correct one:

But the person who is occupied with the Scriptures for the sake of truth has his mind dwelling continually in heaven, making conversation with God at every moment, with his thoughts wandering in yearning for the world to come. This world continually appears to his eyes as something to be disdained, as his mind meditates on the hope to come, and throughout his life he chooses no other task or labour or ministry that is greater than this one.[24]

21. Isaac, *Ascetical Homilies*, 5–6.

22. Brock, *Isaac of Nineveh*, ch. 29, sec. 5.

23. Brock, *Isaac of Nineveh*, ch. 29, sec. 10.

24. Brock, *Isaac of Nineveh*, ch. 29, sec. 11.

* * *

The advice given by these three Syriac saints remains just as pertinent today for anyone approaching the Bible from a starting point of faith as it was for their own contemporaries, well over a millennium ago. Very similar advice will be found in the Greek and Latin Fathers,[25] and indeed what all of them are talking about is precisely the tradition of *lectio divina*, the meditative reading of Scripture. But let St. Ephrem have the final word:

> Who is capable of comprehending the extent of what is to be discovered in a single utterance of Yours? For we leave behind in it far more than we can take from it, like thirsty people drinking from a fountain. . . . The facets of His words are more numerous than the faces of those who learn from them. God depicted His words with many beauties, so that each of those who learn from them can examine that aspect of them which he likes. And God has hidden within His words all sorts of treasures, so that each of us can be enriched by them from whatever aspects we meditate on. For God's word is the Tree of Life which proffers blessed fruits to you on all sides; it is the Rock which was struck in the Wilderness, which became a spiritual drink for everyone on all sides: "They ate the food of the Spirit and drank the draft of the Spirit" (1 Cor 10:3). . . . Anyone who encounters Scripture should not suppose that the single one of its riches that he has found is the only one to exist; rather, he should realize that he himself is only capable of discovering that one out of the many riches which exist in it. Nor, because Scripture has enriched him, should the reader impoverish it. Rather, if the reader is incapable of finding more, let him acknowledge Scripture's magnitude. Rejoice because you have found satisfaction, and do not grieved that there has been something left over by you. A thirsty person rejoices because he has drunk: he is not grieved because he proved incapable of drinking the fountain dry. Let the fountain vanquish your thirst; your thirst should not vanquish the fountain! If your thirst comes to an end while the fountain has not been diminished, then you can drink again whenever you are thirsty; whereas, if the fountain had been drained dry once you had had your fill, your victory over it would have proved to your own harm. Give thanks for what you have taken away, and do not complain about the superfluity that is left over. What

---

25. It is significant that in his section entitled "Scripture, the First Sacrament," Olivier Clément cites Isaac of Nineveh side by side with Origen, John Cassian, and Gregory the Great. Clément, *Roots of Christian Mysticism*, 97–103.

you have taken off with you is your portion; what has been left behind can still be your inheritance.[26]

Bibliography

Alfeyev, Hilarion. *The Spiritual World of Isaac the Syrian*. Kalamazoo: Cistercian, 2000.

Barthélemy, Dominique. *Critique textuelle de l'Ancien Testament 1: 1. Josué, Juges, Ruth, Samuel, Rois, Chroniques, Esdras, Néhémie, Esther*. Orbis Biblicus et Orientalis 50/1. Göttingen: Vandenhoek & Ruprecht, 1982.

Biesen, Kees den. *Simple and Bold: Ephrem's Art of Symbolic Thought*. Piscataway, NJ: Gorgias, 2006.

Brock, Sebastian P. *Isaac of Nineveh (Isaac the Syrian): "The Second Part," chapters IV–XLI*. Corpus Scriptorum Christianorum Orientalium 555 = Scriptores Syri 225. Leuven: Peeters, 1995.

———. "Jacob of Serugh's Verse Homily on Tamar (Gen. 38)." *Le Muséon* 105 (2002) 279–315.

———. *The Luminous Eye: The Spiritual World Vision of St. Ephrem*. 2nd ed. Kalamazoo: Cistercian, 1992.

———. "The Robe of Glory: A Biblical Image in the Syriac Tradition." *The Way* 39 (1999) 247–59.

———. "St. Ephrem the Syrian on Reading Scripture." *The Downside Review* 438 (2007) 37–50.

———. "The Syriac Orient: A Third 'Lung' for the Church?" *Orientalia Christiana Periodica* 71 (2005) 3–17.

———. *The Wisdom of St. Isaac*. Oxford: Fairacres, 1997.

———. *The Wisdom of St. Isaac of Nineveh*. Piscataway, NJ: Gorgias, 2006.

Clément, Olivier. *The Roots of Christian Mysticism*. Hyde Park, NY: New City, 1993.

Ephrem the Syrian. *Commentary on the Diatessaron*. See *Commentaire de l'Évangile concordant; texte syriaque (Manuscrit Chester Beatty 709)*, edited and translated by Louis Leloir. Dublin: Hodges Figgis, 1963.

———. *Commentary on the Diatessaron, Additional Folios*. See *Commentaire de l'Évangile concordant; texte syriaque (Manuscrit Chester Beatty 709); Folios additionnels*, edited and translated by Louis Leloir. Leuven: Peeters, 1990.

———. *Commentary on Genesis*. In vol. 1 of *Sancti Ephraem Syria in Genesim et in Exodum Commentarii*, translated by R. M. Tonneau. Corpus Scriptorum Christianorum Orientalium 152–153 = Scriptores Syri 71–72. Louvain: Imprimerie Orientaliste L. Durbecq, 1955.

———. *Des heiligen Ephraem des Syrers Carmina Nisibena*. Edited by Edmund Beck. 4 vols. Corpus Scriptorum Christianorum Orientalium 218, 219, 240, 241. Leuven: Peeters, 1961–63.

———. *Des heiligen Ephraem des Syrers Hymni de Fide*. Edited by Edmund E. Beck. Corpus Scriptorum Christianorum Orientalium 212 = Scriptores Syri 73. Louvain: Imprimerie orientaliste L. Durbecq, 1955.

---

26. Ephrem, *Commentary on the Diatessaron* (1990), 1:18–19.

————. *Hymnen de Nativitate (Epiphania)*. Edited and translated by Edmund Beck. Corpus Scriptorum Christianorum Orientalium 186–87. Louvain: Secrétariat du CSCO, 1959.

————. *Hymns on Paradise*. Translated by Sebastian Brock. Crestwood, NY: St. Vladimir's Seminary, 1990.

Isaac of Nineveh. *The Ascetical Homilies of Saint Isaac the Syrian*. Translated by Dana Miller. Boston: Holy Transfiguration Monastery, 1984.

————. *Mar Isaacus Ninivita: De perfectione religiosa*. Edited by Paul Bedjan. Paris: Harrossowitz, 1909.

————. *Mystic Treatises by Isaac of Nineveh Translated from Bedjan's Syriac Text with an Introduction and Registers*. Translated by Arent J. Wensinck. Amsterdam: Uitgave der Koninklijke Akademie van Wetenschappen, 1923.

Jacob of Serugh. *160 Unpublished Homilies of Jacob of Serugh*. Edited by Roger Akhrass and Imad Syriany. 2 vols. Damascus: Department of Syriac Studies–Syriac Orthodox Patriarchate, 2017.

————. *Homilies of Mar Jacob of Serugh*. Edited by Paul Bedjan and Sebastian P. Brock. 6 vols. Piscataway, NJ: Gorgias, 2006.

————. *Iacobi Sarugensis Epistulae quotquot supersunt*. Edited by Gunnar Olinder. Corpus Scriptorum Christianorum Orientalium 110 = Scriptores Syri 57. Paris: e Typographeo Reipublicae, 1937.

Kollamparampil, Thomas. *Jacob of Serugh: Select Festal Homilies*. Bangalore: Dharmaram, 1997.

————. *Salvation in Christ according to Jacob of Serugh*. Bangalore: Dharmaram, 2001.

3

St. Ephrem's Mary

Icon of Wonder, Icon of Beauty[1]

JEANNE-NICOLE MELLON SAINT-LAURENT

Marquette University

Introduction

THE IMAGES OF THE Blessed Virgin Mary are multifaceted and point to the mystery of her person and the splendor of her paradoxical roles in salvation history. They have inspired Christian art, architecture, hagiography, exegesis, homilies, and doctrine. While all four Gospels contain references to Mary,[2] the Gospels of Luke and John contain the most developed picture of her.[3] Luke narrates the annunciation of the virgin birth of Jesus (Luke 1:26–38), Mary's visit to her cousin Elizabeth who is also miraculously pregnant (Luke 1:39–56), Mary's song of praise and thanksgiving (Luke 1:46–55), the birth of Jesus in Bethlehem, and the visit of the shepherds (Luke 2:1–20). Luke's picture teaches us about Mary's strength and fidelity to God's will, just as it identifies a contemplative spirit within her: "Mary treasured these things in her heart" (Luke 2:19). The Gospel of John presents Mary as a woman with special access or understanding of Jesus her Son, as is demonstrated in the account of the wedding at Cana (John 2:1–12). She stands at the foot of

---

1. I am honored to present this essay in honor of Father Patrick Hartin, who taught me New Testament at Gonzaga University. I am grateful to Dr. Catherine Brown Tkacz who edited this essay and offered helpful feedback.

2. Mark 3:31–35; 6:3; 15:40–41, 47; 16:1–8; Matt 1:16—2:21; 12:46–50; 13:53–58; Luke 1:26–56; 2:1–52; 8:19–21; 11:27–28; 23:49, 55; 24:12; John 1:1–18; 2:1–12; 19:25–27; 20:1–18; Acts 1:14.

3. For a presentation of Mary in Scripture, see Brown et al., *Mary in the NT*.

the cross, as the dying Jesus entrusts her care to the beloved disciple (John 19:25–27). The portraits of Mary in Luke and John provided a basis from which early Christian exegetes, narrators, and poets would expand.

Christians understood that the mother of Jesus, the mother of God, could be no ordinary woman. The second-century text the *Protevangelium of James* depicts the wondrous conception of Mary by Anna and Joachim, Mary's pure upbringing in a temple, God's selection of Joseph to be the spouse of Mary, and Jesus' birth.[4] The popularity of the story shows how Christians elevated the uniqueness and sanctity of Mary and her family and attests to early Marian devotion.[5] It honors Mary's lineage by clothing her in the Old Testament's symbols of holiness reserved for priests, prophets, and kings.[6] However, the portrait of Mary in the *Protoevangelium* differs significantly from the portrait of her in Scripture. For instance, when Elizabeth asks Mary about her pregnancy, Mary does not praise God with a canticle of praise (cf. Luke 1:46–55). Instead, Mary is afraid.[7]

Within the first century, Mary's virginal conception of the Lord was already much discussed.[8] By the second century, early Christian texts attest to doctrinal interest in Mary.[9] Early Christian philosophers and theologians like Irenaeus of Lyons,[10] Clement of Alexandria,[11] Origen,[12] and Tertullian[13] theologized about the relationship of Mary to her Son, the Incarnate God.[14] Irenaeus interpreted Mary through a typological lens as a new Eve,[15] developing the Pauline theology of Christ as the second Adam (cf. Rom 5:5–21). Mary, as Second Eve, participates in the re-creation of the world and divine

---

4. Despite the popularity of the *Protoevangelium of James* in the early Church, it contains elements that contrast to the orthodox presentation of Mary.

5. Vuong, *Gender and Purity in the Protevangelium*.

6. Scott, "Mary in the Protoevangelium."

7. *Protevangelium of James*, 12.

8. See for example Ignatius' references to Mary's virginity in the letters of Ignatius of Antioch: *To the Smyrnaeans*, 1. See also *To the Ephesians*, 7.2, 19.1; *To the Trallians*, 9.1.

9. Shoemaker, *Mary in Early Christian Faith*. Shoemaker published an important collection of stories from the Patristic and Byzantine tradition: *Traditions of the Dormition and Assumption*.

10. Irenaeus, *Against Heresies*, 3.22.4.

11. Clement, *Miscellanies*, 7.16.

12. See for example Origen, *Homilies on Luke*, 14 (p. 100).

13. Tertullian, *On the Flesh of Christ*, 7, 17, 20.

14. See Graef, *Mary*, 25–37; Shoemaker, *Mary in Early Christian Faith*, 64–99.

15. See Irenaeus, *Against Heresies*, 3.21–22; see also 4.33 (p. 11).

healing of humanity.[16] Her virginal birth of the New Adam, Christ, corrects the mistakes of humanity's first parents.

Indeed, Mary has always been a theologically central figure in Christian theology, because it is through her that Christ received his humanity. It is therefore not surprising that the earliest Christians developed rich literary traditions about Mary's life, lineage, and relationship to Christ, filling in questions that Scripture left unanswered. Indeed, as Stephen J. Shoemaker has shown,[17] devotion to Mary in the early Church began long before 431 when the Council of Ephesus declared Mary the *Theotokos* or God-bearer. Narratives and poetic collections about Mary like the *Book of Mary's Repose, Six Books Dormition Apocryphon* and the *Odes of Solomon*[18] show that Christians honored Mary as the person with the most intimate understanding of her Son. Reflections about Mary generated a corpus of mytho-poetic texts and hymns celebrating the virgin Mary and her exceptional role in the salvation drama.

The Syriac-speaking church centered in Nisibis and Edessa attests to Marian devotion and theological interest in Mary at an early date.[19] Indeed, as Fr. Robert Murray noted already in 1971, "The monuments of early Christian devotion to our lady are, perhaps, more concentrated in the Syriac language field than in any other."[20]

A fitting focus here is St. Ephrem the Syrian (d. 373), doctor of the Church, whom Christian tradition honors as the "Harp of the Spirit." He dons Mary in a raiment of theological and natural symbols, presenting her as the second Eve, a wonder, a bridge between humanity and her Son,

16. See Pasquet, "La relation typologique," 27.

17. Shoemaker, *Mary in Early Christian Faith*, esp. 229–40 where he summarizes this argument.

18. See especially Ode 19 of the *Odes of Solomon* for an important reference to Mary. See Charlesworth, *Odes of Solomon*.

19. Edmund Beck, Robert Murray, Sebastian P. Brock, Kathleen McVey (who translated Ephrem's corpus into English), and Susan Ashbrook Harvey have all contributed important work on Mary in the Syriac tradition, and I build upon their scholarship. Indeed, much of this article is compiling things that they have already written about extensively. Beck showed how the authentic texts attributed to Ephrem (as opposed to the corpus of Ephrem Graecus) contained advanced Marian theology: Beck, "Mariologie der Echten Schriften Ephräms." Murray brought Ephrem's Mariology into Catholic historical theology: Murray, "Mary, the Second Eve." Much of my thinking on Mary has been nourished by the scholarship of my teacher Susan Harvey: "On Mary's Voice"; see especially her *Song and Memory*. Above all I build upon the scholarship of Sebastian P. Brock, especially *Bride of Light* and *Mary in Syriac Tradition*. His *Bride of Light* is a basic starting point for Mary in the Syriac tradition. It contains a collection of hymns to her from the Syriac Churches as well as anonymous dialogue hymns on Mary.

20. Murray, "Mary," 372.

the Incarnate God. Ephrem views Mary through the lens of faith and awe, commemorating her in the mode of expression appropriate for incomprehensible realities of God's love: poetry and hymns. While doctrinal formulations are important, Robert Murray rightly emphasizes how that does not diminish the importance of poetics in theology:

> All theology starts with the human mind reaching out to evoke some echo or reflexion of the ineffable by means of poetic imagery, knowing that the ineffable cannot be pinned down. There follows a period of rising confidence in the intellect's power, then of declining vision and confidence; finally, in decadence, an abject literalism which can no longer distinguish the levels of discourse and discern what was poetic imagery, what was philosophical symbolism, and what was matter-of-fact language. The peaks of theological poetry remain to inspire us again—Ephrem, Dante, Blake, T. S. Eliot. It would be good for the Church if they were put more in the forefront of theological study.[21]

Since Fr. Murray wrote that nearly fifty years ago, there has been considerable attention drawn to the corpus of St. Ephrem and his Mariology; theologians and historians recognize the genius in Ephrem's dynamic and poetic approach to theology and scripture.[22]

Central themes of Ephrem's Mariology are clearly expressed in his *Hymns on the Nativity*.[23] Here Ephrem teaches much about the many paradoxical roles that Mary plays in the drama of the Incarnation. His method of exegesis is distinctive: Ephrem uses a theology of wonder to elevate Mary through his symbolic poetry and parallelisms with other women in the bible, especially Eve.[24] Ephrem commemorates not just her holy otherness, but indeed her very humanity. Mary, in Ephrem's words, knits a body for God within her own body; Ephrem in turn clothes Mary in a garment of poetic hymns of praise: "You [Mary] wove a garment for him; He was

21. Murray, "Mary," 384.

22. The two most important books for illuminating the early Syriac theological tradition and the value of its perspectives were Brock, *Luminous Eye*, and Murray, *Symbols*. For an excellent study of the place of the Bible in Ephrem's world, see Wickes, *Bible and Poetry in Mesopotamia*.

23. Ephrem's *Hymns of the Nativity* (hereafter *Hymn Nat.*) were edited and translated into German: Ephrem, *Hymnen de Nativitate* (hereafter: ed. Beck). The citations and page numbers in this essay refer to Volume 186 (the Syriac text). Kathleen McVey translated the *Hymns of the Nativity* into English, and in this essay I have followed and cited her translations (hereafter: trans. McVey). When I have slightly modified her translations, I indicate this in the notes with "mod."

24. See Bonian, "Mary and the Christian."

extending his glory over all your senses!"[25] Central to Ephrem's theology of wonder was his praise of her virginity, which he presents as a gift of freedom in exchange for her free assent to God's will. Ephrem presents Mary as a teacher for the Church: Mary teaches the community of faith to participate actively in God's divine plan, as she weaves Christ's body in her womb. She also teaches the people of the Church to have a place in their prayer for silence and passive contemplation, as Ephrem presents her as a thankful mother in awe of her child, who reflects on the wonders of God's love within her womb and at her breast.[26]

Syriac Christianity and Ephrem's Context

A brief introduction to the Syriac tradition as well as the context of St. Ephrem clarifies how he elevates Mary in his corpus of Pro-Nicene hymns. Syriac is a dialect of Eastern Aramaic that was spoken in the early centuries of the Common Era around the city of Edessa. A Semitic language with its own script, Syriac flourished as a literary language in both the Sasanian (Persian) and Roman Empires. Texts in Syriac comprise the third largest surviving corpus of literature (after Greek and Latin) from the late ancient period. As one of several dialects of Aramaic, Syriac also served as a *lingua franca* enabling both commerce and religious missionary activity across political boundaries. Syriac remains the liturgical language of the Syriac Orthodox Church, the Syriac Catholic Church, the Assyrian Church of the East, the Chaldean Catholic Church, and many Syrian churches in India. Varieties of Neo-Aramaic are spoken by Christians in Lebanon, Iran, Iraq, Turkey, Syria and the diaspora.

Ephrem of Nisibis ranks among the most important authors of the Syriac tradition. He lived most of his life in the city of Nisibis and worked under the bishop James.[27] At the end of his life, in about 363, Ephrem moved from Nisibis to Edessa after Nisibis became part of the Sasanian Empire. Robert Murray, SJ, called Ephrem, "the greatest poet of the patristic age and, perhaps, the only theologian-poet to rank beside Dante."[28] Ephrem wrote a large corpus in Syriac of hymns, homilies, and prose works. As Sidney Griffith notes, the Syriac tradition remembers Ephrem primarily as a

---

25. Ephrem, *Hymn Nat.* 28.7, ed. Beck, 142; trans. McVey, 216 (mod).

26. For the active and passive nature of Mary's holiness as Ephrem presents it, see Beck, "Mariologie," 30.

27. James attended the Council of Nicaea in 325.

28. Murray, *Symbols*, 31.

teacher.[29] Ephrem's style of religious discourse was more contemplative rather than academic: "based on a close reading of the scriptures, with an eye to the telling mystic symbol (*râzâ*) or 'type' in terms of which God chose to make revelations to the Church."[30] Through his hymnody, Ephrem instructed his church about the mysteries of the Christian faith. Mary herself is a dynamic type or *râzâ* of wonder who in turn teaches the Church to sing wondrous praise or rest in quiet awe before her Son.

Ephrem directed his theological poetry and hymns to the Pro-Nicene Christians, affirming that Christ was truly divine, born of the Holy Spirit (the Sanctifier) and of Mary the Virgin (the Sanctified). The Pro-Nicene communities of Nisibis and Edessa, however, were not a majority. Ephrem and his bishop had several other branches of Christianities with whom they contended, including the Arians, Marcionites, and followers of Bardaisan. The Arians believed that Christ was the Word of God, a divine creature, born at the beginning of time, but not that he shared in the same divine essence as the Father. The Marcionites rejected the Old Testament as well as any allegorical or typological reading of it. The Marcionites believed that a lesser god, erroneously identified as the god of the Old Testament, had created the world. This lesser god hated humanity: "it was this creator who devised the humiliating method of sexual reproduction, the discomforts of pregnancy, and the pains of childbirth, the mere contemplation of which filled Marcion with nausea."[31] Marcion identified the second god as one that was associated with the New Testament: the god of light, goodness, and spirit. Such erroneous theology insulted the Creator and the integrity of the Bible.

The corpus of Ephrem is replete with anti-Marcionite and Anti-Arian theology. In a striking passage from the *Hymns on Paradise*, Ephrem proclaims that the two most important realms that teach us about God are books of the Bible (*seprā*) and Nature (*kyānā*). The faithful must honor, study, and praise all of these, as revealing truths about God:

> In his book Moses described the creation of the natural world,[32]
>
> so that both Nature and Scripture might bear witness to
> the Creator:
>
> Nature, through man's use of it,
>
> Scripture, through his reading of it.

29. Griffith, *Faith Adoring the Mystery*, 6.

30. Griffith, *Faith Adoring the Mystery*, 8.

31. Chadwick, *Early Church*, 39.

32. Ancient readers of the Bible believed that Moses had written the Book of Genesis.

These are the witnesses which reach everywhere,

they are to be found at all times, present at every hour,

confuting the unbeliever who defames the Creator.[33]

The theology of the Marcionites and the Arians misconstrued the Incarnation. In contrast to Marcion, Ephrem celebrates Mary's pregnancy and redefines her childbirth as "miraculous." Ephrem proclaimed that the Word of God in the divine descent of the Incarnation clothed himself in all the limits of humanity in order to restore and heal the image that was lost in Paradise.

Ephrem's Exegesis and Theological Approach

The Bible of the Syriac Church was a bible of great antiquity, the Peshitta. The Old Testament of the Peshitta was translated into Syriac from the Hebrew rather than the Greek, and the New Testament of the Peshitta was translated from the Greek. Ephrem actually knew another Syriac New Testament earlier than the Peshitta text, of which only the Gospels survive.[34] Ephrem also knew a second-century Gospel harmony, the Diatessaron. In the *Commentary on the Diatessaron*, Ephrem (or someone writing in his tradition) presents what Sidney Griffith calls his attitude towards scripture and its interpretation:[35]

> Many are the perspectives of his word, just as many are the perspectives of those who study it. [God] has fashioned his world with many beautiful forms, so that each one who studies it may consider what he likes. He has hidden in his word all kinds of treasures so that each one of us, wherever we meditate, may be enriched by it. His utterance is a tree of life, which offers you blessed fruit from every side. It is like the rock which burst forth in the desert, becoming spiritual drink to everyone from all places. [They ate] spiritual food and drank spiritual drink (1 Cor. 10:3–4).[36]

33. Ephrem, *Hymns on Paradise*, V.2 (English translation on p. 102). Syriac text in Ephrem, *Hymnen de Paradiso*, 16.

34. See Brock, "Mary in Syriac Tradition," 183.

35. Griffith, *Faith Adoring the Mystery*, 16. See also the essay by S. P. Brock in this volume: "Three Syriac Fathers on Reading the Bible."

36. MacCarthy, *Ephrem's Commentary on Tatian's Diatessaron*, 49–50. I was led to it by Griffith, *Faith Adoring the Mystery*, 16.

For Ephrem, Scripture nurtures anyone who receives it in a posture of wonder and awe.

The mysteries of the Trinity, the incarnation, and Christ's nature are truths that God has revealed in scripture, nature, and typology. One must explore theological teachings and read scripture through the lens of faith. It is a fount from which one will never grow thirsty:

> Every time I meditated upon you, I acquired a treasure
> from you.
> Every time I thought of you, a spring gushed from you,
> And I drew as much as I could. Glory to your font!
> Lord, your font is concealed from whoever thirsts not for you.
> Your treasury is empty to whoever hates you.[37]

The person who understood and perfected this response and posture of wonder was Mary. For Ephrem, she epitomizes the wonder of God's love through the miracles that occur in her body; she also teaches the faithful how to approach and praise her Son. As Mary sings to her son, Ephrem speaks through her and instructs his congregation through her imagined speech.[38] Ephrem celebrates the pulchritude of Mary's body, which God fashions as the perfect place for the indwelling of the Son.

The basis of Ephrem's portrayal of Mary is the narrative of Scripture. Ephrem reads the stories of the Old Testament typologically as pointing to the coming of Christ: "connections between persons, objects, and events were sought out and brought together, either as complementing, or contrasting each other."[39] As Sebastian P. Brock notes, Ephrem's typology can be historical (Christ as the new Adam, Mary as the new Eve) or symbolic: earthly realities standing as symbols of heavenly ones.[40] Sometimes Ephrem uses both historical and symbolic typologies at the same time.[41] Ephrem affirms Mary's centrality in the story of salvation, imagining that the righteous of the Old Testament looked and saw that Mary would carry the Messiah. Mary is the mother through whom all believers, even gentiles, are linked to the holy men and women of the Old Testament:

> Mary today has hidden in us the leaven of the house of Abraham;
>
> Let us, therefore, love the poor as Abraham loved the needy.[42]

37. Ephrem, *Hymns on Faith*, 32:3–7 (English translation on p. 196).

38. Harvey, *Song and Memory*.

39. Brock, "Mary in the Syriac Church," 185.

40. Brock, "Mary in the Syriac Church," 185.

41. Brock, "Mary in the Syriac Church," 185.

42. Ephrem, *Hymn Nat.* 1.84, ed. Beck, 11. Trans. McVey, 73.

Ephrem recalls the barren women of the Old Testament who prayed for children, and he contrasts them with Mary:

> Blessed is Mary—who without vigils and
> without prayer—in her virginity
> conceived and bore. The Lord of all,
> the children of her companions who were and will be
> modest, upright; priests and kings.[43]

Mary is the most important woman of scripture, so her commemoration in the Church is vital:

> Worthy of remembrance is the mother who gave birth to Him;
> worthy too of blessings is the bosom that bore Him.[44]

But how does one honor Mary? Through Mary's words, Ephrem instructs his congregation how to understand her and identify her as first among all human beings:

> Most of all those healed, I rejoice, for I conceived him; most of
> all those magnified by Him, He has magnified me, for I gave
> birth to Him.
> I am about to enter his living Paradise,
> and in the place in which Eve succumbed, I shall glorify Him,
> For of all created women, He was most pleased with me,
> [and] He willed that I should be mother to Him,
> and it pleased Him that He should be a child to me.[45]

Ephrem highlights that Mary is the highest of all women ever born, who taught all humanity how to align one's will with the will of God.

She is indeed blessed, as her cousin Elizabeth proclaims in the Gospel of Luke (Luke 1:42). Ephrem imagines further the outworking of this happy state, and it leads him to consider Mary's singular freedom and free will, a favorite topic for Ephrem. For Ephrem, Mary's virginal motherhood is a divine gift that has relieved her of the worries of household life:

> Blessed is she, you are in her heart and mind.
> She, the palace of the king;
> In you is the Son of a king, and the Holy of Holies,

---

43. Ephrem, *Hymn Nat.* 8.16, ed. Beck, 61–62. Trans. McVey, 122 (mod).
44. Ephrem, *Hymn Nat.* 2.6, ed. Beck, 14. Trans. McVey, 77.
45. Ephrem, *Hymn Nat.* 2.7, ed. Beck, 15. Trans. McVey, 77.

for you, the High Priest. She has no anxiety,

nor stress of house or husband.[46]

Thus, for Ephrem, the first step towards understanding Mary is through proper study and reflection upon her words and actions in Scripture, as well as her typological relationship to other central figures of the Bible. As noted above, scripture inspires the response of wonder.

Theology of Wonder, Beauty, and Joy

For early Christian writers, one of the greatest paradoxes is that of the incarnation.[47] God who is all powerful became human in the person of the Incarnate Christ, the Word made flesh. Thus, the response of Creation to the mystery of the incarnation is one of wonder, praise, and thanksgiving, and Mary is at the center. The virginal conception of Jesus or the incarnation of the divine Word in the womb of Mary is mystery that is difficult for the human mind to grasp. Just as the Father's begetting of the Word is a hidden mystery, so is the Word's incarnation in the womb of Mary. Wonder is not just a response to the incarnation but rather another title for Christ:

Today a child was born, and he was called "wonder" [*dúmrā*][48]

for it is a wonder that God reveals Himself as infant.[49]

In her hymns, Mary ponders that she must give Jesus nourishment and feed him as a nursling to live, even though he gives life to all. Even Mary, who knows Christ better than any other person, is puzzled and in awe over Christ's birth. Rather than scrutinize this paradox, she praises and hymns it, offering the Church a model of how a believer should respond to divine mystery. In the sixteenth *Hymn on the Nativity*, Mary sings a reverent lullaby of silence, since no typical song will suffice for the infant Jesus. His birth is full of wonder. God has entered the world, and so Mary shifts from being a mother singing to her child to a prophet, through whom the Spirit speaks. In this one stanza, Ephrem deftly reflects on the multi-faceted dimensions of Mary's holiness, who is both a link to her Son and source of unity within the Church:[50]

46. Ephrem, *Hymn Nat.* 17.5, ed. Beck, 88. Trans. McVey, 154–55 (mod).

47. For the use of the "rhetoric of paradox" in early Christian narrative imagination, see Cameron, *Christianity and the Rhetoric of Empire*, 155–88.

48. Isa 9:6.

49. Ephrem, *Hymn Nat.* 1.9, ed. Beck, 2. Trans. McVey, 64.

50. Bonian, "Mary and the Christian," 49.

You are no ordinary human being that in an ordinary way
I should sing you a lullaby. For Your conception was novel
And Your birth full of wonder. Without the Spirit,
who can sing of You? It is a new utterance
of prophecy that stirs within me.[51]

Mary does not know what to call her Son: he is also Joseph's Son as well as her Lord. That does not prevent her from praising and hymning his arrival, the Son of many, her Lord and Son:

Although you are the Son of the One, I shall call You henceforth
Son of many, for myriads of names
do not suffice for you, For you are Son of God
and Son of Man and Son of Joseph
and Son of David, and Lord of Mary.[52]

If Jesus himself is wondrous, as is his birth, then so indeed is his mother. Mary is a bridge between humanity or the Church and her Son. Ephrem sets Mary apart from other women through discussing her roles and titles, many of which are paradoxical. Mary calls Jesus her Son, but as a member of the Church she is also the betrothed of Christ. Mary is the handmaid of his divinity and the mother of his humanity. The incarnation—the cosmic meeting of heaven on earth—undoes the natural order of the created world. Mary is at the center of this intersection, adorned in the beauty of her Son, who transforms his mother's poverty, identifying Mary as a princess rather than a handmaid:

Suddenly a handmaid has become daughter of the King
by You, Son of the King. Behold, the lowly one [is]
in the House of David because of You![53]
O Son of David, behold, the daughter of the earth
Has reached heaven by the Heavenly One.[54]

Ephrem also highlights that God's choice of a poor girl, a daughter of the poor, to carry the Incarnate Word exemplifies the paradoxical nature of

51. Ephrem, *Hymn Nat.* 16.8, ed. Beck, 84–85. Trans. McVey, 150 (mod).

52. Ephrem, *Hymn Nat.* 6.1–2, ed. Beck, 51. Trans. McVey, 111. See Beck, "Mariologie," 24.

53. Syriac tradition, based on readings of Luke 2:4 in the Old Syriac Gospels and the Diatessaron, believed that Mary, like Joseph, was of the house of David. See Murray, "Mary," 374.

54. Ephrem, *Hymn Nat.* 5.21, ed. Beck, 49. Trans. McVey, 150.

his divine descent. Mary wonders at this as well. In her own words, as Ephrem imagines them, Gabriel's question, Mary's response, and the miraculous events that unfolded began a series of seemingly self-contradictory titles for Mary. She is, as she says, the maidservant of God, but she is also the mother of Jesus' humanity. She is both the mother and child of her Son:[55]

> That day that Gabriel entered
>
> unto my poor presence;
>
> Free woman and maidservant he made me at once;
>
> For I am the maidservant of your divinity and
>
> I am the mother of your humanity—Lord and Son![56]

Ephrem dramatizes the infancy of the Lord tenderly. The Word of all descended, was born as a baby, and pitched his tent among other families and children. The all-powerful God crossed over into the human family. Yet even as a baby, Jesus remains Lord of all, Lord of angels as well as humanity, a wonder we contemplate with Mary:

> He came out and like a babe He sucked milk,
>
> and the Son of the Ruler of All crawled among infants.[57]

Mary's Virginity

Following the tradition of scripture (Matt 1:18; Matt 1:23; Luke 1:27; Luke 1:34–38) as well as orthodox theologians of the early Church, Ephrem emphasizes throughout his corpus the virgin birth of Jesus.[58] Christians had to defend Mary's virginity. Pagan opponents to Christianity, like Celsus, whom Origen refutes, had claimed this. Early rabbinic traditions had charged that Mary was not a virgin but instead had conceived Jesus out of

---

55. See Beck, "Mariologie," 28.

56. Ephrem, *Hymn Nat.* 5.20, ed. Beck, 49. Trans. McVey, 109 (mod).

57. Ephrem, *Hymn Nat.* 4.194, ed. Beck, 43. Trans. McVey, 103.

58. Beck notes that Ephrem is limited and unclear about the teaching of Mary's virginity during the birth of Christ: *virginitas in partu*. See Beck, "Mariologie," 22. Catherine Brown Tkacz notes (in a personal correspondence, Feb. 2020) that it is important not to read into the word "virginity" the idea of "possession of an unaffected hymen." Rather we must consider that what ancient Christians may have intended was "virginal character and actions, never having sexual intercourse." In this way, we can consider that "because Mary conceived virginally and remained a virgin, of course she was a virgin in giving birth, and because giving birth is not a sexual act, she remained a virgin."

wedlock with a Roman soldier.[59] Texts like the *Protevangelium of James*, therefore, that emphasized the miraculous nature of Mary's virginity and her purity from birth, were written in response to such criticism.[60] Syriac writers follow in this tradition and stress the perpetual virginity of Mary, but her perpetual virginity is not a matter that they "pry" into much.[61] As a virgin mother, Mary defies categorization:

> O Lord, no one knows
> How to address Your mother. [If] one calls her "virgin,"
> Her child stands up, and "married" –
> No one knew her [sexually]. But if Your mother is
> Incomprehensible, who is capable of [comprehending] You?[62]

Ephrem identifies Mary as a chaste vessel whom God chose to carry Emmanuel. She is a typological fulfillment of the salvific arc of Noah. Mary constrained herself willingly for the sake of all. God rewards her proper use of her free will:

> Your will, [Mary,] magnified and sanctified you;
> Your Lord increased and adorned you too,
> The animals of Noah were constrained by force
> But you [chose] by your free will![63]

Ephrem presents Mary's virginity as a freedom from the stresses and obligations of a husband. Mary's virginity transformed her body and freed her day for prayer, for single-hearted devotion to God. Angels come to greet her, and this for Ephrem is also a sign that they recognized her holiness:

> Spiritual woman; All of you has become spirit;
> Since you bore the spiritual man.[64]

Elsewhere in his corpus, Ephrem uses the image of light to describe how the miraculous conception of the Word in her body, and the intactness of her virginity, shine out as a sign of God's power within her:

59. Shoemaker, *Mary in Early Christian Faith*, 54. For Origen's response to Celsus' critique, see Origen, *Contra Celsum*, Book I, 34.8.

60. The *Protevangelium of James* described the wondrous conception of Mary by the old woman Anna, Mary's holy upbringing in a temple, and Mary's virginal conception of Jesus, as well as his birth.

61. Brock, "Mary in Syriac Tradition," 185.

62. Ephrem, *Hymn Nat.* 11.1, ed. Beck, 69. Trans. McVey, 131.

63. Ephrem, *Hymn Nat.* 28.1, ed. Beck, 141. Trans. McVey, 214 (mod).

64. Ephrem, *Hymn Nat.* 28.4, ed. Beck, 142. Trans. McVey, 215 (mod).

> As though on an eye, the light settled in Mary,
>
> It polished her mind, made bright and pure her understanding,
>
> Causing her virginity to shine.[65]

Ephrem looks to symbolism and types in nature that prefigure or teach us about the mysterious truth of the virgin birth of Jesus. He articulates the paradox that the incarnate divine beauty that "gladdens all creation" is born from a virgin in the coldest and most sterile months of the year.[66] Adam too, Ephrem reflects, was born from virgin earth. So the New Adam, Christ, must be born from a virgin. Mary's virginal birth is part of the paradox woven into the entire celebration of the birth of the Lord, the incarnation:

> The virgin earth gave birth to that Adam, head of the earth;
>
> the Virgin today gave birth to [second] Adam, head of heaven.[67]

Mary, as both virgin and mother, is a stumbling block for those who do not consider her through the eye of faith. Mary cannot be categorized according to the typical constructions for a woman as "virgin," "wife," or "mother." Her body shows the wondrous indications that she is all of these, and she remains a single human person. She crosses boundaries between the human and divine, as she is a human who miraculously gives birth to the divine:

> It is a wonder and a marvel to the wise ones
>
> It is a vexation and a torment to the learned.
>
> Virginity was hidden; but the breasts were full.
>
> On account of all of this, to him be praises![68]

Ephrem teaches, too, that the unborn God-Man whom Mary carries in her transforms Mary's body as she weaves a body for God. The interplay of these extraordinary activities refashions and glorifies her: "He imprinted himself like a signet ring upon your mind; he whose conception was glorious."[69]

Ephrem teaches his audience to look to Mary as a model of how to receive Christ also in their minds, those who have singlehearted and faithful devotion to him, like a bride to her bridegroom. Mary, because she is a

---

65. Ephrem, *Hymns on the Church* 36.2, as cited and translated by Brock, "St. Ephrem on Christ," 138.

66. Ephrem, *Hymn Nat.* 4.120, ed. Beck, 36. Trans. McVey, 98.

67. Ephrem, *Hymn Nat.* 1.16, ed. Beck, 3. Trans. McVey, 65.

68. Ephrem, *Hymn Nat.* 28.5, ed. Beck, 142. Trans. McVey, 215–16 (mod.).

69. Ephrem, *Hymn Nat.* 28.7, ed. Beck, 142. Trans. McVey, 216 (mod.).

virgin, represents an ideal for all chaste and continent women who likewise will receive Christ when they have learned to perceive him.[70] Mary's virginal conception of Jesus also freed her to love him with a single-hearted devotion, the ascetic vow that all the consecrated virgins and continent married make. Asceticism liberates the worshiper to love freely. It prepares the body for the indwelling of the incarnate God.

Mary's Imagined Speech as Theological Instruction

As Susan Harvey has shown, Ephrem uses a mode of expression known as imagined speech to explore theological questions surrounding the mysteries of Christ's birth.[71] In Scripture, Mary wonders how she can be pregnant since she has not known man (Luke 1:34). The Bible presents Mary as a woman who questions and probes before assenting. Ephrem celebrates in his hymns the Mary who questions, the Mary who wonders, and the Mary who contemplates. She engages in all of these activities in the *Hymns of the Nativity*, modelling also how Christians themselves should approach theological mysteries. She gives thanks. In showing humanity how to give thanks and praise to God, Ephrem creates in Mary a model of piety and wonder. One uses the tongue to sing, not to speak doubts that question the plans of God's love:

> Blessed are you also, Mary, whose name
> is great and exalted because of your Child;
> Indeed you were able to say how much and how
> and where the Great One, Who became small, dwelt in you.
> Blessed is your mouth that gave thanks but did not inquire
> and your tongue that praised but did not investigate.
> Since his mother was bewildered by him, although she bore him,
> Who is sufficient [to know] him?[72]

Songs and responses of thanksgiving, for Ephrem, are fitting modes of expression for exploring the mystery of the incarnation.[73] If the incarnation was difficult for us to understand, what questions filled the mind of Mary, when a man of fire appeared to her and told her that she, a virgin, would

70. Ephrem, *Hymn Nat.* 4.130–32, ed. Beck, 44. Trans. McVey, 99.

71. Harvey, "On Mary's Voice." Greek hymns also use imagined speech as a form of theological instruction, and it is likely that this practice came into the Greek tradition through bilingual Greek-Syriac speakers, like Romanos the Melodist.

72. Ephrem, *Hymn Nat.* 25.14, ed. Beck, 132. Trans. McVey, 203 (mod).

73. See Harvey, *Song and Memory*.

conceive the Anointed Christ, the Divine Physician who would descend to heal and restore the broken nature of humanity?

Ephrem imagines that Christ, as the Word of God soaring above his Creation, takes special care to protect his mother. Ephrem presents Mary as both tender and strong. The Syriac poetic approach to Mary, as Brock notes, is suggestive, "avoiding cut and dried dogmatic statements."[74] Ephrem proceeds therefore with wisdom and awe, as he imagines Mary's words:

"The newborn babe whom I carry carried me"

said Mary; "He lowered His wings,

and took me and placed me between them;

He soared into the air, and promised me:

Both height and depth shall be your Son's."[75]

Ephrem voices through Mary the paradox of Christ's smallness and majesty, his immanence and transcendence.

Mary chants:

Who granted the barren woman to conceive and bear?

One who is many—small and great—

Unto me is all of him—all of him in the universe.[76]

Mary also becomes in Syriac tradition the voice of all women who have ever been falsely accused:[77] "On account of you, behold, I am hated. Lover of all, see I am the persecuted." Ephrem's defense of Mary's virtue and his commemoration for her bravery illustrates Ephrem's theology of justice between the sexes.[78] In the ninth *Hymn on the Nativity*, as Philip Botha has shown, Ephrem urges his congregation to follow the example of faith and strength demonstrated by Ruth, Tamar, and finally Mary: all biblical women with controversial pregnancies. They acted with bravery and boldness to participate in the divine plan of salvation; their commemoration in

---

74. See Brock, "Mary in Syriac Tradition," 183.

75. Ephrem, *Hymn Nat.* 17.1, ed. Beck, 87. Trans. McVey, 153–54 (mod.).

76. Ephrem, *Hymn Nat.* 5.19, ed. Beck, 49. Trans. McVey, 108 (mod.).

77. Mary retains this role in Syriac memory, as we note in a Memra on Ephrem the Syrian: Jacob, *Metrical Homily on Holy Mar Ephrem*.

78. Catherine Brown Tkacz has shown the importance of attending to how biblical women like Susanna and Jephthah's daughter were presented in patristic and medieval exegesis as types of Christ. She notes that the recovery of this theme is important to "deepen the theological understanding of women, especially the spiritual and moral equality of the sexes." See Tkacz, "Women as Types of Christ."

hymnody was meant to silence those who doubted Mary's virginity.[79] In this vein, Ephrem, who wrote hymns for women's choirs, is commemorated in Syriac religious memory as an advocate for justice between the sexes, as Jacob of Sarug [Serugh] notes in his verse homily or Memra on Ephrem.[80] Ephrem himself wrote hymns for women's choirs, instructing that they sing in Church.[81] Because Mary undid the transgression of Eve, Jacob recalls, chaste women chant "Alleluia" with Mary:

> Your silent mouth which your mother Eve closed,
>
> Is now opened by Mary, your sister, to sing praise.
>
> The old woman [Eve] tied a cord of silence around your tongues;
>
> The Son of the virgin loosed your bonds that you may sing out.
>
> The married one put a muzzle of silence on your mouths;
>
> [but] the virgin opened the closed door of your tongues.
>
> Until now, your side[82] was brought low because of Eve;
>
> But from now on, it stands up through Mary to sing Alleluia![83]

Eve–Mary Typology

As discussed above, Mary's story, in Ephrem's eyes, did not begin with the annunciation of Gabriel. Rather, as Ephrem notes, it started with the story of Creation, the story of Adam and Eve, and scripture's presentation of the paradisiacal state to understand the typology of Mary (Gen 2:4—3:24). For Ephrem, as mentioned above, the narratives of the Old Testament contain symbols and types that find fulfillment in the New Testament. Ephrem builds on the typological understanding of Christ as the New Adam and Mary as the Second Eve, and he elevates Mary as the highest of all women in scripture, who undoes the damage her foremother caused. Mary also,

---

79. See Botha, "Bold Women."

80. Jacob presents Ephrem as one who "introduced women to doctrinal disputes; with (their) soft tones he was victorious in the battle against all heresies." Jacob, *Metrical Homily on Holy Mar Ephrem*, 152 (pp. 64–65).

81. Harvey, *Song and Memory*.

82. I.e., the female sex.

83. Jacob, *Metrical Homily on Holy Mar Ephrem*, 108–12 (pp. 50–53). I have modified Amar's translation slightly. On line 111, he translated "gabākén" as "your gender," but I translated it as "Your side." On line 112, I have translated "qām" as "stood up," rather than his "restored."

as Brock notes, has a typological relationship to Adam, corresponding to him in her wondrous childbirth.[84]

Here it is useful to recall the creation narrative as Ephrem presents it in his *Commentary on Genesis*, as the themes are recapitulated in his *Hymns on the Nativity*. In Scripture, God creates Adam and Eve with free will and clothes them in garments of glory. The transgression of the divine command, for Ephrem, was not one of ignorant children but rather of arrogant adults.[85] Adam and Eve were wrapped in a heavenly raiment of glory—and because of that glory—they were naked but not ashamed.[86] When God expels Adam and Eve however from Eden, they lose these garments. It is Mary who will restore this garment to humanity.

Cupidity drives Adam and Eve to eat the fruit of the forbidden tree; even if the serpent had not tempted Eve, Ephrem implies they would have eaten from it eventually, on account of their greed. Eating the fruit, the first occasion of the sin of gluttony, disorders the relationships between God and humanity and between man and woman. The serpent envied Adam and Eve for the unique glory and reason with which they had been created, as well as the "eternal life which is provided by the Tree of Life" that was "promised to them alone."[87] The serpent manages through cunning to take the portion of divinity that could have belonged to Adam and Eve. God had wished, in Ephrem's imagination, to confer immortality onto Adam and Eve. But through eating, that immortality was lost.

Ephrem's reading of the Genesis story will also shape Ephrem's presentation of Mary. Mary will be the ascetic second Eve who does not give into her own wishes but rather offers her body up for the sake of the healing or restoration of the world, denying her own desires to become what God desires for her. Mary regains the immortality that was lost through Eve's disobedience and rebuilds the ruptured relationship between Creator and Creation.[88] Death comes into the world through Eve, and re-creation begins with Mary.[89]

Mary, as a new Eve, assents to God's will, and this contrasts Eve's disobedience. Eve's misuse of her free will led to a rupture in the relationship

---

84. Brock, "Mary in Syriac Tradition," 187.

85. Ephrem, "Commentary on Genesis" 14, in Ephrem, *Hymns on Paradise*, 206.

86. Ephrem, "Commentary on Genesis," 18, in Ephrem, *Hymns on Paradise*, 210.

87. Ephrem, "Commentary on Genesis," 23, in Ephrem, *Hymns on Paradise*, 214.

88. In his classic study of the theology of Ephrem the Syrian, *Luminous Eye*, 26, Sebastian P. Brock noted that one of the most important themes of Ephrem's theology is the gap between Creation and Creator.

89. Pasquet, "La relation typologique," 29.

between God and humanity. Ephrem contrasts Eve and Mary, as he imagines Mary's voice:

> In her virginity, Eve put on
> *leaves of disgrace*, but Your mother has put on
> in her virginity, the *garment of glory*
> that is enough for all, while I gave
> a body as a small cloak to Him who clothes all.[90]

Mary's obedience corrects and heals the relationship that Eve's desires destroyed.

His presentation of Mary as the Second Eve also shapes his portrait of the miraculous nature of the incarnation: a conception that took place through the entry of the Word or Logos into Mary's ear.[91] This compelling image recurs throughout his corpus. In the *Hymns on the Church* he writes:

> Just as from the small womb of Eve's ear death entered in
> And was poured out, so too through a new ear,
> That was Mary's, Life entered and was poured out.[92]

Ephrem draws Mary also into relationship with the Samaritan woman whom Jesus meets at the well in the Gospel of John (John 4:4–26). Ephrem creates a parallel relationship between her and Mary: the Word of God entered Mary's ear and she bore the infant Jesus. The Samaritan woman meets Jesus as an adult, and his word enters her ear, allowing her to drink from the source of all:

> Mary, the thirsty earth in Nazareth,
> conceived the Lord through her hearing,
> Also you, [Samaritan] woman, thirsting for water,
> Conceived the Lord through your hearing;
> Blessed are your ears that drank the source
> That gave drink to the world.[93]

90. Ephrem, *Hymn Nat.* 17.4, ed. Beck, 87–88. Trans. McVey, 154 (mod).

91. Brock, "Mary in Syriac Tradition," 184. See also Pasquet, "La relation typologique," 30–33.

92. Ephrem, *Hymns on the Church*, 49.7, in Ephrem, *Hymnen de Ecclesia [Textus]*, 126.

93. Ephrem, *Hymns on Virginity* 23.5, in Ephrem, *Hymnen de Virginitate*, 82. Trans. McVey, 362 (mod).

This tradition of the Word entering women of Scripture through their ears remains strong in Syriac liturgical memory. In the anonymous dialogue hymns (which Brock dates to the fifth or early sixth century), for example, the hymnist notes that the serpent

> with venomous intention breathed poison in the ears of weak Eve. . . . The Word of the Father made his descent down to the ear through which misfortune had entered in . . . for the snake's insinuation which had wrought destruction, had entered in by the ear. Thus by the gate through which death had come, Life should enter in, and there, in the very place of sin, grace which has come to reign, should abound.[94]

Thus, death entered the world through one woman's free choice—a woman whom the serpent tricked. This action forced Eve (and Adam) to strip off their garments of glory. Christ and his mother Mary, however, will undo this action and give back the garments to Adam and Eve, who together symbolize all of humanity. Ephrem notes that Mary inaugurates a new age for all womankind:

> Man imposed corruption on woman when she came forth
> from him;
> today she has repaid him—she who bore for him the Savior.
> He gave birth to the Mother, Eve, he, the man who was
> never born;
> How worthy of faith is the daughter of Eve, who without
> a man bore a child.[95]

In this occasion, Ephrem imagines, Eve rejoices from Sheol. Christ, the Son of the daughter of Eve, the Medicine of Life, descends to save the mother of his mother, the blessed babe who will crush the head of the serpent who injured her.[96] Eve redeems Mary as Christ redeems Adam.[97]

94. See Brock, *Bride of Light*, hymn 27:4–6 (pp. 92–93). See the reference to this also in Constas, *Proclus of Constantinople*, 283.

95. Ephrem, *Hymn Nat.* 1:14–17, ed. Beck, 3. Trans. McVey, 65.

96. Ephrem, *Hymn Nat.* 13:2, ed. Beck, 73–74. Trans. McVey, 137. See Beck, "Mariologie," 33.

97. Pasquet, "La relation typologique," 41. This theme is also found in Cyrillonas, another early Syriac poet theologian.

Holy Womb, Holy Breast

Ephrem also celebrates in wondrous awe the mystery and holiness of Mary's body. Ephrem's celebration of Mary's body affirms the goodness of the body and creation. Especially in the fourth-century Church, such affirmation contains also a polemic against Marcion and other Christian sects who denigrated the body's goodness. Christ receives his humanity through Mary. Mary's womb and breasts together nurture and sustain Jesus' life, and thus Ephrem focuses his attention on these organs as the sites of divine activity, like the sites of liturgical mysteries. The Word of God descends through Mary's ear and settles in Mary's womb, and thus the womb of Mary itself becomes a tabernacle, a holy of holies. Ephrem accentuates both Mary's corporality and the sanctity of her body, calling special attention to her womb and breasts that housed Jesus and then nurtured him in infancy, providing food, safety, comfort, and survival to the Incarnate God.

Ephrem's focus upon Mary's womb, ' *úbā* in Syriac, would resonate to the ear of the Syriac speaker since it is also the word for baptismal font:[98] a place of rebirth, transformation, hope, and wonder. The womb of Mary, like the baptismal font, changes the life of the individual Christian as well as the life of the Church. Because of the Word's descent into Mary's womb, humanity can be reborn and healed. Mary weaves the body of Christ:

> She wove it and clothed him who had stripped
> himself of his glory;
> She measured and wove it for him who had made
> himself small.[99]

Ephrem also celebrates Mary's sanctified corporality through praising Mary as the nursing mother, nourishing her baby as all mothers. Although she is a virgin, she is gifted with the effects of motherhood. The Word of God becomes a tiny baby in Mary's womb; in what seems a great contradiction, the Word as infant can no longer speak:

> Mary bore a quiet infant
> In him were hidden all our tongues.
> Joseph bore him; in him was hidden
> A silent nature that is older than all.[100]

---

98. McVey, "Images of Joy in Ephrem."

99. Ephrem, *Hymn Nat.* 4:188, ed. Beck, 42. Trans. McVey, 102 (mod).

100. Ephrem, *Hymn Nat.* 4:146–47, ed. Beck, 38. Trans. McVey, 100 (mod). Ephrem's emphasis on the eternity of Christ's nature is thus also an Anti-Arian polemic.

Mary and Joseph for their part teach the church how to approach Christ.

Mary gives the exalted one milk, even though this baby—the incarnate God—is the living breast who revives the dead.[101] Even in the womb of his mother, he never stops creating:

> While the fetus of the Son was being formed in the womb,
> He himself was creating all babies in the womb.[102]

The incarnation is a dance of giving and receiving—and Mary's activity as the mother of the Lord is at the center of this dance:

> From the great treasury of all creation,
> Mary gave to him all that she gave.
> She gave him milk from what he brought into existence.
> She gave him food, from what he had created.
> He gave milk to her as God,
> In turn he was given suck by her as a human being.[103]

Mary's milk symbolizes the miraculous nature of her virginal motherhood as well as Christ's humanity. She wonders at the paradoxical mysteries of her gestures of caring for her baby.

Ephrem expresses his own wonder through the mouth of Mary who ponders:

> How shall I open the fount of milk
> for You, the Fount? How shall I give
> sustenance to You, the All-sustaining,
> from Your [own] table? How shall I approach
> with swaddling clothes the One arrayed in streams [of light]?[104]

Mary undoes the harm of Eve's desires and paradoxically becomes a source of food for her child, who himself feeds the world.

Model of Devotion and Prayer—Prophet and Mystic

Ephrem's typological exegesis was transmitted in the context of the liturgy and meant to lead the believer to greater devotion. Thus Ephrem beautifully

101. Ephrem, *Hymn Nat.* 4:150, ed. Beck, 39. Trans. McVey, 100.
102. Ephrem, *Hymn Nat.* 4:161, ed. Beck, 40. Trans. McVey, 101.
103. Ephrem, *Hymn Nat.* 4:183–85, ed. Beck, 42. Trans. McVey, 102 (mod).
104. Ephrem, *Hymn Nat.* 5:24, ed. Beck, 50. Trans. McVey, 109.

fashions in Mary, too, a portrait of faithful piety to God. Mary teaches the believer how to approach and worship the Lord. Other saints of scripture also show us the importance of wonder in our approach to God:

> John drew near with his parents,
>
> and he worshipped the Son; the brightness rested
>
> on his face; he did not leap
>
> as in the womb; it is a great wonder
>
> that here he worshipped, and there he leaps.[105]

Ephrem considers what Mary may have been thinking when she discovered that she would carry the Christ. This becomes a place for poetic theological expansion and instruction. Ephrem imagines that Mary, as model of so many things, was perhaps at prayer. He likens her to Daniel, whom Gabriel also found at prayer:

> What indeed was the pure woman doing at the moment
>
> When Gabriel was sent down to her?
>
> She saw him perhaps at the moment of prayer,
>
> For Daniel was also at prayer when he saw Gabriel.
>
> For prayer is next of kin to good tidings.[106]

As a figure of contemplative prayer, of bold assent to the will of God, and of wonder at God's activity, Mary teaches all the Church how to worship Christ, her Son. In this way, Ephrem's Mary, as Fr. Stephen Bonian, SJ, noted, "is continuously bringing Mary and the Christian closer together."[107] As Cornelia Horn has shown, later Syriac tradition after the sixth century will build upon the strong portrait of Mary in Ephrem's corpus to show her role as intercessor.[108]

Conclusion

The Council of Ephesus (431) affirmed Mary as the Theotokos, the Mother of God, a title that denoted her doctrinal importance as the individual through whom Christ's humanity is secured.[109] Yet nearly a century before

---

105. Ephrem, *Hymn Nat.* 6:18, ed. Beck, 54. Trans. McVey, 113 (mod).

106. Ephrem, *Hymn Nat.* 2:17, ed. Beck, 17. Trans. McVey, 79–80.

107. Bonian, "Mary and the Christian," 46.

108. But Ephrem does not present Mary as an intercessory figure; that is absent from Syriac sources before the sixth century: Horn, "Ancient Syriac Sources on Mary."

109. The hymns of Ephrem, as Beck notes, lack an exact equivalent or articulation

the Council of Ephesus declared Mary the Theotokos or mother of God, Ephrem developed a theology of Mary in his hymns and homilies that placed her at the center of the drama of the Incarnation. No other author in the early Church gives so much attention to Mary as Ephrem the Syrian. In his *Hymns on the Nativity*, Ephrem expands the character of Mary, giving her a voice of power and affirming Mary as a wonder herself. He silences any imagined detractors who would question Mary's virginity. He praises her body as a holy tabernacle, the place where God met humanity in the most intimate gift of Christ. Mary is a figure who both leads and symbolizes the Church. She is honored in every Syriac Church, even the so-called "Nestorian" Church which rejected the title "Theotokos."[110] Studying the portraits of Mary in the Syriac tradition offers an important balance to her depiction in Byzantine and Western Christian traditions.

Bibliography

Beck, Edmund. "Die Mariologie der Echten Schriften Ephräms." *Oriens Christianus* 40 (1956) 22–39.

Bonian, Stephen. "Mary and the Christian in the Mystical Poetry of St. Ephrem." *Diakonia* 17 (1982) 46–52.

Botha, Phil J. "Tamar, Rahab, Ruth, and Mary—The Bold Women in Ephrem the Syrian's Hymn De Nativitate 9." *Acta Patristica et Byzantina* 17 (2006) 1–21.

Brock, Sebastian P. *Bride of Light: Hymns on Mary from the Syriac Churches.* Piscataway, NJ: Gorgias, 2010.

———. *The Luminous Eye: The Spiritual World Vision of Saint Ephrem.* Kalamazoo, MI: Cistercian, 1992.

———. *Mary in Syriac Tradition.* London: Ecumenical Society of the Blessed Virgin Mary, 1973.

———. "Mary in Syriac Tradition." In *Mary's Place in Christian Dialogue*, edited by Alberic Stacpoole, 182–91. Slough, UK: St. Paul, 1982.

———. "St. Ephrem on Christ as Light in Mary and in the Jordan (Hymns on the Church, 36)." *Eastern Churches Review* 7 (1976) 137–44.

Brown, Raymond E., et al., editors. *Mary in the New Testament: A Collaborative Assessment by Protestant and Roman Catholic Scholars.* New York: Paulist, 1978.

Cameron, Averil. *Christianity and the Rhetoric of Empire: The Development of Christian Discourse.* Berkeley: University of California Press, 1994.

Chadwick, Henry. *The Early Church.* London: Penguin, 1993.

---

of the term "Theotokos," but as we have seen, the idea was certainly present. Beck, "Mariologie," 23. We note further that the dogmas of the Immaculate Conception and the Assumption of Mary are not articulated yet in the theology of Mary in Ephrem, but, as Beck notes, we see in his picture of Mary the suppositions or understandings of Mary's holiness, out of which these dogmas will grow. See Beck, "Mariologie," 39.

110. Brock, "Mary in Syriac Tradition," 182–83.

Charlesworth, James H. *The Odes of Solomon: The Syriac Texts*. Missoula, MT: Scholars, 1978.

Clement of Alexandria. *Miscellanies*. See *Clemens Alexandrinus: Stromata. Buch VII und VIII*, edited by Otto Stählin et al. Griechischen christlichen Schriftsteller der ersten drei Jahrhunderte 17/3. Berlin: Akademie, 1972.

Constas, Nicholas. *Proclus of Constantinople and the Cult of the Virgin in Late Antiquity Homilies 1–5, Texts and Translations*. Leiden: Brill, 2003.

Ephrem the Syrian. *Hymnen de Ecclesia [Textus]*. Edited by Edmund Beck. Corpus Scriptorum Christianorum Orientalium 199, Scriptores Syri 85. Louvain: Secretariat du CSCO, 1960.

———. *Hymnen de Nativitate (Epiphania)*. Edited and translated by Edmund Beck. Corpus Scriptorum Christianorum Orientalium 186–87. Louvain: Secrétariat du CSCO, 1959.

———. *Hymnen de Paradiso und Contra Julianum*. Edited by Edmund Beck. Corpus Scriptorum Christianorum Orientalium 174. Louvain: Secrétariat du CSCO, 1957.

———. *Hymnen de Virginitate*. Edited by Edmund Beck. Corpus Scriptorum Christianorum Orientalium 223. Louvain: Secrétariat du CSCO, 1962.

———. *Hymns*. Translated by Kathleen E. McVey. New York: Paulist, 1989.

———. *The Hymns on Faith*. Translated by Jeffrey Wickes. Washington, DC: Catholic University of America Press, 2015.

———. *Hymns on Paradise*. Translated by Sebastian P. Brock. Crestwood, NY: St. Vladimir's Seminary, 1990.

Graef, Hilda Charlotte. *Mary: A History of Doctrine and Devotion*. Notre Dame: Christian Classics, 2009.

Griffith, Sidney Harrison. *Faith Adoring the Mystery: Reading the Bible with St. Ephraem the Syrian*. Milwaukee: Marquette University Press, 1997.

Harvey, Susan. "On Mary's Voice: Gendered Words in Syriac Marian Tradition." In *The Cultural Turn in Late Ancient Studies: Gender, Asceticism, and Historiography*, edited by Dale B. Martin and Patricia Cox Miller, 63–86. Durham: Duke University Press, 2005.

———. *Song and Memory: Biblical Women in Syriac Tradition*. Milwaukee: Marquette University Press, 2010.

Horn, Cornelia. "Ancient Syriac Sources on Mary's Role as Intercessor." In *Presbeia Theotokou: The Intercessory Role of Mary across Times and Places in Byzantium (4th–9th Century)*, edited by Leena Mari Peltomaa et al., 153–75. Vienna: Austrian Academy of Sciences, 2015.

Ignatius of Antioch. *Letters*. In *The Apostolic Fathers*, edited by Bart D. Ehrman, translated by Kirsopp Lake, 165–277. Loeb Classical Library 24. Cambridge: Harvard University Press, 2003.

Irenaeus of Lyon. *Against Heresies, Book 3*. See *Contre les hérésies: Livre III*, edited by Adelin Rousseau and Louis Doutreleau. Sources Chrétiennes 210–11. Paris: Cerf, 1974.

———. *Against Heresies, Book 4*. See *Contre les hérésies, Livre IV*, edited by Adelin Rousseau et al. Sources Chrétiennes 100. Paris: Cerf, 1965.

Jacob of Sarug. *A Metrical Homily on Holy Mar Ephrem by Mar Jacob of Sarug*. Edited and translated by Joseph P. Amar. Patrologia Orientalia 209 (47.1). Turnhout: Brepols, 1995.

MacCarthy, Carmel. *Saint Ephrem's Commentary on Tatian's Diatessaron: An English Translation of Chester Beatty Syriac MS 709 with Introduction and Notes.* Oxford: Oxford University Press, 1993.

McVey, Kathleen E. "Images of Joy in Ephrem's Hymns on Paradise: Returning to the Womb and the Breast." *Journal of the Canadian Society for Syriac Studies* 3 (2009) 59–77.

Murray, Robert. "Mary, the Second Eve in the Early Syriac Fathers." *Eastern Churches Review* 3 (1971) 372–84.

———. *Symbols of Church and Kingdom: A Study in Early Syriac Tradition.* 2nd ed. Piscataway, NJ: Gorgias, 2004.

Origen. *Contra Celsum.* Translated by Henry Chadwick. Cambridge: Cambridge University Press, 1980.

———. *Werke: Die Homilien zu Lukas in der Übersetzung des Hieronymus und die griechischen Reste der Homilien und des Lukas-Kommentars.* Edited by Max Rauer, translated by Saint Jerome. Griechischen christlichen Schriftsteller der ersten drei Jahrhunderte 49/9. Berlin: Akademie, 1959.

Pasquet, Colette. "La relation typologique Eve–Marie dans la tradition syriaque." *Connaissance des Pères de L'Église* 121 (2011) 27–41.

Protevangelium of James. In *Evangelia Apocrypha,* edited by Constantin von Tischendorf, 1–50. Hildesheim: Olms, 1987.

Scott, Samantha. "A Priest, a Prophet, and a King Walk into the Holy of Holies: A Fresh Look at Mary in the Imagination of the Protoevangelium of James." Seminar paper presented at Marquette University, May 2019.

Shoemaker, Stephen J. *Ancient Traditions of the Virgin Mary's Dormition and Assumption.* Oxford Early Christian Studies. Oxford University Press, 2003.

———. *Mary in Early Christian Faith and Devotion.* New Haven: Yale University Press, 2016.

Tertullian. *La Chair du Christ.* Edited and translated by Jean-Pierre Mahé. Sources Chrétiennes 216–17. Paris: Cerf, 1975.

Tkacz, Catherine Brown. "Women as Types of Christ: Susanna and Jephthah's Daughter." *Gregorianum* 85 (2004) 278–311.

Vuong, Lily C. *Gender and Purity in the Protevangelium of James.* Tübingen: Mohr Siebeck, 2013.

Wickes, Jeffrey. *Bible and Poetry in Late Antique Mesopotamia: Ephrem's Hymns on Faith.* Oakland: University of California Press, 2019.

4

St. Macrina the Younger, the Spirit of Holiness, and the "God-Breathed Scriptures"

ANNA M. SILVAS

University of New England, Armidale, NSW

Introduction: Fr. Hartin and the Way to Approach the Scriptures and the Fathers

ST. MACRINA THE YOUNGER, the Spirit of Holiness and the "God-breathed Scriptures" is my theme. In tracing Macrina's engagement with the Scriptures, I take the opportunity to pay tribute to Fr. Patrick James Hartin's work at Gonzaga University in the area of scriptural hermeneutics, and especially his desire to re-commend to his hearers the interpretive approach of the Fathers of the Church.

Let us begin by focusing on the sensibility of Scripture that is so characteristic of Early Christianity, of the Church Fathers, and of all the traditions of Sacred Liturgy in the ancient Churches, the sense that Scripture has *layers* of meaning, one meaning opening out on another. This has every relevance to Macrina and to her biographer, Gregory, because they certainly shared this sensibility.

Sometime in the mid-twentieth century biblical studies in the Western Catholic Church began a shift to the historical-critical method, which accentuates skepticism of the text, abstracted reasoning, and an analytical "objectivity" that imposes a distance between the reader/scholar and his text.[1] Since then we have had the rise of sub-Marxist and secularizing

---

1. See the magisterial survey of this topic in Joseph Ratzinger's Erasmus Lecture, originally delivered in 1991 and now available in print: Benedict XVI, "Biblical Interpretation in Conflict." "What is needed is *a criticism of criticism*, developed, not from

critiques like that of feminism, post-structuralism and post-modernism. Concomitantly, the approach to patristic literature, or "Early Christian Studies" as it was rebranded, was also affected by the same shift, becoming fraught with ambiguities thereby. It is essentially the same problem: the programmatic skepticism of secular critiques towards the texts of the Christian deep-faith tradition.[2] I myself have experienced the professional tension between being a passionate believer and lover of our Lord Jesus Christ, a child of his Bride the Church, and fielding the secularist imperatives of the contemporary academic setting.

Suffice it to say, that I have long rebelled against these secularizing constraints. I refuse to engage in the writings of the Church Fathers except in the spirit in which they were written, setting a premium on the same faith to which they bore witness and looking to the same goal that led them: the *anagogy* of our life in the Spirit, the perfecting of our life in Christ, the imitation of the Father.

Hence I agree with Fr. Hartin on the importance of our recovering the patristic, liturgical and spiritual approach to interpretation of Scripture.

The Sacred Scriptures are forever re-reading God's ways with man, forever rehearsing and probing the received accounts, and, under pressure of severe crises, and indeed catastrophes, anguishing over, seeking to elucidate more deeply the tenor of God's covenant relationship with Israel. Girard memorably calls it the "internal travail" of Scripture,[3] and we must taste it for ourselves, deeply, in prayer. This forensic attitude, this "searching out," this "digging deeper," is true above all of the prophets—not the false prophets, the appeasers, the mollifiers, deluded and deluding, but the true prophets, signs of contradiction in their own age, credentialed by suffering, to whom the Lord discloses his ways with man from depth unto depth, opening up vista upon vista, always pointing beyond and above. Hebrews 1:1–3 and 1 Peter 1:10–12 encapsulate the slow and varied unfolding of the divine pedagogy in history, till its culmination in the event of Christ. The sublime hymn of Ephesians 1:3–10 marvels at the final revelation of "the Mystery" hidden before all ages.[4] We find the Gospel of John (cf. John 2:11)

---

outside, but simply from within, from critical thought's potential for self-criticism" (p. 100; emphasis added). Ratzinger synthesizes his recommended approach on pp. 114–26.

2. An early sign of a "stock-take" of modernist interpretations was Young, "From Suspicion to Spirituality," 421. For a secular academic's account, see Clark, "From Patristics to Early Christian."

3. Girard, *Things Hidden*, 263.

4. This hymn is discussed elsewhere in this volume: Weinandy, "Paul's Three Hymns," 239–42.

steeped in a profoundly sapiential sense of the energy of God at work in "sacred signs," signs ever leading us inward, onward and upward. These brief pointers should be enough to show that the layered patristic and liturgical hermeneutic of Scripture is in truth a discipleship of the same vibrant "deep reading" approach of the sacred writers themselves.

In the tradition of ecclesial faith, Sacred Scripture has first a literal or historical sense. It is on this first level that historical criticism may have a legitimate and useful contribution to make. The literal sense then opens out upon a number of "spiritual" senses: a moral sense, an allegorical or preferably a typological sense, and an anagogical sense.[5] These "senses" or "layers" of meaning" correspond to the kinds of questions we bring to the text. The literal asks the immediate "who and what, where and when" of the document or text in hand. The moral asks "how must we behave then?" The typological asks: "how does this fit into the deep pattern of salvation history?" The anagogical sense asks: "whither, ultimately, would this lead us?"

These human questionings correspond to the varied ways that the Holy Spirit is ever at work to reclaim us for God, *the living and true God* (1 Thess 1:9), through epic history and picaresque tales, covenantal literary forms, epideictic commandment and case-law, dread theophanies, divine oracles, prophetic appeals, human pleadings full of pathos, warnings and consolations, poetic metaphors, and apocalyptic images. Through all these varied literary forms found in the Scriptures, the educative purpose of the Spirit is always *anagogical*. *Anagōgē* means "leading upward." It is the Spirit of God then, who leads us onward and upward to ultimate realities, from sin, through redemption and the walk of obedience and the cleaving of prayer, to growth in holiness and finally to perfect union with God, to *what no eye has seen, nor ear heard, nor the heart of man conceived, what God has prepared for those who love him* (1 Cor 2:9).

In reading the Scriptures and the Fathers, therefore, we necessarily seek to tap that same Spirit of Holiness that inspired them, and this we do best by the spirit of prayer, and asceticism, and participation in the sacred Liturgy. Such then is our disposition.

Our Macrina Is Always Gregory's Macrina

The fathomlessly deep Johannine spirit is very close to the Marian spirit. After all, at our Lord's bidding, John took Mary into his home after the Crucifixion.

---

5. The classic fourfold sense of Scripture is affirmed in Second Vatican Council, *Dei Verbum*, para. 12, and *Catechism of the Catholic Church*, para. 109–19. See also Fr. Hartin's essay in this volume at pp. 38–39.

It was these two, Mary and John, who in that eternal Hour contemplated the piercing of our Lord's side with a lance, and the water and the blood gushing forth. Decades, and indeed a lifetime passed, and the youngest and longest lived of the Apostles gave us the sublime Fourth Gospel. Who would dare to say that John gives us a distorted picture of our Divine Lord in this Gospel, one that it is filtered through an "ideological agenda" or strained by the necessities of the "rhetorical genre" in which he chose to write? Say rather that the first Christian Pentecost, the anointing of the Spirit who teaches us all things, a lifetime of abiding with the Risen Lord in noetic prayer, the years of familiarity with Mary, and of being an apostolic father in the midst of immense difficulties in the infant Church, matured in him that interior contemplative vision, that transparent inner purity that enabled him to paint for us a radiantly true and most precious verbal icon of our Beloved Lord and God and Savior given us in his Gospel.

Something like this relationship exists between St. Macrina the Younger and her biographer, her little brother, St. Gregory of Nyssa. Except for one epigram of St. Gregory the Theologian, all we know of Macrina is Gregory's Macrina. To be sure, there are those in the reductionist spirit of textual criticism who readily dismiss all that Gregory has to say about his sister as purely a function of literary genre. His narrative is a tissue of predetermined rhetorical topoi—in short, it is all an artful invention. This superior-minded skeptical approach can be exceedingly tiresome, and I will not enter into a countering argument here. Suffice it to say that, allowing by all means for the skillful play of Gregory's rhetorical art, underpinning all he says is a profound, thoughtful and prayerful appreciation of his sister. It matured through a lifetime of severe vicissitudes, through his attendance at her death-bed in July of the year 379, and through the subsequent two or three years when he penned the three works in which he tells us of Macrina: the first, his Letter 19, the second, his Life of Macrina, and the third, the philosophical dialogue, On the Soul and the Resurrection.

An interesting sidelight: one of the oldest apparitions of Mary on record comes from the pen of Gregory of Nyssa, in his Life of St. Gregory Thaumaturgus or the Wonderworker, of the third century AD. Who should Mary be both preceded and accompanied by in this vision, but St. John the beloved disciple.

Who Was Macrina the Younger?

Who then was St. Macrina the Younger? Catherine Tkacz asked me for a description in one sentence. I had two tries, and settled on: "Saint Macrina the

Younger (327–79), the 'Fifth Cappadocian,'[6] Mother of Greek Monasticism, was the first-born child of Saints Emmelia and Basil the Elder, grand-daughter of Saint Macrina the Elder, and elder sister and spiritual mother to Saints Basil the Great, Gregory of Nyssa and Peter II of Sebasteia." She was truly an outstanding spiritual Mother from the Early Church, even if somewhat hidden and unknown in her lifetime and leaving no written legacy of her own. We ask her to be with us now, in Christ, as we take up her story.

Her family lineage goes back to the age of the martyrs, when the Church existed in a tense relationship to the Roman Empire, periodically enduring outbreaks of persecution. Her mother's grandfather died as a Christian Martyr in the Decian persecutions of the 250s. Her paternal grandmother was St. Macrina the Elder, from the city of Neocaesarea, just south of the Black Sea, lying along the great Via Pontica leading to the eastern boundary of the Roman Empire at Satala. Here the Christian church was founded by St. Gregory Thaumaturgus, mentioned above, student and panegyrist of the great Origen of Alexandria. This Macrina was a zealous custodian of the traditions of the church in Neocaesarea. Basil the Great even invoked her name as a guarantor of his doctrinal orthodoxy. She and her husband were forced to live as outlaws in the mountain forests for seven years during the last, particularly savage persecution of Christians under Emperor Maximian. Their son, Basil the Elder, became a successful lawyer and rhetorician in Neocaesarea and married the orphaned Emmelia from Cappadocia. Of their ten children, one died in infancy, and of the other nine, at least four are saints of the universal Church, and two of these Fathers of the Church. This was one outstanding family in Christian history, a splendid example of generational holiness, passing down from martyrs and confessors of the faith, willing, when really put to the test, to break with society's demands, who in their turn passed on the obedience of faith to their children and grandchildren, who in their turn became great saints and leaders of the Church in the later part of the fourth century.

Macrina the Younger was the first-born. She became a spiritual trail-blazer for all her siblings, and even of her own mother. In her early teens—we are in the early 340s here—her father decided on a young man as her future betrothed, but he died before the time of betrothal arrived. She seized on the event to make a radical act of choice. She belonged to a church which was very strong on the idea that Christian marriage was a once-only event in this life. She argued to her parents that her father's decision should be taken as definitive, since her lost future husband was simply

---

6. After Basil the Great, Gregory of Nyssa, Gregory the Theologian, and Amphilochius of Iconium, although in point of time and influence she was their elder.

away on a long journey, and she would see him in eternity. In this way she prosecuted her resolve on a life of virginity for the Lord. She began to deepen her practice of the ascetic life by her mother's side; in the mid-350s she persuaded her mother, by then widowed, to set aside all the privileges of the aristocratic life, and put herself on an equal footing with the servants and virgins. Like a leaven in the house, Macrina inspired her family household, transforming it by degrees into a kind of proto-monastic community. When the youngest-born, Peter, entirely educated by his sister Macrina, came of age, he wanted to follow his sister in a life of virginity and asceticism for the Lord. Thus they worked out how to have a house for monks as part of the community. About ten years later, Peter was ordained a priest by his brother Basil and served the Holy Liturgy for the community. Thus a classic *adelphotēs* ("Fraternity"/"brotherhood"), or monastic community had emerged by the early 360s, comprising a house for women, a house for men, a house for the care of children, and a common "house of prayer" or church. This was the form of community that Basil came back to in about 363, which helped form his own thinking and teaching on the ascetic community. Basil, be it noted, did not initiate Macrina and her community into the monastic life. No, this had already been achieved at Annisa under Macrina's governance, and in fact helped shape Basil's ideas and teaching in the period 363–66. It is for this reason, then, I maintain, that we have every right to think of Macrina as a Mother of cenobitic monasticism and yes, the Mother of Greek Monasticism.

According to Gregory of Nyssa's testimony, in about the year 356/7 Basil returned from years of study in Athens, "puffed up" with the superiority of his own rhetorical powers in comparison with the locals. He commenced a secular career down in Caesarea of Cappadocia, when, during a visit back to the family homestead in Pontus, his elder sister took him in hand, forcibly reminding him of his earlier aspirations. As Basil says, his eyes were opened to the deifying light of Christ. Such was the spiritual integrity to which Macrina had attained, for we all know how hard it is to impress our siblings. Something in her entire life and conduct and character lent power to her remonstrance in words. Basil turned his life around there and then, sought Holy Baptism and Chrismation, and began his quest in the ascetic life that lead him eventually to become a great father of monks. Through her timely intervention, Macrina was a spiritual mother to her own brother, the great Basil.

She was also a spiritual mother to the third of the sons, her brother Gregory, who was about eight years younger. In 364 Gregory chose a secular career as a rhetorician, married, and may even have had a son. Alas, his wife, it seems, died very early in the piece, possibly in childbirth. Gregory was traumatized; he continued his career in the city of Caesarea of Cappadocia facing years of "widowerhood." The Hound of Heaven, however, had other plans for the gifted Gregory. Caught in a spiritual pincer movement, between the influence of his sister and his youngest brother bearing down on him from Pontus, and the influence of Basil, elected metropolitan archbishop of Caesarea in September 370, Gregory accepted being made a bishop himself at the hands of his brother, in 372. It seems that as a newly minted bishop, he went north to Pontus to see his sister, who, he said, was a mother in place of their mother, a spiritual instructress and inspiration. Now Gregory has been called a Father of Christian mystical theology no less.[7] Well, if so, Macrina was his spiritual mother. His first writing was his *On Virginity*, written in about 371. Though unnamed, his sister is discernibly the watermark of the entire work, his exemplar of the loftiest spiritual progress in virginity, and of the upper reaches of the mystical life in Christ. You see it especially in the last chapter, 23.

The Scriptures: The Approach of the Early Christian Church

Let us consider Macrina's engagement with the Scriptures. That means considering Gregory of Nyssa's hermeneutic of the Scriptures, because he uses the same approach to "read" Macrina's life. Gregory follows the approach of the early Christian Church, which in turn was a continuation and development of approaches found within Holy Scripture itself. At the same time, this tradition of interpretation also drew on the hermeneutical tradition of the Hellenistic era as first applied to the Scriptures by the Hellenized diaspora Jew, Philo of Alexandria.

Gregory discusses his approach to interpreting Scripture at length in the letter with which he prefaces his *Homilies on the Song of Songs*.[8] He addressed it to St. Olympias of Constantinople, another holy woman who lived a life of hidden but significant influence in the Church of her time, leaving no literary legacy. The very nature of the book Gregory means to take up begs a discussion of interpretation. On the face of it, it is a series of love songs between lover and beloved, full of sensuous and passionate

7. Daniélou, *Platonisme et théologie mystique*, 6. This judgment was endorsed by Pope Benedict XVI in the first of his two catecheses on St. Gregory given August 29, 2007: "As a great 'father of mysticism' he pointed out in various treatises—such as his *De Professione Christiana (On the Christian Profession)* and *De Perfectione Christiana (On Christian Perfection)*—the path Christians must take if they are to reach true life, perfection." Benedict XVI, *Fathers of the Church*, 72.

8. See Gregory, *Homilies on the Song of Songs*, prefatory letter, 2–13.

language. To Gregory whenever one comes across a scriptural passage that offers no immediate reference to a Godward piety, one treats it as an enigma on a higher register of meaning that brings benefit. He is not too concerned whatever terms are used to describe such forms of spiritual interpretation: "One may wish to refer to the anagogical contemplation of such sayings as 'tropology' or 'allegory' or by some other name. We shall not quarrel about the name, as long as a firm grasp is kept on thoughts that bring a benefit."[9]

"Anagogical contemplation," he says. One could sum up Gregory's entire spiritual disposition with the word "anagogy." Gregory is particularly good in this letter in showing how this leading *onward* and *upward*, was supremely our Lord's own manner, his constant intention in all his teaching. He overwhelms us with examples from the Gospels. It is so true.

Immediately after this passage Gregory uses the beautiful phrase *tēn theopneuston graphēn*, "the God-breathed Scripture," which he also uses in his *Life of Macrina*, and frequently appears in the Cappadocian Fathers.

Reared and Nurtured on the Scriptures

How then, did Macrina come into contact with the Scriptures? Basil the Elder and Emmelia reared all their children in a family atmosphere imbued with the Scriptures. Basil describes his early upbringing: "I was delivered from the deceitfulness of the tradition of those outside, having been brought up from the very beginning by Christian parents. With them I learned from infancy (*apo brephous*) the holy Scriptures."[10]

Gregory attests much the same of Macrina in *Vita Sanctae Macrinae* (hereafter *VSM*[11]), chapter 4, where he describes her childhood education:

> **2.** Her mother was most concerned that the child be educated, but she did not educate her in the customary secular curriculum, which for the most part instructs the early years of study by means of the poems. . . . **3.** But the parts of the God-breathed Scripture that seem more easily learned[12] at a young age: these formed the child's lessons, especially the Wisdom of Solomon, and besides this, whatever bears on the moral life.[13] **4.** Indeed

---

9. Gregory, *Homilies on the Song of Songs*, 2–5.

10. Basil the Great, *De judicio* (Patrologia Graeca 31:653–76); English from Basil, *Ascetic Works*, 77–89.

11. *VSM* in Gregory, *Opera*, 8/1.

12. *Eulēptotera*, probably in the sense of memorized, rehearsed; one manuscript (designated v) has *alēptotera*, "less easily taken up."

13. I.e., the God-breathed Scriptures themselves had to be meted out judiciously to the child.

there was nothing whatever of the Psalter that she did not know, since she recited each part of the psalmody at its own proper time.[14] When she rose from bed, or began her duties or rested from them, or sat down to eat or retired from table, when she went to bed or rose from it for prayers, she kept up the psalmody everywhere. It was like a good travelling companion that never left her at any time.

What Gregory does not mention in his *Life of Macrina*, we learn from autobiographical testimonies of Basil,[15] namely, that their grandmother, Macrina the Elder, played an important role in the education of the children. This is significant, since this Macrina relayed the traditions of the church of Neocaesarea, including the modified Origenism of its Apostle, St. Gregory Thaumaturgus, with all that that implies for an intellectually attentive and contemplative approach to the Sacred Scriptures, which in their case meant the Greek of the Septuagint and the original Greek of the New Testament, largely according to the so-called Byzantine recension.

The Public and Domestic Liturgy of the Church

It is important to stress something here: the cross-over in those days between the chanting of the psalms and of Scripture lessons in the public liturgy of the Church, and the prayer-life of the domestic Church of the family. Woven into the same convergence was liturgical prayer and *Lectio Divina*, the contemplative reading of Scripture. Indeed, the Sacred Liturgy itself might well be described as the Church's collective *Lectio Divina* of the saving words and deeds of God in Sacred History.

There was never a question of *saying* the Psalms in a spoken voice; they were chanted, that's what the word "psalm-ody" means. *Psallō* is to chant, *hadō* is to sing. It was inconceivable to the early Church, and for many centuries, and still is in the Christian East, that the sacred words of the public Liturgy should ever be merely *said* in a spoken voice.

The early Church Fathers show that the Liturgy of the Hours informed the piety of the Christian family. Tertullian, for example, in a famous page

14. This section corresponds with the description of a rudimentary system of Hours in Basil's Letter 2, written in 358 at the very beginning of his ascetic retreat. He was almost certainly imitating Macrina's established practice. See Pierre Maraval's notes to Basil the Great, *Vie de Sainte Macrine*, 69–70, where he points out that even the earliest Christian authors (the *Didache*, Tertullian, Hippolytus, Clement of Alexandria, etc.) recommend certain definite moments of psalmody and prayer through the night and day.

15. Letter 210 in Basil, *Letters*, 3:194–215 at 196–97; and Letter 223 in Basil, *Letters*, 3:286–313 at 298–99.

in his *Letter to His Wife*, describes the prayer life of husband and wife as a carry-over from the liturgy of the Church in liturgical assembly, into the domestic church:

> Together they pray [*simul orant*], together they prostrate themselves [*simul volutantur*], together they undertake their fasts [*simul ieiunia transigunt*] (Matt 6:5,16), mutually teaching [*alterutro docentes*], mutually exhorting [*alterutro hortantes*] (Eph 5:19, Col 3:16), mutually supporting [*alterutro sustinentes*]. Side by side they are in the Church of God [*In ecclesia Dei pariter utrique*], side by side at the Banquet of God [*pariter in convivio Dei*], . . . Psalms and hymns re-echo from one to the other [*sonant inter duos psalmi et hymni*] (Eph 5:19)—indeed they challenge each other to see who could sing the better to God [*et mutuo provocant, quis melius Deo suo cantet*].[16]

At a time when the Church in Milan was under severe duress by the Arian faction, the beleaguered Nicene faithful recruited their spirits by joining together in chanting the psalms and the Liturgy of the Hours. So St. Augustine, who participated in these events, reports:[17]

> It was at this time that the practice was instituted of singing hymns and psalms after the manner of the Eastern churches, to keep the people from being altogether worn out with anxiety and want of sleep. The custom has been retained from that day to this, and has been imitated by many, indeed in almost all congregations throughout the world.

The oldest form of pre-Carolingian chant in the Western Church is the Ambrosian Chant of Milan, and the interesting point is, it followed Syrian models. St. Ambrose and St. Basil the Great corresponded with each other. There is little doubt, therefore, that the Eastern practices being imitated in Milan reflect the practices not only in Syria, but also in adjacent Asia Minor, the very region where Macrina and her family lived.

Allow me to quote Augustine again, on the effect of common liturgical chanting of the faithful in the Church of Milan:

> I wept at the beauty of your hymns and canticles, and was powerfully moved at the sweet sound of your Church's singing. These sounds flowed into my ears, and the truth streamed into

---

16. Tertullian, *To His Wife* 2.8.6–8 (Corpus Christianorum Series Latina 1:393), partly cited in *Familiaris consortio*, no. 13, *Ante-Nicene Fathers*, 4:48.

17. Augustine, *Confessions*, 9.7.15 (pp. 172–73).

my heart; so that my feeling of devotion overflowed, and the
tears ran from my eyes, and I was happy in them.

Not for nothing did this great Church Father declare of our participation in the Liturgy: *it is the part of a lover to sing*.[18] Singing was the
practice of both the public and domestic liturgy of the Church in which
Macrina was reared. The Scriptures were chanted, enacted, and rehearsed
in the local Church gathered together for the Eucharist on the Lord's Day,
and in the daily and weekly round of psalmody, the *sacrifice of praise* by
which they wove like a garland around the Eucharistic core whether in
Church or in the home.

In this ecclesial culture, therefore, Macrina was introduced to chanting
the psalms from her earliest years, grew up with their sacred sounds cours-
ing through her whole body and imprinting themselves in her muscular
memory. Of course she knew them by heart, they pervaded her whole being.
In this way she lived, ate and drank the Scriptures. Gregory testifies in his
Letter 19, that once the family household of Annisa had been transformed
by her leadership, "The psalmodies resounded in her house night and day."
It is this "echoing" of the psalms that primed the mind, and kept the ear of
the heart opened to the visitation of the Word to each soul.

In 376, St. Basil wrote a letter from Annisa itself. He was in the proxi-
mate company of his sister Macrina, staying in the men's quarters with Peter.
In this letter, he accounts for the practice of psalmody in the Christian community in this way. And notice how the Scriptures permeate his discourse:

> But I want you to know that we for our part pray to have
> communities of both men and women *whose citizenship is in
> heaven* (Phil 3:20), who have *crucified the flesh with its affec-
> tions and desires* (Gal 5:24), who are not *anxious about food*
> and *clothing* (cf. Matt 6:25), but who, remaining undistracted
> and *constantly attentive to the Lord* (1 Cor 7:35), *persevere* day
> and night *in supplications* (cf. 1 Tim 5:5). Their mouths do
> not proclaim the works of human beings, but sing psalms and
> hymns to our God unceasingly (cf. Ps 10:2, Eph 5:19), while
> they *work with* their *own hands that they may have something
> to share with those in need* (Eph 4:28).
>
> But as to the charge about the psalmodies with which those
> who slander us especially try to frighten those of simpler sort, I
> have this to say: the customs which now prevail among us are in
> harmony and entire accord with all the churches of God.

---

18. *Sermon* 336.1 (Patrologia Latina 38:1472).

For with us, the people rise early in the night to go to the house of prayer, and in labour and affliction and in continual tears confessing to God, they at length rise from their prayers and commence the psalmody. And at one time indeed they divide into two groups and sing the psalms alternating between the one and the other, both thereby strengthening their meditation of the scriptural phrases and securing for themselves both their close attention and the means of keeping their hearts from distraction. And then again, after entrusting one to lead the chant, the rest sing in response. And so they pass the night in a variety of psalmody, praying in the intervals. Then as day begins to dawn, all of them in common raise with one voice and one heart the psalm of confession to the Lord, each of them making his own the words of repentance.[19]

Gregory also testifies to a Eucharistic focus in the life of the young woman, as she matured in her self-offering to God in ascesis and prayer. Macrina deemed it befitting to her way of life to prepare and bake the bread for the Eucharist with her own hands, and, it appears, partake of the Body of Christ every morning. Daily Eucharistic liturgy was not then the custom, but daily Holy Communion was. Ascetics and devout faithful in certain circumstances, such as not having a priest available, might be allowed to take a supply of the *viaticum* home from the Sunday Offering, and partake of it daily through the week.[20]

The Intellectual and Theological Life

In this section let us briefly touch on Macrina's intellectual and theological life since this too will have a bearing on her engagement with the sacred page.

When Gregory reached his sister's bedside two days before she died, he was reduced to tears at her diminishment. Basil had only died about nine months earlier, and he was still keening terribly over the loss. Now, it was plain that his sister, too, was dying before his eyes. In their first evening together, Macrina took her brother's grief in hand and spoke to him at length on the truth of the immortal life and the certainty that even the body has a share in it. This conversation Gregory took as the basis of a philosophical/theological dialogue, *On the Soul and the Resurrection*,

---

19. Basil, Letter 207, to the Clergy in Neocaesarea. See Silvas, *Macrina the Younger*, 75–77.

20. See Basil, Letter 93, to the Patrician Caesaria, for evidence of this custom.

in which Macrina appears as "the Teacher," a veritable philosopher and theologian of Christian hope.

Which prompts us to ask how Macrina's prayerful, ardent and lifelong immersion in the Scriptures was aided by the training of her intellectual powers. Would she really have been competent to carry on dialectical argument with her brother whose credentials as a rhetorician had impressed even the pagan Libanius?

We can give a tentative "yes" to this query. There are several pointers to the likelihood of Macrina's exposure to the "extern" philosophy and the opportunities she had to be aware of intellectual trends. Her father had been a leading rhetorician in the provincial capital of Neocaesarea. Rhetorical studies which formed the higher curriculum required familiarity with the philosophers. After Basil senior died in ca. 345 and Emmelia moved the family seat to Annisa, a day's journey west, to their estate on the River Iris, his library went with them, especially since his sons were all marked for the same privileged education. This was a family steeped in the tradition of Greek *paideia*. We know that the writings of Origen were available at Annisa, since sometime in the years 359–62 Basil and Gregory Nazianzen made a florilegia of excerpts from his *De principia* (*On first principles*) while in the retreat on the Iris, just a few kilometres from the villa. Besides, a certain respect for the intellectually engaged Alexandrian tradition came with the family turf through Macrina the Elder, as noted above.

Once Macrina had completed her formal schooling at about fourteen years of age, and she was free to do so, one can be sure that she did not studiously ignore the repository of Christian writings which were part of the family's patrimony.[21] Whether through his influence or not, she gained acquaintance with Plato and the questions pursued in the higher "extern" philosophy. Christian apologetic writings, and the answers they gave to the pagan philosophers, taught Macrina that reasoned argument too had its place in the milieu of faith and scriptural meditation in which she was nurtured (and that in a culture in which Hellenism was still very alive) there was a witness-value in being able *to give a rational account* (λόγος) *for the hope*

---

21. Cf. Melania the Elder, a woman of the Roman nobility who gave herself to the ascetic life in Palestine and who was an assiduous reader of Christian classics. Palladius: "She was most erudite and fond of literature, and turned day into night going through every writing of the ancient commentators: three million lines of Origen and two and a half million lines of Gregory, Stephen, Pierius, Basil and other worthy men. And she did not read them once only and in an offhand way, but she worked on them, dredging through each work seven or eight times. Thus it was possible for her to be liberated from the *knowledge falsely so called* (1 Tim 6:20), and to mount on wings thanks to these books. By good hopes she transformed herself into a spiritual bird and so made the journey to Christ." Palladius, *Lausiac History*, 55.3 (p. 136).

within (cf. 1 Pet 3:15). Macrina certainly exercised her own intelligence and eventually developed her own powers of discourse.[22] The *VSM* shows her maturing into the moral reason of self-control and the practical reason of financial administration and the governance of others. So too she did not neglect to make progress in the forensic reason of intellectual enquiry.[23]

In his autobiographical Letter 223 Basil recalls that the inspirer of the ascetic movement in northern Anatolia, Eustathius of Sebasteia, used often to visit Annisa and hold long conversations there especially on matters of Christian asceticism, but also on matters concerning doctrinal strife and Church politics. Macrina, the chorus-leader of the spiritual transformations of Annisa, was scarcely an uninvolved bystander. A factor in Eustathius' regular visits was the location of Annisa along the Via Pontica, the direct route connecting Constantinople and the eastern Frontier across northern Anatolia. Other travellers visited Annisa over the years. The *VSM*, chapter 40, and Basil's Longer Responses 20 make it clear that Annisa was a place of hospitality. Passing comments in *On the Soul* are suggestive. In 8.16 Macrina says: "For I have heard those expounding such views," and then goes on to report their beliefs in reincarnation of souls. Similarly in 1.13: "I hear that Epicurus was led very far in this direction by his theories," implies an exchange of views with visitors. And compare 8.20: "For I have heard those expounding such views" as he goes on to report the belief in the pre-existence of souls entertained by the Pythagoreans, Platonists, and even by Origen. Before we discount these as evidence that Macrina was in a position to listen to or engage and contend with the ideas of "extern" thinkers and Christian theologians, consider the figure of Vetiana in *VSM*, chapter 30. This noble widow divided her time between Annisa and Constantinople, where her father Araxius was a senator. Macrina's name therefore was known in high circles, particularly among the neo-Nicenes, given her relationship to the famous Basil and his allies in the movement. In such quarters, she was looked

---

22. Maraval refers to epigraphic evidence of young girls being styled *filovlogoi* or *filogravmmatoi*: Basil the Great, *Vie de Sainte Macrine*, 49n3.

23. The letters of the Cappadocians bear witness to the high degree of doctrinal and theological argument they expected of their women correspondents, e.g., Gregory's letter to Olympias which prefaces his homilies on the Song of Songs and his Letter 3, *To Eustathia and Ambrosia and Basilissa* (Silvas, *Gregory of Nyssa*, 123–32). For Basil, see Letter 52, *To the Canonicae* (Basil, *Letters*, 1:326–37); Letter 105, *To the deaconesses, daughters of count Terentius* (Basil, *Letters*, 2:198–201); Letter 159, *To Eupaterius and his daughter* (Basil, *Letters*, 2:392–99); Letter 173, *To Theodora* (Basil, *Letters*, 2:448–53). In the letter to the deaconesses (Basil, *Letters*, 2:198), Basil praises women who have kept both their piety and their wits about them in the midst of great doctrinal confusion: "you have not given way to deceptions, surrounded as you are by the gross perversity of those who corrupt the word of truth. You have not abandoned the apostolic proclamation of the truth to go over to the faddish novelty of the day."

up to as a model and a leader of ascetic women and men. These few hints lift the lid ever so briefly on the likelihood of her theological acumen where for the most part the documentation is silent.

Anagogy and the Ascent of Macrina's Life

In the *Life*, Gregory at first portrays Macrina as an exemplar of the "philosophical" life in generic Hellenic terms of progress in the virtues. Even in the extended eulogy of the ascetic life implemented among the virgins at Annisa in *VSM*, chapter 13, their approach to what in Gospel terms is called the "angelic life" is conveyed in Platonic terms: "their philosophy continually aided them towards greater purity by multiplying the goods [= virtues] they discovered." What Basil calls "meditation on scriptural sayings" in his Letter 207, is here styled "meditation on divine things." What this unpacks is that *Lectio Divina*, or assiduous prayerful application to the word of God, was part of Macrina's way of life and that of the community she guided.

But gradually, the *anagogy*, that is, the upward leading of Macrina's life comes into view. Gregory frames her life very much as an interior liturgical progress, reaching by degrees to the ultimate threshold and passing through it into the innermost shrine. He finally discloses the secret of the spiritual life which Macrina attained in the liturgy of her own heart and life. All is by a way of modesty, caution, and reverence: nothing is precipitate, brash or presumptuous, and yet, in the end, the secret of Macrina's liberty, her *parrhēsia* with God is revealed. The veil of the liturgy of the heart pursued by Macrina through her whole life, is finally drawn aside in the following passage:

> Accordingly, it seemed to me that she was then making manifest to those present that divine and pure love of the unseen Bridegroom which she had nourished secretly in the inmost recesses of her soul and was proclaiming the disposition of heart by which she hastened towards Him for whom she longed, so that, freed from the fetters of the body, she might be with him as quickly as possible. For in truth, her race was towards the Beloved, and none of the pleasures of this life diverted her eye to itself.[24]

When Gregory reveals this finality of Macrina's earthly life in Christ, he closes the circle of a strange and paradoxical current in his narrative: a

---

24. Gregory, *Opera*, 396.14; Gregory, *Vie de Sainte Macrine*, 212–16; Silvas, *Macrina the Younger*, 132–33.

perichōresis of headship and submission between Macrina and himself. When he arrives in her room, Macrina pays his priesthood, that is, high priesthood, episcopal dignity, the greatest reverence, struggling in her illness to achieve a *proskynēsis*, head to the floor, from her pallet on the ground. Nevertheless, as Gregory goes on, she very soon presents as the mother and teacher, and he as the little brother and disciple, with everything to learn from her. The roles of headship and submission seem strangely reversed.

But the interplay goes deeper than that. If, in the treasure of the Church, the ministerial priest presses *through the veil* (Heb 10:19–20; cf. 8:11–12) into the holy of holies in the great Offering of Christ's Blood, this, ultimately, is what it serves: that each believer by attentiveness to the call of Christ in the inner liturgy of the heart be brought by the Blood of Christ into that Holy of Holies which is the "secret recesses of the heart." Macrina's consummation of this ascent to the Mystery of Christ shows the interior face of all that the priest would serve sacramentally in the outward liturgy on earth. Gregory, bishop and mystical theologian in the making, knows this very well, and is in awe of this holy woman, his sister, and holds her out as an exemplar for every earnest believer.

The interplay shifts again after her death, when Gregory assumes the high priest and the master liturgist, arranges for death her holy body, which glows, like the relics he bore in his hands in a dream thrice repeated, and leads the liturgical procession to her interment in their parents' grave.

Macrina's Prayer before Death

Mystagogy is another way of describing anagogy as liturgical ascent, i.e., the slow and gradual initiation through the Mysteries into the Mystery of Christ. How far Macrina travelled in this inward liturgical procession is fully disclosed only in the account of her dying hours. If "the Sacred Scriptures grow with the one who reads them," as St. Gregory the Great says, we can see in this culminating hour how deeply the *vademecum* of Scripture had "grown with" Macrina in her race towards the Bridegroom. The truth is, between chanting the psalms, participating in the Liturgy, obeying the commandments, meditating the Scriptures, and cleaving to the Word behind these holy words—or rather allowing that Word to reach down to her and penetrate her whole being—one cannot find the least interstice, the least gap, the least making of a distance. One sees this transparently in the luminous words of Macrina's prayer before death, which as a supremely mystagogical utterance, proves to be but a tissue of Scriptural phrases.

In fact, we shall end this contemplation by revisiting that prayer in its entirely. I have taken pains to indicate the Scriptural phrases and allusions embedded in the text. In fact I have counted at least thirty-five such references. I have often thought how desirable it would be that we should edit all liturgical texts this way, to illustrate how much the Liturgy is indeed the collective *Lectio Divina* of the Word of God. This same use of Scripture informs the theological discourse of the Fathers of the Church, as for example, St. Basil's *Anaphora*, which is the basis of the Fourth Eucharistic Prayer.

Before we begin our ending, let us prepare ourselves by noting a few points. The first part of Macrina's final prayer is a series of appeals commencing with *Su*, that is, an emphatic "you," or preferably "Thou" (ll. 1–8). A series of informative statements about God really addressed to a human audience is not the idea. Recall how the *Te Deum laudamus* opens with repeated expressions of "Te" and "Tibi." Just so Macrina's repeated invocation of "Thou" / You is a cadence of adoration signifying the ever-turning of her life from self to the supreme "Other," to God. Thus her whole being cleaves to the invisible reality of God her Creator, Redeemer and the Bridegroom of her soul.

We discern in these words that the way of the ascent of her soul to the divine beauty, is the descent of that divine beauty incarnate, Jesus Christ. The nexus which coordinates that ascent and descent is humility. Through the co-offering of her whole life in union with the Crucified, she immersed herself in the *kenōsis* of the Son of God, his self-emptying in entire loving obedience to his Father. Macrina takes to herself the prayer of the good thief on Golgotha and counts it all her life is worth to be found, as she puts it in the words of Paul, *co-crucified* with Christ. This is the *tonos*, the stretched bowstring of her whole life, which now nears its consummation.

Her prayer before death has the pattern of a Eucharistic Prayer, an *Anaphora* or *Offering*. It opens with a litany of God's saving acts on our behalf (ll. 1–8). Compare the long *anamnēsis*, the calling to mind of the events of salvation in the earlier part of the Anaphora of St. Basil.

The prayer hinges on something like an *epiclēsis*, when she asks that an angel be sent to lead her in this hour (ll. 9–13). The rest of the prayer consists of *supplications*, or petitions that every sin, weakness and hindrance that might oppose her coming home to God be forgiven and remitted (ll. 14–21). The very final words of the prayer are an expression of her final self-offering to God. The *thanksgiving and Trinitarian doxology*, in the very moment of dying, when Gregory says: "But when she had finished the thanksgiving (*eucharistia*) and had brought her hand to her face for the seal [= sign of the Cross] to mark the end of the prayer, she drew one great deep breath and brought to a close both her prayer and her life."

In the words of Maraval, "Her final prayer and the liturgical context of her last moments make explicit the Christian sense of her entire trajectory . . . the pursuit of the philosophical ideal is none other than the ascent to Christ."[25]

The Waning of the Day: Macrina Turns to God Alone[26]

So then, let us begin, or, to say it more accurately, let us conclude:

1. Much of the day had now passed, and the sun was declining towards the west, but her eagerness did not decline. Instead, the nearer she approached her exodus, the more clearly she discerned the beauty of the Bridegroom and the more eagerly she hastened to the one for whom she longed. Such thoughts as she uttered were no longer addressed to us who were present, but to him to whom she looked away with intent eyes. 2. Her pallet[27] had been turned towards the east,[28] and, withdraw-

---

25. Gregory, *Vie de Sainte Macrine*, 92.

26. Gregory, *Opera*, 8.1.396.15–398.17; Gregory, *Vie de Sainte Macrine*, 216–21; Silvas, *Macrina the Younger*, 133.

27. *Chameunion*, a bed set on the ground. Sleeping on the ground (*chameunia*) was an ascetic practice adopted by Christian monks and nuns.

28. Turning to the East for prayer, literally *orientation*, was practiced across all Christian traditions. In the public liturgy (especially the Eucharist) and private liturgy (prayer) this was a gesture signifying nostalgia for a lost paradise and hope of the world that is to come, *when the orient from on high shall visit us* (Luke 1:78), Christ, *the Sun of Righteousness* who *shall rise with healing in his wings* (Mal 4:2) who bestows on us the resurrection of life, symbolized forever with the dawning of Easter day and every Lord's day (Eph 5:14). In the final hymn of Methodius' *Symposium*, Thecla intones: "From above, O virgins, a voice that wakes the dead has come. It cries out to us: in white robes, bearing your lamps, hasten towards the East to meet the Bridegroom, before the King enters within the gates!" As Pierre Maraval observes, the death of Macrina breathes the same atmosphere. Gregory in his fifth *Homily on the Lord's Prayer* says, "Whenever we turn to the East, it is not as if God were only to be contemplated there, for he who is everywhere is not especially apprehended in any part since he encompasses all things equally, but because our first homeland is in the East—I mean our sojourn in Paradise, from which we fell, for *God planted a paradise in Eden towards the East* (Gen 2:8 LXX), and when we look to the East and recall to our memory how we were cast out from the bright regions of bliss in the East we shall have reason to utter such prayer." Gregory, *Opera* 7.2.65, adapted from Graef's translation: Gregory, *Lord's Prayer, Beatitudes*, 76–77. Of the many ancient testimonies to this practice listed by Graef (in Gregory, *Lord's Prayer, Beatitudes*, 192n125) and by Maraval (in Gregory, *Vie de Sainte Macrine*, 78–79), one might mention John Moschus, *Spiritual Meadow*, 72 (Patrologia Graeca 87/3:2925A) where a man about to undergo martyrdom begs the clemency of being turned to the East for his death. In the mid-1990s William Dalrymple followed Moschus' late sixth-century itinerary. He tells of discovering in the ancient cells of

ing from converse with us, she spoke from then on to God in prayer, making appeal with her hands[29] and murmuring in a low voice, so that we barely heard what she said. This then was the fashion of her prayer, and we need not doubt that it came before God and was heard by him:

Macrina's Prayer before Death[30]

1. It is you[31] O Lord, she said, who have freed us *from the fear of death* [Heb 2:15],

2. You who have made the end of our life here the beginning of true life for us,

3. You who put our bodies to rest in sleep a little while and will awaken them again *at the last trumpet* [1 Cor 15:52],

4. You who return our earth which you fashioned with your hands [cf. Gen 2:7] to the earth [cf. Gen 3:19] for safekeeping and will retrieve again what you once gave, transforming what is mortal and unseemly in us [cf. 1 Cor 15:53] with immortality and grace,

5. You who have rescued us from the curse [cf. Gal 3:13] and from sin, having become both for our sakes [cf. 2 Cor 5:21],

6. You who have *shattered the head of the dragon* [cf. Ps 73:13, 14 LXX] who had seized man in his jaws and dragged him into the yawning abyss of disobedience,[32]

monks around Mar Saba in Palestine "the prayer niche, a small arched cut in the eastern wall of the cell indicating the proper direction for prayer. As I passed from cell to cell, I realized that the prayer niche must be another of those features of the early Christian world which has been lost to modern western Christianity, yet which is still preserved in Islam. No mosque is complete without its *mihrab* pointing in the direction of Mecca": Dalrymple, *From the Holy Mountain*, 304.

29. Or "supplicating" with her hands. Other passages mention the use of her hands in prayer, e.g. "She then stretched out her hand to God and said . . ." (Gregory, *Vie de Sainte Macrine*, 19.3); "Only through the trembling of her lips and the gesture of her hands did we know she was in prayer" (27.1).

30. Gregory, *Opera*, 8.1.397.3–398.17; Gregory, *Vie de Sainte Macrine*, 218–24; Silvas, *Macrina the Younger*, 133–35.

31. The first part of this prayer is a series of expressions beginning with *Su*, i.e., an emphatic "you" (or "Thou"). This insistent repetition of "Thou" is in itself an expression of adoration; it is interspersed with a litany of God's saving acts on our behalf. Compare the encomium of salvation history in the earlier part of the Anaphora of St. Basil.

32. A strong sense of the Fall, and the weakness it wrought in human nature is very much part of Gregory's religious anthropology.

7. You who have opened up for us the way to the Resurrection, having trampled down the gates of Hades [cf. Ps 106:16; Matt 16:18] and brought him *who had the power over death* [Heb 2:14] to naught,

8. You who have given a sign [Ps 59:16] to those who fear you, the symbol of the Holy Cross, to destroy the adversary and to secure our life,

9. O *God the eternal one* [Gen 21:33; Isa 40:28],

10. to whom I have cleaved from my mother's womb [cf. Ps 21:11],

11. *whom my soul has loved* [Song 1:7] with all its strength [cf. Mark 12:30],

12. to whom I have dedicated my flesh and my soul from youth even until now,

13. send an angel of light to be by my side to guide me to the place of refreshment [cf. Pss 65:12; 38:14], to *the water of repose* [Ps 22:2], in the bosom of the holy Fathers [cf. Luke 16:22].

14. You who averted the flame of *the fiery sword* [Gen 3:24][33] and brought to Paradise the man who was co-crucified with you and implored your mercies:

15. *remember me, too, in your kingdom* [Luke 23:42], since I, too, was *co-crucified* with you [cf. Gal 2:19; Rom 6:6], *having nailed my flesh in the fear of you, for I have feared your judgments* [Ps 118:120 LXX; cf. Gal 5:24].[34]

16. Do not let *the terrible abyss* sunder me from your elect [Luke 16:26],

17. or the Slanderer[35] stand in the way to oppose me [cf. Zech 3:1; Rev 12:10],

---

33. *Phloga tēs purines hromphaias* WV, *phloginēn hromphaian* ΨH, S, GM, W-C. Gregory interprets the significance of the fiery sword at the entrance to Paradise at the end of his Second Homily on the Forty Martyrs. "Scripture shows that the fiery sword does not always oppose those who approach Paradise. It stops those who are unworthy, but gives way to the worthy and opens up a clear path to life." Gregory, *Opera: Sermones Pars II*, 10.1, 135–69 at 155–56.

34. This phrase from the Septuagint is cited by Basil in Letter 22 on the monastic life: Basil, *Letters*, 1:129–41 at 140–41.

35. *Ho baskanos*, the Envious One, the Begrudger, the Slanderer.

18. or my sin be uncovered before your eyes, if I have sinned in word or deed or thought, led astray in some way through the weakness of our nature.

19. O you who *have power on earth to forgive sins* [Matt 9:6; Mark 2:10],

20. *spare me, that I may revive* [Ps 38:14], and as I put off my body [cf. Col 2:11] be found before you without stain or blemish [cf. Eph 5:27] in the form of my soul.

21. But may my soul be received into your hands [cf. Ps 30:6] blameless and undefiled *as an incense offering in your sight* [Ps 140:2[36]].

Bibliography

Augustine, St. *Confessions.* Edited by Michael P. Foley. Translated by Frank J. Sheed. Indianapolis: Hackett, 2006.

Basil the Great, St. *The Ascetic Works of St. Basil.* Translated by W. K. Lowther Clarke. London: SPCK, 1925.

———. *The Letters.* Translated by Roy J. Deferrari. 4 vols. Loeb Classical Library 190. Cambridge: Harvard University Press, 1926, 1928, 1930, 1934.

Benedict XVI. "Biblical Interpretation in Conflict: The Question of the Basic Principles and Path of Exegesis Today." In *God's Word: Scripture–Tradition–Office*, edited by Peter Hünermann and Thomas Söding, translated by Henry Taylor, 91–126. San Francisco: Ignatius, 2008.

———. *The Fathers of the Church from St. Clement of Rome to St. Augustine of Hippo.* Grand Rapids: Eerdmans, 2009.

Clark, Elizabeth A. "From Patristics to Early Christian Studies." In *Oxford Handbook of Early Christian Studies*, edited by Susan Ashbrook Harvey and David G. Hunter, 7–41. Oxford: Oxford University Press, 2008.

Dalrymple, William. *From the Holy Mountain.* London: Flamingo, 1998.

Daniélou, Jean. *Platonisme et théologie mystique: Essai sur la doctrine spirituelle de saint Grégoire de Nysse.* Paris: Aubier, 1944.

Girard, René. *Things Hidden Since the Foundation of the World.* Translated by Stephan Bann and Michael Metteer. London: Bloomsbury Academic, 2016.

Gregory of Nyssa, St. *Homilies on the Song of Songs.* Edited and translated by Richard A. Norris. Atlanta: Society of Biblical Literature, 2012.

———. *The Lord's Prayer, The Beatitudes.* Translated by Hilda C. Graef. Westminster, MD: Newman, 1954.

———. *Opera.* Edited by Werner Jaeger. Leiden: Brill, 1958–.

———. *Vie de Sainte Macrine.* Edited and translated by Pierre Maraval. Sources Chrétiennes 178. Paris: Éditions du Cerf, 1971.

Methodius. *Symposium.* Sources Chrétiennes 95. Paris: Éditions du Cerf, 1963.

---

36. The psalm, *par excellence*, of evening prayer.

Palladius. *Lausiac History.* Translated by Robert M. Meyer. New York: Newman, 1964.

Silvas, Anna D. *Gregory of Nyssa, the Letters: Introduction, Translation and Commentary.* Leiden: Brill, 2007.

———. *Macrina the Younger, Philosopher of God.* Turnhout: Brepols, 2008.

Young, Frances. "From Suspicion and Sociology to Spirituality: On Method, Hermeneutics and Appropriation with Respect to Patristic Material." *Studia Patristica* 29 (1997) 421–35.

5

The Function of Scripture in Augustine's *Confessions*

A Ricoeurian Approach

Michael Cameron

University of Portland

Introduction

Even first-time readers of Augustine's *Confessions* are struck by the abundance of biblical quotes, references, allusions, and imitations. Some are extensive, several only a clause, others a mere word or phrase, but they pile up: more than 1500 by one count, roughly six hundred (40 percent) from the Psalms.[1] By what process did the texts make their way off the biblical page and into Augustine's mind, then back out again on to the pages of *Confessions*? Broadly speaking the process had two phases: Augustine reads and digests Scripture for himself in the hermeneutical phase; then he deploys scriptural understanding for the sake of drawing and persuading readers, or the rhetorical phase.[2]

---

1. As noted by Aimé Solignac in Augustine, *Les Confessions* (Bibliothèque Augustinienne 14), 667–79. Latin quotations from *Confessions* come from this edition.

2. Clearly these two phases intermingle; one might well speak of "rhetorical hermeneutics," since we have access to his hermeneutical understanding only through the final text of *Confessions* whose rhetorical agenda seeks the conversion of readers. The paper seeks to understand Augustine's reception of the texts by mean of hermeneutic moves encased in the rhetorical moves of narrative. One can also speak of "hermeneutical rhetoric," a feature of the second part of *Confessions* in Books 11–13. See my "Genesis in *Confessions* 11–12."

Three critical turning points in the narrative of *Confessions* show Augustine's developing relationship to the Bible. The first in Book 3 portrays his unhappy first encounter with Scripture, which reveals points of tension that propel the story of both his attitude to Scripture and his conversion. The second from Book 6 tells of his transformative experience under Ambrose, who helped Augustine to perceive the coherent story in the Bible, which had previously seemed incoherent, and which now opened the possibility of differently understanding Christianity and himself. The third treats the famous garden scene in Book 8 where the strange divine voice commanding "Pick it up! Read it!" turns him decisively toward Scripture and toward a new life. While other important moments with the Bible appear in the story, these suffice to show how Scripture became a surpassing existential force in his life and a critical component in his self-presentation in *Confessions*.

The limited goal of this paper is to take a beginning look at components of the hermeneutical phase of Augustine's encounter with Scripture. The goal is to see how Augustine's ideas about the Bible took shape both in narrative and as narrative. Augustine's experience of coming to terms with the Bible as he lived it moving forward, combined with the achieved perspective from which he looks backward as he writes his story, shape the function of Scripture in *Confessions*.

The paper seeks to cull understanding of Augustine's actual practice from the *Confessions* narrative as a way to uncover a practical understanding of hermeneutics that operates in his work (as opposed to making *Confessions* conform to imported abstract hermeneutical rules). But to assist in throwing light on that actual practice I draw on the practice-oriented hermeneutical studies of Paul Ricoeur. Ricoeur's sharp analysis of narrative has helped scholars in other fields to develop penetrating approaches that have refreshed our understanding of much-trodden texts.[3] I am convinced that Ricoeur's work promises the same for *Confessions*.[4]

---

3. The work of Patrick Hartin exemplifies this approach. See, e.g., his essay, Hartin, "The Role of the Disciples," with explicit reference to Ricoeur (p. 50). See also his essay in this volume, p. 39. For a systematic actualization of Ricoeur's analysis for reading the New Testament, see Schneiders, *Revelatory Text*.

4. Ricoeur has contributed to Augustinian studies both directly and indirectly. Isabelle Bochet surveys the place of Augustine in Ricoeur's thought in *Augustin dans la pensée de Ricoeur*. She quotes Ricoeur: "Augustine has always enjoyed, in my eyes, a sort of preference" (Bochet, *Augustin dans la pensée de Ricoeur*, 7; my translation). Ricoeur plays an indirect but important role in her magisterial study of Augustine's hermeneutical outlook: Bochet, *"Firmament de l'Écriture,"* 16n47. From a different angle, Paul Rigby draws extensively on Ricoeur to study *Confessions* in *The Theology of Augustine's Confessions*.

Hopes for the Bible Dashed! (*Confessions* 3.5.9)[5]

Therefore I undertook to consider the sacred texts and get a sense of them. And lo and behold, the subject matter wasn't "factual" in the pretentious people's opinion, or laid straight-forwardly bare for children's eyes, either, but lowly when I stepped toward her, of lofty dignity when I came up close, and veiled in mysteries. But back then, I wasn't the sort of person who could enter into her, or bend my neck submissively to follow her own strides.

The tone I take now, you see, doesn't show the way I felt when first turning to these writings, which seemed not even worth comparing to the excellence of Cicero. My swollen-headed opinion of my own taste recoiled from their mediocre manner, and my critical eye couldn't pierce into the qualities behind that. In actual fact, this writing is just the sort to grow up alongside small children, but I wasn't going to stoop to being a small child. I was bloated with conceit and seemed—to myself anyway—quite grown up.

This passage mingles the viewpoints of Augustine the teen-aged undergraduate reading Cicero with the critical perspective of Augustine the middle-aged bishop composing *Confessions*. The contrast between the perspectives of Augustine's past ("the way I felt") and present ("the tone I take now") must be teased apart. This relates to comments that he makes about the character of the biblical text and Augustine's character as a reader. In fact, only two lines relate to the young Augustine's views as he describes thinking the Bible unworthy of comparison to Cicero and recoiling from its seeming primitive inelegance. The rest comes from the writer of *Confessions*, who now recognizes Scripture's simplicity as a feature and not a bug, part of the mystery of the text's multi-faceted character. Surface meanings relate easily to less capacious and inquiring minds; yet the very same words carry a sense deep enough to challenge the most demanding and searching minds. This double character of the Bible constantly fascinated the mature Augustine (*Confessions*, 6.4.6; 12.14.17; 12.27.37—28.38).[6]

5. Translations come from Augustine, *Confessions: Translation by Sarah Ruden*. For ease of cross reference, notations of Augustine's text follow the traditional book/section/chapter breakdown reflected in the Bibliothèque Augustinienne volumes and many other translations (e.g., 3.5.9 for Ruden's 3.9).

6. This anticipates the famous and charming image of Gregory the Great two centuries later: "[Scripture] is, if I might put it this way, a kind of river that is both shallow and deep, where a lamb might frolic and an elephant might swim." *Moralia in Iob*, Preface to Leander, iv (Patrologia Latina 75:515; my translation).

Augustine imagines Scripture as a great house whose low doorway required one to bend the neck low in order to "enter into" (*intrare*). But once inside, the house revealed a massive interior with high walls and ceilings that housed a vast space to explore. Augustine reflects on himself as one who was out of sync with the character of Scripture and so blocked from understanding it. He describes his fatal flaw as hardened pride that misunderstood his identity as an adult, when in fact vis-à-vis the text he was an uncomprehending child. But this misjudgment caused him to miss Scripture's beckoning accommodation to enter precisely as a child, a "little one." This misperception cost him the ability "to pierce into" (*penetrare*) the text's inner depths.[7]

Augustine tells the story of pre-conversion recalcitrance in contrast with the divine plan that was already operative and would ultimately prevail. This imitates the arc of the biblical narrative itself, where the contrast between the divine and human planes creates tension that moves his story forward. The divine plan, though inexorable, gets realized only by means of what Robert Alter calls "the refractory nature of man"; this tension is the wellspring of the narrative form.[8] Narratives literarily negotiate the mysterious "hermeneutical problem of the collusion between the inevitable divine plan and the unpredictability of human contingency."[9] Ricoeur sees a similar mysterious collusion driving the passion narratives of Jesus in Mark's Gospel, where a "narrative mediation" similar to the one described by Alter gets inserted between the two levels of drama represented by the absoluteness of "the Son of Man had to be betrayed into the hands of sinners" and the contingency of "and Judas drew near to him."[10]

A story is a series of events that go somewhere, with characters whose actions move the story along. Plots draw on tension and suspense, on characters that develop, and on detours and surprises that culminate in a critical moment when the story crosses over into resolution. The crisis point

---

7. I present Augustine's language as picturing a metaphorical overgrown child unable to enter a house, whereas Ruden's feminine pronoun for Scripture makes his language overtly sexual. If fitting, this double entendre may allude to the contrast between his randy sexual activity at this time, an explicit subject in Book 2, alongside feminine images of Lady Wisdom from the Old Testament books of Proverbs and Sirach, besides anticipating the appearance of personified Lady "Self-Constraint" just prior to Book 8's conversion scene (8.11.27).

8. Ricoeur quotes Alter (*Art of Biblical Narrative*, 33) in "Interpretive Narrative," (in Ricoeur, *Figuring the Sacred*, 182), and continues that "a theology that confronts the inevitability of the divine plan with the refractory nature of human actions and passions is a theology that engenders narrative."

9. Ricoeur, *Figuring the Sacred*, 183.

10. Ricoeur, *Figuring the Sacred*, 183.

brings about "the unity of the supratemporal and the intratemporal."[11] The events of a story contrast with and play off of the implied goal of the story's movement toward a destination ever fixed in the mind of the author, who guides the narration of events toward its intended resolution. The irresolution of events and the ultimate resolution of the story stand in contrast and give the story its tension, which remains even if the reader knows the ultimate end point.

Augustine's narrative mediation in *Confessions* intertwines his story of recalcitrance, ignorance and sin, mired in the inscrutability of his own evil will, and the providential (though likewise inscrutable) saving will of God.[12] This double inscrutability calls forth not disquisition or dissertation but narrative. *Confessions* contrasts the junior Augustine, wise in his own eyes, with the senior, humbler Augustine who appropriates the narratives by entering into them. This dual-level story appears figuratively in Book 2 where Augustine inhabits the character of the rebellious prodigal whose father unalterably longs for his return (Luke 15:11–32). This is more than an illustration, for the story generates the narrative salvation that it portrays. Like the parable, the arc of Augustine's story imitates the arc of the biblical story of salvation, replicating the tension between the divine plan and human recalcitrance. But it does so indirectly, by the mediation of figures: by the detour through impersonation of biblical figures and their stories, and above all, by the inhabitation of voices in the Psalms. Each figure mediates to Augustine the new self being offered by biblical text.

For Augustine to enter into these personae and avail himself of the grace they offer, but to do so he must—and, by the grace of the text, he can—dispossess his prior self, the self that had set the conditions for its own reality and self-affirmation and thus had defected from God. This dispossession enables him to appropriate and to enter into the new "I" that indwells a new reality. *Confessions'* post-mortem of Augustine's failure to accept the Bible in 3.5.9, and his prescription for properly appropriating the text, turns on his analysis of the prerequisite of the reader's humility. This refers not merely to the refusal to vaunt oneself, but more radically to a surrender and relinquishment of ego. Ricoeur's analysis fits this passage well:

> Relinquishment is a fundamental moment of appropriation and distinguishes it from any form of "taking possession." Appropriation is also and primarily a "letting-go." Reading is an appropriation-divestiture. How can this letting go, this relinquishment,

11. Ricoeur, *Figuring the Sacred*, 184.

12. Frances Young speaks of the "overall perspective" of *Confessions* as a "reflection on human existence and God's providence." Young, "*Confessions*," 13.

be incorporated into appropriation? Essentially by linking appropriation to the revelatory power of the text which we have described as its referential dimension. It is in allowing itself to be carried off towards the reference of the text that the ego divests itself of itself.[13]

Ambrose's Single, Sweeping Biblical Story! (*Confessions* 6.4.6, 5.8)

I rejoiced also because the ancient writings of the law and the prophets were no longer presented to me for reading with the kind of gaze that had made them look ridiculous before, when I'd accused your holy followers of holding opinions that in fact they didn't hold.

I was happy in hearing Ambrose say often in his public sermons, as if he were recommending this very carefully as a basic principle, "The letter kills, but the Spirit gives life" [2 Cor 3:6]. He was removing the ritual covering, as it were, from the deeper meaning, to disclose the spiritual sense of things that, when taken literally, seemed to teach what was untenable.

I'd already started to believe that there was no way you could have set out to grant such preeminent authority to this writing throughout the world unless you'd wanted belief in you and the search for you to come about through this very means.

Now that I'd heard plausible explanations for many passages, I proceeded to attribute to the depth of the mysteries there the apparent lack of sense that used to put me off this literature. Its authority appeared to be more worthy of reverence and more deserving of an inviolable trust in that it was within everybody's reach for reading, but it preserved its impressive mystery within hidden significance. It offered itself to everybody with extremely simple words in the most colloquial style, but also required serious minds to exert themselves with concentration.

The result was that it could take everyone in its arms, like true popular writing, and let a few through to you through narrow apertures [Matt 7:13–14]—many more, though, than it could if it didn't loom on such a high peak of authority and at the same time draw whole masses of people into the lap of its pure-hearted humility.

---

13. "Appropriation," in Ricoeur, *Hermeneutics and Human Sciences*, 191. On "reference," see my next note.

Augustine's crucial turn of attitude toward Scripture occurs at Milan under Ambrose, when the bishop's sermons help him to conceive of it as a grand synthetic vision cast as a story of salvation. He speaks of Ambrose untying knotty difficulties among Old Testament texts by referring to a rule encapsulated in Paul's statement of 2 Corinthians 3:6, "The letter kills, and the Spirit gives life." This is often seen as a philosophical clue to insight, or even an escape hatch from embarrassment, into spiritual interpretation that transcended the material realm. But the profound impact of Ambrose seems to require a more richly religious perspective. Ambrose's teaching, derived finally from the great third-century teacher and greatest of early Christian exegetes, Origen of Alexandria, turned Augustine around; it opened his future as priest, bishop and preacher in Hippo, saved him for Nicene Christianity as Saint Augustine and Doctor of the Church, and installed him as thinker without peer in the West until Thomas Aquinas.

With Ambrose's help Augustine could ascribe to Scripture "the depth of the mysteries," bringing together simple and the sophisticated, rough-hewn and elegant, material flesh and non-material spirit, earthly and heavenly. Not just Scripture's accessible composition and style, but even more its conscious appeal to a wide audience of lettered and unlettered, its simultaneous simplicity and depth (logically incongruous though it may be) impressed him most.

Ambrose's insight meant more than pointing out how to solve textual problems using a new method; more positively, it instructed him in the essential thing Scripture is about, its "reference."[14] This insight is reflected in Augustine's repeated early references to God's plan for saving humanity, *dispensatio temporalis*, "the temporal design for salvation" (e.g., *True Religion*, 7.13; my translation). This framework fitted all the disparate elements of the stories and characters of Scripture—particularly the Old Testament passages that had offended Manichean sensibilities—into an intelligible whole.[15] Ambrose did more than uncover the Bible's dual-level metaphysical structure of reality; he opened the possibility of conceiving its coherent world wherein low and high, flesh and spirit, even good and

14. Borrowing categories from the philosopher Gottlob Frege, Ricoeur distinguishes between a statement's "sense" and its "reference": "The sense is the ideal object which the proposition intends, and hence is purely immanent in discourse. The reference is the truth value of the proposition, its claim to reach reality." He translates the extra-linguistic reference to his notion of "the world of the text." See "The Hermeneutical Function of Distanciation," in Ricoeur, *Hermeneutics and Human Sciences*, 140.

15. Just after writing *Confessions*, Augustine dedicated a long work that detailed the unity of the Old and New Testaments, entitled *Contra Faustum Manichceum*. It replied to the Manichean bishop Faustus and his *Capitula* ("Chapters"), an anti-Catholic handbook of biblical questions and answers composed for the Manichean mission field.

evil might be understood together. This suggested to Augustine a whole context for each part; his biblical understanding having been unresolved by Manichean teaching, he now made sense of Old and New Testaments as stages in a single movement toward salvation: the Bible therefore constitutes a diversity-in-unity.

Here the dynamics of narrative begin to operate in Augustine's perception of Scripture. One who thinks of a life as more than a succession of disparate episodes, as having an intelligible coherence, thinks of it in the form of a narrative, i.e., conceives it as a plot. The acts of composition and of reading bring about an arrangement, a sequencing that implies either causation or reasonable inference in a chain that builds anticipation toward the resolution of a story. An aphorism of E. M. Forster makes the point: "the king died, the queen died" is mere chronicle, an episodic succession; but "the king died, the queen died of grief" suggests a dramatic story.[16] With Ambrose's help, Augustine could now see Scripture bringing together far-flung and contrasting characters, events, teachings, rites, as a worthy product and imitation of the one God who reigned over all and still guides the story to salvation's end.[17]

Augustine was able to conjoin disparate elements of the biblical story into a coherence that pointed to a single divine mind at work. He put together heterogeneous elements that included letter and spirit, fear and love, law and freedom. In a word, he espied in Scripture a mediating plot. "The operation of plotting may very broadly be defined as a synthesis of heterogeneous elements."[18] What happens to a person reading a story? Individual events in the narrative no longer stand alone but in relation to other events and to a context; the reader looks for a plot. "The reader expects a configuration," because "reading is a search for coherence."[19] A constructed plot makes each event more than a happening; it contributes to the story's progress, moving it along its course from beginning to end. Narration organizes discrete events into an intelligible whole. That synthesis conjoins features of discord ordered by the primacy of concord that is desired and expected by the story's readers. They follow a story and at each stage imaginatively complete the synthesis of disparate elements incrementally revealed by the plot. The reader gains understanding by the act of following the story, recognizing and surrendering to the action of the plot. The reader understands,

16. Dowling, *Ricoeur on Time and Narrative*, 5.

17. See Augustine's early musing on the unity of Scripture as reflecting the unity of God in *The Catholic Way of Life and the Manichean Way of Life*, 1.17.30: "There is one God of the two Testaments" (Augustine, *Manichean Debate*, 45).

18. What follows depends on Ricoeur, "Life," 431.

19. Ricoeur, "World of the Text," 15–16.

gradually synthesizes, settles an interim view, then receives new narrative, synthesizes again, readjusts, and resettles in a spiral of reception until the story reveals its conclusion.

The net result of this mediation, this act of synthesis, is not just knowledge, but understanding. Understanding subscribes and surrenders to the narrative's mediation, allows it to determine reality and truth, and allows it to order consciousness. It familiarizes the text so as to open a world that might move one to forsake one's accustomed world and to appropriate, or "make one's own," the new world proposed by the text. "Configuration makes possible reconfiguration of a life by the way of the narrative."[20] In this way the text becomes a means of new *self*-understanding that derives not from abstract theoretical knowledge but from practical intelligence, what Aristotle called *phronesis*, which the Latins translated as *prudentia*.[21]

The help of Ambrose was less about a method of reading individual texts and more about ascending to a panoramic reading perspective, a new way of seeing the whole text of Scripture from the perspective of unity. Augustine would later say, "Those pure verbal expressions now seemed to me to come from a single face, and I learned to thrill to the point of trembling" (*Confessions*, 7.21.27).[22] This synthesis suddenly brought the vast Old Testament back into Augustine's understanding of the Bible (he had rejected it as a Manichean), releasing an avalanche of new perspectives that allowed all the formerly opaque and even repulsive characters, events, and sayings to take their place in a grand, overarching scheme. The act of synthesizing these heterogeneous elements, which were perceived and venerated in the Christian canon "set on high, as if on a kind of throne"[23] was made complete in Augustine's own work of synthesis. Paul's statement in 2 Corinthians 3:6 offered less of a new method than a passageway into a new world that Scripture was opening up. The world that reared up from Ambrose's preaching offered a new story, a new vision, along with plausibly different ideas, attitudes, perceptions and values. In short, it offered new possibilities and a new self.

---

20. Ricoeur, "Life," 430.

21. Ricoeur, "Life," 428.

22. This chimes with Augustine's sermon, possibly preached not long after *Confessions*, which deals with Psalm 68:2: "As wax melts from the face of fire, so let sinners perish from the face of God." Augustine says: "So for the time being treat the Scripture of God as the face of God. Melt in front of it." *Sermon* 22.7 in Augustine, *Sermons II*, 46.

23. *Answer to Faustus*, 11.6; see Augustine, *Manichean Debate*, 119. The original: "tamquam in sede quadam sublimiter constituta est." Augustine, *Contre Fauste*, 252.

"Emplotment" names the storyteller's art that acts to "derive a configuration from a succession";[24] it names the capacity to order episodic temporal events into a meaningful totality. This configuration synthesizes events that otherwise resist conjunction. Narrative mediates between disparate events. Emplotment sets up a directed movement under the control of a particular point of view; it gives a historical or literary text the capacity to set forth a story that combines the givens of contingent historical existence with the possibilities of a meaningful sequence with beginning, middle and end. Before writing *Confessions*, Augustine was aware of this "basic law (*lex*) of how to tell stories and of how to suggest sublime truths to lowly people in a lowly way, a law that by definition means you can't have a narrative discourse without a beginning, middle, and end."[25]

A narrative proposes a world to the reader and beckons consideration of entering into it and dwelling in it. The approach is textualist, not originalist. The proposed world exists not behind the text, where the text's social and historical origins reside, and its genetic code reveals the roots of its ideas and stories, which historicism equates with its truth. Detached from the origins of its composition, this world arises from the text itself, whose internal sense and external reference offer a different perspective. To "interpret," as Ambrose helped Augustine to do, is, as Ricoeur writes, "to explicate the type of being-in-the-world unfolded *in front of* the text. . . . For what must be interpreted in a text is a *proposed world* which I could inhabit and wherein I could project one of my ownmost possibilities. This is what I call the world of the text, the world proper to this unique text."[26] The text, therefore, constitutes nothing less than "the projection of a new universe."[27]

Ambrose's preaching put forth to Augustine the world proper to the biblical text. Ricoeur sees this very thing happening in biblical texts generally: "The first task of hermeneutics is . . . to allow the world of being that is the issue of the biblical text to unfold," that is, "the proposition of the world that in the biblical language is called a new world, a new covenant,

---

24. Ricoeur, "Life," 427.

25. *Genesi ad litteram imperfectus liber*, 3.8: "An ista dierum digestio, secundum consuetudinem humanae fragilitatis, ordinata est lege narrandi et humilibus humiliter insinuandi sublimia, qua et ipse sermo narrantis non potest nisi aliqua habere et prima et media et ultima?" Augustine, *Genèse au sens littéral*, 406; my translation. This may echo Aristotle on the structure of narrative in *Poetics* 1450b, as Roland Teske notes in his translation of this passage: Augustine, *On Genesis*, 149n16. Augustine began this work about four years before *Confessions*.

26. Ricoeur, "Hermeneutical Function of Distanciation," in Ricoeur, *Hermeneutics and Human Sciences*, 142.

27. Ricoeur, "Life," 431.

the kingdom of God, a new birth."[28] This world is not the same as our everyday reality; it is instead "another reality, the reality of the *possible*. . . . In theological language this means that 'the kingdom of God is coming': that is, it appeals to our ownmost possibilities beginning from the very meaning of this kingdom, which does not come from us."[29]

Augustine's *Confessions*' story displays two planes of narrative: the story as he lived it forward on the earthly plane in conscious or unconscious resistance to the divine plan, and the story told backward from the viewpoint of his position as believer and bishop aligned with the divine plan. The two viewpoints jarringly, and for Augustine shamefully, contrast for much of the narrative through Book 8 when they collide, creating an intense crisis of soul until the spiritual force breaks through the defenses of resistance by means of a biblical text, and forges his new spiritual identity. Ambrose unknowingly fomented, in Hans-Georg Gadamer's well-known phrase, a "fusion of horizons" in Augustine's mind between, on the one hand, the Bible's cosmically focused story of humanity's long, slow turn (return) to God and, on the other, Augustine's individually focused turn to God. Augustine saw in Scripture, as configured for him by Ambrose, a set of new possibilities, not just new ideas: the possibility of a new life and a reconfigured self.

The Bible Breaks Through! (*Confessions* 8.12.29–30)

> I got control over the onslaught of my tears and got up, construing the chant as a straightforward divine command to open a book and read the chapter I first found there. I had heard that Anthony had been admonished by a reading of the gospel that he had walked in on by chance; what was being read seemed to be speaking to him personally, "Go, sell everything you have and give it to the poor, and you will have treasure in heaven; and come, follow me" [Matt 19:21]. Moved by this omen, he turned to you in no time.
>
> Excited, I returned to the spot where Alypius was sitting: I put down a book of the apostle Paul's letters there when I got up. I grabbed it and opened it, and I read in silence the passage on which my eyes first fell: "Don't clothe yourself in a raucous dinner parties and drunkenness, not in the immorality of sleeping around, not in feuds and competition; but clothe yourself in the

28. Ricoeur, "Philosophy and Religious Language," in Ricoeur, *Figuring the Sacred*, 44.

29. Ricoeur, *Figuring the Sacred*, 45.

Master, Jesus Christ, and do not make provision for the body in its inordinate desires" [Rom 13:13–14].

I didn't want to read further, and there was no need. The instant I finished the sentence, my heart was virtually flooded with a light of relief and servitude, and all the darkness of my hesitation scattered away.

Then I put my finger or some other placeholder in the book, closed it, and with a calm expression on my face told Alypius what had happened. And he, for his part, told me what was happening in himself, which I didn't know about. He asked to see what I had read. I showed him, but he looked beyond the sentence I had read. I wasn't aware what followed. It turned out to be "But accept in faith the one who is weak" [Rom 14:1]. He thought it referred to himself, and he disclosed that to me.

Events happen rapid-fire in this famous and much-studied passage. Mercilessly flaying himself over years of inaction, obsessing over his impotence of will, Augustine rocks his body and pulls out his hair with self-absorbed recrimination. Then suddenly the bubble of his morose reverie pops with the sound of a child's sing-song chant. Augustine hears it as a ventriloquizing command of the divine Presence, "Pick it up! Read it! Pick it up! Read it!" This moment of wrenching self-dispossession is framed with ruthless clarity by three biblical texts and their grammatical dynamics.

We might imagine the scenes arranged like panels of a painted triptych. One side panel pictures the legendary desert monk, Anthony of Egypt, acting out a story recounted in Athanasius's *Life of Anthony*. Still indecisive about spiritual commitment, Anthony wanders past a place of worship as Scripture is being read aloud. He hears Jesus command a young inquirer using five orders given in rapid succession: "*Go, sell* everything you have and *give* it to the poor, and you will have treasure in heaven; and *come, follow* me" (Matt 19:21). Anthony takes the text as aimed directly at himself, surrendering himself to Christ and to the ascetic life. On the other panel of the imaginary triptych, Alypius hears a command from Paul, "*Accept* in faith the one who is weak" (Rom 14:1), and immediately turns his life over to God. Augustine occupies the large central panel, where he opens a codex of Paul's letters and falls upon words that strike like lightning: "*Clothe* yourself in the Master, Jesus Christ, and do not make provision for the body in its inordinate desires" (Rom 13:13–14).

Note the italicized imperative verbs in these texts. By the time of writing *Confessions*, Augustine had often mused on humanity's need for the intervention of authority (*auctoritas*; or perhaps better, "authoritativeness," to avoid the image of raw power, *potestas*), prior to the appeal of reason (*On Order*, 2.9.27; *Confessions*, 6.5.8). People cannot be rationally talked into changes of life, but need authority's knife to cut through human obfuscation to heal reason like a physician, to restore its proper functioning (*True Religion*, 24.45). Authority effectively clothes itself, he had observed, in Scripture's jolts of insight ("The kingdom of God is within you!" [Luke 17:21]) or command ("Do not store up for yourselves treasures on earth!" [Matt 6:19]; "Love your enemies!" [Matt 5:44]; "Turn the other cheek!" [Matt 5:39]; "Sow to the spirit!" [Gal 6:8]; "Do not love the world!" [1 John 2:15]), all in *True Religion*, 3.4.

The passage that Augustine fell upon in Romans features a strong negative action command, a strong positive action command, and a mysterious object of the actions that makes sense of them. The negatively oriented biblical command strips and unmakes Augustine's old self which to this point he had still identified with. Though the negative *non* specifies the direction, no verb is attached. However, by reverse anticipation of what follows, the negative implication is clear: "Put off!" (Ruden: "Don't clothe yourself in . . ."). At the end of the text, a negative of the verb *facere* (do, make) appears; with the object *providentia* (providence), it forms a complete sentence ("Do not make provision for"). But all these negatives make sense only when they give way to the positive command wrapped in the imperative verb *Induite!* "Put on!" (Ruden: "Clothe yourself!"). The third dynamic relates to the object of the command "Put on!" But the thing that one is commanded to "put on" remains oddly undetermined in both the biblical text and in Augustine's story; it is not a physical garment (though the image literally anticipates Augustine's robes at baptism) nor is it a state of mind (though humility was an effect of this action). The "object" is rather a person; he is to clothe himself "in the Master, Jesus Christ." It is not immediately apparent what this phrase means. But in fact Augustine has already explained the meaning of this action before it took place, by using the literary device of "prolepsis," or "anticipation," which outlines a fuller revelation to come in a story or speech.[30] At *Confessions* 7.17.23, Augustine narrated his abortive Plotinian spiritual ascent in images that recall Moses meeting God on Mount Sinai; but in 7.18.24 he temporally shifts to an indeterminate future moment by commenting that he could not "enjoy," that is, sustain, the vision of "That Which Is" "until (*donec*) I took in my arms the mediator between God and human beings, the human Jesus Christ" (referring to 1 Tim 2:5). From there he spells out the hidden operation of Christ, who, unbeknownst to Augustine had been calling and saying (note the string of imperfect verbs,

---

30. Quintilian explains prolepsis in Quintilian, *Institutio oratoria*, 9.2.16–18 (pp. 382–85).

denoting continuous action all through the narrative), "I am the way and the truth and the life" (John 14:6). The Word's distinct profile is characterized there by striking self-emptying and humility that descends from the soaring heights of heaven to earth in the incarnation in order to build "a lowly house out of the mud we're made of" (*Confessions*, 7.18.24). This stupefying act of grace not only provides a model of humility; it adapts the otherwise indigestible divine wisdom for humanity's nourishment, just as a nursing mother adapts her solid food for her child. The sight of the humble God at humanity's feet in the abasement of crucifixion undoes human pride, brings love to birth in the heart, and he raises humanity along with Christ in his resurrection. Having explained all this by anticipation in Book 7, Augustine can invoke it in Book 8, with economy and full resonance, in the command, "Clothe yourself in the Master, Jesus Christ!"

The word of Scripture comes to Augustine from outside, not from within where it might be controlled. It existed before he was and now directs itself to him. The givenness of the word speaks of an enduring design of love that is in continual operation, and of grace that precedes Augustine, to woo and seduce and cajole and haunt him.[31] It is a word of love spoken first by one high above to one far below.[32]

Based on the synthesis that made Scripture whole under Ambrose, Augustine was prepared for Scripture to sound with enormous transforming impact in the garden outside Milan. Worlds collide as the old Augustine yields to the new Augustine conferred by the biblical text. As Augustine "opens" (*aperire*) the codex of Paul in response to the divine voice, the world proposed by Scripture "opens" and bids him enter. "Configuration makes possible reconfiguration of a life by way of the narrative. More precisely: the meaning or the significance of the story wells up from *the intersection of the world of the text and the world of the reader*."[33] In this scene, we might

31. For Jean-Luc Marion these scripture echoes are not "a matter of words said by Saint Augustine but of words first said *to* Saint Augustine by the very one to whom the confession now resays them—words said in the beginning by God, who was first to say his word, or rather who said the first word, as he created the world by it." Marion, *In the Self's Place*, 21.

32. Soon after writing *Confessions*, Augustine answered a letter from a teacher anxious for fresh images that would make the gospel intelligible in the stratified society of Roman North Africa. Augustine encouraged him to picture God showing love for humanity in Christ to be like a member of the upper class freely befriending one of the lower class, i.e., love that is unexpected, gratifying, and surely to be returned: Augustine, *On Instructing Beginners in Faith [De catechizandis rudibus]*, 4.7. See the same work for an image of Christ's descent in love reaching from heaven far down to the depths of his creation (10.15).

33. Ricoeur, "Life," 430.

say with Ricoeur, the "act of reading becomes the crucial moment" for on it "rests the ability of the story to transfigure the experience of the reader."[34] Thus for Augustine to "appropriate" the text of Paul was not to commandeer an essentially alien text, nor was it to project himself into the text against its aims; it was rather to "own" the text that had offered itself to him as it does to readers of all times and places. Like Anthony hearing Jesus and Alypius hearing Paul, Augustine heard biblical words addressed to him.[35] The massive configuration of Scripture as a single story made possible Augustine "accompanying the configuration and appropriating the world proposed by the text."[36] The dramatic *tolle lege* scene marks the moment when Augustine entered the world proposed by the biblical text.

Frazzled Augustine, long frightened of faith's cliff-dive into unknown psychic regions, reads the text and suddenly falls headlong—into the arms of the Spirit. He did not expect the new life into which he fell. No longer the "I" he once knew, in the aftermath of the text's impact, strangely he still says "I"; but somehow it has a richer, more authentic ring. Though the persistent puzzle of his identity is not completely solved—"Who am I?" remains a live question for him, as Book 10 shows[37]—this "I" is somehow naturally welcome. Scripture has conferred a new self, i.e., new self-understanding. Ricoeur pertinently writes that to understand is not to project oneself into the text, but rather "*to receive an enlarged self* from the apprehension of proposed worlds which are the genuine object of interpretation."[38]

This new self, enlarged by Scripture, enters the world that Scripture had opened up, now emerges in prominence in *Confessions*. A memorable passage of Book 9 (9.4.9) brings us into Augustine's experience of this enlarged "I" as he reads the Psalms for the first time. He does not merely

34. Ricoeur, "Life," 431.

35. For Ricoeur the historicist idea that "the hermeneutical task would be governed by the original audience's understanding of the text" is "a complete mistake." "Appropriation" in Ricoeur, *Hermeneutics and Human Sciences*, 192. "When I read," he writes, "the letters of Saint Paul are no less addressed to me than to the Romans, Galatians, the Corinthians, etc."

36. Ricoeur, "Between Text and Readers," 390.

37. See 10.1.1—5.7 for ruminations on this question, along with a further question, "Who are all these people reading my book?"

38. Ricoeur, "Appropriation," in Ricoeur, *Hermeneutics and Human Sciences*, 182–83; emphasis added. A recent Christian initiate has written of her conversion experience in linguistic terms. It is not a once-for-all upheaval, she writes, but "a series of turns—toward an ultimate concern, toward reconciliation, toward a source. And the language of faith toward which I turn, whether by instinct or effort, does not rewrite me by erasure *but by expansion*. It moves me, past and all, out into everything. . . . Tectonic plates of past and present collide and reconfigure with each utterance." Gee, "Language & Conversion," 80; emphasis added.

report his experience, but re-lives his reading in the reader's presence; we hear peals of delight and wide-eyed wonder as he reads over each line and lights upon each word—as well as rumbles of anger against the Manicheans who he feels wronged him. Book 11 enters fully into Scripture's new world, into which he hoped to draw readers to dwell together. A lilting hinge passage in the turn to full concentration on the book of Genesis in Books 11–13 poetically, among many other images, pictures him roaming through the "woods" of the pages of the Scriptures like a furry forager for food in a great teeming forest. Books 11 and 12 treat obstacles to right reading that might threaten the stability of those who would maintain their dwelling in the new world that Scripture has opened up. Book 13 works through the creation account of Genesis 1 exploring the many mysteries that the text embeds and offers to venturesome readers. In essence these last three books reveal the point of view from which *Confessions* has been written; indeed this perspective has been operative since the opening lines of Book 1.[39] *Confessions* does not end so much as stop. As conversion in this temporal life remains for Augustine and his readers an ongoing project, so their search through Scripture never rests. The last lines of Book 13 stress this with a string of verbs, drawn from Matthew 7:7–8, that Augustine often uses (e.g., *Confessions*, 12.1.1) to speak of his ever-restless reading of Scripture: asking, seeking, knocking, answering, finding, opening.

Bibliography

Alter, Robert. *The Art of Biblical Narrative*. New York: Basic, 1981.

Augustine, St. *Les Confessions*. Edited by Martin Skutella et al. 2 vols. Bibliothèque Augustinienne 13–14. Paris: Études Augustiniennes, 1992.

———. *Confessions: A New Translation by Sarah Ruden*. New York: Modern Library, 2017.

———. *Contre Fauste le Manichéen: Livres I–XII*. Edited by Martine Dulaey. Bibliothèque Augustinienne 18A. Paris: Institut d'Études Augustiniennes, 2018.

———. *The Manichean Debate*. Translated by Roland J. Teske. The Works of Saint Augustine I/19. Hyde Park, NY: New City, 2006.

———. *On Genesis: Two Books on Genesis against the Manichees and On the Literal Interpretation of Genesis: An Unfinished Book*. Translated by Roland Teske. Fathers of the Church 84. Washington, DC: Catholic University of America Press, 1991.

———. *Sermons II (20–50) on the Old Testament*. Translated by Edmund Hill. The Works of Saint Augustine III/2. Brooklyn: New City, 1990.

39. Isabelle Bochet comments that "the place of arrival is at the same time a point of departure. For the reading of Scripture is the very mainspring of the work [*au principe même de l'ouvrage*]: indeed, it is what makes possible the new self-comprehension that Augustine presents in the Confessions." Bochet, "Interprétation scripturaire et compréhension de soi," 28; my translation.

———. *Sur la Genèse au sens littéral, livre inachevé*. Edited by Pierre Monat. Bibliothèque Augustinienne 50. Paris: Études Augustiniennes, 2004.

Bochet, Isabelle. *Augustin dans la pensée de Paul Ricoeur*. Paris: Editions facultés jésuites de Paris, 2003.

———. *"Le firmament de l'Écriture"*: *L'herméneutique augustinienne*. Paris: Institut d'Études Augustiniennes, 2004.

———. "Interprétation scripturaire et compréhension de soi: Du De doctrina christiana aux *Confessions* de Saint Augustin." In *Comprendre et interpreter. Le paradigme herméneutique de la raison*, edited by Jean Greisch, 21–50. Paris: Editions Beauchêsne, 1993.

Cameron, Michael. "Augustine Reading Genesis in *Confessions* 11–12: A Case Study in Hermeneutical Rhetoric." In *Augustine and Tradition*, edited by David G. Hunter and Jonathan Yates. Grand Rapids: Eerdmans, forthcoming.

Dowling, William C. *Ricoeur on Time and Narrative: An Introduction to Temps et récit*. Notre Dame: University of Notre Dame Press, 2011.

Gee, Melody S. "Language & Conversion." *Commonweal* 147 (2020) 79–80.

Hartin, Patrick J. "The Role of the Disciples in the Jesus Story Communicated by Mark." *Koers* 58 (1993) 35–52.

Marion, Jean-Luc. *In the Self's Place: The Approach of Saint Augustine*. Translated by Jeffrey L. Kosky. Stanford: Stanford University Press, 2012.

Quintilian. *The Institutio oratoria of Quintilian*. Translated by Horace Edgeworth Butler. Loeb Classical Library 127. Cambridge: Harvard University Press, 1976.

Ricoeur, Paul. "Between the Text and Its Readers." In *A Ricoeur Reader: Reflection and Imagination*, edited by Mario J. Valdés, 390–424. Toronto: University of Toronto Press, 1991.

———. *Figuring the Sacred: Religion, Narrative, and Imagination*. Edited by Mark I. Wallace. Minneapolis: Fortress, 1995.

———. *Hermeneutics and the Human Sciences*. Edited and translated by John B. Thompson. Cambridge: Cambridge University Press, 1981.

———. "Hermeneutics and the World of the Text." In vol. 2 of *Hermeneutics: Writings and Lectures*, translated by David Pellauer, 11–18. Cambridge: Polity, 2013.

———. "Life: A Story in Search of a Narrator." In *A Ricoeur Reader: Reflection and Imagination*, edited by Mario J. Valdés, 425–37. Toronto: University of Toronto Press, 1991.

Rigby, Paul. *Confessions in the Theology of Augustine's Confessions*. Cambridge: Cambridge University Press, 2015.

Schneiders, Sandra. *The Revelatory Text: Interpreting the New Testament as Sacred Scripture*. 2nd ed. Collegeville, MN: Liturgical, 1999.

Young, Frances. "The *Confessions* of St. Augustine: What Is the Genre of This Work?" *Augustinian Studies* 30 (1999) 1–16.

6

Augustine on the Sermon on the Mount

Charity and Just War?

DOUGLAS KRIES

Gonzaga University

ST. AUGUSTINE HELD THAT the Scriptures have a unified goal or meaning or purpose; he understood this view not only to be his own, but the view of the universal Church as well. As a result, in composing the first book of his *On Christian Teaching*—itself the first extended, systematic Christian treatise devoted to the interpretation and teaching of Sacred Scripture—Augustine is particularly concerned to explain what the principle of all Scripture is, for if this principle can be obtained, it will guide and direct all attempts to understand the sacred texts and result, ultimately, in a unity of the Church's interpretation of the Bible. What can this singular goal or purpose or meaning of Scripture be? Perhaps not too surprisingly, Augustine finds the principle of the Bible to be contained in its Charity Precepts, the commands of Moses that Jesus uses to summarize the whole of the law and the prophets: love of God, love of neighbor, and love of self—which latter is implied, Augustine insists, in Jesus's statement to "love thy neighbor as thyself."[1] At first glance, then, nothing would seem to be so opposed to the unified intention of the Scriptures as warfare. Yet Augustine's name has been indelibly connected with war, so much so that one hears over and over again the phrase "Augustine's just war theory."

Augustine himself explicitly says that his long and difficult book treating political affairs and the wars that often characterize them, *The City of*

1. Augustine, *On Christian Doctrine*, 1.35, referencing Matt 22:37–39; Mark 12:29–31; Luke 10:27.

126

God against the Pagans, was precipitated by the crisis of the plundering of Rome by Alaric and the Goths in August of 410.[2] In 412, however, he had apparently still not yet actually begun to write the *City of God*, for in a letter from that year he promises the lay Catholic politician Marcellinus that he will soon begin such a work, which is what Marcellinus truly needs in order to counter adequately pagan claims blaming the fall of the city of Rome on the Christian Church. In the letter of 412, however, Augustine does not simply leave Marcellinus hanging but outlines various paths for responding immediately to these pagan critics who are suggesting to Marcellinus that Christian faith is unsuited to regulating political affairs properly. In particular, Augustine tells Marcellinus how to explain the precepts of the Sermon on the Mount to these pagan detractors who are especially concerned about the Christian teachings regarding turning the other cheek, giving the garment in addition to the tunic, and going extra miles.

Over the centuries, this letter to Marcellinus, which survives as #138 in Augustine's correspondence, has come to be viewed within the Christian tradition as one of the principal sources for the so-called "just war theory." Thomas Aquinas, for example, relies on this text when writing his summary of just war thinking in the *Summa Theologica*, appealing to it in the authoritative position of the *sed contra* of his article on just war and also appealing to it for its understanding of the precepts about the cheek, the garment, and the extended journey.[3] Nevertheless, since *Letter 138 to Marcellinus* was written in response to the events of 410 and especially addresses itself to the question of how Marcellinus should respond rhetorically to those events, one can see how it would be easy enough for readers of the letter today to wonder whether it is simply an emergency, *ad hoc* response to an immediate political crisis—and not something that really stems from Christian faith or the New Testament. Those inclined to pacifism often prefer a more direct interpretation of the precepts about the cheek, the tunic, and the extra miles, and thus could dismiss Augustine's letter. Of course, a defender of just war thinking could point out that simply because a line of thinking emerges as a response to an immediate historical problem, it does not follow that such a line of thinking is false. In this case, however, it turns out that Augustine's thinking about the commands of the Sermon on the Mount did *not* begin with his letter to Marcellinus in 412, and hence any concern that the teaching of the letter is only an emergency, *ad hoc* response is misplaced.

Augustine had returned to Africa from Italy in about 388. He was ordained priest in 391 and soon asked his bishop for a sabbatical period

2. Augustine, *Revisions*, 2.43.

3. Aquinas, *Summa Theologica*, IIa–IIae.40.1.

to be devoted to Scripture study before beginning his priestly ministry. Probably by 393, he was composing a work on *The Lord's Sermon on the Mount*. It was thus not the Goths but the Manichees and perhaps even the Platonists who were more immediately on Augustine's mind as he wrote his two books on *The Lord's Sermon*, although it seems he was not extensively animated by apologetic concerns as he pursued Scripture study within a rather scholarly, leisurely, monastic-like existence.[4] As a result, what Augustine would have to say to Marcellinus in 412 had already been thought through with care some nineteen years earlier in his work on *The Lord's Sermon*.[5] Indeed, the crucial insights about the Sermon on the Mount that enabled the development of the just war theory were already firmly established in Augustine's mind long before the sacking of Rome by Alaric. They originated in a thoughtful, reflective work and were not something simply demanded by the pressures of the moment.

Analysis of the Plan of Augustine's *The Lord's Sermon on the Mount*

The Lord's Sermon on the Mount is a work of two books, the first of which is our principal concern. These books are organized around a plan that Augustine finds within the Sermon on the Mount itself, which comprises chapters 5–7 of the Gospel of Matthew. Augustine's view of the outline of the Sermon begins with the Beatitudes, which he views almost as a sort of table of contents for the entire Sermon. In Augustine's view, the eight Beatitudes are reducible to seven; he can make this claim because the first and the eighth Beatitudes both end with "for theirs is the kingdom of heaven." Numbers one and eight are thus, Augustine claims, essentially the same in thought. Confirmation of the seven themes announced in the "table of contents" that the Beatitudes embody is to be found in the seven Gifts of the Holy Spirit of Isaiah 11:2–3. Augustine had recently been working on his *On the Literal Interpretation of Genesis*, and his treatment of the Sermon

---

4. Since the narrative of Augustine's early life breaks off at the end of Book 9 of the *Confessions* with events of 388, and since Book 10 was not composed until 397, we have relatively less information about Augustine's life during the period when *The Lord's Sermon on the Mount* was written. Still, it does seem probable that his life was more relaxed then than it was after his ordination as bishop of Hippo Regius in 396. See Van Fleteren, "*Sermone domini.*"

5. Thomas Aquinas himself seems to have recognized the connection between *The Lord's Sermon* and *Letter 138* by placing them together in *Summa Theologica*, IIa–IIae.40.1.2.

on the Mount is generally "literal" as well.[6] In appealing to the seven Gifts of the Holy Spirit, however, Augustine is clearly not the least bit hesitant to view the list of the seven qualities ascribed to the Messiah in Isaiah 11:2–3 as precursors to or prefigurations of the Beatitudes of Jesus.[7] These seven themes from the Old Testament are also reflected in the seven articles of the Lord's Prayer, as Augustine will explain later on in *The Lord's Sermon*. We wind up, then, with seven Beatitudes corresponding to seven Gifts of the Holy Spirit, which in turn correspond to seven articles of the Lord's Prayer. These seven themes, moreover, are used to divide and organize the remaining parts of the Sermon on the Mount.[8]

The part of the Sermon that is particularly relevant for Augustine's just war theory is Matthew 5:38–42, which treats the saying "an eye for an eye, and a tooth for a tooth" from Exodus 21:24, the so called *lex talionis* or "law of retaliation":

> You have heard that it was said, "Eye for eye and tooth for tooth." But I say to you, "Do not resist evil. But if anyone strikes you on the right cheek, turn to him the other also; and should anyone want to sue you in court and take your tunic, give him your garment also; and should anyone force you to go one mile, go with him another two miles."[9]

In Augustine's plan for the Sermon on the Mount, this passage falls within the boundaries of the fifth Beatitude: "Blessed are the merciful, for they shall obtain mercy." The fifth Beatitude corresponds of course to the fifth Gift of the Holy Spirit, which is "counsel," or *consilium*, and these two then correspond to the fifth article of the Lord's Prayer: "And forgive us our trespasses, as we forgive those who trespass against us" (Matt 6:12).

Jaroslav Pelikan once suggested that Augustine's organization of the Sermon on the Mount in this rather complicated way is "quite evidently a literary conceit" but that "the parallelism between the Beatitudes and the petitions [of the Lord's Prayer] does enable Augustine to correlate

---

6. By "literal," we refer to the historical or immediate or direct sense of the inspired author rather than to a figurative sense whereby the people or events or topics referred to in the literal sense in some way stand for or prefigure different topics or events.

7. In order to make the list of the Beatitudes correspond to the list of the Gifts, Augustine inverts the order of the latter. He views the Beatitudes as being arranged in ascending order; the Gifts (as they are listed by Isaiah) in descending order. Hence his inversion of Isaiah's list in *The Lord's Sermon*, 1.4.11.

8. Ramsey has offered a helpful schema of Augustine's organization of these seven themes in his "Introduction" to Augustine, *The Lord's Sermon*, 11–12.

9. Translations from the Bible are my own, based on the Latin used by Augustine.

command and promise forcefully and persuasively."[10] On the other hand, Boniface Ramsey states that Augustine's organization of the Sermon seems to be "a tour de force of systematization, for the most part arbitrary."[11] Our assessment is probably somewhere in between: at times Augustine's organizational plan does indeed seem, if not exactly arbitrary, at least forced. Nevertheless, with respect to our text about the *lex talionis* and its correspondence to the Beatitude about mercy, to the Gift of counsel, and to forgiving trespasses, the plan seems to work rather well, as the themes generally do correspond, or at least overlap.

Certainly, mercy and forgiving trespasses overlap; perhaps the one that seems most to be an outlier is the "spirit of counsel," the Gift of the Holy Spirit. The Latin Vulgate renders this *spiritus consilii*; the Septuagint *pneuma boulēs*. Later on in *The Lord's Sermon*, Augustine indicates a knowledge of a particular Greek word that occurs in the Sermon, and he speaks in yet another place of the superiority of the Greek manuscripts of the Sermon, so it seems *possible* that he knows something of the Septuagint's rendering of Isaiah.[12] Be that as it may, however, Augustine clearly does understand *consilium* as having to do with a strategic plan of action, which would correspond to *boulē*.[13] Thus, Augustine's use and understanding of *consilium* may indeed respect well what Isaiah was intending to say about the quality of the messianic ruler announced in Isaiah 11, at least in the Septuagint's translation of it.

What is especially significant in Augustine's linking of "mercy" and "forgiving trespasses" to "counsel" is that it that deepens his commentary on Matthew 5:38–42 in momentous ways. It enables him to argue that the intention of the precepts about the cheek, the garment, and the extra miles is to counsel or advise the aspiring Christian about how to approach others with mercy and forbearance. Mercy thus comes to sight in *The Lord's Sermon* as bearing a much broader connotation that just forgiving wrongs; it becomes a prudential plan or strategy or even a tool for how to help others as well as oneself. As a result, in transitioning from the fourth Beatitude, about how we must struggle, hunger, and thirst, for righteousness, to the fifth Beatitude, Augustine is able to explain the counsel of mercy in this way:

10. Pelikan, "Introduction," xvii.

11. Ramsey, "Introduction," 14.

12. See Augustine, *The Lord's Sermon*, 1.19.58, 2.9.30.

13. Thomas Aquinas links *consilium* from the Gifts of the Spirit to the virtue of *prudentia* and *euboulia* in *Summa Theologica*, IIa–IIae.52.1–2. Even more interesting is Thomas's linking of *consilium* to the fifth Beatitude in *Summa Theologica*, IIa–IIae.52.4: "Et ideo specialiter dono consilii respondet beatitudine misericordiae, non sicut elicienti, sed sicut dirigenti."

In these struggles, when someone experiences difficulty, and moving forward, through conditions rugged and harsh, and surrounded by multiple trials, encounters the massive obstacles of his past life rising up on this side and on that and fears that he will not be able to complete what he has undertaken, he should seize counsel, so that he will merit receiving help! *But what other counsel is there, if not that he who desires divine assistance for his own weakness should bear the weakness of others, and help with it as much as he can? It follows, then, that we should look at the precepts of mercy.* Now, the meek [*mites*] person and the merciful [*misericors*] person seem to be one and the same. But there is this difference, that the meek person, who was treated earlier[14]—although through his piety he does not contradict the divine sentences brought forward against his sins, nor does he contradict those statements of God that he does not yet understand—still confers no benefit on the person he does not contradict or resist. The merciful person, however, offers no resistance in such a way that he does it for the purpose of correcting that person whom he would make worse by resisting.[15]

At this point in *The Lord's Sermon*, Augustine writes that "the Lord therefore goes on to say" the words contained in Matt 5:38–42 about the cheek, the garment, and the extra miles, which were quoted in full above.

What we see here, then, is Augustine using the notion of counsel to help him understand what the Sermon on the Mount means by practicing mercy. It is in connecting counsel and mercy that he will develop his insight into how prudentially to help others become better, and this insight will later enable him to advocate even the practice of warfare within the context of mercy.

Augustine's Analysis of Matthew 5:38–42

Matthew 5:38–42 is one of the passages in the Sermon on the Mount wherein Jesus treats a part of the Mosaic Law with the formulaic expression "You have heard that it was said . . ." and follows it with another formulaic expression,

14. That is, when treating the third beatitude, which begins "Blessed are the meek." In Augustine's interpretation, "meekness" resembles humility before God.

15. Augustine, *The Lord's Sermon*, 1.18.55; emphasis added. Translations of *The Lord's Sermon* used in this essay are my own, but I am aware of and have considered five different English translations listed in the bibliography. The Latin text used is that of Augustine, *De sermone Domini in monte*, edited by Almut Mutzenbecher. Further references to *The Lord's Sermon* will be to book, chapter, and paragraph, and will be given in parentheses in the running text.

"But I say to you. . . ."[16] It is always tempting to interpret these passages of the Sermon as implying a rejection of the precept of the Mosaic Law in question, but such an interpretation would conflict completely with Jesus's claim that he has not come to abolish the law, not even an iota or a dot of it (Matt 5:17–19). Accordingly, Augustine's approach is to claim that in Matthew 5:38–42, Jesus is not abolishing but perfecting the law about retaliation. But how is it possible to "perfect" the *lex talionis*?

Augustine begins his analysis with the perhaps surprising claim that "an eye for an eye" and "a tooth for a tooth" is already a fairly high level of morality. To be sure, it is at the level of "the lesser justice of the Pharisees," but the Mosaic precept already restricts revenge and is thus a big step in the right direction. In other words, Augustine says that what the *lex talionis* does is limit revenge for "an eye" to *one* eye only, and revenge for "a tooth" to *one* tooth only (1.19.56). In fact, when harmed, most people want to return *more* harm than what was received. Desire for revenge thus usually leads to an escalation of conflict with each side upping the stakes in turn. This is especially the case because the one who was innocent and yet was attacked always wants to harm his attacker *more* in order to exact something *in addition* in order to return to the *status quo ante*, and there is indeed a commonly accepted (if not especially noble) notion of justice at work in such a view. To use a modern example, we do not usually just insist that the bank robbers give back the money. They initiated the wrongdoing and did so violently; as a result, we often think that something in addition to a return of the money needs to be extracted from them—at least that is what this lesser understanding of justice suggests. Augustine's point is that the *lex talionis* does not permit retaliation beyond the initial harm done, thereby stopping escalation and restricting conflict. Hence, he asserts, "He who pays back just as much as he has received already forgives something" (1.19.57).

Having claimed, in effect, that the *lex talionis* of the Mosaic Law is one stage between extremes of justice and injustice, Augustine goes on to lay out a whole range of such stages or steps in a process of moving from imperfection to perfection with respect to mercy. These stages may be enumerated as follows:

1. At the lowest level is the person who, with premeditation and malice, harms another human being even though that other human being has done no antecedent harm.

2. Next is the person who thinks that since the initial victim was attacked for no reason, the initial attacker should be harmed not only to the

16. See Matt 5:21–22, 27–28, 31–32, 33–34, 38–39, 43–44.

same extent as the victim, but more. The attacker, after all, was not innocent in attacking. Such ill will must be punished in addition to the actual harm done. This is the case corresponding to my example about the bank robbers. At this level of morality, extra punishment is exacted for violently taking the money to begin with.

3. Then there is the limited revenge permitted by the Mosaic Law. This, as has already been mentioned, is the lesser morality of the Pharisees who insist that only one eye may be extracted for an eye. This is the morality of the *lex talionis* that has already forgiven something and is thus at a level higher than level 2.

4. There is also a higher level at which one demands less harm than one has suffered—for examples, Augustine offers returning only one blow for two received, or cutting off an ear as revenge for plucking out an eye (1.19.57).

5. Then comes the level at which one forgoes hitting back at all; here one does not retaliate at all. This may seem to be the highest form of morality, but Augustine is clear that one who does not retaliate "is approaching the Lord's precept, but yet does not quite reach it" (1.19.57)

6. At the sixth level, Augustine asserts that what Jesus is indicating with the precepts about the cheek, the garment, and the extra miles is that we must demonstrate that we are willing to suffer more for the sake of the wrongdoer. Not hitting back, as in what I have called "level 5," is not enough: "He [Jesus] does not say, 'If anyone strikes you, do not wish to strike him back,' but, 'Offer yourself further to him if he should go on to strike you'" (1.19.57). This "offering yourself further" can be divided into three sub-levels in Augustine's analysis. The precept about the cheek means that if someone strikes at your highest goods—goods having to do with soul or eternal life, and hence symbolized by the *right* cheek—then present or offer lesser, worldly goods (*left* cheek goods).[17] The precept about the tunic and the garment means, according to Augustine, that one should show oneself prepared to suffer again about as much as one has already suffered, for tunics and garments are

---

17. In *Letter 138*, Augustine points out that the "right" cheek in the precept must not be taken in what we might today call a "literal" sense, for then the precept would seem to leave open the possibility of striking back if someone hits us on the left cheek. He also very perceptively points out that a person is more likely to be struck on the left cheek than the right, for most pugilists are right-handed and would therefore punch so that the victim's left cheek be struck. Hence, Augustine concludes, the use of the *right* cheek in the precept is likely to be symbolic of higher rather than lesser goods.

worth about the same.[18] The precept about the extra mile actually, in the Latin text Augustine was following, says that one should "go with him another two" miles (*vade cum eo alia duo*), and hence the precept, in Augustine's analysis, means that one should be prepared to suffer twice as much as one already has (1.19.61).[19]

7. This brings us to a seventh level in which Augustine appeals to the mandate of Christian love as higher still than the precepts of the cheek, the garment, and the additional miles. In a remarkable sentence, he states, "Many have learned how to offer the other cheek but are ignorant of how to love the one by whom they are struck" (1.19.58).[20] Apparently, then, even the precepts about the cheek, the garment, and the extra miles are beneath the precept of "love thy neighbor," which is itself expanded into "love even thy enemies" in Matthew 5:43–44.

It is this seventh level that is critical for present purposes.[21] The three "level 6" precepts (about the cheek, the garment, and the extra miles) could perhaps be interpreted as implying that one may not resist others ever. Indeed, just before turning to the mandate about the striking of the cheek, the Sermon says, "But I say to you, 'Do not resist evil.'" Nevertheless, Augustine points out that Paul, when about to be struck in Acts 22, does not simply accept his blows but offers an objection to his would-be striker, and when he is slapped on the face in Acts 23, he objects again (1.19.58). Even Jesus, Augustine notes (1.19.58), does not simply endure silently his being slapped, but objects (John 18:22–23). If Paul and Jesus do not then simply turn the other cheek in all situations, it seems that such precepts as those under discussion in the Sermon on the Mount are to be followed only on appropriate occasions. Certainly, Jesus eventually turned the other cheek to such a degree that he willingly accepted death on a cross, but in John he challenges those who would strike him. How are such paradoxes to be understood?

---

18. The Latin text Augustine was following included the words *tunica* and *vestimentum*, or tunic and garment. He is puzzled by the two words, for all tunics are garments, but not all garments are tunics. See Augustine, *The Lord's Sermon*, 1.19.59.

19. Augustine also says that there *may* be a symbolic meaning to the phrase "another two," for one mile plus two more would yield the important number three.

20. "Multi enim alteram maxillam praebere noverunt, diligere vero illum a quo feriuntur ignorant."

21. In *The Lord's Sermon*, Augustine does not enumerate so clearly as I have here these seven levels. Nevertheless, as intrigued as Augustine was with the idea of the number seven, it seems unlikely that this division into seven stages was accidental in his mind.

What Augustine says is that one must "be prepared in the heart itself for all things" but not necessarily follow what we might call today the "literal" meaning of the precepts in every situation, for even the precepts of the Sermon on the Mount are to be understood as "referring to the preparation of heart, not to an external deed" (1.19.58–59). In other words, one must always be ready to turn the cheek, to give the garment, to go the extra miles, and the like, but the time for actually doing such acts is when it is appropriate. But when is it appropriate? Augustine's response seems to be that it is appropriate when doing such acts is in accord with the highest precept, the Charity Precept, of loving one's neighbor. Stated differently, it seems that there may be certain times when loving the neighbor demands that one *not* turn the cheek, give the garment, or go the extra miles.

What times would these be? Augustine's response is that these three precepts do *not* forbid "the punishment that avails for correction," since "this also pertains to mercy." Yet he immediately qualifies this by adding that neither does he intend to hinder a course of action wherein "one is prepared to endure more at the hand of him whom he wishes to be corrected" (1.20.63). Most people who seek punishment do so out of hatred, but there is a kind of punishment that comes from "a largesse of love" (*dilectionis magnitudo*), and as a result is only possible for those who also have the disposition to endure much in order to correct. This sort of punishment, then, that proceeds from charity also belongs, paradoxically, to mercy itself. The example that Augustine appeals to, perhaps not surprisingly, is that of a parent, especially a father, correcting a wayward son:

> This most suitable example is provided, so that it may be suf-
> ficiently clear that sin can be punished in love rather than aban-
> doned to impunity, so that the one punishing may wish the one
> on whom he inflicts punishment not to be wretched by means
> of punishment but happy by means of correction. Yet such a
> person should be prepared, if need be, to endure with a tranquil
> mind more harm from him whom he wishes to be corrected,
> whether he has the authority to compel him or not. (1.20.63)

Augustine's position, then, is that the overriding precept or command or law must be love of neighbor (including those neighbors who might be understood as enemies). Love of neighbor means that we wish for the neighbor's wellbeing, and the way to obtain wellbeing for the neighbor, the counsel says, is through mercy in all its forms. Sometimes people will be brought to wellbeing through that form of mercy that includes turning the cheek and enduring even more harm instead of striking back. Sometimes, though, charity and its counsel of mercy might require a sort of correction that is achieved through punishment. In other words, sometimes turning the other cheek might *not* be the most merciful thing to do. To push Augustine's line of thinking to its logical conclusion, it seems that sometimes one may have a responsibility or duty to correct, and in such cases it would seem that not doing so would be an imperfection, i.e., a sin.[22] These would be, one assumes, slight sins, but sins nonetheless.

Augustine places two restrictions on the practice of correction. First, the one who would practice it must have the authority and intention to do so appropriately. In his example of the wayward son, it is the father who corrects because it is he who "in the order of human affairs has been given authority [*potestas*]" and because it is he who would "punish with the same intention [*voluntas*] that a father has towards his little son" (1.20.63). Thus, even if one has the authority to correct, one must still have the intention or preparation to endure anything if endurance rather than correction is what is necessary for the wellbeing of the wrongdoer.

The second qualification, which is perhaps obvious from the foregoing, is that not only must one always be prepared to turn the other cheek, but generally one must actually do so. There may be a temptation to say that Augustine waters down the Sermon on the Mount by saying that correction is always or almost always legitimate for those with authority. Yet the above analysis shows that *only* those who have attained the seventh level are in a position to correct, and they only attained the seventh level by antecedently limiting any inclinations to retaliation.

Return to the *Letter* to Marcellinus

In writing to Marcellinus in *Letter 138*, about nineteen years after writing *The Lord's Sermon on the Mount*, Augustine is asked to return to the precepts about the cheek, the garment, and the extra miles. As was mentioned in the introduction, Marcellinus has been in a controversial exchange with sophisticated pagans who think that the Christians are in some sense responsible for the collapse of the empire and the sacking of the city of Rome, and he has asked Augustine for advice on how to argue back against his adversaries. The critics of Christianity are especially concerned with the moral precepts advanced in the Sermon on the Mount and are claiming that such precepts lead to the conclusion that "the preaching and teaching of Christ are not at all suitable for the morals of a republic."[23]

---

22. One notes that in Augustine's view, the fourth Gift of the Holy Spirit, the one prior to counsel, is fortitude or courage.

23. Augustine, *Letter 138*, 2.9. All quotations from *Letter 138* will be taken from the

Augustine's advice to Marcellinus is to proceed in two ways; both of the arguments he urges come directly out of the earlier work on *The Lord's Sermon*. First, Augustine explains that the sort of endurance or forbearance of evil advanced in the Sermon on the Mount really is good counsel or advice. He does not take Marcellinus through the various stages of mercy that he outlined in the earlier work, but he does explain more directly just how not returning evil for evil "works" against one's enemies:

> [H]e who conquers evil with good patiently foregoes temporal conveniences in order to teach how such things, the excessive love of which made the evil man evil, are scorned for the sake of faith and justice. In this way, the wrongdoer might learn from the very person whom he wronged what sort of things they are for the sake of which he did wrong. Repenting, he is overcome not by ferocious violence but by the benevolence of forbearance, and is thus brought to concord. (2.11)

This attempt to transform a malefactor through mercy is a particularly good strategy under certain circumstances and in certain situations: "The right time for this to be done is when it seems that it will be profitable for him for whose sake it is done, so that correction and concord will be achieved in him" (2.11). The martyrs in particular, he goes on to say, adopted this method of converting wicked people. Nevertheless, forbearance is good advice for all good people: "Thus, a just and pious man ought to be prepared to endure patiently the malice of those whom he seeks to make good, so that the number of the good grows, rather than add himself, through like malice, to the number of the wicked" (2.12).

Augustine's suggestion that there are certain times and situations in which forbearance is to be practiced for the benefit of malefactors of course leads directly into his second suggestion for Marcellinus, which is that he point out to the pagan critics that at certain times and in certain situations forbearance is not profitable. A distinction must be made between possessing a disposition or readiness or preparation in the heart (*praeparatio animi*) to practice the sort of forbearance advocated by the precepts about the cheek, the garment, and the extra miles on one hand, and actually doing those acts on the other. To be sure, "these precepts of patience are always to be retained in readiness in the heart, and benevolence, which prohibits returning evil for evil, must always be abundant in the will" (2.14). Nevertheless, sometimes patience is *not* in the best interests of the one requiring correction: "With respect to those who, contrary to their own will, need to

translation of Tkacz and Kries in *Augustine: Political Writings* and will be referenced by chapter and paragraph in parentheses in the running text.

be set straight, many things must be done with a certain benevolent harshness (*asperitas benigna*). Their welfare rather than their wishes must be
considered" (2.14). This sort of "benevolent harshness" is often required in
correcting a son—an example Augustine uses in both the *Letter* and, as we
have already seen, in *The Lord's Sermon*.[24]

In *Letter 138*, Augustine goes on to apply this suggestion about benevolent harshness to warfare, which is something that he did *not* do in the
earlier work on the Sermon on the Mount. Now he points out that Christians may indeed even wage war when it is needed to correct those who are
wayward and who cannot be turned to good by means of patient endurance
of harm. "Accordingly, if this earthly republic kept the Christian precepts,"
he says, "wars themselves would not be waged without benevolence, so that,
for the sake of the peaceful union of piety and justice, the welfare of the conquered would be more readily considered. He whose license for wrongdoing
is wrested away is usefully conquered, for nothing is less prosperous than
the prosperity of sinners" (2.14).[25]

Conclusion

It is surely the case that, after the disastrous events of August 410, the question of warfare and military virtue became more urgent for Augustine.
Nevertheless, it cannot be said that, under political pressure, he quickly
developed the just war theory, and particularly its interpretation of the Sermon on the Mount, as an *ad hoc* response to pagan rhetoric. The essential
principles of the just war theory were in place much earlier in his two books
on *The Lord's Sermon on the Mount*. It was there that Augustine first laid out
his view that the hard sayings and precepts of the Sermon on the Mount,
while requiring a will and a heart thoroughly formed by charity and mercy,
did not preclude the possibility that correction of wrongdoing was likewise an act of charity and mercy. The precepts of the Sermon, howsoever
sublime, still require that they be subsumed under the Charity Precepts
stipulating love of God and love of neighbor.

By August 410, it was also the case that the principle of the unity of
the whole of Scripture through the Charity Precepts was already firmly in
place in the first book of Augustine's *On Christian Doctrine*, which was

24. Augustine's insistence on the proper authority of the one who would correct
enters more explicitly into his thinking about justice and warfare in Augustine, *Against
Faustus*, 22.75.

25. It should not be overlooked that this passage begins with a conditional statement introduced by "if."

written in 397. Given such a principle, whatever the Sermon on the Mount intended to say, it could never be understood properly as asserting anything that would work against love of God, neighbor, and self—the hard case of war notwithstanding. If forswearing all violence would result in a failure to perform charity to a neighbor, then forswearing all violence cannot be the meaning of the Sermon.

Since the example Augustine uses to drive home this point in *The Lord's Sermon on the Mount* is the case of a boy requiring discipline from a parent, perhaps it is appropriate to conclude with the famous passage of a sermon Augustine preached at Eastertime, 407, on 1 John 4:9, that employs the same illustration to make the same basic point about charity and discipline:

> A father beats his boy; a slave-dealer fawns upon him. If you should propose two things, blows and fawnings, who would not choose fawnings and flee from blows? If you should look to the persons, love lashes out, iniquity fawns. See what we are pointing out, that the acts of men are distinguished only from the root of love. For many things can happen that have a good appearance on the exterior and do not proceed from the root of love. Even thorn bushes have flowers. But some things seem harsh, seem savage, but they are done for discipline under the direction of love. Once for all, therefore, a short precept is presented to you: Love and do what you will.[26]

This "precept" of "Love and do what you will" (*dilige, et quod vis fac*) is only, of course, a shorter version of the Charity Precepts of *On Christian Doctrine*. The "and do what you will" part of the precept has an arresting quality about it, but of course if one has true charity for God and neighbor, in doing what one wills one will be doing what the love of God and neighbor wills. In loving sinners, Augustine goes on to explain in the sermon, sometimes one shows love by means of silence, sometimes by means of crying out against them, sometimes by means of pardoning—but sometimes by means of punishing.[27]

Bibliography

Aquinas, Thomas. *Summa Theologica*. Translated by the Fathers of the English Dominican Province. New York: Benziger Brothers, 1947.

26. Augustine, *Tractates*, 7.7–8.

27. Augustine, *Tractates*, 7.8. The transgressors Augustine particularly has in mind in this sermon are the Donatists.

Augustine. *Against Faustus the Manichean*. In *Augustine: Political Writings*, edited by Ernest L. Fortin and Douglas Kries, selections translated by Michael W. Tkacz and Douglas Kries, 220–29. Indianapolis: Hackett, 1994.

———. *Commentary on the Lord's Sermon on the Mount*. In *Commentary on the Lord's Sermon on the Mount with Seventeen Related Sermons*, translated by Denis J. Kavanagh, 19–200. Fathers of the Church 11. Washington, DC: Catholic University of America Press, 1951.

———. *De sermone Domini in monte*. Edited by Almut Mutzenbecher. Corpus Christianorum Series Latina 25. Turnhout: Brepols, 1967.

———. *Letter 138*. In *Augustine: Political Writings*, edited by Ernest L. Fortin and Douglas Kries, selections translated by Michael W. Tkacz and Douglas Kries, 205–12. Indianapolis: Hackett, 1994.

———. *The Lord's Sermon on the Mount*. Translated by John J. Jepson. Ancient Christian Writers 5. Westminster, MD: Newman, 1948.

———. *The Lord's Sermon on the Mount*. In *The New Testament I and II*, edited by Boniface Ramsey, translated by Michael G. Campbell, 23–114. The Works of Saint Augustine I/15–16. Hyde Park, NY: New City, 1999.

———. *On Christian Doctrine*. Translated by R. P. H. Green. Oxford World's Classics. Oxford: Oxford University Press 1997.

———. *On the Sermon on the Mount*. https://www.newadvent.org/fathers/1601.htm.

———. *The Preaching of Augustine: "Our Lord's Sermon on the Mount."* Edited by Jaroslav Pelikan. Translated by Francine Cardman. The Preacher's Paperback Library 13. Philadelphia: Fortress, 1973.

———. *Revisions*. Translated by Boniface Ramsey. The Works of Saint Augustine I/2. Hyde Park, NY: New City, 2010.

———. *Tractates on the First Epistle of John*. Translated by John W. Rettig. Fathers of the Church 92. Washington, DC: Catholic University of America Press, 1995.

Kries, Douglas. "Augustine and the Flexibility of True Justice." In *Augustine in a Time of Crisis: Politics and Religion Contested*, edited by Boleslaw Z. Kabal et al., 343–58. Cham: Springer Nature Switzerland AG, 2021.

Pelikan, Jaroslav. "Introduction." In *The Preaching of Augustine*, edited by Jaroslav Pelikan, vii–xxi. The Preacher's Paperback Library 13. Philadelphia: Fortress, 1973.

Ramsey, Boniface. "Introduction." In *New Testament I and II*, edited by Boniface Ramsey, 11–16. The Works of Saint Augustine I/15–16. Hyde Park, NY: New City, 2014.

Van Fleteren, Frederick. "*Sermone domini in monte, De*." In *Augustine through the Ages: An Encyclopedia*, edited by Allan D. Fitzgerald, 771. Grand Rapids: Eerdmans, 1999.

7

On Biblical Typology

RICHARD J. OUNSWORTH, OP

Blackfriars, Oxford University

I HAVE RECENTLY GIVEN a retreat to some student brothers of the Dominican Order in the United States, on the topic of "Finding Christ in the Old Testament," and the subject matter raised a certain amount of alarm among some of the young friars. Were we not, they asked, "baptizing" the Old Testament? Is it not contrary to the fundamental tenets of modern biblical criticism to find meanings in the scriptures of Israel that could not possibly have been intended by the original human authors of those scriptures? Does it not even smack of supersessionism to suggest that the fullest meaning of the Old Testament can only be gleaned by those who accept the teachings of the New?

These are legitimate concerns, and it is perhaps worth admitting at once that there is a certain sense in which any authentic Christian reading of the OT is necessarily supersessionist—what one might call a kind of "soft supersessionism"—if it is supersessionist to claim that only in the light of Christ can the full authentic meaning of the law, the prophets and the writings be established. Certainly we would not expect a non-Christian exegete of the OT, especially a believing Jewish one, to accept such a claim; it is quite likely, and unfortunate, that such an exegete might find it positively offensive.[1] A Christian cannot, however, shy away from such a claim, since it is a claim made by Christ himself: "'Oh, how foolish you are, and how slow of heart to believe all that the prophets have declared.' Then beginning with Moses and all the prophets he interpreted to them the things about

---

1. On this point, see especially the helpful and nuanced remarks of Moberly, "Isaiah and Jesus," notably 234–35.

himself in all the scriptures" (Luke 24:25, 27). One of the most striking things about these verses is the universality of the claim: it is not just that the coming of Christ is prophesied in one or two places in the OT, but *all the scriptures* contain things about Christ.

The typological approach is a vital aspect of Christian exegesis of the OT, in part precisely because it steers a path between a harder-than-necessary supersessionism on the one hand, in which it is claimed that the OT provides nothing of value to Christian theology other than an amount of background information of purely academic interest, and on the other hand an indifferentism which implies that, for the people of Israel at least, nothing has changed with the coming of Christ, who now offers an alternative path to salvation to the Gentiles which has nothing to do—except perhaps analogously—with the covenant between God and Israel. Between these two extremes, typological interpretation seeks to explore the many, sometimes surprising ways in which that covenant and the record of the salvation history of God's chosen people is precisely ordered to its own fulfilment in the person, the passion, death and resurrection of Jesus of Nazareth.

Three traits of typology demonstrate its validity. First, typological interpretation, particular Christological typology, is fundamental to the manner in which the NT understands the OT; secondly, this approach to the OT, far from being a radical break with the Jewish tradition, is in fact founded upon the scriptures of Israel themselves and the ways in which they portray the reliable, consistent workings of God and his faithfulness to his people; thirdly, some of the theological speculations of the Jewish people in the intertestamental period, as witnessed by the post-biblical literature of the people of Israel, develop the biblical tradition of typology further towards the phenomenon to be found in the NT.

I have written at length elsewhere[2] about how one might go about defining what typology is, recognizing that it is not itself a biblical term, and that in neither testament do we find either an explicit definition or any kind of philosophical discussion as to what is and is not a legitimate or authentic typological interpretation. There is no need, therefore, to repeat the argumentation at length, but let it suffice to say that it follows a suggestion offered by Frances Young[3]: "taking our cue from places where the word 'type' is explicitly used, we may be able justifiably to identify other examples of the procedure where the terminology is not explicit." A consideration of passages in the NT which use word *tupos* and its cognates reveals a number of important points.

2. Ounsworth, *Joshua Typology*, 32–40.
3. Young, *Biblical Exegesis and Christian Culture*, 193.

First, the larger number of relevant passages have words in the *tupos* word-group used in the sense of an example, and the fundamental meaning of *tupos* here is that of a formative impression. The "type" in each case is a mediating term between the original source of the image, Christ and/or the gospel, and the material which is ultimately to be stamped with that image, which is a group of people. We take just two examples to clarify this point: Philippians 3:17 and 1 Peter 5:3. Paul makes it clear from the beginning of Philippians 3 that in his own apostolic mission he has been conformed to Christ, not only explicitly in verses 12–14, but also implicitly by the parallelism between his description of his own biography with that of Christ: the possession of natural entitlements (vv. 4–6 paralleling Phil 2:6), abandonment thereof (vv. 7–8 paralleling 2:7–8), leading to the possibility of death (v. 10 paralleling 2:8b) but also of resurrection and exaltation (vv. 10–11 paralleling 2:9–11). It is with this point of his own conformity to Christ established that Paul goes on to urge the Philippians to conform themselves to him in turn, as he does much more straightforwardly in 1 Corinthians 11:1. There is a further degree of mediation in the Philippians passage: those who conform themselves to Paul (who is the *tupos*) are themselves to be marked (*skopeite*) as models to be imitated (Phil 3:17). That the conformity of all is ultimately to Christ, and importantly that the source of that conformity is Christ's own causative power, is then immediately emphasized again in the last two verses of the chapter which, moreover, invoke a sense of the *vertical* relationship between Christ and the believers. We shall see later on the vital importance of this vertical dimension of typology, that is to say one in which the possibility of a typological relationship between two people, events etc. separated in time in space is established upon the basis of the heavenly origin of the pattern that both share.

Helpful in exploring this notion is terminology proposed by Richard M. Davidson,[4] who speaks of the relationship between a *Nachbild* and a *Vorbild*: a *tupos* can be either the impression that is formed or that which forms the impression, or—crucially—both at once, so that a particular person, event etc., may be simultaneously a *nachbildliche Vorbild* and a *vorbildliche Nachbild*. But the reason that this is possible is that there is always, originating in the heavens, which is to say originating in the divine will and providence, an *Urbild*. In the case of Philippians discussed above, if St. Paul presents himself as at once *nachbildliche Vorbild* and *vorbildliche Nachbild* then it is upon the basis of Christ himself as the *Urbild*. Much the same notion can be found, e.g., in 1 Corinthians 15:47–48 and 1 Thessalonians 4:16; neither is it distinctive to Paul: 1 Peter 5:3 urges the leaders of the

---

4. Davidson, *Typology in Scripture*.

community to be models for their flock rather than domineering over them; implicitly he offers himself as a model of how to be a model (v. 1) and immediately after the charge points towards Christ the chief-shepherd as the *Urbild*. Moreover, here again we are implicitly pointed towards the heavenly status of the *Urbild* both as the source of the formative power of the type and as the ultimate destiny thereof (v. 4).

A second important discovery from our examination of the *tupos* word-group comes from 1 Corinthians 10, where Paul speaks of the events of the wilderness wanderings, and particularly the deaths of the faithless generation who worshipped the golden calf and failed to enter into the promised land through disbelief. Here it is not only that the wilderness generation are "types of us" (1 Cor 10:6) but the whole historical sequence of events. The Exodus, the miraculous provision of water and food, the wilderness murmurings and the punishments that followed: these things happened to the Israelites typologically, and were subsequently recorded in the scriptures so that the people of the new covenant might learn from the type. It is because the type is recorded that it is possible to avoid being conformed to the overthrown Israelites and be conformed instead to that remnant that did make it to the Promised Land. Two distinct, though inseparable, advantages belong to Paul's readers: on the one hand, a knowledge of the history of the relationship between God and his people; on the other, the insight to recognise that this written *Heilsgeschichte* reveals the underlying patterns that shape that history and thus the opportunity to conform themselves to the right models and not to the wrong ones. We must emphasise that, for St. Paul, the formative patterns would be there anyway, but the fact that they are written in scripture makes it possible for us to benefit from them, and makes possible the paraenesis which is Paul's purpose.

The source of the power of the *tupos*, then, to mold the history of God's people, is not ultimately its literary quality but that supernatural power, power of heavenly origin, which Paul so strongly emphasises: the food, the drink, the rock are all *pneumatikos*–"and the Rock was Christ" (1 Cor 10:4). That same supernatural power inheres in the saving events which conform to those of the past, particularly in the Eucharist (v. 16) which is the "table of the Lord" (v. 21). The formative relationship between the People of Israel and the Christian community is an ontological one, with the events of salvation history shaped according to the saving purposes of God with the eschatological community of the Church as their end. That is, Paul is claiming that the events were types at the time, and have not become so with the benefit of hindsight, even if their typical nature need not have been apparent at the time.

It must be admitted, however, that such conclusions would not be plausible if it were not for much clearer uses of the *tupos* word-group to claim explicitly that there is a formative relationship between something in the OT and something subsequent. Here we can mention Romans 5:14, which speaks of Adam as a "type of the coming one" and 1 Peter 3:21, which relates the flood to baptism. Acts 7:44 and Hebrews 8:5 make explicit reference to Exodus 25:40 in a strictly vertical typology—that is to say, the relationship is not between things separated in time or geographically but between the heavenly sanctuary and the earthly temple or tent. In Hebrews 9:24 this same idea is taken up again, with the claim made explicit that the *purpose* of the antitype (the tabernacle, seemingly meaning the Jerusalem temple by a sort of diachronic metonymy) has been accomplished in the present age by the once-for-all sacrificial entry of Christ into the heavenly temple. We have, then, not an interpretation of an OT event as a type of something in the present age but an interpretation of something in the present age as an antitype of something written about in the OT but still extant, or perhaps very recently defunct (but spoken of as continuing).

Central to what is going on in all of these texts, and therefore to the NT concept of typology, is the notion of correspondence or isomorphism: Christian baptism has in common with the Flood not only the bare fact of flowing water, but the rescue of a chosen remnant, so that there is an isomorphism of significance. As the sin of Adam had an enduring effect in human history, so the righteous obedience of Christ has a corresponding, though also intensified, effect upon humanity; the temple is of the same design as that shown to Moses and thus corresponds to it. Hebrews and Acts differ from the other passages in making no appeal to a historical correspondence. In Romans 5 the typology is historical, but unlike 1 Peter 3 is both a negative and an intensive typology. That is to say, Christ's obedience is the converse of Adam's trespass, and the effect of the former is the converse of that of the latter; moreover, the effect of the former is also more powerful than that of the latter: "And the free gift is not like the effect of that one man's sin . . . if, because of one man's trespass, death reigned through that one man, much more will those who receive the abundance of grace and the free gift of righteousness reign in life through the one man Jesus Christ" (Rom 5:16–17). This notion of intensification is, by contrast, not obviously implied in 1 Peter. We note also one further set of differences: in 1 Peter we have a typology of a salvation-historical event corresponding to an aspect of the Church's life, in Romans a correspondence between two particular people and the effects of their actions, and in Hebrews an eternal or heavenly reality corresponding to a building—but also a Jewish liturgical rite, the entrance of the High Priest into the Holy of Holies, corresponding to the death and exaltation of Christ which is indeed the ultimate salvation-historical event.

On turning to the OT to look for the roots of the complex notion of typology that we have discovered in the NT, we find first of all that, *pace* a number of OT scholars[5], the vertical as well as the horizontal (historical) dimension is readily apparent. In the Psalms and other liturgical texts there is a clear invocation of a correspondence between the tabernacle or temple and heaven, and between Israel's liturgy and the eternal heavenly liturgy. Related to this, Horace D. Hummel notes in Exodus 15 and Judges 5, to which we may add Daniel 7, analogies (which I would argue are ontological, not merely verbal) between the cataclysmic events of Israel's earthly history and their metahistorical counterparts, the cosmic war between good and evil played out in the heavenly court.[6]

Nevertheless, by far the most common typological relationships are drawn between historical events, and most especially with reference to the Exodus. Creation and the flood, exile and restoration, the eschatological new covenant of Ezekiel and Jeremiah, as well as (e.g., in Wisdom) the intellectual or moral growth of the individual, are all described in terms of the deliverance of the people of Israel out of Egypt through the Red Sea. This archetype has also been proposed (e.g., by N. T. Wright)[7] as that which lies behind much of the NT and even behind Jesus' own self-understanding as well as, less contentiously, the ministry of John the Baptist. Certainly the resonances of the Exodus event are heard throughout the NT and into the post-apostolic period. It may well be the case that the OT description of the Exodus is based, either fully or in part, on the experiences of exile and restoration, rather than vice versa, so that the typology here is as it were a reverse-horizontal one. In fact, it is quite natural that there should be some sort of retrojective aspect to any kind of historical typology: the likening of the later event to the earlier one not only shapes our understanding of the later one, but also plays a part in reformulating our understanding of the earlier, and this in turn will of course strengthen the identification between the two.

Importantly, a backwards-horizontal typology of the temple cult is found in that same literature which expresses most clearly the vertical typology of the temple cult. Moreover, if Mary Douglas's reading of Leviticus is right[8], then the Priestly understanding of the cult included a threefold analogy between the geography of the temple, the anatomy of the sacrificial

---

5. E.g., Rad, "Typological Interpretation of the OT."
6. Hummel, "OT Basis of Typological Interpretation."
7. Wright, *Jesus and the Victory of God.*
8. Douglas, *Leviticus as Literature.*

animal and the narrative of Exodus 19 and 24. Geographical, historical and biological, vertical and horizontal, are all incorporated in one powerful set of typological resonances centring on the temple. This should be no surprise given the centrality of the temple and its cult in late Second Temple Judaism, and it can be no coincidence that so much of the NT typology we have considered revolves either around the liturgy of the temple or the sacraments of the early Christian communities.

But while it is often within the context of liturgy that typological evocation takes place in the OT, that does not by any means imply that such a context is of the essence of typology. To find that essence, it is wise to follow a similar path to that we took with regard to the NT, which is to look for what we might think of as typological terminology, and here we take our cue from Michael Fishbane, whose work on this topic[9] remains the most comprehensive and helpful. He proposes that the commonly occurring constructions "just as . . . so" (e.g., Ezek 20:36; Isa 11:16; Josh 3:7) is a good starting point, though Fishbane does not notice that this and similar constructions are not only used to delineate horizontal—that is, historical—typologies, but also vertical ones, for example, at Exodus 27:8. Nevertheless Fishbane does go on to include "cosmological-historical" among his typological categories, along with "historical," "spatial" and "biographical." The historical and the biographical—the latter really a subset of the historical—are by far the most common. In the case of biographical typologies, repetitions of words, phrases and whole narrative pericopes, especially in the primeval and patriarchal narratives, serve to establish Noah as a second Adam (see above on 1 Pet 3), to present Jacob or David as another Abraham, to relate Joshua or Elijah to Moses, and so on. We also find the individual biography related typologically to the history (or future) of a whole nation, as when in Jeremiah 9:3–5 the prophet takes up a number of key terms from the description of Jacob in Genesis to portray the deceitful and perverse nature of the Israel of his own day: Jacob the trickster is a type of the Israel that is named after him, which is thus given a corporate identity. This then serves not only as chastisement, which is the overt purpose of the passage, but also to imply hope, that through testing (v. 7) the people of Israel might be refined and prepared for the purpose for which they have been called, just as Jacob had to struggle with the Lord at Peniel.

Historical typologies similarly can have either a purely retrospective or a prospective nature in the OT. In the former mode, the description of one historical event serves as the model for the description of another. The crossing of the Jordan is clearly modelled on the crossing of the Red Sea,

9. Fishbane, *Biblical Interpretation in Ancient Israel.*

for example. In the same way, it has been argued that the narratives of the return from exile in Ezra, Nehemiah and Chronicles have been shaped at least in part by the desire to portray it as a second exodus, with Ezra in particular being a new Moses. This use of retrospective exodus typology is first found in chapter 15 of Exodus itself, in which the power of God in leading his people across the water is the same power that is to lead them to conquer the Canaanites. (It might well be, as Hummel argues, that the roots of this typological thinking lie in liturgy, if Exodus 15 is a primitive hymn of some kind.) The prospective mode of historical typology then depends upon the same supposition, that these foundational patterns underlie the life and history of the people of Israel, revealed not only by Israel's past history *per se* but even more by its narration, showing the power of God and giving the hope of a future that reiterates them. Once again exodus and conquest form the most common motif, and not just in the exilic period: Hosea 2:15 offers Israel a new consecration to the Lord "as at the time when she came out of the land of Egypt."

An important aspect of prospective historical typology is that very often the future event involves an intensification of the type. This is closely related to the increasingly explicit notion of a "new age," which emerges strongly in Deutero-Isaiah and then intensifies in the proto-apocalyptic writings of, for example, Zechariah. Thus Isaiah 43:16–28 is closely modelled on Exodus 15, but goes on to make a contrast with the former times: "Thus says the Lord, who makes a way in the sea, a path in the mighty waters, who brings forth chariot and horse, army and warrior. 'Remember not the former things, nor consider the things of old.'" Occasionally this contrast is made in more detail as in Isaiah 52:12: "For you shall not go out in haste, and you shall not go in flight, for the Lord will go before you, and the God of Israel will be your rear guard." Jeremiah 31:31–34, picked up explicitly in Hebrews 8, suggests that the covenant of Sinai (explicitly linked to the exodus) is a foreshadowing of a much greater covenant yet to come. This is closely related to the standard Rabbinic rhetorical device of *qal wahomer* which Paul uses to draw eschatological conclusions in, for example, Romans 5. In the OT (and Rabbinic texts such as P Rabbati 48:2; P de-Rab. Kahana 9:2) the argument runs thus: "if the past has been thus, how much more will the future be"; in the NT we have "if the past was thus, how much more is the present" (e.g., Rom 5; 2 Cor 3:7–8; Heb 9:13–14).

When we come to what Fishbane calls "cosmological-historical" typologies, the promised future is likened not to a past historical event but to a primordial one; the age to come will have the features not of past human history but of the apocalyptic milieu of the creation. Such, for example, is the promise of Isaiah 65:17–25, but the idea is already present in first Isaiah

(11:6–9). Isaiah 51 and Psalms 74, 78 and 89 similarly draw a link between the creative power of God manifested before the ages and the power of God to redeem Israel that will be manifested at the end.

Particularly significant along these lines is Isaiah 11:15, which portrays the deliverance of Israel from her enemies in terms of God's smiting of the sea. This passage exemplifies the mediating aspect of types which we found in the NT: given the preceding section, in which the future is portrayed in terms of a return to Eden, we are justified in supposing that the smiting of the sea is a creation motif, drawing on the common Ancient Near Eastern mythology of creation as the victory of God or his agent (Marduk, Baal) over the sea deity or monster (Tiamat, Leviathan). The reference to God's *ruah*, his wind or spirit, brings to mind Genesis 1:2, and the dividing of the waters into seven streams cannot be equated straightforwardly with the dividing of the Red Sea; and yet there clearly is reference to the latter event in the mention of passing over the river dry-shod. It is not a case of *either* creation or exodus, but of *both*, as is the case more explicitly in Isaiah 51:9–11. We have both the parallelism of *Endzeit* and *Urzeit* and the evocation of a salvation-historical event, and thus the mediating type, that of the exodus, is re-interpreted in terms of primordial and eschatological apocalyptic event: salvation history is the stage upon which is played out the eternal drama of God's creative and redemptive power, and once again it is this power which gives the historical type its strength to form and mold human history and draw it to its eschatological conclusion.

What we are seeing here, in a sense, is what Katherine Grieb refers to as the "combination of spatial and temporal realism,"[10] as the distinction here proposed between the horizontal and the vertical dimensions begins to be called into question. For Grieb, this is something "unusual"[11] in the Letter to the Hebrews, and it is true that Hebrews' use of the contrast between the two tents to allude at once to the historical move from the old covenant to the new and the cosmological movement of Christ the High Priest between the earthly and the heavenly realms is particularly distinctive. However, our investigations would suggest rather that Hebrews has simply followed a trajectory already established: the historical realities of past and present are related to realities which are—what shall we say?—parahistorical and heavenly in their *locus*. If we speak of the historical as the horizontal dimension and the cosmological as the vertical dimension of typology, then we find ourselves obliged to imagine a world in which two dimensions at right angles to one another are somehow fused, plaited together, folded into one another in a

10. Grieb, "Identity of Jesus in Hebrews," 209.
11. Grieb, "Identity of Jesus in Hebrews," 209.

mind-bending origami; must we appeal to M. C. Escher for help in visualizing the interweaving dimensions of the typological universe?

This sense that the future, very often the *hoped-for*, realities and the eternal things of the heavenly realm are closely related, even identical, is found perhaps even more clearly in the fourth category of OT typologies, those of a spatial nature. As with the previous category these are not unique to Israelite theology, but once again are so enthusiastically taken up by it from its religious milieu that we cannot cast them out as alien without doing grave violence to the OT. Here, the correspondences are between places of religious significance, explicitly stated (e.g., 2 Chr 3:1) or implied by various literary techniques. Psalm 46, for example, probably a pre-exilic text, attributes to Jerusalem the life-giving river proper to Eden (Gen 2:10). As with the previous category, it is in the exilic and post-exilic periods that this typology really develops, especially again in projective typologies: Isaiah 51:2 and Ezekiel 36:35 explicitly portray the land to which the people will return as a new Eden (the following chapter of Ezekiel—the raising of the dry bones—perhaps continuing the same theme with implicit reference to the creation of Adam in Eden). Similar ideas can be found in Joel 2:3 and Zechariah 14:8–11.

The application of Eden and of Sinai typologies came to focus especially on Mount Sion and the temple. Ezekiel sees a heavenly vision of the new temple while "on a very high mountain" (40:2), the blueprint of which he must relate, just as Moses on Mount Sinai saw the *tupos* of the tabernacle. So Ezekiel is a new Moses and his envisioned temple becomes a type of the heavenly sanctuary—the vision, and the typology, is at once a horizontal/eschatological one in which the future is cast in terms of the past, and a vertical one in which the temple is portrayed as a projection into the temporal world of the eternal heavenly realities. At the same time the new temple is infused with both Eden and Sinai associations, Eden representing the primordial pre-history in which vertical and horizontal distinctions are inevitably brought together, and Sinai representing the founding moment of Israel's history as a covenant people, but also the heavenly dwelling of the Most High. There is a transfer of Sinai images to Mount Sion in, for examples, Isaiah 2 and Psalm 68:16–18, the latter explicitly making the claim that the Lord has somehow moved from one to the other, so that the place in which the vertical ascent to heaven itself is made is now Jerusalem. We note at the same time that the portrayal of Sinai in Exodus 24 involves retrojective temple typology—the building of an altar and pillars, performance of sacrifice and most notably the pavement of sapphire.

Therefore, in the exilic and post-exilic prophecies regarding the temple, the future for Israel is the eternally-present reality stored up in heaven, precisely the idea Paul applies to the individual Christian, with temple language, in 2 Corinthians 5 (cf. Phil 3:20). It is in eschatological writings that the purely vertical temple typology, which was by no means unique to Israel, becomes interwoven with horizontal typology, both prospective and retrospective, to form a distinctive tapestry in which the eternal is depicted in the history and future of the people of God.

This Escheresque interweaving of historical and vertical typologies only strengthens in the intertestamental period, an important feature of which is the phenomenon of "re-written bible." Josephus's *Jewish Antiquities* is the most substantial example; others include the Genesis Apocryphon and the Book of Jubilees. Very often these works, like the Books of Chronicles before them, betray a clear ideological purpose in their selection, expansion and suppression of biblical materials, but underneath this phenomenon typology is often at work, the portrayal of two distinct events or characters being brought closer together by literary means. Other texts of the Second Temple period also model their descriptions of (sometimes more recent) events and personalities on those of the Hebrew Bible: the character of Tobit shows clear affinities with that of Job, and the story of the Book of Esther has strong literary as well as narrative affinities with the Joseph story in Genesis. In Joseph and Aseneth, we are told that Aseneth "was in every respect similar to the daughters of the Hebrews; and she was tall as Sarah and handsome as Rebecca and beautiful as Rachel" (Joseph and Aseneth 1:5). Thus she is typified by the wives of the patriarchs, a typology which is developed throughout the work even as she also becomes, like Ruth, a type of the penitent proselyte (thus mediating between patriarchs and proselytes). In 1 Maccabees 5:48, the words of Judas are a conflation of the three passages in the OT in which Israelites request passage from Sihon, king of the Amorites (Num 21:22; Deut 2:26–29; Judg 11:19); in this way the Maccabean struggle is placed in typological relationship with the conquest, and so the Maccabean regime becomes legitimated and those who adhere to it are encouraged, in an implicit typological paraenesis, to see themselves as heirs of the original conquerors of Canaan.

The same kind of typological modelling is found not only in historical but also in prophetic documents of the period: the War Scroll models its prediction of the eschatological battle between the Sons of Light and the Sons of Darkness on various battles between Israel and her enemies in the OT, whether by the lightest of allusions or seemingly direct quotation (e.g., 1QM 11:6b–7a = Num 24:17–19). In some cases, the directly-quoted passage is explicitly claimed to be "about" the situation of the sectarians: "From ancient times thou hast fore[told the hour] when the might of thy hand (would be raised) against Kittim, saying *Assyria shall fall by the hand of no man, the hand of no mere man shall devour him"* (Isa 31:8, quoted in 1QM 11:11). This method of biblical interpretation, in which a biblical prophecy is reinterpreted in respect of a new situation not obviously envisaged by the prophet, is best exemplified among the Dead Sea Scrolls by the Pesher on Habakkuk (1QpHab). Along with many other works of biblical interpretation found in caves 1 and 4, it seems to go beyond typology, since the middle term is lost, as it were: this is not a matter of a second application of the scriptural text alongside the original, but the complete occlusion of the first, the end of a process of re-orienting biblical prophecy along more apocalyptic and eschatological lines that began in the Persian period. Yet it might be argued that it is the prophecy itself, rather than its attendant historical circumstances, that has become the "type," the mold waiting to be (ful)filled, as a more apocalyptic understanding of prophecy developed in which the words themselves were a direct heavenly revelation. Events of the future, or more recent past, might be foreshadowed then not by events of the past (under the guiding hand of God as Lord of history) but by words spoken in the past by the prophets (under the direct inspiration of God as Lord of the future).

Yet it cannot be necessary to insist on including this last example among those of typology in the intertestamental period, for this reason: a type is always more than just a set of words—it is both the words and that to which the words refer, as typology elevates the realities to which the words refer to the rank of symbol. However, such texts do provide, alongside many others, cumulative evidence of two things: a continued and growing tendency to look to the past in order to make sense of the present and express hope in the future; and alongside this a tendency to look to heaven for a source of hope and understanding. These two tendencies might seem at odds, yet are constantly present in the same texts, because the heavenly origin of the past prophecies (the fact that they are an *Urbild*, to use the language proposed above, makes it possible that their true application should be to a contemporary situation or a still-distant future unrelated to the original prophet. In the War Scroll, the confidence of the sectarians in the fulfilment of the prophecies of final victory is related to the relationship of their own armies to the hosts of heaven: "For thou wilt fight with them from heaven. . . . For our Lord is holy and the King of Glory is with us together with the Holy Ones. Valiant [warriors] of the angelic host are among our numbered men, and the Hero of war is with our congregation" (1QM 11:16; 12:6–7).

Thus the confidence of the sectarians in their future vindication depends upon their vertical relationship with the heavenly realm, and their present situation corresponds to a heavenly reality. Mimetic correspondences are created in the texts between different historical situations and between those historical situations and the eternal realities which are played out in them. The identity of the community is strengthened by these inter-dependent horizontal and vertical correspondences.

We should hasten to add that it is not just the profoundly sectarian and perhaps quite unrepresentative writings of the Dead Sea Scrolls and other rather outré apocalyptic literature that increasingly link the verti-cal and horizontal dimensions: one of the most notable developments in the thought of wisdom literature, a striking difference between Proverbs and Ecclesiastes on the one hand and the Wisdom of Solomon or Sirach on the other, is the bringing together of wisdom and history. Wisdom of Solomon, for example, shows how the principle of divine wisdom which emanates from the throne of God, portrayed in terms reminiscent both of middle Platonic language and that of apocalypticism (Wis 7:24–30) is the guiding spirit of the history of Israel (chs. 10–19); and that history and its relationship with eternal wisdom is portrayed using a retrospective typology, casting the situation of the people of Israel in Egypt quite overtly in terms of the situation of the Jews of the Alexandrian diaspora, with an ultimately paraenetic purpose.

One final area in which some significant development may have taken place during the Second Temple period is in liturgical typology. The Book of Jubilees throughout relates the feasts and sacrifices of the temple typologi-cally to the events of the past, so that for example the Feast of Weeks is kept at one and the same time for the celebration (and the ensured continua-tion) of the harvest and in commemoration of the promises made to Noah and to Abraham: "the feast is twofold and of two natures" (Jubilees 6:21). Failure to observe the feasts properly will put the people of Israel out of touch with their own history and simultaneously they will cease to repre-sent to the world the eternal patterns in the cosmos established at creation (see especially 6:32–38). For the keeping of the feasts is no mere temporal phenomenon: "It is an eternal decree and engraved upon heavenly tablets for all the children of Israel" (49:8). Levi and his successors re-enact the eternal liturgy of the heavens (31:18) as they re-enact the events of salvation history. This is typological not only inasmuch as mimetic correspondences are explicitly drawn between the cult and historical events (or heavenly/cosmic realities) but because the cult, by so corresponding, is able—indeed essential—to *create* those correspondences in turn in the people of Israel. So the type once again has mediating power.

The Book of Jubilees shares a certain sectarian character with (some of) the Dead Sea Scrolls, so both sets of texts might be thought unrepresentative of mainstream thought. However, it is difficult to point to any text created during the period in question which is demonstrably mainstream. Perhaps the most we can hope to do is identify straws in the wind, and another of these is the writings of Philo. To engage on a profound analysis of his biblical hermeneutics is well beyond the scope of this brief essay, but we should admit that it comes closest in this period of Judaism to the purely allegorical and ahistorical. This does not mean that there is nothing typological in it, of course: Philo thinks it important to keep to the letter of the Law as well as its deeper meaning (see, e.g., *De migratione Abraham* 89) and indeed the personal mental/spiritual growth which the OT is ultimately about is in many instances made possible precisely by attentiveness to the surface meaning of the text. Neither does he deny the facticity of the historical events that are related, including the giving of the Law to Moses on Sinai. So we might say that Philo sees the whole of scripture as a *tupos*, molded by the divinely ordained order of things and by the equally divinely ordained history of Israel, and in turn having the power to mold the insightful reader and actor-out of these laws and histories into full maturity.

It must be significant, though, that this mediating notion is found in Philo especially in his consideration of the laws of the cult. The temple itself is a microcosm of the universe, with the High Priest having a distinctive character, almost a corporate personality, as he participates in the eternal cosmic worship (see, e.g., *De specialibus legibus* 1:66 and 1:114–16). At the same time, the individual soul is a microcosmic temple, unified through worship with the divine Logos and so brought into perfect correspondence with the heavenly reality, through the mediation of the earthly cult, in which the High Priest is the *mimema* of the true man, the "priest" of the rational soul. These ideas are similar in kind to those of Sirach regarding the High Priest as the embodiment of Wisdom ordering both the universe and the soul of the righteous. Philo also uses a geographical typology, arguing in *De plantatione* 46–50 that Exodus 15:17–18, which speaks of God's command to Moses to plant Israel, and particularly his sanctuary, on the mountain of his inheritance means that Israel is on the site of Eden—a geographical but also a primordial-historical typology, but quickly brought to a strictly vertical dimension: Eden, as a type of Israel, properly refers to the universe as God's sanctuary, an "outshining of sanctity . . . a copy of the original" (*De plantatione* 50). This is explicit language of vertical temple typology.

What, then, can we say about the trajectory that leads from the OT to the New via the development of thought to which a surprising amount of the intertestamental literature bears witness? As the Jewish people looked more and more intently to their history to make sense of their present and to give them hope for the future, they found in that history, and manifested by the way it was inscriptured, the patterns that demonstrated God's creative and redeeming power. This power was the ultimate source of their hope and of the meanings they were able to draw out of their history. Meanwhile the endeavor represented by wisdom literature continued to seek the same patterns in the unchanging realities of the world; but the two projects, never separate or expressly distinguished in ancient Israel, grew closer together and became almost indistinguishable, as the literature of wisdom and apocalypticism came to see Israel's history as the canvas onto which were projected, as it were, the eternal truths emanating from God's heavenly throne. Whether these patterns were unearthed in historical events or personages or in the rhythm of the seasons and the liturgical calendar—or increasingly in some combination of both—their heavenly source gave them the power to shape the people of Israel, their lives and their future in accordance with God's plan.

The discovery and expression or evocation of these patterns that mediate divine power always took place along both the horizontal axis of history and the vertical axis between earth and heaven, but the two became increasingly intertwined. This change took place above all in two areas: liturgy and eschatology, and these areas continued to predominate in the earliest Christian literature. In the NT itself we note how often typology is related to baptism and/or the Eucharist—in 1 Corinthians 10, in 1 Peter 3, and so on. The symbolic re-enactments of cardinal moments in salvation history conform those who are now participating in the culmination of that history to the eternal realities they make manifest. The developing theological relationship between vertical-*cum*-horizontal typology may have been in two directions at once, with the early Christian understanding of the sacraments both encouraging and encouraged by trends in typological thinking that had already begun, especially in association with cult, in Judaism.

Alongside the growth of sacramental typology, the eschatological tension that suffuses early Christianity allowed further developments in the use of heavenly personalities as types. Already Daniel 7 presented the "one like a son of man" as a type of Israel's *future*, a representative figure in both a literary sense and in the sense of an agent, a real heavenly personality in which the people of Israel participate. This was developed in 1 Enoch, in which the Son of Man is more explicitly a pre-existent figure, described as "the prototype of the before time" (46:2); this is part of a strong tendency in 1 Enoch to make the creation, and the flood, types of the end of the age. But the NT can see Christ himself as a type of the Christian believer's *present* as well as future: insofar as we participate in Christ's corporate personality (are "in Christ") we already achieve the life of the age to come which exists eternally in heaven. This idea is clearly expressed in Ephesians 2, for example (especially vv. 4–6), and it is intriguing that at the end of this chapter the body of believers is likened to the temple: Christ is the fulfillment of the type of the temple, and so the believers who are molded into his image (cf. 4:15 and Rom 8:29) are being molded into a temple, in fact into the heavenly sanctuary of which the temple in Jerusalem is but a shadow. Christ then becomes for Christians the ultimate type, the mold in which, especially through the mediation of the sacramental life, they are being cast in the image of God.

An image I commonly use to explain typological readings of the OT, whether speaking at parish missions in Wales or to ferociously bright young friars in Missouri, is that of potato prints. Recall from your childhood days how you would cut a large potato in half and then carve some kind of pattern or image onto the cut surface, to be used with oil paint to stamp repeated patterns onto a sheet of paper. Now suppose that the paper in this case is not clean, uncreased, flat and smooth, but tatty, torn, stained and wrinkled— how difficult it would be under those circumstances to discern that any kind of pattern was repeated. What might make it easier to recognise the pattern? Perhaps to have seen the potato. This is precisely what the NT is telling us: we might not have seen with unveiled eyes the absolute reality of God and the final consummation of all things, "but we do see Jesus" (Heb 2:9). We have seen the potato, and now when we look back at the written history of God's dealings with humanity, and especially with his chosen people—at that tatty, stained and torn record of a history marked on our side by sin and faithlessness—we can see how there descended from heaven, in many and various ways, the imprint of God's saving love. Jesus Christ is that imprint, "the exact imprint of God's very being" (Heb 1:3), the *Urbild* of God, as it were. The claim implicit in typological readings of the OT—a claim made more or less explicitly in the NT and to which a Christian reading of the OT cannot but be faithful—is that in having seen Christ we have received the cipher that decodes the deepest meanings, the Christological meanings, to be found "in all the scriptures."

This claim, that only in the light of Christ can the full meaning of the OT be discerned, is "at heart a conviction that the vision of God, the world and the people of God in Israel's Scriptures is taken to its fullest limit and best realizes it rich potential in the person and work of Jesus."[12] We must, however, recognize that the discerning of types, particularly types of Christ, in the OT is not a one-way process: it is not only that our knowledge of Jesus illumines our reading of the OT, but also that an ever-deeper engagement in that reading in turn deepens our understanding of Christ, his person and the meaning of his saving work. The NT shows us that it was precisely by means of this engagement that the earliest Christians—the Apostles themselves, in-deed—came to understand how it was that the crucified prophetic preacher

12. Moberly, "Isaiah and Jesus," 235.

from Galilee was not only the Messiah of Israel but also, and precisely as such, the Savior of the world. The Gospels clearly assert, moreover, that it was Jesus himself who established this exegetical method. Not only after his resurrection on the road to Emmaus, but even during his pre-Easter ministry, he directed his hearers to the Scriptures of Israel to assert his identity and to help those with ears to hear to understand his mission.

Let us take just three examples, all of which proved fruitful to my re-treatants, though none are by any means original to me. A few very brief remarks may be offered, simply to illustrate some of the possible Christological implications of following Jesus's own indications regarding his OT types. We shall consider the Son of Man, Jonah, and the bronze serpent in the wilderness.[13] As far as the first of these is concerned, it is relatively uncontroversial to place this expression on the lips of the historical Jesus, though the debate about what he meant by it is by no means settled.[14] It directs us, though, to re-examine Daniel 7 in the light of Christ, and recognise that the victory represented there of Israel over the nations that have oppressed God's chosen people is not a military one, whether led by a human Messiah or a heavenly one, but is the victory of the Cross and the Resurrection, an eschatological victory but one that (for the present time at least) has the appearance of folly to the Greeks and scandal to the Jews. At the same time, though, there is a deeper typology at work, for the vision of the Son of Man in Daniel not only points forward to Christ but back to Adam, the original Man of whom all are sons and daughters.[15] To be clear, this is a link that is established in the Book of Daniel itself; so the typological relationship between Christ and the Danielic Son of Man not only sheds light on the meaning of the OT text, but also brings new Christological insights, as light is shone in *both* directions: we see that in Christ's victory over sin and death, the *imago Dei* is restored, and that with it the role of humanity as God's earthly vice-regent, exercised now by the Church in anticipation of the second coming of the Son of Man and the final consummation of creation.

While Jesus without serious question referred to himself as the Son of Man, we are on less solid historical ground regarding the Sign of Jonah, which appears at Matthew 16:4 and Luke 11:29 but not the Markan parallel (Mark 8:12). Moreover, Matthew's and Luke's versions emphasise different aspects of the story of Jonah as parallels to Christ, respectively the burial of Jesus and his prophetic ministry. Yet if we allow the typology, we can explore

13. A fourth example, more original but more difficult to show as originating in the preaching of Jesus, is that of Joshua the son of Nun; this is elaborated in detail in Ounsworth, *Joshua Typology*.

14. See for example Burkett, *Son of Man Debate*.

15. On this point see Farrer, *Study in St. Mark*, 258–64.

more implications even that those explicit in the Gospel texts. For example, we might find in Jonah the paradigmatic example of the prophet who succeeds in failure: his prophetic ministry brings about repentance and thus his prediction is not borne out, so that he fails the test of prophetic authenticity offered by Deuteronomy 18:22.[16] Or we might draw some parallel between the suffering, seemingly both physical and existential, of Jonah in the heat of the sun outside the city of Nineveh, a suffering apparently intended to be educative in some way, and the way in which Jesus himself "learned obedience through what he suffered" (Heb 5:8), and so come through Jonah to a deeper appreciation of the way in which Christ paid the price of God's merciful act of redemption, an act in which he invites the willing but costly participation of human beings, beginning with his own incarnate Son.

It is upon Christ's atoning death that our final brief example also touches. John records that Jesus tells Nicodemus, "just as Moses lifted up the serpent in the wilderness, so must the Son of Man be lifted up" (John 3:14). The scholarly literature on this point tends to focus much more on the "lifted up" than on the serpent part of this saying[17], not least because this is just the first of the three very distinctive "lifted-up" sayings in the Fourth Gospel (the others being 8:28 and 12:32) that parallel the three passion predictions in the Synoptics and thus contribute to the distinctiveness of John's theological vision. That this is so does not at all mean that we may not take these distinctive sayings as another point of entry for interpreting Christ in the light of the OT, however: setting aside the thorny question of the historical reliability of the Fourth Gospel, we must insist that the Gospels not only communicate authentically the principle established by Christ himself that the OT speaks of him and his ministry, but also must be the first places we look for clues as to where in particular we should look for such typologies. For this reason, it is right to consider both the *lifting up* of the serpent and the bronze serpent *per se* as pointing towards the meaning of Christ crucified.

In this regard two points immediately suggest themselves. The first is that the serpent has already featured at a fairly crucial (pun intended) point in the story of salvation, namely at Genesis 3.[18] Is this just a coincidence? May we not at the very least speculate that in the crucifixion of

16. On the topic of prophetic failure and success, see Hayes et al., *Delay of the Parousia*.

17. See, for example, Hays, *Echoes of Scripture*, 333–35.

18. It will no doubt be pointed out that the Hebrew words are not the same at Genesis 3 and Numbers 21. The Greek in both places is *ophis*, however, as it is at John 3:14, and indeed in references to the temptation in Eden at 2 Corinthians 11:3 and Revelation 12 and 20.

Christ we see, paradoxically, that it is not Christ who is destroyed but the ancient serpent, the deceiver, his lies and his wiles finally skewered upon the tree of life. Can we not go further, and say that while the tempter in Eden offers to humanity the false promise of equality with God, to be grasped with the gift of knowledge, it is the authentic self-offering of Christ on the Cross that promises true knowledge, and with it a genuine theosis for all who are of the light?

Secondly, within the more particular context of the story of Numbers 21, we should ask why it is that Moses is instructed to raise up a serpent and not some other thing. It is because the people of Israel are being fatally bitten by poisonous serpents as punishment for their sinful murmuring against God in the wilderness. So we may say that the serpent on the pole (in the Greek of Numbers 21:9 a *sēmeion* or "sign") is a depiction of the consequence of this rejection of God, a portrayal of the effects of sin. This is entirely consonant with John's theological vision of the crucified Christ as a manifestation, at one and the same time, of the love of God for the world and of what it looks like for that love to live out a human life in the context of a world that hates the light. This typology then highlights the way in which, for the believer, to gaze upon the crucified is to look steadfastly at the consequences of human sinfulness.

These last few paragraphs have been mere sketches of the ways in which an imaginative search of the OT, following the cues of Jesus himself, for types of Christ may shed new light on his identity and the meaning of his saving work. The vital point to note, even if my suggestions be thought over-fanciful, more suited for the homily perhaps than for systematic theology, is that the principle of biblical typology is more than just the baptism of the OT. Yes, Christians claim unashamedly that the Scriptures of Israel are fully understood only in the light of Christ; but we equally claim that Christ can only be fully understood in the light of the many and varied types of him that we find in those scriptures, so that the imaginative study of the OT becomes a vital part of Christology and soteriology today, as it was when the first Christian texts were being composed under the inspiration of the Holy Spirit two thousand years ago.

Bibliography

Burkett, Delbert R. *The Son of Man Debate*. Cambridge: Cambridge University Press, 1999.

Davidson, Richard M. *Typology in Scripture: A Study of Hermeneutical Typos Structures*. Berrien Springs, MI: Andrews University Press, 1981.

Douglas, Mary. *Leviticus as Literature*. Oxford: Oxford University Press, 1999.

Farrer, Austin. *A Study in St. Mark*. London: Dacre, 1951.

Fishbane, Michael. *Biblical Interpretation in Ancient Israel*. Oxford: Oxford University Press, 1985.

Grieb, Katherine. "'Time Would Fail Me to Tell': The Identity of Jesus Christ in Hebrews." In *Seeking the Identity of Jesus Christ: A Pilgrimage*, edited by Beverley Roberts Gaventa and Richard B. Hays, 200–14. Grand Rapids: Eerdmans, 2008.

Hayes, Christopher M., et al. *When the Son of Man Didn't Come: A Constructive Proposal on the Delay of the Parousia*. Minneapolis: Fortress, 2016.

Hays, Richard B. *Echoes of Scripture in the Gospels*. Waco, TX: Baylor University Press, 2016.

Hummel, Horace D. "The Old Testament Basis of Typological Interpretation." *Biblical Research* 9 (1964) 38–50.

Moberly, Walter. "Isaiah and Jesus: How Might the Old Testament Inform Contemporary Christology?" In *Seeking the Identity of Jesus Christ: A Pilgrimage*, edited by Beverley Roberts Gaventa and Richard B. Hays, 232–48. Grand Rapids: Eerdmans, 2008.

Ounsworth, Richard. *Joshua Typology in the New Testament*. Wissenschaftliche Untersuchungen zum Neuen Testament 2/328. Tübingen: Mohr Siebeck, 2012.

Philo. "On Noah's Work as a Planter (*De Plantatione*)." In vol. 3 of *Philo*, translated and edited by F. H. Colson and G. H. Whitaker, 205–305. Loeb Classical Library 247. Cambridge, MA: Harvard University Press, 2014.

Rad, Gerhard von. "Typological Interpretation of the Old Testament." In *Essays on Old Testament Interpretation*, edited by Claus Westermann, 17–39. London: SCM, 1963.

Wright, N. T. *Jesus and the Victory of God*. London: SPCK, 1996.

Young, Frances. *Biblical Exegesis and the Formation of Christian Culture*. Cambridge: Cambridge University Press, 1987.

8

Susanna and the Son of Man in the Gospel of Matthew[1]

CATHERINE BROWN TKACZ

Bishop White Seminary

SCHOLARSHIP IN SERVICE OF the faith characterizes Patrick Hartin's career. His research is rigorous and always undertaken with an eye to nourishing and developing the understanding and spirituality of those God entrusts to his pastoral care. In his lifetime he has both seen with excitement the Church's affirmation of the value of historical biblical scholarship (*Divino Afflante Spiritu*, 1943) and also witnessed with concern the ensuing, unfortunate neglect of the unity of the Bible and the disparagement of typology. For he recognizes typology as a venerable form of exegesis operative within the Jewish Scriptures and then validated for Christians by Jesus own' use of it, making it an essential means of perceiving and exploring the unity of the Bible. Hartin's own preaching treats the role of typology and explains it to the faithful.[2]

Respect for Fr. Hartin and his life's work prompts this essay. Often over the years he and I have discussed our respective intellectual projects in hand, and always he has warmly welcomed and encouraged my work.[3] The present

---

1. The germ of this material was first presented at the Monastery of Our Lady of the Rosary, cloistered Dominican community then in Buffalo, New York, in July 2018, to the novices.

2. For instance, Fr. Hartin treated Isaac as prefiguring Christ in his sermon for the Second Sunday of Lent (Year B), February 25, 2018, Our Lady of Fatima Church, Spokane, Washington.

3. A number of times he has commended it publicly, as when he spoke of my "working so tremendously with the Old Testament typology of women as types of Christ, particularly with attention to the Greek Old Testament." Hartin, "Interpreting the Bible."

essay draws on some of those studies, especially my recovery of the Christian tradition of interpreting women as types of Christ[4] and my analysis of the structure and meaning of the pre-Christian Book of Daniel.[5] Focal in that analysis is the first woman interpreted by Christians as a type of Christ: Susanna. The synoptic Gospels themselves present her as a prophetic foreshadowing of Christ in his passion, as will be discussed below.[6]

Her role as a type of Christ in the Gospels proves to be complementary with the role of Daniel's primary vision in the revelation of Christ. The importance of Susanna and the Son of Man in Matthew's Gospel provides a striking instance of the new Christian exploration of the balance of the sexes, a motif found occasionally in the Old Testament which became a widespread pastoral theme in text and art in the early Christian era.[7] What Jesus and the Evangelist did with the Book of Daniel shows the unity of the predictive import of both prophecy and typology, the dynamic counterpart to prophecy. This is accomplished through sustained reference to a man's vision and a woman's ordeal.

The Book of Daniel shows a notable recognition of the spiritual equality of the sexes and the potential for children as well as adults to serve God.[8] The balance of the sexes which was evident in the Book of Daniel was then emphasized in the Gospels.[9] The prophet book itself is well known for having two equal halves, first court tales and then visions. At the time of Jesus, Susanna's history was still in its original position as the first chapter of the Book of Daniel. The original structure of that book emphasized two prophetic elements, one in each half of the book, one female, the other male. The first chapter of the first half, the historical half, is devoted to a woman who turns out to be *the* prophetic type of Christ with the greatest influence in the synoptic Gospels: Susanna is a type of Christ in his Passion. The first chapter of the second half, the half recounting Daniel's visions, opens with one "like a son of man," a prophetic vision of Christ, and "the Son of Man"

---

4. Eleven women are so interpreted: see in the following notes the essays on Susanna, the first and most important of the eleven. For the other women see Tkacz, "Susanna and Jephthah's Daughter" (this identifies several women); Tkacz, "'Here Am I'"; Tkacz, "Esther and Purim"; and Tkacz, "*En colligo duo ligna*," which focuses on the Sareptene but also documents Jael in this role. My monograph on the whole tradition, also identifying the two other women, is forthcoming: *Women as Types of Christ.*

5. Tkacz, "Pre-Christian Book of Daniel."

6. First presented in Tkacz, "*Aneboēsen phōnēi megalē.*"

7. Tkacz, "Doctrinal Context."

8. First noted by MacKenzie, "Meaning of the Susanna Story." See also my "Pre-Christian Book of Daniel."

9. Tkacz, "Jesus and Spiritual Equality."

turns out to be *the* self-designation used by Jesus as a prophetic indicator of himself, his passion, and his Second Coming.

Long has it been known that Daniel, with two hundred New Testament citations, ranks with Isaiah and the Psalms as the Old Testament books most quoted and alluded to in the NT.[10] Moreover, "two hundred New Testament citations" has become "230 New Testament citations," for one must add new information published in 2006, identifying thirty additional references to Susanna in the Synoptic Gospels: seventeen quotations in Matthew (fifty-two words in Greek), seven quotations in Mark (twenty-seven words) and six quotations in Luke (twelve words).[11] Thus the importance of that one prophet book within the Gospels is greater than previously thought.

Remarkably, in the first century BCE Jewish scholars in Palestine re-edited one book and one book only of the Jewish Scriptures: Daniel.[12] That historical fact suggests that the Holy Spirit was preparing for the importance of that prophet book in the life and teachings of Jesus.

The Son of Man and Jesus' Self-Revelation in Matthew

Jesus wove Daniel's first vision into his ministry and prophecy. Eighty-four passages in the Gospels record that Jesus called himself "the Son of Man."[13] More than any other evangelist, Matthew attests this, doing so thirty times.[14] As important as the *Egō eimi* statements are in the Gospel of John are the "Son of Man" statements in the synoptic Gospels, and for the same reason: these are prominent ways—perhaps the most prominent ways—that Jesus revealed his identity, not just as the Messiah, but God

---

10. E.g., Evans, "Daniel in the New Testament," 490.

11. Tkacz, "*Aneboēsen phōnēi megalēi*," 433, 469, 472–73.

12. Previously it has been documented that the synoptic Gospels overwhelmingly cite the history of Susanna from the new, Jewish Palestinian edition of the Book of Daniel, which later Theodotion preserved in his edition of the Bible: Tkacz, "*Aneboēsen phōnēi megalēi*," 474–75; Barthelémy, *Devanciers d'Aquila*, 144–48; Di Lella, "Textual History of Theodotion-Daniel," 595–96, 604–5.

13. Brown, *Death of the Messiah*, 1:507, and vol. 2, Appendix VIII; Tkacz, *Alētheia Hellēnikē*, 47–48.

14. "Son of Man": Matt 8:20; 9:1; 10:23; 11:19; 12:8, 32, 40; 13:37, 41; 16:13, 27, 28; 17:9, 12, 22; 18:11; 19:28; 20:18, 28; 24:28, 30 *bis*, 37, 39, 44; 25:31; 26:2, 24 *bis*, 45, 64. In addition to these thirty passages in Matthew, "Son of Man" occurs twenty-six times in Luke, fifteen in Mark, and thirteen in John. With reason W. D. Davies considers that "Lord" and "Son of Man" are "primary for Matthew." Davies, *Sermon on the Mount*, 96–99.

incarnate.[15] Though some scholars hold that Jesus' usage of "the Son of Man" is not "authentic" or "pure," or that it is incompatible with Jesus being "sane,"[16] scholars who affirm the validity of Jesus' action include Pope John Paul II and Raymond Brown.[17]

Matthew throughout his Gospel reported Jesus' words drawing on the Book of Daniel and then, in the final chapter, Matthew himself drew on the language of Daniel's vision. As an aid to exploring this, here are the few pertinent verses from Daniel's description of that "vision" (*horama*: Dan 7:1)[18]:

> [v. 9] I beheld till thrones (*thronoi*) were placed and the Ancient of Days[19] sat (*ekathēto*): his garment was white as snow (*Kai to enduma autou hōsei chiōn leukon*), . . . his throne (*thronos*) like flames of fire. . . . [v. 10] . . . The judgment sat (*kritērion ekathisen*) . . . . [v. 13] I beheld there in my vision (*horamati mou*) of the night, and lo, with the clouds of heaven one like a son of man came[20] (*meta*[21] *tōn nephelōn tou ouranou ōs huios anthrōpou erchomenos*[22] *ēn*) even unto the Ancient of Days.[23] . . . [v. 14] [And the Ancient of Days gave him] power and glory

15. The point was made in a novel way by Ford, "Son of Man—Euphemism?" Others who affirm that Jesus himself is the source of the self-title "Son of Man" include Caragounis, *Son of Man*, 165; Zorn, "Jesus' Self-Designation"; Sabourin, "About Jesus' Self-Understanding"; Longenecker, "Self-Designation of Jesus."

16. Not a "pure form" or an "authentic interpretation" of Daniel: Casey, *Son of Man*, 56–61. Not sane: Knox, *Death of Christ*, 58, 65–67; Higgins, *Son of Man*; discussed by Caragounis, *Son of Man*, 150–51nn67, 72.

17. John Paul II, "Jesus Christ, Son of Man"; Caragounis, *Son of Man*; Brown, *Death of the Messiah*, 1:507, 2:1473–88; Ratzinger, *Jesus of Nazareth*, 321–25. See also n15 above.

18. I use the Douai Rheims translation in this essay, sometimes adjusting the diction or word order to mirror the Greek. For instance, *thronos* I always translate "throne" rather than sometimes "seat." *Horama* is in LXX Dan 7:1, 2, 7, 13, etc. In Theodotion-Daniel are both the cognate verb *horaseis* and the phrase *etheōroun en horamai mou tēs nuktos*, "I saw in my vision of the night." The phrase is also in Theod Dan 7:7, 15; and LXX 7:13. The predicate *etheōroun* recurs in Dan 7:9 (both Theodotion and LXX).

19. On this unique name, in Dan 9, 13, 22, see Tkacz, "Pre-Christian Book of Daniel," 187–88. Arrestingly, this name, *to Palaios tōn Hēmerōn*, is a variant of Daniel's epithet for one of the false Elders who condemned Susanna: him Daniel named *pepalaiōmene hēmerōn kakōn* (Theod Dan 13:52). In short, the true Judge is the reverse of the false judge.

20. I revised the word order here to preserve that of the Greek.

21. LXX: *epi*.

22. LXX: *ērcheto*.

23. The LXX lacks the articles with "ancient of days."

(LXX: *doksa*)[24] and a kingdom (*basileia*) . . . that shall not be destroyed. (Dan 7:9–10, 13–14)

An angel explained much of the vision to him, concluding by repeating, "And judgment shall sit (*kritērion kathisei*)" (Dan 7:26).[25] Phrases, ideas and diction from Daniel's record of this vision recur in the Lord's teaching. The specific form *erchomenos* ("coming") Jesus used thrice and other forms of the verb, eight more times.[26]

Since 1920[27] the standard approach to the Son of Man sayings (hereafter "SM sayings") has been to start by categorizing them, although the resulting systems show no consensus on either how to classify them or how to assess their authenticity.[28] The approach taken here is to accept the Gospel of Matthew as a coherent, authoritative text. After all, what the celebrant proclaims after reading the Gospel lection at mass is "The Word of the Lord," not "A first-century document." It is fitting to consider both how Jesus' auditors would have understood his words initially and also how his followers, after he had arisen and instructed them, would have apprehended more of his meaning. In short, Matthew's account is a report of what occurred, and that report is embedded in narration which interprets (through ordering, selection of events and details, rhetoric, etc.) and clarifies what occurred. A benefit for the reader of and listener to the Gospel is being able to recreate, to some degree, the experience of those who were first encountering Jesus.

In Matthew's Gospel, the first six citations of Old Testament prophecies are made by the narrator, thrice also naming the prophet (Jeremiah and Isaiah).[29] Next Jesus declared he had come to fulfil the law and the prophets (Matt 5:17) and thereafter both he and the narrator quoted and sometimes named prophets.[30] Interwoven through Jesus' discourses during the three years of his public ministry are his statements about the Son of Man, referring

24. Theodotian Daniel has *timē*.

25. LXX: *hē krisis kathisetai*.

26. *Erchomenos*: Matt 16:28; 24:43; 26:64. Other forms: Matt 10:23; 11:19; 16:27; 18:11; 20:28; 24:27, 44; 25:31.

27. Foakes-Jackson and Lake, *Beginnings of Christianity*, 1:368–84. Bultmann popularized their three-part schema: Bultmann, *Theology of the New Testament*, 1:30.

28. For details of scholars and schema and controversies, see Caragounis, *Son of Man*, 145–67.

29. Matt 1:23 quoting Isa 7:14; 2:6 quoting Mic 5:2; 2:15 quoting Hos 11:1; 2:18 naming and quoting Jeremiah (Jer 31:15); and 3:3 and 4:14, each naming and quoting Isaiah (Isa 40:3; 9:1).

30. Jesus does this (the list here excludes the Son of Man passages, listed in n14 above): Matt 8:17; 9:13; 11:10; 12:7; 13:14–15; 15:8–9; 21:13, 15–16, 42; 22:44; 24:3 (citing Dan 9:27), 31; 26:31. Narration: Matt 12:17–21; 13:35; 21:4–5; 27:9–10, 35, 43, 46.

to himself. This self-designation is initially provocative and mysterious. Is it a reference to Ezekiel? To Daniel's first vision? Whatever its background, Jesus elevated the phrase into a title, a change expressed in the Greek by adding articles to the Old Testament phrase, in effect putting capital letters on it.[31] The words *huios anthropou* in Dan 7 have become ho *huios* tou *anthrōpou* in the Gospels.[32] A "son of man" has become "the Son of Man."

Matthew's first report of Jesus using the phrase seems a puzzling aside. A scribe had declared he wanted to follow Jesus, who replied, "The foxes have holes and the birds of the air nests, but the Son of Man has nowhere to lay his head" (Matt 8:20). Quite different is the next SM saying, in which Jesus asserted his authority: in response to the crowd's questioning his forgiving a paralytic's sins, Jesus healed the man, explaining that healing as a sign to show that the Son of Man has the power to forgive sins (Matt 9:6).

Calling aside his twelve disciples (Matt 10:1),[33] Jesus empowered them to heal and commissioned them to preach to and to heal the house of Israel. This will not be finished, he observed, before the Son of Man "comes" (10:23). This predicate is *elthēi*, from *erchomai*, a verb prominent in Daniel's first vision. Thus, privately, the first hint of the importance of that vision has been given to the twelve.

The next SM saying is highly public. The Lord told the multitude that this generation rejected John the Baptist for neither eating nor drinking, but contrarily rejected the Son of Man also, who came (*ēlthen*)[34] eating and drinking (Matt 11:18–19). Shortly afterwards, when the Pharisees objected to the hungry disciples' plucking and eating grain on the sabbath, Jesus responded with a building series of comments that indicate more and more clearly his divinity. First he implied this with types: he drew a parallel between himself and David, who fed at need on the Temple's loaves of propitiation, setting aside the law (Matt 12:4), and Jesus then compared himself to the Temple itself, declaring, "there is here a greater (*meizon*) than the Temple" (Matt 12:6).[35] Quoting from Hosea, Jesus made the words of The Lord his own

---

31. On the role of articles in New Testament Greek, see Sandmel, "Son of Man," 355. This wording, with the articles, is evidently in all manuscripts: see the apparatus of Aland et al., *Greek New Testament*. Others agree that Son of Man is a title, derived from Daniel 7: e.g., Caragounis, *Son of Man*, ch. IV. Another instance within the New Testament of the use of articles is in Jesus' dialogue with the woman at the well (John 4:10–11): he told her of the "water of life" (*hydōr zōn*) and the idea arrested her so she asked about it as "the Water of Life" (*to hydōr to zōn*).

32. This change, of course, probably reflects something distinctive in the Aramaic Jesus presumably was speaking.

33. *Tous dōdeka mathētas autou.*

34. From *erchomai.*

35. "Greater than" presents himself as superior to the type, the Temple: on

speech: "I desire mercy and not sacrifice" (Hos 6:6 in Matt 12:7). These words can evoke recollection of a nearby verse in Hosea which foretells that God will revive [someone] after two days, raising [him] up on the third day, so that [he] lives (Hos 6:3). With that evocation of prophecy hovering, Jesus spoke directly about the sabbath in a way that implied his divinity, for he concluded this speech with emphasis by final position on "Son of Man": "For the Lord of the sabbath is the Son of Man" (Matt 12:8).[36]

The intimation of divinity is again in the next SM statement. Jesus said blasphemy will be forgiven, but not blasphemy against the Holy Spirit; that speaking against the Son of Man will be forgiven, but not speaking against the Holy Spirit (Matt 12:31–32). By equating speech against himself with blasphemy, he presented himself, the Son of Man, as divine.

Then a sign (sēmeion) was asked, and Jesus offered Jonah as a prophetic prefiguration of himself, mysteriously alluding to his passion: "Just as (hōsper) Jonah was in the belly of the whale three days and three nights, just so (houtōs) the Son of Man will be in the heart of the earth for three days and three nights" (Matt 12:40).[37] Male and female models of repentance and wisdom follow: he presented the men of Ninevah and the Queen of Sheba as judges of this generation because, behold, a greater (pleion) than Jonah, a greater (pleion) than Solomon is here (Matt 12:41–42).

The next SM speech Matthew recounted expands Jesus' range of predictive materials to include parables. First Matthew reminded us that the Psalms foretold this: "I will open my mouth in parables" (Ps 77:2 in Matt 13:35). Then Jesus recounted the parable of the sower to the crowds, after which in private he explained it to the twelve, first identifying the sower as "the Son of Man" (Matt 13:37). He added, "the Son of Man shall send his angels" (Matt 13:41) to gather the wicked and cast them into the furnace. "Then shall the just shine (eklampsousin) as the sun" (Matt 13:43).[38] Clearly this is a prophecy of divine judgment, with the Son of Man instrumental.

The pivotal use of the title is in Jesus' private catechesis of his twelve disciples when they have arrived in Cesarea Philippi.[39] He asked them,

---

syntactical ways of indicating typology in scripture, see, e.g., Ounsworth, "On Biblical Typology," 146.

36. I reorder the sentence according to the Greek: kyrios gar estin tou sabbatou ho huios tou anthropou.

37. On the rhetorical pattern of "Just as . . . so" to indicate typology, see Fishbane, Biblical Interpretation, 352–53. He cites Josh 3:7; 4:14, 23; Isa 11:16; and a variant pattern in Hos 2:17.

38. The idea and predicate (eklampsousin) are from Theod Dan 12:13; the LXX has phanousin. Cf. Wis 3:7: analampsousin.

39. On the identification of women among the larger group of Jesus' disciples, see

"Whom do men say that the Son of Man is?" (Matt 16:13). After some reply John the Baptist, Elijah, Jeremiah or another prophet, Jesus asked them personally, "But whom do you say that I am?" Peter then professed, "You are the Christ, the Son of the living God" (Matt 16:15–16).[40] Jesus' clear equation of "Son of Man" with himself is matched by the clarity of Peter's response. What follows is the Lord's prophecy "to his disciples" (Matt 16:24) of his Second Coming and the Last Judgment: "For the Son of Man shall come (*hos huios tou anthrōpou erchesthai*[41]) in the glory (*doksēi*) of his Father with his angels, and then will he render to every man according to his works" (Matt 16:27). They will "see the Son of Man coming (*ton huion tou anthrōpou erchomenon*)[42] in his kingdom (*basileiai*)" (Matt 16:28). This epitomizes Daniel's first vision: the son of man coming in glory to judge and set up the eternal kingdom. For the first time, Jesus used more of the details from Daniel's first vision (Dan 7:9). He had already been using *erchomai*, a verb focal in Daniel's report of that vision. Now Jesus used the exact form of that verb and more of the language and specifics from that vision. Daniel saw one like a "son of man coming (*huios anthrōpou erchomenos*) with the clouds of heaven before the Ancient of Days, to judge and receive the kingdom (Dan 7:13).[43] Jesus' term, "glory" (*doksēi*) simultaneously echoes Daniel's first vision and also anticipates the imminent event of the Lord's Transfiguration.

This session of Jesus with the twelve was the turning point: hereafter the Lord's Son of Man predictions were more detailed. This first private and detailed SM saying prophesied the Second Coming. After that Jesus explicitly predicted his passion and resurrection, sometimes through SM sayings. Only near the end, only to the unbelieving Sanhedrin would he again deliver a SM speech, making it the fullest reference to the Second Coming in the language of Daniel. Until then, between Peter's profession of faith and the trial before the high priests, Jesus' SM speeches ceased to be public but were

---

Butler, "The Importance of Retrieving the 'Women of Galilee,'" in this volume. She also treats a SM speech related to these women (Luke 24:4–7; Butler, "Women of Galilee," 206). Much needed is a study of the diction of *hoi mathētai* and *mathētai* (without the article) within the individual Gospels to refine our knowledge of when the noun may be generic and when it is specific to "the twelve disciples." The article is in, e.g., Matt 18:1; 19:23, 25; and several passages cited below.

40. One notes that uniquely Jesus here calls Peter "Simon *bar-Jonah*," right after the Lord has referred to the sign of Jonah. Naming Simon thus may indicate in a novel way that Simon-Peter is in the line of Jesus, spiritually.

41. From *erchomai*.

42. From *erchomai*.

43. *Meta tōn nephelōn tou ouranou ōs huios anthrōpou erchomenos ēn.*

given to the twelve disciples in private. Matthew's Gospel thus shared with the faithful what had initially been imparted only to the twelve.

The point is worth clarifying. The early SM sayings were to "the multitudes" (Matt 11:19) or large groups in which the scribes and Pharisees were vocal (Matt 12:8, 32, 38, 40). Likewise the parable of the sower Jesus told to "great multitudes" (Matt 13:2, 32), but then he sent them away, went inside with his disciples (13:36) and explained to them that the sower is the Son of Man (13:37, 41). That private catechesis of the twelve culminated in Peter's pivotal profession of faith in the divinity of the Son of Man (Matt 16:15–16) and Jesus' prophecy of his Second Coming (Matt 16:27–28). Thereafter he imparted his SM sayings to the disciples (Matt 17:21; 18:1, 11), to Peter and the disciples on the coast of Judea (Matt 19:1, 28),[44] to the Twelve apart (*kat' idian*) while going to Jerusalem (Matt 20:17, 18, 28), to them privately (*kat' idian*) on the Mount of Olives (Matt 24:3, 30 *bis*, 37, 39, 44; 25:31), to the Twelve (*tōn dōdeka*)[45] at the Last Supper (Matt 26:20, 24), and at Gethsemane to Peter, James, and John (Matt 26:37, 45). Ultimately, he spoke fully of the Son of Man to the Sanhedrin (Matt 26:62).

What followed the pivotal private catechesis was the Transfiguration, when three disciples had the evidence of their own eyes that the Son of Man was indeed native to heavenly glory. Moreover, both the event of the Transfiguration and Matthew's diction in describing it recall Dan 7:9, for the prophet had seen the resplendent Ancient of Days and "his garment was white (*leukon*) as snow." Likewise, the three disciples saw Jesus transfigured and "his raiment became white (*leuka*) as light" (Matt 17:2).[46] Notably Jesus called his Transfiguration a "vision" (*horama*) when he instructed his disciples to tell it to no one until the Son of Man had arisen (Matt 17:9); *horama* is the word Daniel used to identify his experience (Dan 7:1, 3).

Earlier Jesus had used the self-designation "Son of Man" when comparing himself to John the Baptist (Matt 11:19); he renewed this comparison in the SM speech which follows the Transfiguration. As John suffered, "so the Son of Man shall suffer," Jesus explained (Matt 17:12). In Galilee, he elaborated in detail: "The Son of Man shall be betrayed into the hands of

---

44. That he is speaking only to the twelve is indicated by the article with the noun—*hoi mathētai* (Matt 19:23, 25)—but is definitely shown by his saying that his auditors shall sit on twelve thrones (*thronous*) judging the twelve tribes of Israel (Matt 19:28).

45. Aland et al., *Greek New Testament*, notes that some manuscripts add *mathētōn*.

46. Most manuscripts have *phōs* in Matt 17:2, but it is interesting that the Vulgate has *nix* ("snow") as in Dan 7:9. The structure of the clause *ta de himatia **autou** egeneto **leuka** hōs to phōs* (Matt 17:2) mimics Dan 7:9 (*Kai to enduma **autou** hōsei chiōn **leuka***), though the only words in common (emboldened in this note) are *autou* (his) and *leukon / leuka* (white).

men, and they shall kill him, and on the third day he shall rise again" (Matt 17:21–22). Soon he explained, "For the Son of Man is come (*ēlthen*[47]) to save that which was lost" (Matt 18:11).[48]

Next, in Judea Jesus foretold to Peter and the other disciples that "when the Son of Man shall sit on the throne of his glory (*thronou doksēs*), you also shall sit on twelve thrones (*thronous*) judging (*krinontes*) the twelve tribes of Israel" (Matt 19:28). Here the ideas and very diction of "throne" and "judgment" are reprised from Daniel's first vision, in which he beheld thrones (*thronoi*) placed, and, once the Ancient of Days assumed a throne (*thronos*), it was a time of judgment (*kritērion*, Dan 7:9–10).[49]

For Jesus' most specific prophecy of his passion and the last one expressed as a SM saying, he took his disciples apart (*kat' idian*):

> Behold, we go up to Jerusalem, and the Son of Man shall be betrayed to the chief priests and the scribes, and they shall condemn him to death. And shall deliver him to the Gentiles to be mocked, and scourged, and crucified, and on the third day he shall rise again. (Matt 20:18–19)

He clarified the purpose of this, stating that "the Son of Man is . . . come (*ēlthen*)[50] . . . to give his life a redemption for many" (Matt 20:28). Thereafter, until the Last Supper, all of Jesus' remaining SM sayings, by Matthew's account, refer not to his Passion but to his Second Coming. These pronouncements he uttered in Jerusalem.

On the Mount of Olives two days before the Pasch (Matt 26:1), the disciples asked Jesus privately for a sign marking the end of the world. He replied at length (chapters 24–25), quoting from "Daniel the prophet" and seven times speaking of the Son of Man. A linguistic note is helpful here, for modern translations blur a distinction in the Greek: this passage repeatedly uses the verb *erchomai* ("come") from Daniel's vision, and also the noun *parousia*, often translated "coming." That noun, however, is from *pareimi*, 'to be present,' and might more accurately be rendered Abiding Presence, as it

---

47. From *erchomai*.

48. Aland et al., *Greek New Testament*, omit v. 11, implicitly dismissing it as an interpolated variant from Luke 19:10. However, Matt 18:11 is in Jerome's Vulgate (*venit enim Filius hominis salvare quod perierat*), indicating that it was in the ancient manuscripts he had consulted: *Biblia Sacra iuxta vulgatam versionem*. The modern Vatican edition of the Vulgate, for use in worship, lacks the verse in question, presumably in imitation of the consensus of modern biblical scholars: *Nova Vulgata Bibliorum Sacrorum editio*.

49. The specific four-word Greek phrase for "on the throne of his glory" (Matt 19:28), however, is not in the Old Testament but occurs several times in the *parables*: Caragounis, *Son of Man*, 171.

50. From *erchomai*.

refers to the state that Christ will bring into being when he returns. Many would render *parousia* as "arrival" and construe it as the moment of return. I suggest it may indicate both the instantaneous bringing about of his Abiding Presence, never to end, and also that unending presence itself.

Therefore, the phrase Abiding Presence will be used here for the noun *parousia*, to highlight the relationship between it and the verbs of "coming":

> [v. 3] The disciples came to him privately, saying: Tell us when shall these things be? And what shall be the sign of thy Abiding Presence, and of the consummation of the world? And Jesus answering, said to them: . . . [v. 15] When therefore you shall see the "abomination of desolation"[51] which was spoken of by Daniel the prophet (*Daniēl tou prophētou*), standing in the holy place: . . . [v. 27] For as lightning cometh (*astrapē exerchetai*[52]) out of the East, and appeareth even unto the West: so shall the Abiding Presence of the Son of Man be. . . . [v. 30] And then shall appear the sign of the Son of Man in heaven (*en ouranōi*) . . . and they shall see "the Son of Man coming in the clouds of heaven with much power and majesty" (*ton **huion tou anthrōpou erchomenon epi tōn nephelōn tou ouranou** meta dynameōs kai doksēs pollēs*)[53] . . . [v. 37] As in the days of Noah, so shall also the Abiding Presence of the Son of Man be. . . . [v.39] So also shall the Abiding Presence of the Son of Man be . . . . [v.44] Be ready, because at what hour you know not the Son of Man will come (*erchetai*). . . . [Matt 25:31] And when the Son of Man shall come (*elthēi*) in his glory (*doksēi*), and all the angels with him, then shall he sit (*kathisei*) upon the throne (*thronou*) of his glory (*doksēs*).[54]

In addition to the full quotation verbatim of eight words from Daniel 7:13 (emboldened above), Jesus echoed the diction of coming, glory, heaven, the accompaniment of angels, sitting on a throne, and the idea of judgment. Throughout, the sevenfold reiteration of "the Son of Man" clarifies that these details are deliberate echoes of Daniel's vision, now explained more fully by the Son of Man himself.

The next two SM sayings Jesus gave privately to his disciples, at the Last Supper and in Gethsemane. These prophecies foretold his betrayal: "The Son of Man indeed goeth, as it is written of him, but woe to that

51. *Bdelugma tēs erēmōseōs*: exact quotation from Dan 9:27.

52. From *erchomai*.

53. Matt 24:30, Luke 21:27, quoting Daniel 7:13. The Greek for "with clouds of heaven" is unique to Daniel and is not in the *parables*: Caragounis, *Son of Man*, 172.

54. Matt 24:3, 15, 27, 30, 37, 39, 44; 25:31.

man by whom the Son of Man shall be betrayed" (Matt 26:24). And in Gethsemane, the third time that he awakened the sleeping trio of disciples: "Behold the hour is at hand, and the Son of Man shall be betrayed into the hands of sinners" (Matt 26:45).

The culmination of all the SM sayings concluded his trial before the Sanhedrin. Silent at first, at last the Lord spoke, a speech imbued with Daniel's first vision: "Hereafter you shall see the Son of Man sitting (*kathēmenon*) at the right hand of the power [of God], and coming in the clouds of heaven" (. . . *ton huion tou anthrōpou . . . erchomenon epi tōn nephelōn tou ouranou*, Matt 26:64).[55] This is the fullest use of Daniel's first vision—details, language, direct quotation. The sitting in judgment is in Dan 7:9, 10. The coming of the Son of Man is in Dan 7:13: *epi tōn nephelōn tou ouranou ōs huios anthrōpou erchomenos ēn*. Jesus quoted eight words from that verse: the two-word phrase "son of man," the present participle for "coming," and a five-word phrase for "in the clouds of heaven." By juxtaposition to that quotation, the word "sitting" is shown to be a ninth word taken from that vision. In Jesus' statement, it is because God transcends time that the Son of Man can simultaneously sit beside God the Father and come in the clouds of heaven. This is the Parousia, simultaneously the Arrival *and* the Abiding Presence. Thus is Daniel's vision reanimated by Jesus. And the Sanhedrin recognized Jesus' declaration as a claim to divinity.[56] Caiaphas tore his robe and declared, "He has uttered blasphemy."

The surprising clincher of the series is a reference by the Evangelist himself to Daniel's first vision (Matt 28:2–3). Because this passage does not use the words "Son of Man" one might miss its pertinence to this discussion. In a seven-word phrase Matthew described the angel who had appeared with a great seismic upheaval at the tomb of the Lord, rolled the stone aside, and sat upon it: "his face was like lightning (*astrapē*)."[57] This recalls Jesus' declaring that his Abiding Presence will be like lightning (*astrapē*, Matt 24:27). Matthew continued, "and his garment was white as snow": *kai to enduma autou leukon hōs chiōn* (Matt 28:3).[58] The first four words are taken, in exact order, from Dan 7:9, which, describing the Ancient of Days, reported that his garment was *hōsei chiōn leukon* (white as snow). In each case, the final three words are also identical, differing only in word order,

55. *Ap arti opsesthe ton huion tou anthrōpou kathēmenon ek deksiōn dynameōs kai erchomenon epi tōn nephelōn tou ouranou* (Matt 26:64). Compare Mark 14:62; Luke 22:69.

56. "In the final analysis, it was Jesus' claim to be the Son of Man . . . that brought about his condemnation by the Sanhedrin." Caragounis, *Son of Man*, 245, also 164.

57. *Aggelos gar kyriou katabas ex ouranou . . . hē eidea autou hōs astrapē* (Matt 28:2, 3). The angel appeared after *seismos . . . megas*.

58. See also Matt 17:2, discussed above, and Mark 9:3; Luke 9:29; Acts 1:10.

hōs being a variant of *hōsei*. That statement had been alluded to in Matthew's account of the Transfiguration, now it is used in full.

And to whom does this resplendent angel speak? Women. "Mary Magdalene and the other Mary" (Matt 28:1). The seismic arrival and action of the angel so terrified the guards that they became "as dead" (*nekroi*, v. 4), but the women withstood the presence of the heavenly messenger. He commissioned the women (*gynaiksin*) to bear the news to the disciples (*tois mathētais*, v. 5). Earlier, the Transfiguration with its echoes of Daniel's first vision had been shown only to Peter, James and John; now the echoes of that vision recur at the empty tomb, witnessed only by women and attested by them first to the remaining eleven and through them to all Christians through the ages.

The most reasonable assessment of the SM sayings is that Jesus uttered them and that he did so because he knew their meaning and intended it. I suggest that Jesus emphasized "the Son of Man" as his main self-identification because it is an incarnational title. That is, God inspired Daniel to see in his first vision "one like a son of man" coming in the clouds of heaven to become the enthroned judge because God was preparing for his followers to recognize that their God, their judge, whose kingdom is eternal, is Incarnate. Jesus elevated the spare phrase "son of man" into the arresting title "the Son of Man" to highlight the powerful importance of his human nature in salvation. The titles "Son of God" and "the Lord" could not convey that. It is easy to overlook that in "the Son of Man" the word "man" (*anthrōpos*) means "human being." Yes, Jesus is in fact male, and therefore "man" in both senses, human and male. But the title Son of Man emphasizes his human nature, and the specific *anthrōpos* whose son he is, is the woman Mary. The wording of the title points to his humanity; Jesus' use of the title points to his divinity. "Son of Man" is the incarnational title par excellence.

Yet many modern scholars think that Jesus could not have understood the implications of calling himself the Son of Man and theorize that after his death his followers devised the title and pretended he had used it. In response Raymond E. Brown argues that if one holds that "later Christians 'retrojected' the phrase onto Jesus," then:

> one faces two major difficulties: Why was this title so massively retrojected, being placed on Jesus' lips on a scale far outdistancing the retrojection of "the Messiah," "the Son of God," and "the Lord"? And if this title was first fashioned by the early church, [not Jesus,] why has it left almost no traces in nonGospel NT literature, something not true of the other titles?[59]

---

59. Brown, *Death of the Messiah*, 1:507.

Pointedly, Chrys Caragounis, asks, "What clear or convincing arguments are there to show that while the Church could create the concept of Son of Man, Jesus could not?"[60] A related criticism is the doubt that the Lord would have revisited his own statements, notably in thrice uttering "Son of Man" prophecies of his imminent sufferings.[61] Surely, however, in a span of three years a teacher offering the same course a number of times should be expected to return to key points of his message, especially as finals approach. That is simply good pedagogy.

In sum, thirty-one passages in Matthew draw definitely from Daniel's first vision. Three quotations of seven-to-eight words from that vision confirm that each SM saying by Jesus may be taken as a deliberate allusion to it. Thirty passages use the title Son of Man, which in the Old Testament is a two-word phrase (accounting for sixty words overall in Matthew).[62] Also, diction from the vision is echoed, with forms of *erchomai* (come) used eleven times,[63] *doksa* (glory) five times, *thronos* (throne) twice, *leukos* (white) twice, and, at least once each, the following: *kritērion* and cognates (judgment), *kathēmenon* (sit), *horama* (vision), *basileia* (kingdom).[64] These strengthen the association of Daniel's primary vision with Jesus' prophecies. So do the other quotations from Daniel's visions, e.g., a three-word phrase from Dan 9:27 in Matt 24:15 and the evocation of Dan 12:13 in Matt 13:43.[65] Finally, the full quotations from Daniel 7 make indisputable that the primary referent for all the SM sayings is that vision: eight words in Matt 24:30, nine in Matt 26:64, and seven in Matt 28:3 (twenty-four words). Thus over one hundred words from throughout the Gospel of Matthew are clearly derived from Daniel 7, the most frequent borrowing being "the Son of Man." Nearly all of this was uttered by Jesus himself.

Susanna and Matthew's Passion Narrative

Quite different is the role of Susanna's history within Matthew's Gospel, for this coordinated, sustained constellation of parallels is entirely in the

60. Caragounis, *Son of Man*, 157.

61. Brown, *Death of the Messiah*, 2:1476–80, reviews scholars who raise that objection.

62. In the Gospels the phrase is expanded with the articles into a four-word phrase; only the two words of the original phrase constitute the borrowing from Daniel.

63. See n26 above.

64. *Doksa*: Matt 16:27; 19:28; 34:30; 25:31 *bis*; *thronos* in Matt 19:28 *bis*; 25:31; *basileia*, e.g., in Matt 16:28; *kritērion* and cognates (judgment) in Matt 19:28; *leukos* in Matt 17:2; 28:33; *kathēmenon* in Matt 26:64; *horama* in Matt 17:9.

65. See n38 above.

narration. The Gospel writers, especially Matthew, found in the history of Susanna nothing less than a detailed narrative template for the synoptic accounts of the arrest, trial and death of Christ.[66] The many parallels between the experiences of Susanna and Jesus span their entire ordeals and are often expressed in the Gospels through direct verbal borrowings from Susanna's history: Each is arrested in a garden and endures two trials. In the first trial, each is condemned to death by the "elders of the people" on the testimony of two false witnesses. The judge of the second trial proclaims, "I am innocent of the blood of this one." When death is imminent, Susanna and Jesus each "exclaimed in a great voice, 'My God,'" Susanna continued, "Behold! I die!" Her words foreshadow the actual death of Jesus. Yet, until I published these findings in 2006, the longest treatment of Susanna and the Gospels had been a footnote in a Dutch dissertation.[67]

At least thirty aspects of the experience of Jesus in his Passion as recounted by Matthew correspond to the experience of Susanna. Often more than details of experience are common to Susanna and Jesus. The number and length of direct verbal parallels between the history of Susanna and Matthew's account of the Passion is striking: five individual terms,[68] one set of two words, five three-word phrases, two four-word phrases, two five-word clauses, and two six-word clauses, differing only in name (Susanna, Jesus) or personal pronoun (her, him). These seventeen verbal parallels comprise fifty-two words of Matthew 26–27. That is, Matthew may draw upon the history of Susanna at least as extensively as upon Psalm 22.[69]

Here are the specific parallels:

Matt 26:2—"After two days." Jesus prophesied when his betrayal would occur, using a temporal reference that echoes a detail in the history of Susanna. Matthew reported Jesus' prophecy, when he neared Jerusalem, that "after two days (*hēmeras*) is the Pasch, and the Son of Man is betrayed

---

66. This section is derived from Tkacz, "*Aneboēsen phōnēi megalēi*," 452–68. Consult that essay for fuller bibliography and syntactical discussions as well as for the role of Susanna's narrative in Mark and Luke. For the first outlines of this thesis, see Tkacz, "Singing Women's Words," 308–9; Tkacz, "Susanna and Jephthah's Daughter," 281–84. For Susanna in this role in art see esp. my essay "Susanna as a Type of Christ."

67. Tilborg, *Jewish Leaders in Matthew*, 92–93n2. I argue that the numerous parallels between the accounts of Susanna and of the Lord's passion establish her as a type of Christ, but Hamilton surprisingly thinks they preclude typology and indicate only a "story." Hamilton, "Blood and Secrets," 126n64.

68. Jewish exegesis "a single word" can "recall a whole context." Doeve, *Jewish Hermeneutics in the Synoptic Gospels*, 134.

69. On Psalm 22 in the Passion narratives, see esp. Brown, *Death of the Messiah*, 2:1455–65, who notes, "no psalm offers a parallel to the basic Gospel outline of Jesus' passion." Brown, *Death of the Messiah*, 1452.

and crucified" (Matt 26:2).[70] Immediately Matthew reported the gathering of the chief priests to plan the capture of Jesus by subtlety (26:3–4), Judas' arrangement with them to betray Jesus soon followed (26:14–16), and then Judas betrayed the Lord in the garden (Matt 26:47–49). The temporal parallel for Jesus' being betrayed "after two days" is in Susanna's experience: after the Elders conspired against her, it was "on the third day (hēmeras)" that they accosted her in the garden (Theod Sus. 14–15).[71]

Matt 26:3—"The Elders of the People." To identify those who condemned Jesus, Matthew three times used the distinctive phrase "elders of the people" (*presbyteroi tou laou*).[72] He used it first when the elders plotted against Jesus a few days before the Pasch (Matt 26:3). The identical phrase is used in the history of Susanna to explain why the people credited the testimony of the Elders: they were believed "as elders of the people" (*hōs presbyterois tou laou*).[73] The phrase is as rare in the Old Testament as it is in the New. Used originally to designate the authoritative rulers, the phrase is later found in Isaiah's warning that the Lord will judge the "elders of the people" and in the specific case of the "Elders of the people" who condemn Susanna wrongly.[74] Thus the phrase in Matthew indicates both those who had the primary responsibility to behave righteously and also the seriousness of their defection. The same double-edged meaning is evident in the history of Susanna.

Matt 26:2–4—The intention to condemn to death. Two days before the Pasch, the high priests planned how they might take Jesus by treachery and "put him to death" (*apokteinōsin*).[75] Likewise the Elders treacherously plotted to arrange a legal death for Susanna, for they intended to accuse Susanna of adultery, a capital offense, if she did not submit to them.[76]

The garden. Susanna and Jesus were alike in habitually seeking the solitude of a specific garden, she for refreshment and cleansing, he for prayer. All

---

70. Thus one of Jesus' references to the Son of Man occurs in the same sentence with the first parallel to Susanna's history. No one on first reading could see that here both strains of Daniel material are conjoined.

71. "Theod Sus" refers to wording exclusive to Theodotian; "LXX Sus" refers to wording exclusive to LXX, and "Sus" refers to wordings in common.

72. Matt 26:3, 47; 27:1, see also Matt 21:23.

73. Theod Sus 41.

74. Theod Sus 41.

75. Matt 26:2–4. The term *apokteinō*, "kill, put to death," is used twelve times in the Gospels: notably, Jesus foretold his death (Matt 16:21; 17:23; Luke 18:33; cf. Luke 20:14–15).

76. Theod Sus 20–21. For the verb in the history of Susanna, see Collins, *Commentary on Daniel*, 422n11.

four Gospels show that Jesus often went to this garden and that his disciples knew this.[77] For Susanna's daily walk, see Theod Sus 7, 15. The earliest, enduring tradition of depicting Susanna shows her in prayer in the garden.[78]

Matt 26:14–16—The plot to entrap: The Elders and Judas. The Elders in the history of Susanna plotted against her, betrayed her, falsely testified against her and condemned her. Thus they foreshadowed the religious leaders who condemned Jesus, the false witnesses against him, and Judas. The Elders and Judas knew that the one they wished to apprehend habitually resorted to a garden. On the Elders' knowledge, see Sus 8, 12, 15. As one of Jesus' disciples, Judas would have known that the Mount of Olives was his customary retreat. Like the Elders, Judas exploited that knowledge to surprise the object of his sinful interest.

Matt 26:37, 40, 43–45—The few companions are no protection. Both Jesus and Susanna took two or three persons with them into the garden: Jesus brought three disciples (26:37), and Susanna was accompanied by two serving women (Sus 15). In each case, however, the companions were unavailable during the ensuing ordeal. Jesus' disciples slept while he suffered in agony; Susanna's servants were absent when she was accosted. Slight though this parallel may seem, it became standard in later paired depictions of Susanna and of Christ in Gethsemane: Susanna was depicted in a garden, the maidservants departing in the background, while in the foreground the Elders approach; beside this was depicted Christ in Gethsemane, the disciples asleep while Judas and the soldiers approach.[79]

Matt 26:47—"The Elders of the People." Matthew used this distinctive phrase for the second time when recounting Judas' agreement with the "elders of the people" to betray Jesus: *presbyteroi tou laou*, as in Matt 26:3 and Theod Sus 41.

Matt 26:47–50—The arrest in a garden. Susanna and Jesus were each in a garden when they were betrayed and taken into custody (Matt 26:47–50; Sus 19–27).

Matt 26:57–75—The first trial. Both Susanna (Sus 28–41) and Jesus endured two trials. This itself is unusual in Sacred Scripture and may be unique to Susanna and Jesus. The first trial of each was by the Jewish

---

77. Luke and John stated that it was Jesus' custom to go to this garden and that his disciples knew this (Luke 22:39; John 18:1–2). Matthew and Mark demonstrated this, for instance, recounting that after the Last Supper he returned with his disciples to the Mount of Olives to pray (Matt 26:30, 36; Mark 14:26, 32).

78. Tkacz, "Susanna as a Type of Christ," 105–7, 110–16, 122–23, 126–27, figs. 1–10.

79. For instance, in manuscripts of the *Biblia Pauperum* (thirteenth–sixteenth centuries) and the stained glass of the Frauenkirche, Munich; Tkacz, "Susanna as a Type of Christ," 122–23, 126–27, figs. 8–10.

community and the innocent was condemned. Moreover, two judges presided at the first trial, and only one judge, a different one, presided at the second. This, too, is unusual in Sacred Scripture and may be unique to Susanna and Jesus.

Matt 26:59—The pre-trial intention to condemn. Matthew was explicit that the Sanhedrin from the start intended to condemn Jesus: They sought false witness "against Jesus, that they might put him to death" (*kata tou Iēsou hopōs auton thanatōsōsin*). The identical point is made, and in these words, in the history of Susanna. The Elders from the start intended to condemn her: they were full of wicked plans "against Susanna, to put her to death" (*kata Sousannēs tou thanatōsai autēn*: Sus 28). These parallel clauses share five words: the preposition *kata*, the name of the intended victim, the article *tou*,[80] the appropriate form of the pronoun *autos*, and the verb, *thanatoō*, otherwise rare in the Gospels.[81] Both passages express purpose in comparable ways and in the same position in the sentence.[82]

Matt 26:59–62—The charge. Both Jesus and Susanna were charged with a capital offense, one which by Mosaic Law was punished by stoning. The charge against Jesus was blasphemy, a charge his opponents had raised before, notably in John 8.

Matt 26:59–62—The accused is innocent; the accusers are guilty. In each case the accused was innocent, but ironically the accusers were guilty of the charge they laid against the innocent. In Babylon, the Elders accused Susanna of adultery although it was they who were guilty of trying to coerce her sexually. In the same way, "The authorities accuse Jesus of blasphemy and yet it is they who blaspheme the Son of God."[83]

Matt 26:59–62—False witness. False witness was critical in the first trial of Susanna and also the first trial of Christ. Furthermore, Matthew's diction and phrasing echo the account of the trials of Susanna. The Elders presented their fabricated charge against her and concluded their official statement by saying, "We are witnesses to these things" (*tauta martyroumen*).[84] Susanna in prayer set the situation before God, affirming that he knows that "they have

---

80. In Matt 26:59 *tou* agrees with "Jesus" (i.e., it is masculine genitive singular) and precedes the name; in Theod Sus 28 *tou* follows the name and serves as the articular genitive (i.e., it is neuter singular), governing the infinitive and expressing purpose. On the articular infinitive in Matthew's passion narrative, see Tkacz, *Aneboēsen phōnēi megalēi*," 455n35.

81. *Thanatoō* in the Gospels: Matt 10:21, 26:59, 27:1; Mark 13:12, 14:55; Luke 21:16.

82. Theod Sus 28 uses the articular infinitive (*tou thanatōsai autēn*), and Matt 26:59 uses *hopōs* with the subjunctive (*hopōs auton thanatōsōsin*).

. 83. Davies and Allison, *Matthew*, 3:537, 533.

84. Theod Sus 41.

falsely given witness against me" (*pseudē mou katemartyrēsan*).[85] Inspired, Daniel declared that "these [men] have falsely borne witness against her" (*pseudē gar outoi katemartyrēsan autēs*).[86] After Daniel's questioning revealed the Elders' perjury, the people condemned them as "false witnesses" (*pseudomartyrēsantos*).[87] That same diction recurred in the high priests' trial of Jesus. Matthew used the noun for "false witnesses" (*pseudomartyrōn*: Matt 26:60). Moreover, Matthew's statement about false witness against Jesus uses every element in Susanna's statement about false witness against herself. The evangelist wrote of "false witnesses against Jesus" (*pseudomartyrian kata tou Iēsou*) and Susanna told God the Elders had "falsely given witness against me" (*pseudē mou katemartyrēsan*).[88]

Matt 26:60—Two false witnesses. Matthew specified that two (*duo*) false witnesses accused Jesus of blasphemy.[89] Likewise two (*duo*) false witnesses had accused Susanna.[90]

Matt 26:62—The judge stands. When the two false witnesses had testified, then the high priest, acting as the judge, stood (*anastas*) and asked Jesus, "You answer nothing?" In the history of Susanna the judges stood (*anastantes*) to testify falsely against her (Sus 34). Until now, scholars have been unable to find a precedent in the Bible for a *judge* standing.[91]

Matt 26:63—The falsely accused innocent is silent at the trial. Both Jesus and Susanna were silent at their trials. Neither responded to false accusations made in a manipulated legal situation predetermined to condemn them. During the Sanhedrin trial, when the false accusations were made, Jesus held his peace. Susanna did the same. The two Elders had testified falsely against her: only a pair of refuting witnesses could have negated their accusation. Nothing she could have said would have legally protected her. Immediately after the trial she prayed in "a great voice" to God, demonstrating her articulate voice, but during the trial she held her peace.[92]

85. Theod Sus 43.

86. Theod Sus 49.

87. Theod Sus 61.

88. Matt 26:59 and Theod Sus 43. The elements of these phrases are *martyreō, kata, pseudo*, and a personal direct object (*mou* or *tou Iēsou*) governed by *kata*.

89. Specifying the number of false witnesses as two (*duo*) may indicate that the Sanhedrin were satisfying the Jewish law requiring two witnesses (Deut. 17:16): Senior, *Passion of Jesus*, 92–93; Luz, *Evangelium nach Matthäus*, 4:175n16.

90. Theod Sus 34, LXX Sus 36.

91. The rising of the high priest has been likened to the rising of the unjust witnesses in Ps 26(27):12 (*epanetēsan*) and Ps 34(35):11 (*anastantes*): Davies and Allison, *Matthew*, 3:526–27. Yet the Psalms refer to witnesses, not a judge, who stands while testifying.

92. Theod Sus 35, 42–43.

Matt 26:66—Condemned to death. At the end of Jesus' first trial the council declared him liable to the penalty "of death" (*thanatou*)." Similarly, at the end of Susanna's first trial the assembly condemned her "to be put to death" (*apothanein*: Theod Sus 41)

Matt 26:64–66—Condemned to death for his own words. Though Jesus was silent in response to false testimony, at other moments in his trial he did speak. Matthew recorded that the high priest asked Jesus to respond to the testimony (Matt 26:62), while the Elders did not ask Susanna. Further, when the high priest adjured Jesus in the name of the living God to say whether he is the Christ (Matt 26:62), he then spoke, whereas Susanna was silent during her whole trial. This may appear to negate any parallel between Susanna's silence and Jesus'.

The difference is merely in strategy, however. The Elders and the high priest were alike in intending to condemn their innocent victims. Susanna's testimony would scarcely have benefitted the Elders (even though she alone could not have legally prevailed against their double witness), so they did not ask her to speak. In contrast the high priest hoped to elicit from Jesus what might appear to be culpable statements. When the high priest called upon Jesus "by the living God" to say if he was "the Christ, the Son of God," then Jesus spoke, delivering his final SM speech and quoting from Daniel's first vision: "Thou hast said it. Nevertheless I say to you, hereafter you shall see the Son of Man sitting on the right hand of the power of God, and coming in the clouds of heaven" (Matt 26:63–64). In response, the high priest accused him of blasphemy.

Matt 27:1—The pre-trial intention to condemn. For a second time Matthew made the point that those judging Jesus intended from the start to condemn him to death, and this time the match between the Gospel and the history of Susanna is even stronger in circumstance and language. Matthew recorded that the next morning the elders intended to condemn Jesus to death: "the elders took counsel against Jesus for the purpose of condemning him to death" (*hoi presbyteroi . . . kata tou Iēsou hōste thanatōsai auton*). The diction and phrasing are from Susanna's history, which recorded what happened on the morning of the first trial: "the Elders came full of wicked device against Susanna in order to condemn her to death" (*presbytai kata Sousannēs tou thanatōsai autēn*).[93] The passages share six words: the subject *presbyteroi* / *presbytai*, the preposition *kata*, the name of the intended victim, the article *tou*, the appropriate form of the pronoun *autos*, and the infinitive *thanatōsai*. Both passages share the

---

93. Theod Sus 28.

subject "elders" (*presbyteroi*) and express purpose with the same verb, and even the same form of that verb, the infinitive.[94]

Matt 27:1—"The Elders of the People." The third iteration of the distinctive phrase "elders of the People" (*presbyteroi tou laou*) in the account of the Passion is in Matthew's report of their constant purpose to condemn Jesus. Thus the phrase is used when recording their intention to connive at his death (Matt 26:3–4), their sending a throng to arrest him (Matt 26:47), and their intention to condemn him as they approach Pilate (Matt 27:1). As discussed above, the identical phrase, "Elders of the people," is used in the history of Susanna.

Matt 27:3—Condemned. Judas returned the payment to the high priests when he saw that the one he had betrayed was "condemned" (*katekrithē*). This verb is also used both for reporting the condemnation of Susanna (*katekrinan*) and again in Daniel's rebuke of the people: You condemned (*katekrinate*) a daughter of Israel.[95]

Matt 27:4—Innocent blood. Judas declared to the high priests that he had betrayed "innocent blood" (*haima athōion*).[96] His is the first of two speeches in Matthew's account of the Passion treating innocence or guilt regarding innocent blood. Notably, in the entire New Testament the word *athōios* ("innocent") occurs only in these two speeches.[97] They bracket the second trial of Jesus, i.e., the trial by Pilate. That is, Daniel's declaration that he was "innocent" (*athōios*) "of the blood of this one" (*tou haimatos tautēs*)[98] is echoed first in Pilate's declaration that he was "innocent" (*athōios*) "of the blood of this one" (*tou haimatos toutou*)[99] and again in Judas' admission of guilt.[100] Furthermore, Daniel's words were the prelude to her second trial which saves her; Judas' words were the prelude to Christ's second trial, and death.

The other uses of the terms "innocent" (*athōios*) and "blood" (*haima*) in the history of Susanna are pertinent to Matthew's account. The term *athōios* which frames the second trial of Jesus is found twice at the heart of

---

94. Daniel uses *tou* with an articular infinitive; Matthew uses *hōste* to govern the infinitive.

95. Theod Sus 41 and Sus 48.

96. Matt 27:4. Judas' phrase is also found in Jer 19:4 and in Deut 27:25: Moo, *Old Testament in the Passion*, 199.

97. As noted also by Brown, *Death of the Messiah*, 1:640n9, 835.

98. Theod Dan 1[13]:46. The pronoun *tautēs* ("this one") is feminine, to agree with Susanna.

99. Matt 27:24. The pronoun *toutou* ("this one") is masculine, to agree with Jesus.

100. Brown, *Death of the Messiah*, 1:640n9, 835; Gundry, *Old Testament in Matthew*, 144.

the second trial of Susanna. Daniel started his interrogation of the Elders by asserting that they had inverted the Law by oppressing the "innocent" (*athōious*), whereas, Daniel reminded them, the Lord says: "The innocent (*athōion*) and the just thou shalt not kill."[101] This identifies Susanna as "innocent" in precisely the term Judas would use of Jesus.

Moreover, this diction frames each second trial. Jesus' second trial is framed by Judas' and Pilate's references to their guilt or innocence of his blood, and Susanna's second trial is framed by references to innocence and to her blood. Daniel's declared himself innocent of the blood of Susanna before her second trial. Her history concluded that innocent blood (*haima anaition*) was saved on that day (Sus 62). The identity of diction both points to the identity of the sin of the wrongdoers and also highlights the contrast between the saving of Susanna's blood and the shedding of Jesus'.[102]

Matt 27:11–14—The Second Trial. Jesus underwent a second trial, so that the civil authorities might legally execute Him. This trial culminated in a public disclaimer of guilt by Pilate, the judge at his second trial. Susanna also experienced a second trial (Sus 47–61). She had been condemned to death and was on the way to execution when a public disclaimer of guilt by Daniel halted the procession and prompted her second trial, in which Daniel was judge.

Matt 27:12, 14—The falsely accused innocent is silent at the trial. During the Sanhedrin trial, when the false accusations had been made, Jesus had held his peace (Matt 26:63). Before Pilate, also, when the chief priests and elders accused him, he answered nothing (Matt 27:12), and again when Pilate asked if he did not hear what was testified against Him, Jesus answered never a word (Matt 27:14). Jesus, like Susanna, chose not to speak fruitlessly.

Matt 27:20—The innocent is to be put to death. The high priests persuaded the people that they should "destroy [Jesus]" (*apolesōsin*). The same verb is used in the history of Susanna when she was led "to be destroyed" (*apolesthai*; Theod Sus 45).

Matt 27:23—The innocence of the accused is affirmed. Pilate declared that the accused Jesus had done nothing wrong, and Susanna declared in prayer that she had done nothing which the Elders had maliciously charged against her. These two expressions of the innocence of a condemned person use the same verb (*poieō*; see also Theod Sus 43).

---

101. Sus 53. Daniel was referring to Exodus 23:7.

102. For detailed analysis of the contrasts between the outcomes for Susanna and for Jesus, see Tkacz, "*Aneboēsen phōnēi megalēi*," 468–69.

Matt 27:24—A judge declares himself innocent of this one's blood.
Finding the people insistent upon crucifixion, Pilate publicly declared his innocence: "I am innocent of the blood of this one." Daniel had made the same declaration: "I am innocent of the blood of this one." In the entire Bible only two persons, Daniel and Pilate, uttered this statement, and they did so publicly, immediately after a trial in which a falsely accused innocent had been condemned. It is the typological likeness between the persons being judged, Susanna and Christ, that made it fitting for Matthew to report Pilate's words as echoing Daniel's:

Pilate's words: *Athōios eimi apo tou haimatos toutou.*[103]

Daniel's words: *Athōios* [or *Katharos*] *egō apo tou haimatos tautēs.* [Theod Sus 46]

Both statements begin with a word for "innocent." In the fourth-century Codex Vaticanus, the oldest complete copy of the Bible, both passages have the identical word, *Athōios.*[104] Each statement next expresses "I am," Pilate by the predicate alone, *eimi* (am), and Daniel by the subject alone, *egō* (I). Last is a four-word prepositional phrase in the genitive, governed by the preposition *apo* and with the object comprised of the article *tou* followed by the noun *haimatos* (blood) and ending with the demonstrative pronoun "this [person]" in the appropriate gender.[105]

This significant parallel is expressed in art. For instance, the Brescia Casket, a late fourth-century ivory reliquary shows it: in the presence of Jesus, a seated Pilate washes his hands, recalling his words, and, in the presence of Susanna, a seated Daniel holds his arm in a gesture of speech, recalling his words.

Matt 27:25—All the people. After Daniel and Pilate made this statement, "all the people" (*pas ho laos*) responded—in opposite ways. The two judges were diametrically opposite in character, so, not surprisingly, they spoke with opposite effects, at opposite moments with respect to the second trial, with opposite accuracy, and with opposite responses from the people.[106] Daniel's words were pivotal. He spoke, and "all the people" (*pas ho laos*) were led by him (Theod Sus 47). As a result of Daniel's words, a

103. Some Gospel manuscripts include the word *dikaiou* in Pilate's statement, yielding, "I am innocent of the blood of this *just* one." See the apparatus in Aland et al., *Greek New Testament.*

104. Biblioteca Apostolica, vat. graec. 1209.

105. Schlatter and Gundry note the verbal parallelism: Schlatter, *Matthäus,* 775; Gundry, *Old Testament in Matthew,* 144.

106. As St. Jerome noted in *Commentarii in Danielem* (CCL 75A:949.819–29).

second trial would be held, Susanna would be freed, and "innocent blood" would be saved (Sus 62). In contrast, Pilate's words ended his attempts to free Jesus. The second trial was already over and Pilate had tried in vain to induce the crowd to release Jesus. Although he knew Jesus was innocent, Pilate yielded to the crowd and sent Jesus to the Cross. Pilate spoke, and "all the people" (*pas ho laos*) declared, "His blood be on us and on our children." Though in Babylon "all the people" had vindicated the innocent Susanna, in Jerusalem "all the people" insisted that The Innocent Himself be executed. The phrase that someone's blood is "on somebody" or "upon somebody's head" is a biblical idiom assigning responsibility for a death. In the context of the Bible, the dramatic statement made by "all the people" to Pilate is an unprecedented acceptance of guilt for the death of someone. At the same time, it was also an unconscious prayer for salvation, the salvation brought by the death and resurrection of this particular someone, the One whose blood atones for sin.[107]

Matt 27:31—Led to execution. Susanna, like Jesus, was led to execution: "And she was led away to be destroyed" (*kai apagomenēs autēs apolesthai*: Theod Sus 45).[108] Matthew reported of Jesus: "and they led him away to crucify him" (*kai apēgagon auton eis to staurōsin*). The two passages are parallel, beginning with the same conjunction, then the same verb, next the same pronoun, and finally a verb or verbal phrase for death.

Matt 27:43—The innocent trusts in God. When Jesus was on the Cross, Matthew recounted that the elders mocked Him, paraphrasing Scripture: "He trusted in God [*pepoithen epi ton theon*], let him deliver him." Clearly the context and idea are much indebted to Psalm 21(22) which Jesus would soon quote from the Cross. That psalm had recounted, "All who see me laugh me to scorn, saying, 'He had faith in the Lord [*ēlpisen epi kyrion*], that he would deliver him; let him deliver him.'" (vv. 8–9). But the language Matthew recorded—the initial predicate and the use of the article in the following prepositional phrase—*pepoithen epi ton theon*—seems to derive from the statement that Susanna "trusted in the Lord" (*pepoithuia epi tōi kyriōi*) or "trusted in the Lord her God" (*epepoithei epi kyriōi tōi theōi autēs*).[109] This statement is also a paraphrase from the Psalms, Psalm 111:7. In sum, both Matthew and the history of Susanna made a psalm reference to the faith of the innocent one. Though

---

107. Tkacz, "Literary Studies of the Vulgate," 209–12, 218–19.

108. The Douai translation has "be put to death."

109. Theod Sus 35 and LXX Sus 35. As Sarah J. K. Pearce notes, this passage is striking for explicitly referring to "*her* God." Pearce, "Echoes in Susanna," 19, 20.

paraphrasing a different psalm, Matthew nonetheless drew from Susanna's history the diction of its psalm reference to her faith.

These psalm references have poignantly different roles in the two histories. Susanna's narrator affirmed her faith when she was enduring her first trial, when the Elders had abused the legal process in order to unveil her and, with their hands on her head, were about to give their lying testimony. The account called attention to her steadfast faith when her suffering was acute, as she wept and looked up to heaven (v. 35), expecting an unjust and hideous death. For Jesus, however, the allusion to the psalms came when he was on the Cross, actually dying an unjust and hideous death. Moreover, the reference was made not by Matthew as narrator, to praise Jesus' fidelity, but by those who had connived unjustly at Jesus' death, to taunt Him. Matthew thus conveyed both a parallel with and a contrast to Susanna through a reference to the thought of Psalm 21(22), as expressed in language from the history of Susanna.

This blending of Psalm 21(22) and Susanna is also apparent, dramatically, in the words of Christ on the Cross.[110]

Matt 27:46, 50—Great-voiced prayer before death. The most striking parallel between Susanna's history and Matthew's Passion narrative is between Jesus' outcry on the Cross before dying and Susanna's outcry in prayer before imminent death. Quite rare is the collocation of the specific predicate *aneboēsen* ("he/she exclaimed") with the phrase *phōnēi megalēi* ("with a great voice"). Moreover, this rare collocation, when used specifically of a person on the point of death, is unique to only one woman and one man in the Bible: Susanna in the Old Testament and Jesus in the New.[111] Each passage names the speaker and precedes the utterance by a second verb of speech. Each person cried out a prayer that opens with the word "God." Susanna was about to die; Jesus died:

> then exclaimed Jesus in a great voice, saying, "*Eli!* . . . My God! . . ." And Jesus again crying with a great voice, yielded up the ghost.[112]

> *aneboēsen ho Iēsous phōnēi megalēi legōn, Ēli . . . Thee mou . . . kraksas phōnēi megalēi aphēken to pneuma.*

110. For the importance of Psalm 21(22) in the Gospels and Christian commentary and for the contrasting Jewish interpretation of this psalm, see Tkacz, "Esther, Jesus, and Psalm 22."

111. The phrase *phōnēi megalēi* with a verb of crying out is a biblical idiom for heartfelt exclamation, found seventy times in the Bible. Tkacz, "*Aneboēsen phōnēi megalēi*," Appendix.

112. My translation, to present the verbal parallels in full.

> Then exclaimed in a great voice Susanna, and said, "O God . . .
> Behold I die." (Theod Sus 42–43)
>
> *aneboēsen de phōnēi megalēi Sousanna kai eipen, Ho theos . . . kai*
> *idou apothnēskō.*

Susanna's cry when she had been condemned to death foreshadowed both Jesus' cry when he knew he was about to die and also his second cry (v. 50) when he in fact died.

Jesus on the cross could well have uttered Susanna's words. Indeed, in the fifteenth century over sixty manuscripts record Lenten sermons beginning with her words and then ascribing them to Christ on the Cross.[113] For Susanna prayed: "O Eternal God, who are the knower of hidden things, who know all things before they occur, you know that they have born false witness against me, and behold! I die! although I have done none of these things which they have maliciously fabricated against me."[114] The whole of what she prayed was true of Jesus as well. He, like Susanna, was innocent. Against him also have elders of the people maliciously used false witness to secure condemnation. He, too, could cry out, "Behold! I die!"

"My God, my God, why hast Thou forsaken me?" (Psalm 21[22]:1) is the cry Matthew recorded. Other echoes of Psalm 21(22) are in the Passion narrative, and it is easy to recall, at Jesus' cry, the rest of the Psalm, including the Psalmist's reminder of "the afflicted" whom the Lord "has not despised but has heard when he cried to him" (v. 24).[115] When Susanna, afflicted, cried out in prayer, God did not despise her but heard and delivered her, as St. Augustine noted.[116] The evident reuse by Matthew of the narrative framing of her prayer to introduce Jesus' cry on the cross underscores the same irony as does Jesus' quotation of Psalm 21(22).

The many parallels between Susanna and Jesus show how she prefigured the Lord in his Passion. The differences between them emphasize the completeness of Jesus' sacrifice: whereas God in justice had delivered the innocent Susanna from an unjust execution, God in mercy allowed the innocent Jesus to undergo unjust execution in order to gain salvation for mankind.[117] God chose a woman to prefigure his Son in his Passion to show that truly women equally with men are called to holiness.

---

113. Based on my research in Oxford, etc., especially at the Hill Museum and Manuscript Library, on fellowship in spring 2018. For details see Tkacz, *Women as Types of Christ.*

114. My translation.

115. Senior, *Passion of Jesus*, 139–40.

116. Augustine, *Ennaratio in Ps 21* (CCL 38:124–25).

117. For details, see Tkacz, "*Aneboēsen phōnēi megalēi*," 468–69.

Conclusion

Both Daniel's first vision of the Son of Man and Susanna's ordeal are thus pertinent in this Gospel. Intriguingly, Matthew used the two sets of Old Testament material in different ways. Susanna's role as a type of Christ is established through the compact use of fifty-two words, including six-word clauses, from her sixty-four-verse history, exclusively in the passion narrative, chapters 26–27. In contrast, Jesus' repeated allusions to Daniel's first vision occur throughout two thirds of the Gospel. Jesus used the key phrase, "Son of Man," in his ministry and affirmed the vision as eschatological prophecy as he neared his Passion by using diction and phrases of seven-to-eight words from that vision. The SM material is in over thirty-one passages and comprises over one hundred words. It is diffused and complementary with the concentrated Susanna material: Matthew's Gospel records evocations of Daniel's first vision in chapters 11–13, 16–20, 24–26, and again in 28; this surrounds this Gospel's borrowings from Susanna's history, within chapters 26–27. The influence of Daniel pervades the Gospel.

Mindful of the vehement reaction of Caiaphas to Jesus' declaration, we should not be surprised by the subsequent Jewish rejection of both the Christian recording of Jesus' use of Daniel and also the broader Christian use of Susanna's history. The re-dating of Daniel and Susanna's removal from the Christian-Era Jewish canon came swiftly.[118] This was part of a larger pattern documented by Professor Emanuel Tov of the Hebrew University of Jerusalem, identifying several "nationalistic" Jewish sites which revised the pre-Christian Greek toward a "proto-Masoretic" Hebrew, itself undergoing anti-Christian revision.[119] This move to undercut Christian interpretation by demoting Daniel and removing Susanna shows the great importance of Daniel's vision of the Son of Man and of Susanna, the vindicated type of Christ.

The revised date of the composition of Daniel is now the consensus of modern biblical scholars, who place it in the second century BC. The linguistic evidence, however, including the borrowings of Akkadian and Persian loan words, indicate that the whole book, including Susanna's history, could have been composed during the Captivity.[120] The assumption

---

118. On Susanna's removal from the canon, see esp. Tkacz, *Alētheia Hellēnikē*. Jewish legal scholar Bernard S. Jackson first suggested she was removed because of her obvious parallel with Jesus: Jackson, "Susanna and Singular Witnesses," 2:40.

119. Tov, "Greek Texts from the Judean Desert," 10–11. See also his study, "Qumran Non-Biblical Texts?" 71. For a magisterial overview, see Tov, "Differences between LXX and MT S T V," 125–37. See also Tkacz, *Alētheia Hellēnikē*.

120. This is conceded by, e.g., Moore, *Daniel*, 29, 92–93, and Di Lella, *Daniel*, 47, 74.

that Daniel was a second-century composition makes it susceptible to dismissal as non-prophetic,[121] and thus seems to invalidate Jesus' use of "the Son of Man" and to render irrelevant the evangelists' use of Susanna's history in recounting the Lord's passion. The decisive issue is the Incarnation. If Jesus was and is God, then he was right that Daniel was a prophet, and Jesus' affirming and advancing Daniel's vision of the Son of Man was fresh prophecy. If Jesus is God, then it was fitting for the woman Susanna to prefigure God incarnate.[122]

Susanna as a type of Christ, Daniel's vision of the Son of Man coming in clouds of glory to judgment. A holy woman's ordeal, a holy man's vision, both from the Book of Daniel: the first provides the Gospels' primary type of Christ in his Passion, the second provides Jesus' own dominant self-identification.[123] The balance of the sexes is seen here, and it appears that God intended this, that the Lord orchestrated history so that a woman and a man could be complementary prophetic indications of the good news, and this was done for the profoundly apposite reason that "male and female," revealed in Genesis as created in the image of God, were revealed anew through Christ as created for sanctification.

Bibliography

Aland, Kurt, et al., eds. *The Greek New Testament*. 4th rev. ed. Stuttgart: Deutsche Bibelgesellschaft, 2001.

Barthélemy, Dominique. *Les devanciers d'Aquila: Première publication intégrale du text du fragments du Dodéceprophéton*. Vetus Testamentum Supplements 10. Leiden: Brill, 2014.

Biblia Sacra iuxta vulgatam versionem. Edited by Bonifatius Fischer, et al. 2nd ed. Stuttgart: Württembergische Bibelanstalt, 1975.

Brown, Raymond E. *The Death of the Messiah: From Gethsemane to the Grave: A Commentary on the Passion Narratives in the Four Gospels*. 2 vols. New York: Doubleday, 1994.

Bultmann, Rudolf. *Theology of the New Testament*. 2 vols. London: SCM, 1968.

Notably, the Hebrew and Aramaic of the Book of Daniel are Exilic, affirming its date as 570–536 BC: Gigot, "Daniel, Book of."

121. John J. Collins vaunts the modern rejection of Daniel as prophet: Collins, "Current Issues in Daniel," 1–2.

122. To think that a woman prefigured God incarnate was so revolutionary that perhaps Jesus himself had to explain it on the road to Emmaus. Otherwise, the Holy Spirit imparted the typology.

123. Prior to this essay, Tim Meadowcroft was the only scholar both to deem "Son of Man" as Jesus' "self-designation" and likewise to draw on my interpretation of Susanna in the Gospels. Meadowcroft, "Lessons from Daniel," 404n28.

Caragounis, Chrys C. *The Son of Man: Vision and Interpretation*. Wissenschaftliche Untersuchungen zum Neuen Testament 38. Tübingen: Mohr, 1986.

Casey, Maurice. *Son of Man: The Interpretation and Influence of Daniel 7*. London: SPCK, 1979.

Collins, John J. *A Commentary on the Book of Daniel*. Minneapolis: Fortress, 1993.

———. "Current Issues in the Study of Daniel." In vol. 1 of *The Book of Daniel: Composition and Reception*, edited by John J. Collins and Peter W. Flint, 1–15. Vetus Testamentum Supplements 83/1–2. Leiden: Brill, 2000–2001.

Davies, W. D. *The Setting of the Sermon on the Mount*. Cambridge: Cambridge University Press, 1962.

Davies, W. D., and Dale C. Allison, Jr. *A Critical and Exegetical Commentary on The Gospel According to Saint Matthew*. 3 vols. International Critical Commentary. Edinburgh: T. & T. Clark, 1988–97.

Di Lella, Alexander. *The Book of Daniel: A New Translation with Notes and Commentary on Chapters 1–9 by †Louis F. Hartman, CSSR; Introduction and Commentary on Chapters 10–12 by Alexander A. Di Lella, OFM*. Anchor Bible 23. Garden City, NY: Doubleday, 1978.

———. "The Textual History of Septuagint-Daniel and Theodotion-Daniel." In vol. 2 of *The Book of Daniel: Composition and Reception*, edited by John J. Collins and Peter W. Flint, 586–607. Vetus Testamentum Supplements 83/1–2. Leiden: Brill, 2000–2001.

Doeve, Jan Willem. *Jewish Hermeneutics in the Synoptic Gospels and Acts*. Assen: Van Gorcum, 1953.

Evans, Craig A. "Daniel in the New Testament: Visions of God's Kingdom." In vol. 2 of *The Book of Daniel, Composition and Reception*, edited by John J. Collins and Peter W. Flint, 490–527. Vetus Testamentum Supplements 83/1–2. Leiden: Brill, 2000–2001.

Fishbane, Michael. *Biblical Interpretation in Ancient Israel*. Oxford: Oxford University Press, 1985.

Foakes-Jackson, Frederick John, and Kirsopp Lake. *The Beginnings of Christianity*. 5 vols. London: Macmillan, 1920–33.

Ford, Josephine Massingberd. "The Son of Man—A Euphemism?" *Journal of Biblical Literature* 87 (1968) 257–66.

Gigot, Francis E. "Daniel, Book of." In vol. 4 of *Catholic Encyclopedia*, edited by Charles G. Herbermann et al., 620–21. New York: Appleton, 1908.

Gundry, Robert H. *The Use of the Old Testament in Matthew's Gospel*. Leiden: Brill, 1967.

Hamilton, Catherine Sider. "Blood and Secrets: The Re-telling of Genesis 1–6 in 1 Enoch 6–11 and Its Echoes in Susanna and the Gospel of Matthew." In *"What Does Scripture Say?" Studies in the Function of Scripture in Early Judaism and Christianity, 1: The Synoptic Gospels*, edited by Craig A. Evans and H. Daniel Zacherias, 90–141. London: T. & T. Clark, 2012.

Hartin, Patrick J. "Neglected Roots for Interpreting the Bible." Lecture for Socratic Club, Gonzaga University, November 11, 2011. https://www.youtube.com/watch?v=bLNdmdI4zb8.

Higgins, Angus J. B. *Jesus and the Son of Man*. Philadelphia: Fortress, 1964.

Jackson, Bernard S. "Susanna and the History of Singular Witnesses." In vol. 2 of *Essays in Honour of Ben Beinart: Jura legesque antiquiores necnon recentiores*, edited by Wouter de Vos, 37–54. Johannesburg: Juta, 1978.

John Paul II, Pope. "'Jesus Christ, Son of Man,' General Audience of April 29, 1987." In *A Catechism on the Creed, vol. 2: Jesus: Son and Savior*, 141–45. Boston: Pauline Books & Media, 1996.

Knox, John. *The Death of Christ: The Cross in New Testament History and Faith*. London: Collins, 1967.

Longenecker, Richard N. "'Son of Man' as a Self-Designation of Jesus." *Journal of the Evangelical Theological Society* 12 (1969) 151–58.

Luz, Ulrich. *Das Evangelium nach Matthäus*. 4 vols. Evangelisch-Katholischer Kommentar zum Neuen Testament I/4. Düsseldorf: Benzinger, 2002.

MacKenzie, Roderick A. F. "The Meaning of the Susanna Story." *Canadian Journal of Theology* 3 (1957) 211–18.

Meadowcroft, Tim. "Belteshazzar, Chief of the Magicians: Lessons from the Career of Daniel." In *Living in the Family of Jesus: Critical Contextualization in Melanesia and Beyond*, edited by William Kenny Longar and Tim Meadowcroft, 381–408. Archer Studies in Pacific Christianity. Auckland: Archer, 2016.

Moo, Douglas J. *The Old Testament in the Gospel Passion Narratives*. Sheffield: Almond, 1983.

Moore, Carey. *Daniel, Esther, and Jeremiah: The Additions: A New Translation with Introduction and Commentary*. Anchor Bible 44. Garden City, NY: Doubleday, 1978.

Nova Vulgata Bibliorum Sacrorum editio. Vatican: Libreria Editrice Vaticana, 1979.

Pearce, Sarah J. K. "Echoes of Eden in the Old Greek of Susanna." *Feminist Theology* 11 (1996) 10–31.

Ratzinger, Joseph. *Jesus of Nazareth: From the Baptism in the Jordan to the Transfiguration*. Translated by Adrian J. Walker. New York: Doubleday, 2007.

Sabourin, Leopold. "About Jesus' Self-Understanding." *Religious Studies Bulletin* 3 (1983) 129–34.

Sandmel, Samuel. "Son of Man." In *In Time of Harvest: Essays in Honor of Abba Hillel Silver*, edited by Daniel Jeremy Silver, 355–67. New York: Macmillan, 1963.

Schlatter, Adolf. *Der Evangelist Matthäus. Seine Sprache, sein Ziel, seine Selbständigkeit.* 2nd ed. Stuttgart: Calwer, 1933.

Senior, Donald. *The Passion of Jesus in the Gospel of Matthew*. Wilmington: Glazier, 1985.

Tilborg, Sjef van. *The Jewish Leaders in Matthew*. Thesis: Katholieke Universiteit te Nijmegen, 1972.

Tkacz, Catherine Brown. *Alētheia Hellēnikē: The Authority of the Greek Old Testament*. Etna, CA: St. Palamas Monastery, 2011.

———. "*Aneboēsen phōnēi megalēi*: Susanna and the Synoptic Passion Narratives." *Gregorianum* 87 (2006) 449–86.

———. "The Doctrinal Context for Interpreting Women as Types of Christ." *Studia Patristica* 40 (2006) 253–57.

———. "*En colligo duo ligna*: The Widow of Zarephath and the Cross." In *Early Christian Iconography*, edited by Markus Vinzent and Allen Brent, 53–68. Leuven: Peeters, 2013.

————. "Esther as a Type of Christ and the Jewish Celebration of Purim." *Studia Patristica* 44 (2010) 183–87.

————. "Esther, Jesus, and Psalm 22." *Catholic Biblical Quarterly* 70 (2008) 709–28.

————. "'Here Am I, Lord': Preaching Jephthah's Daughter as a Type of Christ." *The Downside Review* 434 (2006) 21–32.

————. "Jesus and the Spiritual Equality of Women." *Fellowship of Catholic Scholars Quarterly* 24 (2001) 24–29.

————. "Literary Studies of the Vulgate: Formula Systems." *Proceedings of the Patristic, Medieval and Renaissance Conference* 15 (1990) 205–19.

————. "Singing Women's Words as Sacramental Mimesis." *Recherches de Théologie et Philosophie médiévales* 70 (2003) 275–328.

————. "Susanna as a Type of Christ." *Studies in Iconography* 29 (1999) 101–53.

————. "Susanna and the Pre-Christian Book of Daniel: Structure and Meaning." *The Heythrop Journal* 49 (2008) 181–96.

————. *Women as Types of Christ, East and West.* Etna, CA: St. Palamas Monastery, 2022.

————. "Women as Types of Christ: Susanna and Jephthah's Daughter." *Gregorianum* 85 (2004) 278–311.

Tov, Emanuel. "The Nature of the Greek Texts from the Judean Desert." *Novum Testamentum* 43 (2001) 1–11.

————. "The Nature of the Large-Scale Differences between the LXX and the MT S T V, Compared with Similar Evidence in Other Sources." In *The Earliest Text of the Hebrew Bible: The Relationship between the Masoretic Text and the Hebrew Base of the Septuagint Reconsidered*, edited by Adrian Schenker, 121–44. Atlanta: Society of Biblical Literature, 2003.

————. "A Qumran Origin for the Masada Non-Biblical Texts?" *Dead Sea Discoveries* 7 (2000) 57–73.

Zorn, Raymond O. "The Significance of Jesus' Self-Designation 'Son of Man.'" *Vox Reformata* 34 (1980) 1–21.

9

The Importance of Retrieving
the "Women of Galilee"

SISTER SARA BUTLER, MSBT, STL

University of St. Mary of the Lake, Mundelein, IL

WHO ARE THE "WOMEN of Galilee"? Many will remember the three names mentioned in chapter eight of Luke's Gospel: Mary Magdalene, Joanna, and Susanna. But there were more; Luke says there were "many others." (Luke 8:2–3) Under the impulse of the feminist critique, women Scripture scholars have succeeded in finding in and "behind" the text of the four Gospels evidence that our Lord Jesus Christ, from the beginnings of his public ministry, was accompanied not only by the twelve apostles but also by a group of women disciples. In the Synoptic Passion Narratives, they are referred to as the women from Galilee, and as a group they constitute a kind of female counterpart to the Twelve.[1]

Like the Twelve,[2] the women of Galilee belonged to the larger group of disciples and within that group they had a distinct identity. Like the Twelve, they left behind houses, brothers, sisters, mother, father, children and lands (Matt 19:29; cf. Luke 14:26) to travel through the towns and villages of Galilee with Jesus. Unlike the Twelve, the women of Galilee stayed with the Lord during his crucifixion and accompanied his body to the tomb.

---

1. Among the many studies on this topic, Carla Ricci's *Mary Magdalene* is the most complete. I am using Bauckham, *Gospel Women*, for its support and critique of the feminist studies, and Calduch-Benages, *Perfume*, for a more recent feminist contribution. Bauckham and Calduch-Benages are both in a constructive dialogue with Ricci's work.

2. See Brown, "The Twelve," for the critical questions concerning the designation of the Twelve as "apostles."

Unlike the Twelve, they were the first witnesses of the empty tomb, and, at least in one Gospel (Matt 28:9), the first to see the Lord risen from the dead. (According to Mark 16:9 [from the "longer ending"] and John 20:14–17, it is Mary Magdalene alone who is the first.) The women of Galilee are the ones who carried the good news of the empty tomb and the resurrection to the remaining members of the Twelve on Easter Sunday.

It is common knowledge that certain women from Galilee watched the crucifixion, accompanied Jesus' body to the tomb, and returned to find the tomb empty on Easter morning. We read this in the Gospels of Passiontide and Easter. What contemporary scholars have retrieved is solid evidence that a distinct and sizable group of women disciples (not just the handful whose names we know) accompanied Jesus from the outset—the beginning—of his public ministry. These women did not show up for the first time at the Cross; they did not just make a "cameo" appearance. They had been with Jesus and the Twelve throughout his mission in Galilee, and they belonged to his "inner circle."[3] Their commission was not fulfilled when they carried the news of the resurrection to the apostles; they did not retire. On the contrary, they were the primary and indispensable eyewitnesses to the resurrection, and they continued to proclaim the Risen Lord in the life of the early church.

For obvious reasons, retrieving the role of the women of Galilee has been a matter of special interest to women scholars. Due to their diligence and imagination, the women of Galilee have stepped out of the shadows during the past forty years. Today we confidently classify them as "disciples,"[4] and even "apostles" (in the Pauline sense[5]), and we recognize them as models for women called to the apostolic life and various public ministries in the church. Most women scholars appeal to this tradition to challenge the feminist critique of Christianity and its narrative of the "total oppression" of women. Some also appeal to it to support their conviction that women should be eligible for ordination to the priesthood.[6] I will point out, however,

---

3. According to Luke 8:1–3, both men and women belong to Jesus' inner circle. See Ricci, *Mary Magdalene*, 51–55; Bauckham, *Gospel Women*, 199–200.

4. As Meier notes in *Marginal Jew*, 70–83, scholars have been reluctant to call them "disciples" until recently. See the discussion in Ricci, *Mary Magdalene*, 177–85. Meier (*Marginal Jew*, 82) concludes that the Twelve alone belong to a "still smaller subset, an inner circle within the group of [the] committed, itinerant disciples."

5. Namely, "those who had been commissioned by the risen Christ himself in resurrection appearances" (Bauckham, *Gospel Women*, 180). See also Brown, "The Twelve," 151.

6. According to D'Angelo (*Women and Christian Origins*, 106), this tradition refutes "the bizarre argument that, since Jesus chose only men as 'apostles,' women should be excluded from the ministerial priesthood." I will leave the question of women's

that early Christian sources appeal to Jesus' women disciples to make the case that Jesus intended to reserve the priesthood to men. In any event, the retrieval of the women of Galilee is important because—without displacing the Blessed Virgin Mary[7]—it enlarges the circle of New Testament role models for women. It gives women new confidence in the Gospel's support for a "discipleship of equals" in the church.

Since St. Mary Magdalene is the leader and the best known of the women of Galilee, I will begin by recalling the recovery of her role as the "Apostle to the Apostles." Next, I will show how women scholars have also retrieved "the women of Galilee" as a group who can rightly be called "apostles to the apostles." Feminist Scripture scholars have broken through the exegetical silence that left these women and their indispensable witness in the shadows. Finally, I will propose that the retrieval of the women of Galilee contributes to a vision of the church in which the complementarity of the sexes is acknowledged and women's full collaboration is promoted.

The Rehabilitation of St. Mary Magdalene, the "Apostle to the Apostles"

On June 10, 2016 the Holy See announced that the liturgical memorial of St. Mary Magdalene would be elevated to the rank of "feast" on the Roman calendar, the same rank as that of the twelve apostles. On July 22, 2016 this feast, complete with its proper Preface for an "Apostle to the Apostles" (*de apostolorum apostola*),[8] was celebrated for the first time. This liturgical upgrade was made at the express wish of Pope Francis and was meant to call attention to the dignity of women, the new evangelization, and the mystery of God's great mercy.[9] The decision serves to correct a long-standing tradition, preserved not only in the liturgy but also in art, drama, popular piety, and scriptural scholarship, that views Mary Magdalene more as a repentant sinner than a primary witness of Christ's resurrection.[10]

ordination as deacons/deaconesses to one side. The interested reader may consult my essays in *New Diaconal Review* archives (May 2011 and November 2012) and *Josephinum Diaconal Review* (Fall 2015).

7. See Johnson, *Truly Our Sister*, 137–206, for a reconstruction of the "historical Mary" that parallels this research in many respects.

8. The Latin text is available on the internet.

9. See Roche, "*Apostolorum Apostola*." Archbishop Roche says it is right that the liturgical celebration of this woman should have the same rank as that for the celebration of the Apostles in the General Roman Calendar because it underlines the special mission of this woman who is an example and model for all women in the church.

10. See Warner, *Alone*, 224–35. The 1969 Missal of Pope Paul VI began to address this when it dropped the identification of St. Mary Magdalene as "penitent."

Mary Magdalene in the Christian West: A Penitent

For centuries, the Latin Church identified Mary Magdalene, a woman from whom the Lord cast out seven demons (cf. Luke 8:2; Mark 16:9[11]), as a sinner. Why? First, because Luke's Gospel introduces her immediately after reporting the story of the sinful woman (generally thought of as a prostitute) who crashed the dinner party Simon the Pharisee had thrown for Jesus. (Luke 7:36–50). Second, because she is remembered as someone released from demonic possession.[12] While persons possessed by demons are not usually thought of as sinners, and are not presented as such in the Gospels, St. Jerome (347–419) made this association in her case. He thought the seven demons that possessed the Magdalene represented the full number of vices.[13] Pope St. Gregory the Great (ca. 540–604) endorsed Jerome's interpretation in a homily,[14] and from there it passed into the common tradition in the Latin West. In other words, Mary Magdalene was identified with the un-named sinner or prostitute who wept at Jesus' feet, dried them with her hair, kissed them, and anointed them with ointment from an alabaster flask in the home of a man named Simon. The confusion was then compounded. On the assumption that Jesus was probably anointed by a woman only once, Luke's story of the sinful woman was conflated with two other accounts: Matthew's and Mark's account of an anointing by an unnamed woman in the home of Simon the leper shortly before the Passover (Matt 26:6–7; Mark 14:3–4) and John's account of the anointing of Jesus' feet by Mary of Bethany in the home of Lazarus, also at a supper held shortly before the Passover (12:1–3; cf. 11:2)! The confusion of Mary Magdalene with Mary of Bethany seems to have been made on the basis of their shared name, Mary.

As a result of these similarities, all three—Mary Magdalene and Mary of Bethany and the sinful woman in chapter 7 of Luke's Gospel— were taken to be one and the same person. This interpretation, which presumes there was only one anointing by one woman, took hold in the

11. Mark 16:9–20 is the "longer ending."

12. Scholars today assume this demonic possession represents a serious pathology, perhaps a recurring mental illness or chronic disease. See Ricci, *Mary Magdalene*, 92, 131–35.

13. Ricci, *Mary Magdalene*, 34–35n16. In a letter to Marcella (Epistle 59.4: Corpus Scriptorum Ecclesiasticorum Latinorum 54:545), St. Jerome wrote: "Mary Magdalene is that same from whom seven demons had been expelled; so that where sin abounded, grace superabounded."

14. Pope St. Gregory the Great wrote: "This woman, whom Luke calls a sinner, John names Mary. I believe she is the same Mary of whom Mark says that seven demons were cast out. How should we interpret the seven demons except as the totality of vices?" *Homiliae in Evangelia*, II, 33, translated in Gregory, *Forty Gospel Homilies*, 269.

West, and the Magdalene became the patron of women penitents. Until quite recently, in fact, the gospel reading for her feast day was the story of the repentant prostitute from Luke 7.[15] Although scholars over the ages, especially since the sixteenth century, have succeeded in distinguishing the three women (called the "three Marys"), this tradition, and the many legends that accompanied it, continued to influence how St. Mary Magdalene is remembered. In the sanctoral cycle of the Eastern Church, Mary Magdalene, Mary of Bethany, and the repentant woman of Luke 7:36–50 all have their own feast days.[16] Spiritual writers and homilists in the West, however, not only rolled the three Marys into one, but also drew a dramatic contrast between Mary Magdalene, the penitent, and Mary, the sinless Virgin Mother of God. According to a fifth-century poem, the Virgin Mary, "alone of all her sex . . . pleased the Lord."[17]

Women Scholars Correct This Exegetical Distortion

Christian feminist theologians denounce this tradition as a distortion that obscures the authentic Gospel portrait of Mary Magdalene.[18] They point out that contemporary scholarship finds no warrant for identifying her with the sinful woman who anointed the Lord in the house of Simon the Pharisee, nor any warrant for equating her demonic possession with personal sin. At least one male scholar who recognized this distortion deemed it "harmless."[19] Feminist scholars, on the other hand, refuse to tolerate it because it is untrue and it deprives faithful women of an invaluable role model.[20] The liturgical recognition of Mary Magdalene as the "apostle to the apostles," and what the Christian East would call "equal to the apostles,"[21] represents a major breakthrough. It was achieved largely

15. The 1969 Missal of Paul VI replaced this gospel with John 11:1–2, 11–18.

16. According to Ricci, *Mary Magdalene*, 32n6, Mary of Bethany is celebrated on March 18; the repentant sinner of Luke 7 on March 31; and Mary Magdalene on July 22.

17. See Warner, *Alone*, xvii. Warner quotes Caelius Sedulius's poem in Herbert Musurillo's translation: "She . . . had no peer/ Either in our first mother or in all women/ Who were to come. But alone of all her sex/ She pleased the Lord."

18. For a thorough review of this scholarship, see Hinsdale, "St. Mary of Magdala."

19. Ricci, *Mary Magdalene*, 33, reports that New Testament scholar Ferdinand Prat dismissed this confusion as unproblematic.

20. Johnson, *Friends of God*, 146, says "the distortion that shifts the story of a leading apostolic woman into someone remembered mainly as a sinful transgressor is a deep untruth."

21. See Tkacz, "Singing Women's Words," 297, for evidence that Mary Magdalene, along with the other "myrrh-bearers," was designated *isapostolos*.

by feminist scholars and it is well worth celebrating. St. Mary Magdalene is now increasingly held up as a role model for women in the church. She is an icon of "discipleship" and "friendship" with Christ,[22] and revered as the primary witness to his resurrection. She is a saint who supports our apostolic vocation and invites our imitation.

The recovery of the saint's traditional designation as an "apostle" was part of this effort.[23] Like the disciples on Easter evening (John 20:25) and St. Paul (1 Cor 1:9), she testifies to the resurrection: "I have seen the Lord!" (John 20:18) Like them, she was commissioned by the Risen Lord himself to spread this good news. Many of the Catholic faithful are now aware of her rehabilitation from penitent prostitute to apostle to the apostles. But Mary Magdalene was not alone. She was clearly the leader of the group of women disciples, the women of Galilee. If the truth about Mary Magdalene has been exegetically distorted, it is not surprising that the women in her band have also remained in the shadows, at least in the Latin West. Restoring the image of Mary Magdalene as the "apostle to the apostles," then, has led to the retrieval of the women of Galilee. In fact, some ancient Christian authors, e.g., Hippolytus of Rome (ca. 170–235) and St. Jerome, gave them the same title—"apostles to the apostles."[24]

The Retrieval of the Women of Galilee, "Apostles to the Apostles"

The revival of interest in Mary Magdalene is only one item in a larger project, namely, re-reading the Gospels (in fact the whole New Testament) in search of the full truth about the status of women in the church. It is only in recent times that women have been allowed to earn advanced degrees in theological

22. See Moltmann-Wendel, "Motherhood or Friendship." As Johnson (*Truly Our Sister*, 37) likewise points out, "Jesus' life was shaped not only by relation to his mother but also by adult friendship with his women disciples, chief among whom was Mary Magdalene."

23. The tradition has been traced by Nürnberg, "*Apostolae Apostolorum*."

24. Tkacz, "Singing Women's Words," 297. For an English translation of their texts, see Backes, "*Apostola Apostolorum*," 67. In his commentary on the *Song of Songs*, Hippolytus writes, "And after this with a cry the synagogue expresses a good testimony for us through the women, those who were made apostles to the apostles, having been sent by Christ to those to whom first the angels said 'Go and announce to the disciples, "He has gone before you to Galilee. There you shall see him."'" St. Jerome writes in the preface of his commentary on the Book of Zephaniah: "the risen Lord appeared first to women, and those women were apostles to the apostles [*apostolorum . . . apostolas*], so that the men were put to shame for not having sought out the Lord, whom the weaker sex had already found."

and biblical studies.[25] Once initiated into these fields, women have noticed the influence of a male, or androcentric, bias in the reading of the sources, and have sought to correct it by asking new questions and devising new tools of interpretation. The search for the backstory of the women of Galilee is part of this agenda. Mary Magdalene has been subject to a distortion that has had adverse consequences for women. The group of women which she headed suffers, not from distortion (for the rest were not thought to be prostitutes), but from being forgotten and passed over, that is, from silence.[26]

Women from Galilee: Only Transitional Figures?

Until recently, Gospel commentaries written by men remember the women of Galilee chiefly for their role in Jesus' passion, death, burial, and resurrection. And, since the women's eyewitness testimony to the empty tomb and the Risen Lord was not thought to count as reliable in a court of law, and since it was not reported in St. Paul's formulation of the kerygma (1 Cor 15:3–7), scholars have rarely made the women themselves the subject of serious scholarly investigation. Interest in them has often been confined to working out how many women stood at the foot of the cross and whether there is some way to discern which proper names correspond to which unnamed women, e.g., Is Salome the mother of the sons of Zebedee or someone else?[27] Let us consider the texts in which they appear.

According to the Passion narratives of the Synoptic Gospels, Jesus' disciples, including many women from Galilee, accompanied him when he went to Jerusalem to celebrate the Passover. Some of the women who "looked on from afar" (Matt 27:55; Mark 15:40)[28] as the Lord Jesus hung on the cross and died are personally identified: Mary Magdalene, Mary the mother of James and Joses, Salome, and the mother of the sons of Zebedee. Several of these women—Mary Magdalene with "the other Mary" (Matt 28:1) or with Mary the mother of James, and Salome (Mark 16:1)—accompanied his body to the grave. They made note of where he lay, expecting to return with spices and ointments to anoint him after the mandatory Sabbath rest. And early on Sunday morning they did return (Luke 24:10 adds Joanna at this point), only to find the tomb empty. One or two angels, or

25. Ricci, *Mary Magdalene*, 46.

26. Ricci, *Mary Magdalene*, 19–28.

27. See, for example, Brown, *Death of the Messiah*, 2:1014–19.

28. As Ricci points out (*Mary Magdalene*, 165n1), Luke typically shows an "apologetic concern for the apostles," and he reports that "all his acquaintances and the women who had followed him from Galilee stood at a distance and saw these things (23:49)."

men in dazzling garments,[29] announced that Jesus had risen from the dead and sent them to give this news to the disciples.[30] According to Matthew 28:9, Mary Magdalene and "the other Mary" met the Risen Lord on the way. He greeted them, and, falling prostrate at his feet, they worshipped him. The disciples, however, did not believe the women.

The Synoptic accounts vary in several respects, and the Fourth Gospel (19:25–20:18) offers a still different version of what happened. According to John, Mary Magdalene stood at the very foot of the cross, along with the Mother of Jesus and her sister, Mary of Clopas.[31] Two secret disciples from Jerusalem, Joseph of Arimathea and Nicodemus, saw to Jesus' anointing and burial. Early on the first day of the week Mary Magdalene went to the tomb alone, saw that the stone had been taken away, and ran to tell Peter and the Beloved Disciple that the Lord's body was gone. They examined the evidence and returned home, but she remained at the tomb, weeping. When Jesus called her by name she recognized him and rejoicing ran to tell the disciples "I have seen the Lord!" Matthew (28:9) and Mark (16:11) corroborate John's account that Jesus appeared first to Mary Magdalene.

Exegetes have been concerned to harmonize the discrepancies among the various versions of these events and to assess the relative importance of the women's testimony, in view of reports that the disciples did not believe them. (Mark 16:9–11; Luke 24:11) They have often treated the women participants as necessary, but transitional, figures in the narrative that links the cross to the appearances of the Risen Lord to the Eleven. The women could not be ignored because the male disciples did not see where Jesus was buried and evidently did not plan to look for his tomb, but they were transitional in the sense that the narratives culminate in Christ's appearance to the apostles and his commission to them to bear witness to the world.[32]

Women Scholars Correct This Exegetical Silence

Women scholars maintain that the women of Galilee were the protagonists in this series of events, not just transitional figures. They have followed

29. One angel or young man in Matthew and Mark; two in Luke.

30. Matthew (28:7, 8, 10) says to "his disciples" and Jesus' "brethren"; Mark (16:7), to "his disciples and Peter"; Luke (24:9,10), to "the eleven and all the rest" and "the apostles."

31. Does John name three or four women at the foot of the cross? Brown (*Death of the Messiah*, 2:1014) thinks there are four; Bauckham (*Gospel Women*, 208) thinks there are three.

32. Bauckham, *Gospel Women*, 278–79, defends this view against the opinion of Witherington, "On the Road."

up clues and traces in the gospel texts to demonstrate that these women were not only essential eyewitnesses to the Lord's resurrection; they were associated with him right from the beginning of his ministry in Galilee. To establish this, women scholars have recovered the importance of a text that male exegetes passed over quickly. It is the short passage in Luke's Gospel that identifies the women of Galilee as a stable group, Luke 8:1–3: "And immediately he [Jesus] went through the cities and villages proclaiming and announcing the good news of the kingdom of God *and* the Twelve [were] with him, and some women who had been cured of evil spirits and diseases: Mary called Magdalene, from whom seven demons had gone out, and Joanna the wife of Chuza, Herod's superintendent, and Susanna, and many others, who assisted him with their resources."[33]

Until quite recently, New Testament scholars did not regard this information as particularly significant. Feminist scholar Carla Ricci describes this as "the text exegetes forgot,"[34] and cites as proof the report of a contemporary exegete who in 2002 said: "Luke 8:1–3 has the dubious honour of being a New Testament pericope that has not been studied in any of the specialist reviews for the past hundred years."[35] It is women scholars who have found and followed up on the clues in this passage that identify the women disciples in Jesus' public ministry mentioned in Luke 8 with "the women from Galilee" in the Passion Narratives.[36] What prompted their search and how did they uncover the story of these women?

Excursus on Feminist Principles of Interpretation

Interest in the status of women in the New Testament and in the church was fueled by the feminist critique of Christianity. Proposed in 1949 in Simone de Beauvoir's, *The Second Sex*,[37] and repeated in 1968 in Mary Daly's *The Church and the Second Sex*,[38] it laid blame for the oppression of women on Christianity and in particular, the teaching and practice of the Catholic Church. Feminist critics scoured the Scriptures, church teaching, theology, and church history. They called attention to evidence that

---

33. This translation is from Calduch-Benages, *Perfume*, 70.

34. Ricci, *Mary Magdalene*, 29.

35. Witherington, "On the Road," 133.

36. In 1963, Martin Hengel paved the way, however, by addressing the question from the perspective of historical Jesus scholarship. See his essay "Maria Magdalena."

37. Beauvoir, *Le deuxième sexe* (1949), was published in English in 1953.

38. Daly's book was republished by Harper & Row with a post-Christian introduction in 1975.

seemed to support the view that Christianity regards women as inferior to men and relegates them to "second place."

Christian feminist theology responds to this critique, accepting some elements and rejecting others.[39] One step in its method is the discovery and retrieval of elements in Scripture and Tradition that defend the equality of women. The investigation of the women of Galilee arose from this research. Women who earned advanced degrees in biblical and theological studies noticed in the existing (namely, male) commentaries on the Gospels a certain indifference to the biblical evidence concerning the participation of women in Jesus' mission. They were determined to uncover the full story behind Luke 8:1–3, and they used the tools of historical-critical research to do so.[40] For example, they noticed that rabbis in Palestine during Jesus' time did not accept women into the circle of their disciples; not only that, women were segregated, that is, generally excluded from social and public life, and even prevented from studying the Torah. For a celibate male teacher to take unchaperoned women along with him and other men on his preaching tours, then, was both revolutionary and scandalous.[41] The very novelty of the report in Luke 8:1–3 gives scholars confidence in its authenticity.[42] Consultation of the extracanonical Gospels provided additional insight into the importance and influence of Jesus' women disciples and the leadership of women, especially Mary Magdalene.[43]

Women exegetes have also brought the women of Galilee out into the open by applying the feminist "hermeneutics of suspicion."[44] In order to

39. Catholic feminist theologians are both apologists for Christian faith, insofar as they respond to the feminist critique, and critics, for example, in their complaint that the Christian tradition as handed on by the "patriarchal" Church has suffered a "massive distortion." See, for example, Carr, *Transforming Grace*, 95, 162; Johnson, *She Who Is*, 29.

40. For a description of this method, see the Pontifical Biblical Commission, *Interpretation of the Bible*, I, A.

41. Ricci, *Mary Magdalene*, 85–91.

42. Ricci, *Mary Magdalene*, 43–44.

43. Ricci, *Mary Magdalene*, 146–48. These texts are the *Gospel of Mary* [Magdalene], *Pistis Sophia*, and the *Gospel of Philip*.

44. See Pontifical Biblical Commission, *Interpretation of the Bible*, I, E, 2: "Feminist hermeneutic has not developed a new methodology. It employs the current methods of exegesis, especially the historical-critical method. But it does add two criteria of investigation. The first is the feminist criterion, borrowed from the women's liberation movement, in line with the more general direction of liberation theology. This criterion involves a hermeneutic of suspicion: Since history was normally written by the victors, establishing the full truth requires that one does not simply trust texts as they stand but look for signs which may reveal something quite different. The second criterion is sociological; it is based on the study of societies in the biblical times, their social

break through the general silence of the Gospels concerning the disciple-ship of women, they devised principles and tools for investigating what was *not* reported and what was *not* said.[45] For example, according to Elisabeth Schüssler Fiorenza, "androcentric [that is, male-centered] language mentions women only when their presence is exceptional or causes a problem, not in normal situations."[46] According to this principle, it should be presumed that the women were with Jesus and the Twelve all along, not just from time to time.[47] What would be the point of repeatedly mentioning them, once their presence has been announced?[48] Again, since the New Testament uses the ge-neric masculine, any translation or interpretation should be taken as inclusive of women unless proven otherwise.[49] By applying the feminist hermeneutics of suspicion and drawing imaginatively on their own experience,[50] women scholars have broken the silence of the Gospels about the women who fol-lowed Jesus throughout his public ministry in Galilee.

Women Scholars Direct New Attention to Luke 8:1–3

With this in mind, let us look again at Luke 8:1–3, the only text in the gospels that directly attests to the presence of women in Jesus' ministry in Galilee.[51]

stratification and the position they accorded to women."

45. Ricci, *Mary Magdalene*, 19–28. Bauckham, *Gospel Women*, xiii–xxi, also dis-cusses this approvingly, but he offers a critique of a certain "one-issue" exegesis that fails to take note of what can be found in the Gospel texts themselves. The hermeneutic of suspicion is also used to seek out hitherto unnoticed presuppositions or traditions that appear to legitimate injustice.

46. Schüssler Fiorenza, *In Memory of Her*, 44.

47. In his apostolic letter *On the Dignity and Vocation of Women* (*Mulieris Dignita-tem*, 1988), sec. 13, Pope St. John Paul II says only that women "often" (*saepe*, rendered as "sometimes" in the Vatican's translation) accompanied Jesus as he journeyed with the Apostles.

48. Ricci, *Mary Magdalene*, 61; Bauckham, *Gospel Women*, 110.

49. Schüssler Fiorenza, *In Memory of Her*, 45. Matthew 14:21 (see also 15:38), for example, reporting the multiplication of the loaves and the fishes, notes that Jesus fed five thousand men, not counting women and children. Bauckham does not appeal to the same example (where "men" may not in fact be a true instance of the generic mas-culine, but only a shorthand for indicating a large number), but he acknowledges the force of Schüssler Fiorenza's principles in *Gospel Women*, 112n7, 199–202. On this basis Bauckham assumes that women were included among the seventy-two disciples Jesus sent out on mission (Luke 10:1–20). The principles involved in adopting this reading strategy need careful analysis, it seems to me, for it is open to manipulation.

50. Moltmann-Wendel, *Women around Jesus*, exemplifies the use of imagination in reconstructing women's experience.

51. See Ricci, *Mary Magdalene*, 51–110; Bauckham, *Gospel Women*, 110–21;

"And immediately he [Jesus] went through the cities and villages proclaiming and announcing the good news of the kingdom of God *and* the Twelve [were] with him, and some women who had been cured of evil spirits and diseases: Mary called Magdalene, from whom seven demons had gone out, and Joanna the wife of Chuza, Herod's superintendent, and Susanna, and many others, who assisted him with their resources."[52]

According to this translation of what is only a single sentence in the Greek, both the Twelve and the women—those who are named and "many other" women—accompanied and served Jesus.[53] Women scholars prefer the textual variant that says the women served "him," that is, Jesus, rather than "them," Jesus and the Twelve.[54] Whereas the Twelve were introduced earlier (Luke 6:13–16), the women are introduced here for the first time. The sentence is precisely about them. It is a not just a "summary" of what has gone before, as was commonly held in the past; it is a "narrative statement that describes a prolonged situation or portrays an event as happening repeatedly within an indefinite period of time."[55] Even though the women of Galilee are not mentioned again until Jesus' passion, then, it should be assumed that they were present throughout his ministry.

Women scholars point out the value of this short text. It provides "startling information."[56] The news that women left their homes to follow an itinerant Master is "absolutely astonishing."[57] It sheds light on the liberating practice by which Jesus broke with the customs and conventions of his time. It is "a 'privileged trace' of a female following that is virtually silenced by all the evangelists."[58]

What is the source of Luke's testimony to the women's prior participation in Jesus' Galilean mission? Carla Ricci, drawing on the thesis of Thorleif Boman,[59] suggests that Luke has his own source, in fact, that his special material comes from a tradition "kept and mainly handed on by women."[60]

Calduch-Benages, *Perfume*, 70–74.

52. Calduch-Benages, *Perfume*, 70.

53. Calduch-Benages, *Perfume*, 71.

54. See Ricci, *Mary Magdalene*, 156–58; Calduch-Benages, *Perfume*, 71. They regard this as significant, for it puts the women, like the men, in a relationship of service to Jesus.

55. Calduch-Benages, *Perfume*, 71–72, quoting Co, "Summaries in Acts," 56–57. Bauckham, *Gospel Women*, 110, cites with approval the same source and its definition.

56. Ricci, *Mary Magdalene*, 53.

57. Calduch-Benages, *Perfume*, 75.

58. Calduch-Benages, *Perfume*, 82.

59. Boman, *Jesus Oberlieferung*.

60. Ricci, *Mary Magdalene*, 44, 70–73. Bauckham, *Gospel Women*, 190–91, also

According to this hypothesis, the "women's tradition" would have been a single account, extending from the birth of the Baptist to Jesus' Ascension, that preserved the memories of which women were the witnesses, hearers, and custodians. The silence of the other Gospels would reflect the fact that their authors did not have access to the special "women's tradition" on which Luke's Gospel depends.

There is a growing consensus that Luke intends to draw a certain parallel between the women of Galilee and the Twelve, two identifiable groups within the larger body of disciples.[61] Luke associates the two groups by naming three leading members of the women, Mary Magdalene, Joanna the wife of Herod's steward Chuza, and Susanna—although there are also "many others"—just as elsewhere (8:51; 9:28) he names three leading members of the Twelve, Peter, James, and John. Again, he always names Peter and Mary Magdalene first in these lists.[62]

Luke 8:1–2 is the first time that the three women whose names are supplied appear in the Gospel. What they have in common is the fact that Jesus has cured them of "evil spirits and infirmities." We are told that Jesus cast out seven demons from Mary Magdalene. There is no account of their cures, however, and there are no "call stories" as there are for the leading members of the Twelve. It is possible, however, that the cures they received functioned as a call.[63] Whatever the case, they are repeatedly described as "following" Jesus in the Passion Narratives.

Like the Twelve, the women of Galilee have left their homes and families to accompany Jesus,[64] though they apparently brought with them or retained control over some of their earthly goods. What this text says equally of the women and of the Twelve is that they were "with Jesus" as he traveled through Galilee. Being "with Jesus" is the essence of discipleship in Luke,[65] and since the women are the ones who stand by Jesus in the end, following him to the cross and to the grave, Jesus must have regarded and treated them as his disciples.[66]

---

favors this hypothesis, and he attempts to identify and account for "gynocentric" narratives (Bauckham, *Gospel Women*, 14–16).

61. Bauckham, *Gospel Women*, 281n54, takes issue with Ricci's view (*Mary Magdalene*, 54) that the women and the Twelve are quite distinct from "the disciples."

62. Calduch-Benages, *Perfume*, 76. Hengel, *Maria Magdalena*, 248, noticed this, and Ricci, *Mary Magdalene*, 146–49, points out that the Gnostic gospels feature a rivalry between Peter and Mary Magdalene.

63. Meier, *Marginal Jew*, 77, makes this suggestion.

64. Matt 19:27, 29; Mark 10:28–29; Luke 5:28; 18:29.

65. Bauckham, *Gospel Women*, 112–14.

66. Meier, *Marginal Jew*, 79–80.

The Nature of the Women's Ministry to Jesus

Like the Twelve, the women of Galilee accompanied Jesus in his travels, but unlike the Twelve, they also "ministered to him" (or to "them") out of their resources. The reference to their "ministry" has traditionally been understood to mean that they carried out typical women's roles, like acquiring and preparing food. Contemporary scholars point out, however, that while the women evidently put their material and economic resources at the disposal of Jesus and the Twelve,[67] we should not imagine that they only provided meals and paid the bills. Using the feminist hermeneutic of suspicion, they notice that while Luke often uses the verb *diakoneo* to refer to service at table (4:39; 10:40; 12:37; 17:8), he also uses it to refer to the "missionary-service" that Jesus himself exercises and recommends to his followers (22:26–27).[68] Luke 8:3b could be translated: "and many other [women] who were using their resources while going on mission in his name."[69]

Being "with" Jesus as he proclaimed the kingdom surely implies that they received the same theological and spiritual "formation" as the Twelve during his public mission. Did they engage in preaching? Were they sent out with the seventy-two disciples?[70] We do not know, but this passage allows us to revise the common picture of Jesus accompanied by an all-male traveling band. Mary Magdalene, Joanna, and Susanna and *many other women* were right there with the Twelve, not just as serving maids but as collaborators and contributors to the mission.[71]

Re-reading the Passion Narratives

Two passages from the Passion Narratives, one from Mark's Gospel and another from Luke, confirm the truth of the women's presence and participation in Jesus' mission after the fact. Mark 15:41 notes that the women who

67. For Bauckham, *Gospel Women*, 114–15, "the true male counterpart to women's 'service,' as described in Luke 8:3, is not preaching or leadership but the abandonment of home and family by the twelve."

68. "Let the greatest among you become as the youngest, and the leader as one who serves. For which is the greater, one who sits at table or one who serves? Is it not the one who sits at table? But I am among you as one who serves." Calduch-Benages, *Perfume*, 80, suggests this.

69. Calduch-Benages, *Perfume*, 80–81, citing the study by Karris, "Women and Discipleship," 9–10.

70. Bauckham, *Gospel Women*, 112, thinks that they were.

71. Calduch-Benages, *Perfume*, 82, suggests that along with domestic chores the women were "praying, witnessing, helping the needy, and talking about deep questions" with Jesus and the disciples.

looked on Jesus' crucifixion from afar were "the women who, when he was *in* Galilee, followed him and ministered to him." In other words, they not only "followed" Jesus him from Galilee on this occasion, as Matthew 27:55 suggests; they belonged to his company back home, as his disciples, and were accustomed to "ministering" to him there.[72] The second testimony is in Luke's report of the Easter morning encounter of the women of Galilee with the two men in radiant apparel at the tomb. "'Remember how he told you, while he was still in Galilee,' the men say, "that the Son of Man must be delivered into the hands of sinful men, and be crucified, and on the third day rise.' And they remembered his words" (24:6–8). They *did* remember, because they had been there. They were among the disciples to whom Jesus predicted his passion, privately, during the Galilean ministry.[73]

Re-reading the Passion Narratives against this background, it is possible to evaluate the information they provide about the women of Galilee in a new light. The women are the protagonists that link Jesus' death and burial to his resurrection. They are the ones who knew where to find his tomb and were determined to give him a proper burial. They are the first eyewitnesses of the empty tomb, and—at least for Matthew and John—of the Risen Lord Jesus. They model the proper response to the Easter revelation by falling at his feet and worshipping him. And they are the ones who receive the commission: "Go to my brethren" (Matt 28:9; John 20:17).

According to Bauckham, there is no evidence to suggest that the role of the women in the resurrection stories has been depreciated or limited in the gospel narratives of Matthew, Luke, and John, as some feminist scholars suspect.[74] Where male prejudice against their testimony is explicitly evoked (Luke 24:11), he maintains, it is "so that it may be decisively overturned."[75] This group of women constitutes an indispensable link between Jesus' cross and his resurrection. They are, in fact, the primary witnesses to his burial and resurrection.

Much more can be said of some of the women of Galilee named in the Gospels. Scholars like Richard Bauckham have explored in detail their life circumstances and possible relationships. For example, Mary of Clopas may

72. Schüssler Fiorenza, *In Memory of Her*, 319–23, explores the implications of Mark's account and believes that he intends to contrast the fidelity of the women with the cowardice of the men disciples.

73. See Luke 9:22, 43–44. Bauckham, *Gospel Women*, 113, notes that the third prediction (Luke 18:32–33) is addressed only to the Twelve.

74. Bauckham maintains (*Gospel Women*, 276–95, especially n43) that the feminist exegetes are mistaken in thinking that reports of the male disciples' disbelief represent "a denigration of the women's witness."

75. Bauckham, *Gospel Women*, 285. In his opinion, 286, "the effect of the narratives will be to refute and to reverse assumptions of male priority and female unreliability."

be Mary of Nazareth's sister-in-law, and she and Clopas may be the disciples on the road to Emmaus;[76] Joanna, wife of Herod's steward Chuza, may be the woman named "Junia" in Paul's letter to the Romans.[77] And so on. In addition to Mary Magdalene and Joanna, and Susanna, who is not heard from again, the Passion narratives name Salome, Mary the mother of James and Joses, and Mary of Clopas; they refer to, but do not name, the mother of the sons of Zebedee and "the other Mary."

Scholars today have a new appreciation of the importance of eye-witness testimony to the resurrection in the early Christian community.[78] This leads them to grasp the significance of the fact that the names of the women of Galilee who saw the Risen Lord are included in the gospel tradition. It must be that they were well-known figures, and that they continued to serve as witnesses in the early Christian community. Their names are important, and readers should not try to reduce their number or combine them.[79] There were *many* women in this group, and different oral traditions recall different memories and personalities. Whereas later readers may regard the women who witnessed Jesus' death, burial, and empty tomb only as transitional figures on the way to his appearances to the Twelve, this does not necessarily represent the viewpoint of their contemporaries. As against the view that only the witness of men counted in first-century Judaism, Bauckham believes that the witness of the women of Galilee was "highly respected" and valued by their contemporaries.[80] They were "apostles to the apostles," certainly, but they were more than that. They were themselves eyewitnesses, commissioned by the Risen Lord to testify to his victory over death to everyone they met. This would make them "apostles," at least by Paul's definition.

Some were remembered by name—Mary Magdalene and Joanna, introduced in Luke 8, bear witness to the Easter mystery; also, Mary the mother of James and Joses, and Salome. Perhaps Mary of Clopas belongs to this group. Others are remembered as belonging to this group, but are not named: the mother of the sons of Zebedee and the "other Mary." These are not the only women witnesses, however, for there were also "many other women" (Matt 27:55; Mark 15:40), including of course the Virgin Mary, the mother of Jesus. These women saw the Risen Lord and they

76. Bauckham, *Gospel Women*, ch. 6.

77. Bauckham, *Gospel Women*, ch. 5.

78. Bauckham, *Gospel Women*, deals with this in ch. 8. He points out that they "acted as apostolic eyewitness guarantors of the traditions about Jesus, especially his resurrection but no doubt also in other respects" (Bauckham, *Gospel Women*, 295).

79. Ricci, *Mary Magdalene*, 171–77; Bauckham, *Gospel Women*, 297–300.

80. Bauckham, *Gospel Women*, 286.

continued to bear testimony, at least in the Jerusalem church and per-haps even in Rome.[81] Like Mary Magdalene, they too could claim: "I have seen the Lord" (John 20:18). Remember: this is what the apostles said to Thomas: "We have seen the Lord!" (20:25). And this is how Paul claims his status: "Am I not an apostle? Have I not seen Jesus our Lord?" (1 Cor 1:9). We cannot imagine that the women apostles "retired" once they delivered the message on Easter morning!

Some Implications of the Retrieval
of the Women of Galilee

According to contemporary scholarship, the traveling band that accom-panied Jesus during his Galilean mission included a body of women, "the women of Galilee." This research encourages readers to assume that the women disciples heard the same message, saw the same miracles, and shared the same joys and hardships as the Twelve. We may assume that the women of Galilee and the Twelve had virtually the same spiritual and theological "formation." During Jesus' passion, death, and resurrection, the women emerge as the protagonists and the primary witnesses of courage and fidelity, and they actively proclaim the good news. Should we agree, then, with those who claim that their shared life and mission in what is called the "Jesus movement" was a "discipleship of equals"?[82] Should we conclude, further, that the retrieval of the women of Galilee supports the access of women to the ministerial priesthood?

"Discipleship of Equals" and the Ordination of Women

First, was the "Jesus movement," and is the church today, a "discipleship of equals"? We can confidently answer "yes." As contemporary New Testament scholarship illustrates, Jesus' teaching and example support the spiritual equality of women and men,[83] and the presence of the women of Galilee in his traveling band is a particularly striking confirmation of this. Contem-porary church teaching explicitly asserts that women and men are equally

---

81. Bauckham, *Gospel Women*, 109–202. He speculates that Joanna may be the "Ju-nia" Paul greets with her husband Andronicus (once known as "Chuza") as his relatives and fellow prisoners, "prominent among the apostles" (Rom 16:7).

82. Recall that during Jesus' Galilean ministry, the Twelve had not yet been assigned the specific tasks that belong to the apostolic ministry after the Resurrection.

83. See the overview in Tkacz, "Jesus and Spiritual Equality" and Mary Healy's re-cent overview, "Women in Sacred Scripture."

made in God's image and have the same dignity and human rights. It also claims, citing Galatians 3:28, that there is no inequality in Christ and in the church arising from the difference between the sexes. Women and men have a common baptismal dignity, filial grace, call to holiness, gift of salvation, hope, and love.[84] This discipleship of equals, then, is rooted in Baptism, that is, in the sacraments of Christian Initiation. Equality, however, does not imply identity. This truth holds both for the equal dignity of the sexes and for the equal dignity of the laity, the clergy, and those who belong to a religious state approved by the church.

In the divine design, the complementarity of the sexes is compatible with their genuine equality as human beings.[85] Women and men possess the same human nature, but they possess it differently, not only for the sake of generating new life but also, more generally, as an invitation to interpersonal communion and fruitfulness.[86] May we not assume, then, that the Lord sought and found in the ministry of the women of Galilee something different from what he expected from the Twelve? May we not suppose that their love and fidelity was "the ideal and necessary response . . . to his gift of himself for the salvation of the world"?[87] In the Catholic tradition, the distinctive characteristics of women's spirituality have been thoroughly explored with reference to the Blessed Virgin Mary as the premier model. The retrieval of the women of Galilee—Jesus' adult women friends and disciples, active in his ministry—invites a further elaboration of this theme.

By divine institution there are in the Church many diverse gifts and functions. "Although by Christ's will some are established as teachers, dispensers of the mysteries and pastors for the others, there remains, nevertheless, a true equality between all with regard to the dignity and to the activity in the building up of the Body of Christ."[88]

Second, does the retrieval of the women of Galilee support the priestly ordination of women? Some feminist scholars believe that it does, and they

84. Paul VI, *Lumen Gentium* (Dogmatic Constitution on the Church), sec. 32. In *Mulieris Dignitatem*, John Paul II reiterates and defends this teaching with respect to the status of women.

85. See my essay, "Embodiment."

86. According to the Congregation for the Doctrine of the Faith's "Letter to the Bishops of the Catholic Church on the Collaboration of Men and Women in the Church and in the World," no. 8, the "equal dignity of man and woman as persons is realized as physical, psychological and ontological complementarity."

87. According to Healy, "Women in Sacred Scripture," 50, Jesus valued the love and fidelity of his women companions. For an early but still valuable discussion of the difference in men's and women's ministry, see Galot, "Femme dans l'Église."

88. Paul VI, *Lumen Gentium*, sec. 32. The remainder of this article elucidates how the diversity of vocations contributes to the Church's unity and mission.

appeal to the "discipleship of equals" in support of their position. If women were not only disciples, but apostles (by Paul's definition), and if they went on mission and proclaimed the good news, what is to prevent us, they ask, from concluding that women as well as men in the Jesus movement exercised the leadership functions that would later be associated with the ordained priesthood, and that Catholic women today should have equal access with men to priestly ordination?[89] It is important to notice that feminist scholars who pursue this line of reasoning are generally raising questions about the magisterium's claim that in choosing only men to belong to the Twelve, Jesus established a perennial norm for the ministerial priesthood, and that the practice of the apostolic church confirms this.[90] Relying on a widespread scholarly consensus developed by means of the historical-critical method, they argue that it is impossible to prove that Jesus' constitution of the Twelve is relevant to the question. They accept the theory that the ordained ministry, and in particular its priestly character, emerged only gradually, under the guidance of the Holy Spirit and that "the presbyter-bishops described in the N[ew] T[estament] were not in any traceable way the successors of the Twelve apostles."[91] The implication is that the sacramental power exercised by the ordained "resides in the Church and can be given to those whom the Church designates or acknowledges without a lineal connection to the Twelve."[92]

Clearly, this version of a discipleship of equals fails to correspond to Catholic teaching on the vocation of the Twelve, the dominical institution of the sacrament of holy orders, the New Testament priesthood, the hierarchical structure of the church, and apostolic succession.[93] This reconstruction, which has roots in the sixteenth-century Reformation,[94]

---

89. See Schneiders, "Did Jesus Exclude Women?"; Schüssler Fiorenza, "The Twelve"; Schüssler Fiorenza, "Apostleship of Women."

90. See the Congregation for the Doctrine of the Faith's Declaration on the Question of the Admission of Women to the Ministerial Priesthood (*Inter Insigniores*), 1–2, and Pope John Paul II's apostolic letter to the bishops of the Catholic Church on Reserving Priestly Ordination to Men Alone (*Ordinatio sacerdotalis*), 2.

91. See Brown, *Priest and Bishop*, 72. At times, this line of reasoning is accompanied by the hypothesis that the discipleship of equals in the early Jesus movement was suppressed in the apostolic era for the sake of gaining credibility in the Greco-Roman world. Such is Schüssler Fiorenza's proposal, *In Memory of Her*, 251–65.

92. Brown, *Priest and Bishop*, 55, reports the academic consensus.

93. All of these doctrines are revisited in debates about the ordination of women to the ministerial priesthood.

94. Martin Luther, for example, held that since the Twelve prefigure the whole church, the gifts Christ entrusted to them belong to the rest of the baptized as well. He abandoned the belief that Holy Orders is a sacrament.

investigates the data of the New Testament without regard for its interpretation in the unbroken tradition of the church. It privileges the findings of historical scholarship over the witness of the Tradition and calls into question the "settled doctrine" of the Catholic Church regarding Jesus' institution of a New Testament priesthood.[95]

Mary and the Women of Galilee in Patristic Testimony

What does the witness of the Tradition contribute? When I claimed that the contemporary retrieval of the women of Galilee supports the church's teaching on an all-male priesthood, I had in mind the appeal made to their example in documents of the early church. In the few documents that deal with it, the question of women's admission to the priesthood was decided by appeal either to certain passages in the letters of St. Paul[96] or to the will of Christ known from his choice of men only to belong to the Twelve and from the practice of the apostolic church, in which no woman was appointed bishop or priest.[97] The argument, in fact, contrasts his choice of the Twelve with his failure to choose the Virgin Mary, Mary Magdalene, or any of the worthy women in his company, including the women of Galilee.

The most explicit formulation of this argument is found in the *Panarion* (or *Medicine Chest*) of St. Epiphanius of Salamis, written around AD 377.[98] Epiphanius makes his appeal to the divine will regarding women and the priesthood principally by reference to Mary.[99] The argument is this: If God wanted women to be priests, he would have found no one more worthy than the mother of his Son, but he did not confer the priesthood on her, nor did he even entrust Baptism to her. Christ called no woman to belong to the Twelve, and no woman was ever appointed to succeed the apostles as bishop

95. *Catechism of the Catholic Church* §1577: "The Lord Jesus chose men (*viri*) to form the college of the twelve apostles, and the apostles did the same when they chose collaborators to succeed them in their ministry." For a reply to objections that the Twelve are not identical with the "apostles," and that they had no successors, see Müller, *Priesthood and Diaconate*, 38–39.

96. The "Pauline ban" is found in 1 Corinthians 14:34–35 and 1 Timothy 2:12.

97. In its formal response to this question, the magisterium depends chiefly on the example of Christ recorded in the Gospels and the practice of the apostolic church. See Congregation for the Doctrine of the Faith, *Inter Insigniores*, 2–3, and John Paul II, *Ordinatio sacerdotalis*, 1–2.

98. Epiphanius, *Panarion*, 1.1–9.5. Some of the arguments here are found in earlier texts, e.g., the *Didascalia* and the *Constitutiones Apostolicae*. Congregation for the Doctrine of the Faith, *Inter Insigniores*, nn7–8, cites all three sources.

99. Epiphanius is denouncing the Collyridians, a heretical sect that appointed women priests to offer sacrifice to the Ever-Virgin Mary.

or presbyter, or preside over the mysteries. Therefore, it is God's will to call only men to the ministerial priesthood.[100]

This argument was passed down in the canonical tradition in a "Marian" form, that is, Christ's will with regard to the priesthood was understood by considering the position of Mary vis-à-vis the Twelve. In 1210, Pope Innocent III formulated it this way: "Although the Blessed Virgin Mary was of higher dignity and excellence than all the Apostles, it was to them, not her, that the Lord entrusted the keys of the kingdom."[101] This tradition preserves the judgment that the priesthood is reserved to men, and at the same time shows that Mary was not called to it despite her great dignity, not because of some deficiency pertaining to her sex.

The point I wish to make, however, is that the women of Galilee also play a part in this traditional argument. In fact, the retrieval of their existence as a group that was part of Jesus' inner circle, along with the Twelve, renders this argument more plausible and extends it to all women. Unlike the Virgin Mary, these women accompanied Jesus and the Twelve throughout his Galilean ministry and were commissioned by him as apostolic witnesses to his resurrection. We may suppose, on these grounds, that these women disciples were more likely candidates for the priesthood than Jesus' mother Mary. St. Epiphanius may suppose that God's will for women is known by means of Mary, but he does not rely exclusively on her admittedly unique vocation. He adds to his argument: If God had wanted to call women to be priests, he could have called "the women who followed Christ from Galilee . . . or any of the holy women who were privileged to be saved by his advent <and> who assisted him with their own possessions . . . or any woman on earth."[102] In other words, Jesus had many worthy women in his company, but since they were not chosen for the office of priesthood, neither is any woman.

---

100. Epiphanius, *Panarion*, 79:2.1–4.1. Epiphanius accompanies this with an argument that women were not called to the Old Testament priesthood and have never offered sacrifice to God. "If it were ordained by God that women should offer sacrifice or have any canonical function in the church, Mary herself, if anyone, should have functioned as a priest in the New Testament." Epiphanius, *Panarion*, 79:3.1.

101. This line of reasoning was treated as a principle by medieval canonists and theologians. See the unofficial commentary on *Inter Insigniores*, found in United States Catholic Conference, *From "Inter Insigniores,"* 60, 63–65, and John Paul II, *Ordinatio sacerdotalis*, art. 3.

102. Epiphaniuis, *Panarion*, II.79:7.4. Along with the "women of Galilee," Epiphanius mentions other women associated with the Lord Jesus: "Martha the sister of Lazarus and [her sister] Mary," "the woman of Canaan or the woman who was healed of the issue of blood."

The retrieval of the women of Galilee, then, does not necessarily suggest that women are called to the ministerial priesthood. Those who appreciate the logic of this ancient argument understand that if Jesus chose neither his mother nor any of the worthy women in his company to belong to the Twelve (viz., to be priests, to exercise priestly functions), he evidently did not intend to open this vocation to women. Clearly, however, his choice does not represent a "sexist" discrimination against women. What then? Should we not assume that the ministry of women (in addition to their "ministry" as mothers) has some distinctive and valuable feminine characteristics? According to the magisterium, the ministry of women has its own style and authority—the moral authority of holiness, and their ministry manifests the charismatic, as distinct from the institutional, aspect of the church.[103] This part belongs to the priesthood of the baptized, and to women in a special way.[104] The church's pastors expect that the "*active collaboration* between the sexes precisely in the recognition of the difference between man and woman" will be mutually enriching.[105]

In an ecclesiology of communion, equal discipleship does not exclude a variety of gifts, and full participation in the church is the prerogative not of the clergy but of the saints. The retrieval of the women of Galilee enlarges the circle of New Testament role models for women and invites them to take their place in the life and ministry of the church as disciples and "apostles," called to testify to the resurrection and commissioned to bear witness to the good news in the world.

Bibliography

Backes, Julian R. "*Apostola Apostolorum*: Observations on the Proper of St. Mary Magdalene in the *Breviarium Praemonstratense*." *Antiphon* 21.1 (2017) 66–71.

Bauckham, Richard. *Gospel Women: Studies of the Named Women in the Gospels*. Grand Rapids: Eerdmans, 2002.

Beauvoir, Simone de. *The Second Sex*. Translated by H. M. Parshley. New York: Knopf, 1953.

Boman, Thorleif. *Die Jesus Oberlieferung im Lichte der neueren Volkeskunde*. Gottingen: Vanderhöck & Ruprecht, 1967.

Brown, Raymond E. *The Death of the Messiah: From Gethsemane to Grave: A Commentary on the Passion Narratives in the Four Gospels*. 2 vols. New York: Doubleday, 1994.

103. See John Paul II, *Mulieris Dignitatem*, sec. 27.

104. Galot, "La femme dans l'Église," 206–10, opens this question for further exploration.

105. See the Congregation for the Doctrine of the Faith's Letter on the Collaboration of Men and Women 4.

————. *Priest and Bishop: Biblical Reflections.* New York: Paulist, 1970.

————. "The Twelve and the Apostolate." In *The New Jerome Biblical Commentary,* edited by Raymond E. Brown et al., 1377–81 (135–57). Englewood Cliffs, NJ: Prentice-Hall, 1990.

Butler, Sara. "Embodiment: Women and Men, Equal and Complementary." In *The Church Women Want: Catholic Women in Dialogue,* edited by Elizabeth A. Johnson, 35–44. New York: Crossroad, 2002.

Calduch-Benages, Nuria. *The Perfume of the Gospel: Jesus' Encounters with Women.* Translated by Pascale-Dominique Nau. Roma: Gregorian & Biblical 2012.

Catechism of the Catholic Church. https://www.vatican.va/archive/ENG0015/_INDEX.HTM.

Carr, Anne E. *Transforming Grace: Christian Tradition and Women's Experience.* San Francisco: Harper & Row, 1988.

Co, Maria Anicia. "The Major Summaries in Acts: Acts 2,42–47; 4,32–35; 5,12–16: Linguistic and Literary Relationship." *Ephemerides Theologicae Lovanienses* 68 (1992) 49–85.

Congregation for the Doctrine of the Faith. *Inter Insigniores:* On the Question of the Admission of Women to the Ministerial Priesthood. October 15, 1976. https://www.vatican.va/roman_curia/congregations/cfaith/documents/rc_con_cfaith_doc_19761015_inter-insigniores_en.html.

————. "Letter to the Bishops of the Catholic Church on the Collaboration of Men and Women in the Church and in the World." https://www.vatican.va/roman_curia/congregations/cfaith/documents/rc_con_cfaith_doc_20040731_collaboration_en.html.

Daly, Mary. *The Church and the Second Sex.* New York: Harper & Row, 1968.

D'Angelo, Mary Rose. *Women and Christian Origins.* Edited by Ross Shepard Kraemer and Mary Rose D'Angelo. New York: Oxford University Press 1999.

Epiphanius. *Panarion of Epiphanius of Salamis: Books II and III.* Translated by Frank Williams. 2nd ed. Leiden: Brill, 2013.

Galot, Jean. "La femme dans l'Église." *Gregorianum* 68 (1987) 187–213.

Gregory the Great, Pope. *Forty Gospel Homilies.* Translated by David Hurst. Piscataway, NJ: Gorgias 2009.

Healy, Mary. "Women in Sacred Scripture: New Insights from Exegesis." In *Ruolo delle Donne nella Chiesa: Atti del Simposio promosso della Congregazione per la Dottrina della Fede,* 43–54. Libreria Editrice Vaticana, 2017.

Hengel, Martin. "Maria Magdalena und die Frauen als Zeugen." In *Abraham unser Vater: Festschrift Otto Michel,* edited by Otto Betz et al., 243–56. Arbeiten zur Geschichte des antiken Judentums und des Urchristentums 5. Leiden: Brill, 1963.

Hinsdale, Mary Ann. "St. Mary of Magdala: Ecclesiological Provocations." *Catholic Theological Society of America Proceedings* 66 (2011) 67–90.

John Paul II, Pope. *Mulieris Dignitatem.* https://www.vatican.va/content/john-paul-ii/en/apost_letters/1988/documents/hf_jp-ii_apl_19880815_mulieris-dignitatem.html.

————. *Ordinatio sacerdotalis.* https://www.vatican.va/content/john-paul-ii/en/apost_letters/1994/documents/hf_jp-ii_apl_19940522_ordinatio-sacerdotalis.html.

Johnson, Elizabeth A. *Friends of God and Prophets: A Feminist Theological Reading of the Communion of Saints.* New York: Continuum, 2000.

————. *She Who Is: The Mystery of God in Feminist Theological Discourse.* New York: Crossroad, 1992.

————. *Truly Our Sister: A Theology of Mary in the Communion of Saints.* New York: Continuum, 2003.

Karris, Robert J. "Women and Discipleship in Luke." *Catholic Biblical Quarterly* 56 (1994) 1–20.

Meier, John P. *A Marginal Jew: Rethinking the Historical Jesus.* Vol. III, *Companions and Competitors.* New York: Doubleday, 2001.

Moltmann-Wendel, Elisabeth. "Motherhood or Friendship." In *Mary in the Churches,* edited by Hans Küng et al., 17–22. New York: Seabury, 1983.

————. *The Women around Jesus.* Translated by John Bowden. New York: Crossroad, 1982.

Müller, Gerhard Ludwig. *Priesthood and Diaconate.* San Francisco: Ignatius 2002.

Nürnberg, Rosemarie. "*Apostolae Apostolorum*: Die Frauen am Grab als erste Zeuginen der Auferstehung in der Vaterexegese." In *Stimuli: Exegese und ihre Hermeneutik in Antike und Christentum: Festschrift für Ernst Dassmann,* edited by Georg Schöllgen and Clemens Scholten, 228–42. Jahrbuch für Antike und Christentum: Supplement 23. Münster: Aschendorff, 1996.

Paul VI, Pope. *Lumen Gentium.* https://www.vatican.va/archive/hist_councils/ii_vatican_council/documents/vat-ii_const_19641121_lumen-gentium_en.html.

Pontifical Biblical Commission. *The Interpretation of the Bible in the Church.* March 18, 1994. https://www.vatican.va/roman_curia/congregations/cfaith/pcb_doc_index.htm.

Ricci, Carla. *Mary Magdalene and Many Others: Women Who Followed Jesus.* Translated by Paul Burns. Minneapolis: Fortress 1994.

Roche, Arthur. "*Apostolorum Apostola.*" *L'Osservatore Romano.* https://press.vatican.va/content/salastampa/it/bollettino/pubblico/2016/06/10/0422/00974.html#apos.

Schneiders, Sandra M. "Did Jesus Exclude Women from the Priesthood?" In *Women Priests,* edited by Arlene Swidler and Leonard Swidler, 227–33. New York: Paulist, 1977.

Schüssler Fiorenza, Elisabeth. "The Apostleship of Women in Early Christianity." In *Women Priests,* edited by Arlene Swidler and Leonard Swidler, 135–40. New York: Paulist, 1977.

————. *In Memory of Her: A Feminist Theological Reconstruction of Christian Origins.* New York: Crossroad, 1983.

————. "The Twelve." In *Women Priests,* edited by Arlene Swidler and Leonard Swidler, 114–21. New York: Paulist, 1977.

Tkacz, Catherine Brown. "Jesus and the Spiritual Equality of Women." *Fellowship of Catholic Scholars Quarterly* 24 (2001) 24–29.

————. "Singing Women's Words as Sacramental Mimesis." *Recherches de Théologie et Philosophie médiévales* 70 (2003) 275–328.

United States Catholic Conference. *From "Inter Insigniores" to "Ordinatio Sacerdotalis": Documents and Commentaries.* Washington, DC: United States Catholic Conference, 1996.

Warner, Marina. *Alone of All Her Sex: The Myth and the Cult of the Virgin Mary.* New York: Knopf, 1976.

Witherington, Ben, III. "On the Road with Mary Magdalene, Joanna, Susanna, and Other Disciples—Luke 8,1–3." In *A Feminist Companion to Luke*, edited by Amy-Jill Levine with Marianne Blickenstaff, 133–39. London: Sheffield Academic 2002.

Swidler, Arlene, and Leonard Swidler, eds. *Women Priests: A Catholic Commentary on the Vatican Declaration*. New York: Paulist, 1977.

10

The Christian Psalter

Patrick Henry Reardon
All Saints Antiochian Orthodox Church, Chicago

AMONG THE CLEAREST AND most evident ideas in the Apostolic corpus is that of the Book of Psalms as a manual of *Christian* prayer. Indeed, such was the persuasion of the Church from the very beginning. Thus, the New Testament tells us to address one another with psalms (Eph 5:19), to teach and admonish one another with them (Col 3:16), and to sing them (Jas 5:13).

After the Lord's Ascension the believers turned immediately to the Book of Psalms for guidance. The Church's first canonical act, choosing a replacement for Judas, was explicitly based on a text from the Book of Psalms (Acts 1:20). Again, two psalms were quoted and interpreted in that first sermon on Pentecost Day (Acts 2:25–35). The Psalter is the Old Testament book most frequently cited in the New Testament.

It was the risen Lord who taught the first Christians to discover "in the Law of Moses and in the Prophets and in the Psalms" the Spirit-given references to himself (Luke 24:44).[1] It was in that very first gathering on Easter that the Christian Church began to discern the significance and the importance of the Psalms in their thought and worship.

Put simply, the Psalter is a book of Christology; it is Christology in prayer form. This is the reason why, if Christians are to engage in truly Christian prayer—prayer "in Christ"—then the Psalms must be an integral and important element of that prayer. Thus, in what appears to be our first extant example of the use of a psalm in Christian worship, one observes that its impulse and interest are entirely Christological (Acts 4:24–30

---

1. Unless otherwise noted all translations of biblical texts and ancient sources are my own.

quoting Psalm 2). Prayer "in the name of Jesus" (Acts 4:30 again) readily takes the form of psalmody.

It is remarkable how this thesis of Christology in the Psalms was shared by Christian authors who were otherwise so diverse: Eustathius of Antioch, Ambrose of Milan, John Chrysostom, Cyril of Alexandria, Augustine of Hippo, Gerohus of Reichersberg, Bernard of Clairvaux, and Martin Luther.

Just to limit ourselves, for now, to the last name on that list, we observe that Luther so consistently interpreted the Psalms in the light of the New Testament and Christian theology that this approach even determined how he *translated them* into German. He insisted on reading / praying the Psalms precisely *as a Christian*, through a Christian filter that determined their theologically correct meaning, or *sensus*.[2]

The *Voices* in the Psalter

When Christians the Psalms, they are faced with a particular challenge not usually found in other prayers. This challenge arises from the Psalter's *diversity of voices*, or what the Church Fathers called a plurality of persons, or "faces," *prosōpa*.

This phenomenon is not common to most other forms of prayer. Normally, when I address God, the "voice" of the prayer is first person, whether singular or plural. I pray either as "I" or "we." We petition the Holy Spirit to "come and abide *in us*," for example, or beseech the Lord, "take *from me* the spirit of sloth." We adopt this "first person" voice as a natural assumption.

It is a serious mistake, however, to bring this same assumption—uncritically—to praying the Psalms. Indeed, to do so may lead to some very disordered prayer. For instance, if I think of myself as the "voice" who says, "reward me according to my innocence," or "my heart is not lifted up," I am plunged into a serious conflict with truth, because I know there is not a speck of "innocence" in my heart, which is—in addition—almost always "lifted up."

In respect to this variety of "voices," the Psalms exemplify a larger interpretive concern pertinent to Holy Scripture: In the Bible, divine revelation takes place, not only when God speaks to man, but also, on occasion, when man speaks to God, and even when man speaks to man on God's behalf. All of these instances are the "voices" of revelation.

Philo, a Jewish contemporary of the New Testament, commented on this phenomenon: "The statements (*logia*) are partly spoken in the person (*prosōpon*) of God through the mouth of the prophet, partly revealed as God's

---

2. See Luther, "Translation of the Psalms," 219; Luther, "Preface to the Psalter."

will in question-and-answer form, and partly uttered in the person (*prosōpon*) of Moses while he was under the influence of the Spirit and in ecstasy."[3]

The whole Bible is God's Word, even in those words by which man speaks to God. Revelation is conveyed, not only when the Lord tells Habakkuk, "the just shall live by his faith," but also when Habakkuk inquires, "O Lord, how long shall I cry, and You will not hear" (2:4; 1:1)? In Habakkuk—as in Moses, Jeremiah, Ezekiel, and others—revelation takes on the quality of "conversation"—or *dialogia*.

This complex quality of divine revelation is—if possible—even more pronounced when the Bible is read through Christian eyes. We should have expected as much, since it was Jesus who raised the point. He raised it, in fact, in respect to the Book of Psalms:

> David himself said by the Holy Spirit: "The Lord said to my Lord, 'Sit at My right hand, until I make Your enemies Your footstool.'" Therefore David himself calls Him 'Lord'; how is He then his Son? (Mark 12:36–37)

With this exegetical question, Jesus dropped a very large hint that even the words "Lord" and "Lord" were possessed of more than one reference in the Psalter.

"Conversation" is especially a trait of the Psalms, where we discover, not only ourselves speaking to God about Christ, but also Christ speaking to his Father about us, and so on. The voices will vary, not only in each psalm, but also during the course of a single psalm.

According to Justin Martyr, the Jews who rejected Jesus were deceived by a failure to recognize this variety of "voice" references. The Divine Word, said Justin, "sometimes speaks as from the person (*apo prosōpou*) of God, the Ruler and Father of all, sometimes as from the person (*apo prosōpou*) of Christ, sometimes from the person (*apo prosōpou*) of the peoples answering the Lord or His Father."

Justin went even further, arguing that pagan literature itself had analogies to this "conversation" quality of the biblical writings; he told Marcus Aurelius, "You may observe this even in your own writers, when one writer speaks for all but introduces other *persons in conversation (prosōpa dialegomena).*"[4]

Justin's term, *prosōpon*, had a long history as a literary and theatrical term. Its original meaning, "face,"[5] had been adapted to the stage, to mean

3. Philo, *Life of Moses*, 3.188.
4. Justin Martyr, *First Apology*, 36.
5. Homer, *Odyssey* 19.361.

the mask worn by the actor who portrayed some dramatic character.[6] From that reference it was a short step for *prosōpon* to signify the character himself—the "part" played by the actor.[7]

The theatrical sense of *prosōpon* was very familiar to the early Christians. We find it in Origen, for example: "Actors in a theatrical drama are not what they say they are or what they seem to be, in accord with the character (*prosōpon*) they assume."[8] This word (as well as a variant, *prosōpeion*) occasionally has the same meaning in Athanasius, Basil, Chrysostom, and others. The Christian adaptation of this theatrical term to the understanding of biblical literature suggests a perception that Holy Scripture is the presentation of a *drama*.

This dramatic quality of Holy Scripture is arguably most obvious in the Psalms, I believe, because of their enhanced sense of immediacy. In the Psalter, biblical narrative takes on a more personal and existential quality. Praying the Psalms—speaking to God in those inspired words—renders drama inescapable.

For example, when I simply *read* of his fight from Saul, I may manage to put some distance between David and me. To recite his psalm on that occasion, however, places my feet directly into David's sandals. *I* am no longer safe from the machinations of Saul! David's words become my script: "The sorrows of the nether world surrounded me, the snares of death confronted me" (Ps 17 [18]:5; 2 Sam 22:6). In praying this psalm, I assume the voice of David. I take on—in dramatic form—the character of that persecuted just man, and I identify myself with the Suffering Servant, of whom David was a prefiguration—the Man who "made peace through the blood of His cross" (Col 1:20). When I recite the lines of this psalm, in short, its reference is not reduced to the things that happen to be going on in my individual life. I am playing a part, rather, in the larger and transforming drama of redemption.

Already in the New Testament, we observe the recognition of various "voices" in the psalms. Thus, the author of the Epistle to the Hebrews declares that the Father spoke to his Son in the words of a psalm: "Your throne, O God, is forever and ever" (1:8; Ps 45 [44]:6). Moreover, this same author asserts, the voice of God's Son, as though in the very moment of the Incarnation, used a psalm to address his Father: "Therefore, when He came into the world, He said: 'Sacrifice and offering You did not desire, but a body You have prepared for Me. In burnt offerings and sacrifices for sin You had no

6. Demosthenes, *Orations* 19.287.

7. Epictetus, *Dissertations* 1.29.45.

8. Origen, *On Prayer* 20.2.

pleasure.' Then I said, 'Behold, I have come—In the volume of the book it is written of Me—to do Your will, O God'" (10:5–7; Ps 39 [40]:6–8).

When Christians pray the Psalter, then, the words are not spoken in their own voice. They put on, rather, what St. Paul called "the mind of Christ." Through the inspired lines of these two psalms, the Holy Spirit inserts their prayer into the conversation—the *dialogia*—of the Father and the Son. This form of prayer is not some sort of mental juggling but the Holy Spirit's elevation of the mind: "These things we also speak, not in words which man's wisdom teaches but which the Spirit teaches, deliberating (*sygkrinontes*) spiritual things with spiritual" (1 Cor 2:13, 16).

Identifying "the Man"

We begin, naturally, with Psalm 1. This is not just "the *first* psalm," as though simply to designate its place in a sequence. It is, rather, Psalm *One*, rather, in the sense of an *archē*; it serves as the principle, the font or source, for all the psalms. Psalm 1 enunciates the fundamental thesis of the whole Psalter. It expounds the theme that holds all the psalms together; namely, "the blessings of the man" (*'ashrei ha'ish*) whose "delight (*hepets*) is in the Lord's *Torah*, and on his *Torah* he will meditate day and night." Psalm 1 expresses the piety, the *eusebeia*, of the Torah, structured chiefly on obedient adherence to the will of God. Its fundamental petition is "Thy will be done," *genetheto to thelēma Sou, fiat voluntas Tua*.

The Book of Psalms is the devotional text of the godly and the obedient. It expresses the thoughts, concerns, difficulties, sentiments, and praises proper to those who serve the Lord in obedience to his Torah. Praying the psalms is a disciplined habit integral to a life of service to God in obedience to his will. The Psalter may be described as *Torah*-service expressed in prayer.

Psalm 1 begins, *'Ashrei ha'ish 'asher lo halak ba'atsat resha'im*—"the blessings of the man who walks not in the counsel of the godless." And our first task, on which all our understanding must depend, is to identify this "man." He is not just any man. The Hebrew noun employed here is not only masculine in gender; it is specifically male in reference: *'ish*, not *'adam* ("human being"). The importance of this distinction was very clear to the early translators. In the Greek of Septuagint, it is rendered *anēr*, not *anthrōpos*; in the traditional Latin, it is *vir*, not *homo*.

This "man," if the Psalms are to be prayed as *Christian* prayer, can be no other than the "one mediator between God and men, the man Christ Jesus" (1 Tim 2:5). The "blessed man," the *beatus vir* at the heart of the

Psalter, commented St. Augustine, "is to be understood of our Lord Jesus Christ, that is, of the lordly man."[9]

The precise wording and full canonical setting of Psalm 1 indicates something more than a moral ideal. It identifies the Christological principle at the base of Christian prayer. To grasp the burden of this principle, I suggest a comparison with the Christian understanding of Psalm 8, of which we have an extremely primitive Christian interpretation. Surely the man, the 'ish, in Psalm 1 is identical to the 'enosh (poetic form of 'ish) in Psalm 8, the psalm that inquires, *mah–'enosh ki tivkerenu vuben 'adam. ki tiphkedenu*—"What is man that you are mindful of him, And the son of man that You visit him?"

In fact, the New Testament does identify the man in Psalm 8. The Epistle to the Hebrews quotes the passage in detail:

> Somewhere somebody (*pou tis*) testified, saying, "What is man that You are mindful of him, / Or the son of man that You take care of him? You have made him a little lower than the angels; You have crowned him with glory and honor and set him over the works of Your hands. You have put all things in subjection under his feet."

The author of Hebrews goes on to identify this man who was made a little lower than the angels and then was crowned with glory and honor, all things being put into subjection under his feet:

> Now, we do not, as yet, see all things put under him, but we see Jesus, who was made a little lower than the angels, for the suffering of death crowned with glory and honor, that He, by the grace of God, might taste death for everyone.

The author explains:

> For it was fitting for Him, for whom *are* all things and by whom *are* all things, in bringing many sons to glory, to make the author of their salvation (*ton archēgon tes sōtērias*) perfect through sufferings.

9. "De Domino nostro Iesu Christo, hoc est, de homine dominico, accipiendum est." St. Augustine of Hippo, *Enarrationes in Psalmos* 1.

The Mystery of Christ

Although all of the Psalter refers to Christ and is properly to be prayed within the context of that reference, certain passages of the Psalms have from the beginning enjoyed a special prominence.

A ready example is the opening line of Psalm 109 (Hebrew 110): "The Lord said to my Lord: Sit thou at my right hand." In the traditions reflected in the Synoptic Gospels, Christians remembered that Jesus had cited that verse in controversy with some of his rabbinic opponents (Mark 12:36; Matt 22:44; Luke 20:42) and that the context of his citation was the decisive and great kerygmatic question, the question of the Lord's identity: "What think ye of the Christ? Whose son is he?" In those few words of the Psalter, "the Lord said unto my Lord," Christians learned that Jesus is not only David's descendent but also his pre-existing Lord. He is the son not only of David, but of God.

Having mysteriously addressed the identity of Christ, that same line of the psalm then goes on to speak of his triumphal enthronement. Scarcely any words of any psalm were more beloved of the first Christians than "Sit thou at my right hand." They were quoted in the first sermon of Pentecost (Acts 2:34) and became the foundation of some of the most important Christological and soteriological statements of the New Testament (Mark 16:19; Rom 8:34; Eph 1:20; Col 3:1; Heb 1:13, 8:1, 10:12, 12:2).

Then, that same verse of the psalm goes on to refer to those who oppose the victory of Christ: "Until I make thine enemies thy footstool." Once again, those few words were to lay the basis for important dimensions of eschatology in the New Testament (Acts 1:35–36; 1 Cor 15:25; Eph 1:22; Heb 10:12–13; and perhaps 1 Pet 3:22).

The remaining lines of this same psalm speak of still other grand dimensions of Christian doctrine. Most specifically, this is the psalm that identifies Jesus as "a priest forever according to the order of Melchizedek," and this identification is made the major theme of the Epistle to the Hebrews, our psalm cited repeatedly throughout the development of that letter.

With so much Christian theology concentrated in a single psalm, and so much of it in the very first line of that psalm, it is no wonder that Psalm 109, the *Dixit Dominus*, rather quickly assumed a notable place in Christian worship, particularly on the Lord's Day. The use of this psalm as the solemn opening of Sunday Vespers, a feature still prevalent in the Western Church, seems to have its roots in the third century.

To treat adequately the place of the Psalms in Christian prayer would be the work of several lifetimes, one suspects. It would involve, for example, a lengthy discussion of the Psalms in Christian meditation on the Passion of the Lord. Jesus himself died with words of the Psalter on his lips (Mark 15:34 quoting Psalm 21:2; Luke 23:46 quoting Psalm 30:6) and was imitated in this respect by the Church's first martyr (Acts 7:59).

Images and even whole lines from the Book of Psalms are found within the Gospel accounts of the Lord's sufferings. The Psalter speaks of the vinegar and gall (Matt 27:34 from Psalm 68:22), the dividing of Jesus' garments (Matt 27:35 and John 19:24, citing Psalm 21:19), the distance of his friends (Mark 15:40 from Psalm 37:12), and the blasphemies of his enemies (Matt 27:39–44, citing Psalms 21:8–9; 108:25).

The Christocentricity of the Psalter is not simply a matter of identifying certain select passages as "messianic." Rather, the Tradition of the Church regards Christology as the proper key to the whole Psalter. This appropriate Christian attitude toward the Book of Psalms is the fruit of daily praying those Psalms within the Church's worship, centered around the Sacraments.

Praying the Psalms as Christians means praying them with the "mind of Christ" and illumined by the Christian Mysteries. Correct ("orthodox") understanding of the Psalms (or, indeed, any other part of the Bible), then, always involves Christ. Thus, whether interpreting all or only part of the Book of Psalms the older Christian commentators spontaneously looked at each psalm through the lens of the "life in Christ."[10]

Bibliography

Luther, Martin. "Defense of the Translation of the Psalms." In vol. 1 of *Word and Sacrament*, translated by E. Theodore Bachman, 209–23. Luther's Works 35. Philadelphia: Fortress, 1960.

———. "Preface to the Psalter." In vol. 1 of *Word and Sacrament*, translated by E. Theodore Bachman, 253–57. Luther's Works 35. Philadelphia: Fortress, 1960.

10. It is no accident that those exegetes who were not disposed to adopt a sustained christological interest in the Psalms, such as Theodore of Mopsuestia and Theodoret of Cyrus, were ultimately judged (at Constantinople II in 553) to have a defective Christology.

11

Jesus Becoming Jesus

*The Primacy of Christ in
Paul's Three Hymns*

THOMAS G. WEINANDY, OFM CAP.

Capuchin College, Washington, DC

I AM PLEASED TO have been asked to contribute an essay in honor of Fr. Patrick J. Hartin. While I am a systematic and historical theologian, and so, unlike Fr. Hartin, not a Scripture scholar myself, yet I have always had a great love and appreciation of the Bible. In recent years I have focused my study and academic writing on the theological interpretation of the New Testament—primarily on the Gospels.[1] In this essay I would like to continue this effort.

Introduction

In this essay I want to examine the three Pauline hymns found in Colossians 1:15–20, Ephesians 1:3–14, and Philippians 2:5–11. I wish to focus on the theology or Christology within the three hymns. Since I will concentrate on the christological content of these hymns, I will not fully address some scriptural issues—for example, the dating of these particular epistles, the historical background or antecedents to these hymns, or the question of the Pauline authorship of these letters and the hymns within

---

1. See my *Jesus Becoming Jesus: Synoptic Gospels.* See also my *Jesus Becoming Jesus: John.*

them.[2] Rather, my thesis will concern the universal primacy of Jesus as Savior as found within these hymns, and the manner in which they conceive him obtaining his universal and cosmic primacy as the supreme Lord and Redeemer. In other words: How did Jesus, as YHWH-Saves, become Jesus–YHWH-Saves, that is, how did Jesus enact his name so that his name bears universal and definitive saving primacy? I will conclude with a brief theological summary of my findings.[3]

Before proceeding to my christological exegesis, I want to give two reasons why I have chosen the present study. First, the hymns themselves are of major doctrinal significance—as to who Jesus is as the person of the Son of God existing as man and as to the manner of his salvific work. Second, and this is the immediate motivation, there is a great deal of contemporary discussion, in the light of religious pluralism, as to the singularity of Jesus in the midst of other religions and their respective founders. The Congregation for the Doctrine of the Faith in *Dominus Iesus* addressed these issues and provided clarification as well as dispelling erroneous understandings. It did so by emphasizing that Jesus is truly the Word of God incarnate and so possesses the fullness of truth. Moreover, through his death and resurrection, Jesus freed humankind from sin's condemnation with its ensuing punishment of death, as well as offering his everlasting risen life to all who believe in him.[4] Although such arguments distinguish Christianity and Je-

---

2. Not only is there debate concerning the dating of these letters, but also Pauline authorship. I will hold, as do many Scripture scholars, that Paul is the author of these epistles. By holding for Paul's authorship rather than a later Pauline disciple one must, therefore, acknowledge earlier rather than later dates of their writing. In this light Raymond E. Brown dates Philippians between AD 56–63, Colossians from AD 54–56, and Ephesians in the 60s. Brown, *Introduction to the New Testament*, 484, 600, 621. Margaret Y. MacDonald argues that, if Paul is the author of Colossians, it was written between AD 57 and 63 and that Ephesians, while appearing to be dependent upon Colossians and so written after it, was nonetheless written within the same period of time—mid-50s to early-60s. MacDonald, *Colossians and Ephesians*, 17–18. Bonnie B. Thurston places the date for the Letter to the Philippians, depending from where it was written in the course of Paul's travels and imprisonments, between mid-50s to the early 60s. Thurston and Ryan, *Philippians*, 28–30. Peter S. Williamson also dates Paul's authorship of Ephesians between AD 61–63. Williamson, *Ephesians*, 13–15.

I will first treat the hymn within Paul's Letter to the Colossians since the majority of scholars hold that this letter was written prior to his Letters to the Ephesians and Philippians.

3. Because I will be engaged in a christological interpretation of the Colossian, Ephesian, and Philippian hymns, their precise dating, although somewhat important, is not decisive for determining their theological doctrine.

4. The Declaration *"Dominus Iesus"* speaks of the dangers "of relativistic theories which seek to justify religious pluralism" (*DI* 4). In response to this relativizing of truth "it must be firmly believed that, in the mystery of Jesus Christ, the Incarnate Son of

sus as its founder from other religions and alternative religious founders, I do not believe *Dominus Iesus* adequately expressed the full uniqueness of Jesus as the universal Savior and definitive Lord.

Although implicit within *Dominus Iesus*, the Declaration did not explicitly state that Jesus' saving actions established a new salvific order, that is, that his saving actions brought about the possibility for humankind to enter into a radically new relationship with the Father in the Holy Spirit. Likewise, *Dominus Iesus* did not emphasize that to partake of the saving benefits of Jesus' death and resurrection, one must personally be united to him. The christological lacuna within *Dominus Iesus* is then the singular manner in which the faithful come to participate in and so reap the benefits of Jesus' saving transformative work. All those who believe in the risen Lord Jesus are united to him in communion with the Spirit and so become holy and righteous children of God the Father, something that was not possible prior to Jesus' death on the cross and the Father raising him gloriously from the dead. Only because of these saving acts could Jesus, as the risen Lord, pour out his Holy Spirit upon all who believe. It is this "living in saving Spirit-filled communion" with the risen Lord Jesus, this being "in Christ," that establishes him fully as the ever-living universal Savior and radically distinguishes him from all other religious founders; and again, it is this unique salvific facet that is not satisfactorily treated in *Dominus Iesus*. These two complementary truths, nonetheless, further accentuate the singularity of Jesus as the universal Savior and his uniqueness as the definitive Lord. Moreover, such an understanding of Jesus bears upon the nature of God the Father's will. Did the Father directly and positively will that Jesus, and he alone, be the universal Savior and singular Lord? Or, did the Father also actively espouse and so purposely initiate other religions with their respective founders?[5] The three Pauline hymns provide, as we will

---

God, who is 'the way, the truth, and the life' (Jn. 14:6), the full revelation of divine truth is given" (*DI* 5; see also 6–9). Moreover, "It must therefore be firmly believed as a truth of Catholic faith that the universal salvific will of the One and Triune God is offered and accomplished once for all in the mystery of the incarnation, death, and resurrection of the Son of God" (*DI* 14). Therefore, "one can say and must say that Jesus Christ has a significance and a value for the human race and its history, which are unique and singular, proper to him alone, exclusive, universal, and absolute" (*DI* 15).

5. Such questions take on new urgency in the light of the statement that Pope Francis signed on February 4, 2019, when visiting Abu Dhabi (Francis, *Human Fraternity*). This document stated: "The pluralism and the diversity of religions, color, sex, race and language are willed by God in his wisdom, through which he created human beings." God positively willed male and female, as well as different races and nations. Did he, in the same overt positive manner, will Christianity and Islam and so absolutely will not only Jesus as the founder of Christianity, but also Mohammed as the founder of Islam? For a christological response to this Abu Dhabi document, see my "Will of

see, clear arguments and decisive answers, based upon divine revelation, to these theological, christological, and soteriological issues. With the above in mind, we can now turn to Paul's Letter to the Colossians and the christological hymn contained therein.

Colossians

Christ's Primacy within
the Order of Creation

In writing to the church in Colossae, Paul is addressing a Christian community that he did not found. Rather, the Gospel was first proclaimed by Epaphras, a "faithful minister of Christ on our behalf [Paul's] and has made known to us your love in the Spirit" (Col 1:8).[6] Paul prays on their behalf that they would increase in their knowledge of the Gospel and, in so doing, "lead a life worthy of the Lord" (Col 1:10). Paul reminds the Colossian faithful that God the Father "has delivered us from the dominion of darkness and transferred us to the kingdom of his beloved Son, in whom we have redemption, the forgiveness of sins" (Col 1:13–14). With this concluding greeting, Paul immediately embarks on the lyrical verses that comprise the hymn:[7]

> He [the Greek is "who," referring back to the Father's beloved Son] is the image of the invisible God, the first-born of all creation; for in him all things were created, in heaven and on earth, visible and invisible, whether thrones or dominions or principalities or authorities—all things were created through him and for him. He is before all things, and in him all things hold together.
> He is the head of the body, the church; he is the beginning, the first-born from the dead, that in everything he might be pre-eminent. For in him all the fullness of God was pleased to dwell, and through him to reconcile to himself all things,

God the Father."

6. All Scripture passages are taken from the Revised Standard Version, Catholic Edition, unless otherwise noted. Moreover, all Scripture citations in this section are taken from Colossians 1:15–20 unless otherwise noted.

7. Most scholars believe that Paul is not the author of this hymn, but rather that he employed material from an already existing hymn used within liturgical settings. More than likely this hymn was well known among the Colossian faithful: MacDonald, *Colossians and Ephesians*, 65–66. Besides MacDonald's commentary on the hymn (pp. 58–70), see Fee, *Pauline Christology*, 292–313.

whether on earth or in heaven, making peace by the blood of his cross. (Col 1:15–20)

The first strophe of the hymn declares that Jesus, as the Father's beloved Son, "is the image [the Greek is "icon"] of the invisible God." This "imaging" is twofold. First, since "image" directly refers to the Father's Son, the hymn is defining the divine identity of the Son and, in so doing, defining the divine identity of the Father as well. God the Father is "Father" in that he eternally begets his divine Son, who then is the Father's perfect divine image.[8] The Father and the Son are perfectly who they are only in relationship to one another. If the Father did not beget his beloved Son as the perfect icon of himself, he would not be the perfect Father, for his Son would not be his perfect divine image. Similarly, if the Son is not the perfect image of his Father, he would not properly be the Father's divine Son.[9] Thus, we perceive that the one God is the inter-relationship between the Father and the Son for the Father begets his beloved Son as the perfectly begotten divine image of himself.[10]

Second, while the Son as God is the perfect image of his divine Father, the hymn specifies that the Son is the image of the *invisible* God. To be the

8. This is why Paul, in his Letter to the Ephesians, states that all earthly fatherhood takes its name from God the Father (see Eph 3:15). God the Father is the divine exemplar of all fatherhood since he begets the perfect divine image of himself in the begetting of his Son, and he does so by giving to his Son all that he is as God—his very divine nature. Human fathers give themselves in the begetting of their children who are then in their images, though only to a greater or lesser degree, and so they are not perfect images of their fathers. Human fathers, nonetheless, do reflect the fatherhood of God the Father.

9. Human beings are created in the image and likeness of God (see Gen 1:26; 2:7). However, because they are created, human beings are not and cannot be perfect icons of God for they are not eternally divine. They are images of God in that they were created in the likeness of the Father's perfect icon, his Son. It is through his Son, as we will see shortly, that the Father creates human beings and all else that exists.

10. Although the Holy Spirit is not mentioned within the Colossian hymn, within the Latin theological tradition the Holy Spirit is understood to be the mutual love shared by the Father and the Son, and so proceeds from the Father and the Son. Because the Son is the *beloved* Son of the Father, one could argue that the Father begot his Son in the love of the Holy Spirit. The eternal, ever-present motivation within the Father is the Holy Spirit's imbued paternal love within the Father to beget his beloved Son. Thus, the Holy Spirit conforms the Father to be the loving Father of his beloved Son. Moreover, the Son, having been begotten in the love of the Father, the love of the Holy Spirit, loves his Father in the same love, in the same Holy Spirit, in whom he is begotten. Thus, the Holy Spirit imbues the Son with a filial love for his Father. The one God is, therefore, the inter-relational ontological communion of life and love between the Father, the Son, and the Holy Spirit. For a fuller exposition of this understanding of the Trinity, see my *The Father's Spirit of Sonship*.

image of the invisible God implies that the divine Son made visible his invisible Father. The Son as God could not be the visible image of God since he himself as God is as equally invisible as his invisible Father. Thus, the Son, as the perfect icon of his Father, must, in some manner, visibly manifest in his being the perfect image of his Father so as to make visible his Father. This visible iconic manifestation is most fully enacted, as we will see, when the Father sends his beloved Son into the world as man. The Incarnation is the consummate iconic expression of the Son being the visible image of his Father and so the fullest visible expression of his invisible Father—when the Father's beloved Son comes to exist as the man, Jesus.[11] Nonetheless, the primordial manifestation of the Son being the perfect image of his Father is found in the first act of creation, for the Father's Son is "the first-born of all creation." How can the invisible Father's beloved Son be eternally begotten and yet be the visible first-born of all creation? This is a complex question, but the proper answer to it is essential for understanding the theological and christological depth of the Colossian hymn.

To address this issue, we need to examine what immediately follows. He is "the first-born of all creation" because "in him all things were created, in heaven and on earth, visible and invisible, whether thrones or dominions or principalities or authorities—all things were created through him and for him. He is before all things, and in him all things hold together." Because the Son is the perfect image of his Father, the Father performs his act of creation in and through his beloved Son. Thus, in the act of creation, the Father is manifesting that his Son is his perfect divine image, for if he were not the perfect icon of the Father, the Father could not create anything in or through him. Only a being who exists eternally as God can bring into being that which is not divine. Only if the fullness of divine being is *in him* can all beings come to be *in* and *through* him. He is, therefore, "before all things" not only in the sense of his being "above" all things as the transcendent God, but also as existing before all things as the eternal God. Since all things come to be in and through him as the one who is before all that is, the Son "holds" all things together, that is, the whole of creation, the entire cosmos, comes to be and remains in existence only by being united to him. While "creation" is a distinct ontological order of its own, it can only be held together in the ever-enduring, unbreakable, and intimate co-inhering relationship with him who is its Creator, with him who enfolds the fullness of his Father's divine being. Moreover, because it was the Son in and through whom all creation came to be, the Son's act of creation is not

11. Paul states in his Second Letter to the Corinthians that those without faith are kept "from seeing the light of the Gospel of the glory of Christ, who is the likeness [Greek: "icon"] of God (2 Cor 4:4).

simply a visible manifestation of his divine Sonship, but equally a manifestation of his Father. The act of creation which makes visible the Son is the
same act that reveals the Father. As the Father's perfect image, the Son, in
the act of creation, makes visible his invisible Father—him who is the sole
source of being and fount of all life.

Thus, to be "the first-born of all creation" cannot mean that the Father
created him as the first creature and then created all else in and through
him. Rather, what is first manifested, what is first seen in the act of creation
is not simply that which is created, but him in whom and through whom
all is created. To be "first-born of all creation" connotes that what is first
revealed in the act of creation, what is first made visible, what lies behind
and makes possible the act of creation is the divine Creator-Son in whom
and through whom all comes to be. Because the beloved Son is eternally
begotten of the Father, he rightly becomes "the first-born of creation" in
that the Father, in creating all things in and through his eternally begotten
Son, is first and foremost manifesting his beloved Son. Thus, the eternally
begotten Son is now the "first born of all creation" for he is the first to be
revealed in the act of creation, the act wherein all else comes to be in and
through him. Moreover, because all things come to be in and through the
Son, the Son, in the act of creation, makes visible the source of all life and
being—the invisible Father.

Such an understanding is in keeping with the Prologue of John's Gospel and its interpretive relationship to the first creation story in the book of
Genesis. The first phrase at the onset of the Prologue echoes the first words of
Genesis—"In the beginning." In the beginning, that is, before the beginning
began, the Word already was with God and was God. "All things were made
through him, and without him was not anything made that was made." The
reason is that in the Word "was life, and the life was the light of men. The light
shines in the darkness, and the darkness has not overcome it" (John 1:1–5).
For John, the eternal Word is the life-giving light. Within Genesis, into the
darkness of nothingness, God spoke his word: "'Let there be light,' and there
was light. And God saw that it was good" (Gen 1:3). The first thing that God
created, even prior to the sun, moon, and stars, was "light." That first light
manifested the eternal light, the eternal being that is God, and in that divine
life-giving light all else would come to be. More specifically, literally in the
light of Jesus, John recognizes that the primordial divine light is the life-giving light of God's eternal Word. What God reveals in his first act of creation
is not simply himself; rather the Father is manifesting his divine Word, his
beloved and good Son. The first word that God speaks, "Let there be light,"
is the very word that reveals the Word, for the Word is the life-giving light
in and through whom all else comes to be. What then is the first thing that

God creates? In accordance with the words of the Colossian's hymn, God's first act of creation is the revelation of his beloved Son, "the first-born of all creation"—the primordial visible life-giving light of the invisible Father in whom and through whom all else comes to be. Again, the eternally begotten beloved Son of the Father is the first-born of all creation, for in his light, the primordial divine light, all else comes to be.[12]

This theological meaning authorizes the proper understanding of what is affirmed within the Old Testament Wisdom literature. Wisdom, speaking on behalf of herself, declares: "The Lord created me at the beginning of his work, the first of his acts of old. Ages ago I was set up, at the first, before the beginning of the earth." Before the depths, the mountains, the fields, the heavens "I was beside him [God], like a master workman" (Prov 8:22–31; see also Wis 7:22; 8:1). The beloved Son, as the icon of his Father, possesses all divine wisdom and this filial wisdom was first visibly manifested "at the beginning of his work," in God's primordial act of creation, "the first act of old," when he declared: "Let there be light." This is confirmed in the Book of Sirach: "Wisdom was created before all things, the prudent understanding from eternity" (Wis 1:4).[13] The Father, in first creating light, reveals his life-bearing divine master craftsman, his beloved Son, in whom and through whom all comes to be and is held together.[14] That all is created in and through the Father's beloved Son is, therefore, founded both on his Son being eternally

12. The Letter to the Hebrews reinforces this interpretation. The Son of God, who "reflects the glory of God and bears the very stamp of his nature," is he "through whom" he [God] also "created the world," and who now upholds "the universe by his word of power" (Heb 1:2–3). As the perfect Son of the Father, the Son bears the very stamp of the Father's being. He, therefore, is rightly employed by the Father as the one in and through whom the Father creates. John 1:3 also states that "all things were made through him, and without him was not anything made that was made." See also 1 Cor 8:6 where Paul declares that the Father and Jesus, his Son, are collaborators in the creation of all things.

13. Fee argues that the hymn does not allude to the Wisdom literature since in the Greek Wisdom (*Sophia*) is feminine and so contrary to the Father begetting a "Son" and not a "Daughter." Fee, *Pauline Christology*, 295. If such a restricted identity was made, Fee would be correct. However, although Wisdom is feminine in the Greek, divine wisdom is given to all human beings—both men and women. What would now be perceived is that God's Word as the Father's Son possesses the fullness of divine wisdom which finds it source not in a divine "Mother" but in God "the Father."

14. To interpret the Wisdom literature within the full context of the New Testament revelation, then, fully addresses Arius' misinterpretation. Arius argued that since Wisdom was "created" at "the beginning of his [God's] work," the Son/Word of God had to be a creature and not truly divine. However, if God's first act of creation is, in the creation of light, the revelation of his Son/Word, then the Son/Word, while fully divine, is the first act at the beginning of his work. The Council of Nicaea (AD 325) condemned Arius' position and declared that the Son is equally God as the Father is God.

begotten as his perfect divine image as well as his being "the first-born of all creation." The first-born of all creation, that which is first manifested within the created order, is the eternally begotten beloved Son, the Father's perfect divine image. Moreover, in being the first-born of all creation, not only is the eternally begotten Son made known, but also, in the visible making known of the Son, the invisible Father is made visible. The visible manifestation of the eternal Son as the first-born of all creation, is, by its very nature, the visible iconic expression of the Father as well.

Two further interrelated points need to be made within this first strophe of the Colossian hymn. First, what the Son is proclaimed to create is specified, that is, all that is "in heaven and on earth, visible and invisible, whether thrones or dominions or principalities or authorities." This specificity highlights that nothing resides outside the Son's creative power and that, therefore, he is supreme over all. Scholars speculate that Paul or the hymn is combatting erroneous Gnostic beliefs that may have been present at the time and disturbing the Colossian Christian community. Gnosticism held that there were various hierarchical orders of heavenly beings that mediated between God and the material world. God as Creator, therefore, was not immediately and intimately related to human beings. The Colossian hymn refutes such a notion. The Son, as the Father's perfect divine image, in whom and through whom all was created, even whatever heavenly beings there might be, is present to all that he creates because all of creation is held together or co-inheres in him alone, and not within some successive mediating hierarchy of heavenly invisible beings.[15]

Moreover, although until now I have not emphasized this point, all was created not only in and through the Father's beloved Son but also *for him*. The Father created everything in and through his Son for the explicit reason, the final goal or end, that the whole of creation, the whole cosmos and all that exists therein, is his paternal gift to his beloved Son. That the Father positively willed to create everything for his beloved Son is then supremely relevant when addressing the singular significance of the Son in relation to other religions. In creating all in and through the Son, the Father is equally assuring that all of creation was on behalf of his Son, and for the sake of his Son alone. As the Father's first-born of all creation, the Son is pre-eminent within that creation and, therefore, all primacy within creation belongs to him alone and to no other.[16] Thus, in beholding the first-born of

---

15. Later, within his letter, Paul states that Jesus, the incarnate Son, through his work of redemption, "disarmed the principalities and powers and made a public example of them, triumphing over them in him" (Col 2:15). See also Eph 1:21.

16. This primacy of the Son, that all was created for him, is a theological aspect that is missing within the document *Dominus Iesus*, yet is essential for fully grasping the definitive singularity of the Son in relationship to founders of other world religions.

creation, all of creation, particularly men and women, created in the image of that first-born, are to hold in reverence and awe the Father's beloved Son and to him alone is to be given all glory, honor and praise.[17] Moreover, such esteem and worship are due to the Father's beloved Son for, as the perfect image of the Father, he has made known, made visible to the whole of creation the invisible Father—the fountain of all being and life. This revelation of the Father is likewise declared in John's Prologue: "No one has ever seen God; the only Son, who is in the bosom of the Father, he has made him known" (John 1:18). This making visible of the invisible Father, this making known of the Father, finds its culmination within the Incarnation wherein the Father's beloved Son comes to exist as man.

Before moving to the second strophe of the hymn, which speaks of the Incarnation and Jesus' salvific work, note the elegant completeness of what God has done. The Father, in creating all that has come to be in and through his Son, and importantly, for his Son, has literally created a situation wherein he is able to manifest the pre-eminent glory of his Son. The future Jesus, the Father's incarnate Son, will display his glory through his saving death and, most dramatically, within his resurrection, by becoming the first-born from the dead, and thus becoming the head of his body, the church. In and through these events, Jesus merits and so takes possession of the whole of the re-created creation—the very gift that the Father bestowed upon him from the very beginning. In other words, the Father by creating everything in and through his Son, established the necessary precondition, the *sine qua non*, that allows the anticipated future Jesus to become Jesus–YHWH-Saves, the one who will be pre-eminent in every way—both as the first-born of all creation and as the first-born of the new creation. The Father orchestrates this entire sweep of history, from beginning to end, on behalf of his Son, for his Son is the Beloved. With these thoughts in mind we can now turn to the second strophe of the Colossian hymn.

Christ's Primacy within the Order of Redemption

Having professed the primacy of the Father's beloved Son within the order of creation, the second strophe of the hymn declares his primacy as the Father's incarnate saving-Son. The argument begins with the declaration of

---

17. Paul later states that believers have, through baptism, "put off the old nature with its practices and have put on the new nature, which is being renewed in knowledge after the image of its creator" (Col 3:10). The image of the creator in whose image Christians are being renewed is that of the Father's Son for he is himself the perfect icon of his Father.

the primacy itself and then presents the causal actions by or through which such primacy was achieved. This redemptive primacy, this ultimate consequence, is manifested in that "he [the incarnate Son, Jesus] is the head of the body, the church." The reason he is the head of his body, the church, resides in his being "the beginning," that is, the origin of his body, the church. The reason he is the originate beginning of his body, the church, is due to his being "the first born from the dead."[18] Jesus' resurrection, as the perfect, glorious, incarnate image of his Father, establishes that "in everything he might be pre-eminent." Now what made possible his pre-eminence in every way is founded upon the fact that "the fullness of God was pleased to dwell" in him. Moreover, he merited such primacy because "through him [God was pleased] to reconcile to himself all things, whether on earth or in heaven, making peace by the blood of his cross."

The actual historical sequential causal order can be more fully elaborated in this manner. Because Jesus is the Father's incarnate beloved Son in whom the fullness of God dwells, he was able to overcome the evil of sin and death that had infected God's good creation, a creation over which he already held primacy. He did this through his sacrificial death on the cross, the making peace with God through the pouring out of his blood—the offering of his holy and innocent life to his Father for the reparation of sin. In so doing, he who created all that exists had now reconciled in himself all that exists, on earth and in heaven, that is, as all creation holds together in and through him, so now the re-created order holds together in and through him. Due to his saving death, Jesus merited his glorious resurrection as the first born from the dead and so he is the beginning of the new creation. As the first to be resurrected, he became the head of his body, the church, so that all who are members of his body, the church, will also rise to glory in and through him. Thus, this twofold primacy, that of being the beginning, the first born of all creation, and that of being the beginning, the first born from the dead, means that the risen Jesus, as the Father's beloved Son, is also the eschatological end of all creation, particularly those who are members of his body, the church. Their consummate end will be eternal life in, with, and through him. As the glorious Lord and Savior Jesus Christ declares in the Book of Revelation: "I am the Alpha and the Omega, the first and the last, the beginning and the end" (Rev 22:13).

With this summary overview of the second strophe of the hymn and its relation to the first strophe clarified, it is necessary to examine a number

18. In Psalm 89, God promises David: "I will make him [David] the first-born, the highest of the kings of the earth" (Ps 89:27). This promise is fulfilled in Jesus being the first-born from the dead for not only is he the living-head of his body, the church, but he is also the ever-living king of God's kingdom.

of points in more detail in order to fully appreciate what the hymn is declaring. First, in the Greek there is an "and" that unites the two strophes. So, the Father's beloved Son holds primacy within creation, "and" (likewise or moreover) he also holds primacy within redemption. The "and" is followed in the Greek with an emphatic "he," that is, "he himself," and not someone else, is also the head of his body, the church.[19] No one surpasses him within the order of creation *and* no one surpasses him in the order of redemption, for he alone is the head of his body, the church.

Second, as "the first-born of all creation," the Son was the source of being and life within creation, so now as the risen incarnate Son, "the first-born from the dead," Jesus is the source of new life—the life-giving head of his body, the church. In his earlier letters Paul speaks of Christians being members of Christ's body and so members of one another (see Rom 12:5; 1 Cor 12:12, 27). Here in this later letter, to the Colossians, he emphasizes that Jesus is the head of his body precisely because, as risen, he is the source of the body's life, and the life that he gives to that body is that of the Holy Spirit (see also Rom 8:2; 1 Cor 12:12–13; 2 Cor 1:22; Eph 1:13–14, 22–23; 5:23). Moreover, God gives various gifts and ministries of the Spirit "for the building up of the body of Christ, until we all attain to the unity of the faith and the knowledge of the Son of God, the mature manhood, to the measure of the stature of the fullness of Christ" (Eph 4:12–13). Colossians itself states that by holding fast to Jesus, the head of the body, the body is "nourished and knit together through its joints and ligaments, grows with growth that is from God" (Col 2:19). As the Son of God holds all of creation together, so Jesus, the incarnate Son, as head holds his body together. Further, the growth in maturity implies, as does Jesus being "the first-born from the dead," that those who are members of his living body will also rise from the dead upon Jesus' return in glory. As Paul states in his First Letter to the Corinthians: "But in fact Christ has been raised from the dead, the first fruit of those who have fallen asleep" (1 Cor 15:20). There is an order for Paul: "Christ the first fruits, then at his coming those who belong to Christ" (1 Cor 15:23).[20] At the resurrection, then, "Christ will be all in all" (Col 3:11).

Third, that "the fullness of God was pleased to dwell" in him is the foundational truth from which all of Jesus' saving actions flow and,

---

19. For another examination of this point, see MacDonald, *Colossians and Ephesians*, 61.

20. In conformity with Colossians, Paul immediately states: "Then comes the end, when he delivers the kingdom to God the Father after destroying every rule and every authority and power. For he must reign until he has put all his enemies under his feet. The last enemy to be destroyed is death. 'For God has put all things in subjection under his feet'" (1 Cor 15:24–27).

therefore, why he is pre-eminent within the new order of redemption. Here, nonetheless, there is an ambiguity. The Greek does not have the word "God," but rather it states simply that "in him *the fullness* was pleased to dwell." Within Gnostic thought, "fullness" denoted the realm of all the semi-divine beings that existed between, and so connected, God and human-inhabited earth—the heavenly domain of the thrones or dominations or principalities or authorities mentioned in the first strophe. Thus, if one does not speak of "the fullness *of God*," but simply of "*the fullness*," the hymn is professing that Jesus, and not any or all of these other spiritual beings, possesses "the fullness," that is, he is the one, and the only one, that mediates between, and so conjoins, God and the world in which humans dwell. Translators, in an attempt to clarify to what "fullness" refers have added "of God." They do so because later in the letter Paul states: "For in him [Jesus] the whole fullness of deity dwells bodily, and you have the fullness of life in him, who is the head of all rule and authority" (Col 2:9–10). The two renditions are complementary and bring out the full truth of what the hymn is expressing. Jesus, as the Son of God Incarnate, possesses the full divinity of God his Father and, because Jesus possesses bodily the fullness of God, he as man possesses the fullness wherein he alone, and not some spiritual disincarnate being, mediates human beings' relation to the transcendent God. Precisely because Jesus is the Father's incarnate divine Son, he immediately mediates man's relationship to his Father—he fills "the gap" between God and man because he is fully God and fully man.[21]

Fourth, what is also significant, but often overlooked, is the rather peculiar phrase that "in him" "the fullness" or "the fullness of God" was "*pleased to dwell*." A "fullness," or even a "fullness of God," is not a person and, therefore, normally is not said to take "pleasure" in anything including the pleasure of indwelling. Now, this "fullness" or "fullness of God" dwells in Jesus. But who is Jesus? Jesus is the Father's beloved Son existing as man. Thus, it is the Father's Son, he who possesses the fullness of his Father's divinity, who is pleased, as God, to dwell as man upon the earth. "In him," the man Jesus, the Son of God, in the fullness of his divinity, is pleased to dwell. The Son takes pleasure in his human existence as man, and the reason he is pleased is that, as the incarnate visible Son, he mediates through his own humanity humankind's full relationship with his invisible Father. This mediation is explicitly stated in what follows.

Fifth, Jesus, he in whom the fullness of God is pleased to dwell, is the one through whom all things are reconciled, "whether on earth or in the

---

21. For other discussions of the understanding of "fullness" and "fullness of God," see Fee, *Pauline Christology*, 308–9; MacDonald, *Colossians and Ephesians*, 62–63.

heavens, making peace by the blood of his cross." All the things, the entire cosmos, which includes sinful humankind and all heavenly beings, achieve reconciling-peace with God through the sacrificial death of Jesus upon the cross. The Father, recognizing that his beloved incarnate Son has achieved such reconciling-peace, raises him gloriously from the dead as the first born, the beginning, of the new creation. Jesus, then, is the first to obtain the merited fruit of his own reconciling sacrificial death, and thus becomes the life-giving head of his body, the church. Paul expresses more fully the life-giving nature of Jesus' resurrection when he later states in relation to baptism:

> You were buried with him [Christ] in baptism, in which you were also raised up with him through faith in the working of God, who raised him from the dead. And you, who were dead in your trespasses and the uncircumcision of your flesh, God made alive together with him, having forgiven us all our trespasses, having canceled the bond which stood against us with its legal demands; this he set aside, nailing it to the cross. He disarmed the principalities and powers and made public example of them, triumphing over them all in him. (Col 2:12–15)

Those, therefore, who are united to him as members of his body, the members of the church, share in his new risen life. "Therefore, if anyone is in Christ, he is a new creation; the old has passed away, behold, the new has come" (2 Cor 5:17).

Sixth, the hymn began by declaring that the beloved Son "is the image of the invisible God." The humanity of Jesus is the supreme icon of the invisible God, for he who is the man Jesus is the Father's Son. To behold Jesus, the Son, is to behold his Father (see John 12:45; 14:9). To be members, then of Christ's risen humanity, to live within the church, is to share in his Sonship and so become his iconic image and, therefore, become, in him, adopted children of the Father. "For you did not receive the spirit of slavery to fall back into fear, but you have the spirit of sonship. When we cry, 'Abba! Father!' it is the Spirit himself bearing witness with our spirit that we are children of God, and if children, then heirs, heirs of God and fellow heirs with Christ" (Rom 8:14–17; see also Gal 4:6–7). Because of our sonship in Christ, "we all, with unveiled faces, beholding the glory of the Lord, are being changed into his likeness from one degree of glory to another; for this comes from the Lord who is the Spirit" (2 Cor 3:18). This transformation into the ever-increasing glorification in Christ Jesus culminates when we share fully in his resurrected glory at the end of time, and so become fully children of his Father in communion with his Holy Spirit.

The entirety of the Colossian hymn is a lyrical presentation of the manner in which Jesus became Jesus–YHWH-Saves. The first strophe, by declaring that the beloved Father's Son is the image of the invisible God provides the theological foundation for Jesus' primacy, for all things were created through, in and for him. All that is created, whether heavenly or earthly, co-inhere or are held together within his creative sustaining power. Moreover, within the Son's act of creation, he reveals, as the Son, his invisible Father, who is the fount of all being and life. Furthermore, the created order now becomes the stage upon which the Son will enact his saving acts wherein he will establish his saving primacy. The second strophe subsequently emphasizes that it is through his saving acts that Jesus merits his resurrection so as to be the first-born from the death. Jesus thus becomes Jesus for he becomes the head of his body, the church, in whom he reconciles all those united to him with his Father, having made peace by the blood of his cross. As YHWH-Saves, Jesus, in whom the fullness of divinity dwells bodily, then, holds primacy of place within the order of creation and redemption, for all possess their existence in him; and only in him do those who believe have eternal life with the Father in communion with the Holy Spirit. At this juncture we can turn to the Letter to the Ephesians.

The Primacy of Christ in the Ephesian Hymn

Scripture scholars argue that the Colossian hymn influenced Ephesians 1:3–14 both in liturgical style and in christological content.[22] Such similarity is immediately evident in the opening verses. God the Father of our Lord Jesus Christ is to be blessed because he has "blessed us in Christ with every spiritual blessing in the heavenly places."[23] First then, the spiritual blessing that pertains to the divine realm is that the Father "chose us in him [Jesus Christ] before the foundation of the world." As in the Colossian hymn, the primacy of Christ is determined by the Father from all eternity, for his primordial pre-eminence is manifested in that all human beings were chosen to abide in him before the creation of the world. In conformity with Colossians, he is "the first-born of all creation" in that human beings come

22. See MacDonald, *Colossians and Ephesians*, 206–7. Besides MacDonald's commentary on the hymn (pp. 196–214), see also Schnackenburg, *Ephesians*, 44–69; Williamson, *Ephesians*, 27–44.

23. MacDonald states: "There is general consensus among interpreters that the form of Eph 1:3–14 draws its origin from the extended blessing (*barakah*) found in the OT and Jewish worship." MacDonald, *Colossians and Ephesians*, 206. See also Fee, *Pauline Christology*, 343–44. All Scripture passages in this section are from Ephesians 1:3–14 unless otherwise noted.

to be only in so far as they are destined to be, and so abide, in him. To be chosen *in* Jesus Christ means that he, in accordance with the Father's will, is the reason or end for which human beings were created. The creation of humankind has no rationale in itself. The purpose of its coming to be is to exist in Christ Jesus. In other words, as in Colossians, to be chosen *in* Christ is to be created *for* Christ. Men and women were fundamentally created to live in Christ as the Father's gift to him.

Second, while we were eternally chosen in Christ and for Christ, we were, in so being chosen, to "be holy and blameless before him [the Father]," that is, to be as holy and as sinless as Jesus, the Father's Son. To ensure this, the Father "destined us in love to be his sons through Jesus Christ, according to his will, and to the praise of his glorious grace which he freely bestowed on us in his Beloved." While primacy belongs to Jesus, the Father's beloved Son, yet so much did the Father love us that through his Beloved we too are able to become the Father's holy and blameless sons. We become beloved children of the Father by abiding in Jesus, his beloved Son. This is the express will of the Father to whom we owe praise for the grace that he has bestowed upon us.

Third, this filial relationship with the Father in and through his Son Jesus, an intimate transformative communion with the Father that exceeds that of merely being his creatures, is achieved only by means of Jesus' saving acts. "In him [Jesus] we have redemption through his blood, the forgiveness of our trespasses, according to the riches of his [the Father's] grace which he lavished upon us." Here we have clear echoes of the Colossian hymn—"through him [Jesus] to reconcile to himself all things, whether on earth or in heaven, making peace by the blood of his cross" (Col 1:20). The blood that Jesus shed on the cross brings peace because that redemptive-blood obtained for us the forgiveness of our sins. By abiding in Jesus, the Father's beloved Son, we are reconciled in his very self and, therefore, we are at peace with the Father, for we now abide in his Son as his holy and blameless children.

Fourth, while reference to his sacrificial saving death on the cross is clearly expressed, Jesus' resurrection is implied, but in a manner that it is taken for granted.[24] Only if, as professed in Colossians, Jesus becomes the risen glorious Lord, "the beginning, the first-born from the dead" as merited in his saving death, is it possible for God's eternal will to be accomplished, that is, that we abide in him, the Father's Son, as holy and blameless children of the Father (Col 1:18). Thus, we were chosen before the foundation of the

---

24. Shortly following the hymn, Paul does state that the Father displayed his power "when he raised him [Jesus] from the dead" (Eph 1:20).

world not only to exist in Christ in whom we were created, but we were also, according to God's eternal will and purpose, to be recreated in his resurrected filial likeness as children of his Father. In accord with Colossians, we perceive here the twofold primacy of Christ-Jesus is pre-eminent within the order of creation and within the order of redemption, for human beings were predestined, and so chosen, before the foundation of the world to abide in Christ both as our creator and as our redeemer.

Fifth, the Ephesian hymn now comes to its culminating climax. All of the above is true because the Father has made known "the mystery of his will, according to his purpose which he set forth in Christ as a plan for the fullness of time, to unite all things in him, things in heaven and things on earth." The supreme mystery, a mystery that the Father willed from before the foundation of the world and inaugurated in creation, is that, in the fullness of time, at the end of history, everything in heaven (the thrones, dominions, principalities and authorities enumerated in the Colossian hymn), and on earth (those human beings who abide in Jesus) be united to, summed up, or taken up into and so find fulfillment in [Greek, *anakephalaiōsis*] Christ-Jesus, the risen incarnate, Spirit-filled Father's beloved Son. The truth of this mystery expresses Jesus' supreme primacy and absolute pre-eminence within the whole of the cosmic order—he is universal Savior and definitive Lord.[25]

Lastly, the Ephesian text concludes by professing that we who have believed in Christ "were sealed with the promised Holy Spirit, who is the guarantee of our inheritance until we acquire possession of it, to the praise of his [the Father's] glory." Here we find the essential role of the Holy Spirit. He who makes it possible for men and women to find their fulfillment in and with Jesus, and ultimately the whole of creation, is the Holy Spirit, for it is the Spirit who transforms us, in our being united to the risen Jesus the Son, into holy and blameless children of the Father. This indwelling transformative recreation in the Holy Spirit is the guarantee that we will achieve the fullness of our divine inheritance—eternal life in communion with Jesus at the end of time (see 2 Cor 1:22).

All that Paul declares within the Ephesian hymn, similar to that contained in Colossians, is an articulation of Jesus becoming Jesus–YHWH-Saves. What is unique in Ephesians is Paul's emphasis that the whole of human history, from beginning to end, wherein Jesus becomes Jesus is in accordance with his Father's preconceived plan, his eternal will, the mystery

---

25. Though, unlike the Colossian hymn, the Ephesian hymn does not mention Jesus being the head of his body, the church, yet this supreme mystery of all finding unity in Christ is a similar christological expression of this one reality–all creation will be recreated in Christ by being in communion with him who is the head of his body, the church.

of uniting all things in Jesus, his beloved Spirit-filled Son incarnate. The primacy of Jesus is achieved, and so merited, in his fulfilling his eternal Father's plan, in his becoming Jesus–YHWH-Saves. Such absolute pre-eminence will be fully displayed, in accordance with his Father's will, when Jesus returns in glory and the whole of creation will share fully in his risen glory and in particular human beings will become fully children of his Father in communion with the Holy Spirit. For the entirety of such a lavish and marvelous plan the Father is to be praised, blessed and glorified.

The Primacy of Christ in the Philippian Hymn

We come now to the last Pauline hymn within our study: Philippians 2:5–11. This hymn is more straightforward and more christologically focused than the previous two hymns. As with the other two, scholars debate as to whether Paul actually is the author of the hymn or whether he was employing an already existing hymn. Either way, the hymn clearly professes the primacy of Jesus and the reasons why he is pre-eminent above all.[26]

Paul exhorts his readers that, if they wish to complete his joy, they are to be "of the same mind, having the same love, being in full accord and of one mind."[27] In order to be in such mutual loving accord, they are to "have the same mind among themselves, which was in Christ Jesus." At this point, Paul proclaims the hymn that illustrates the mind of Jesus Christ.

Christ Jesus, "though he was in the form of God, did not count equality with God a thing to be grasped, but emptied himself, taking the form of a servant, being born in the likeness of men." Here we find two contrasting actions. First, while Christ Jesus "was in the form of God, he did not count equality with God a thing to be grasped." To be "in the form [*morphē*] of God" is for Christ Jesus to possess the same eternal divine nature as God. However, this implies that Christ Jesus is not the only "one" who is God. There must be "someone" else who is also in the form of God. Moreover, if he were not divine in a different manner from the other who is also divine, there would be no divine "other" with whom he would be equal, and so an equality to which he might choose to grasp. Thus, there must be two eternal subjects who are both equally God. Yet, Jesus, as an historical man, is not in the form of God and, therefore, not equal to God. Similarly, Jesus is the Christ in that he, as an historical man, is fully anointed with God's Holy Spirit. He was not

---

26. For commentaries on the Philippian hymn, see Fee, *Pauline Christology*, 372–401; Martin, *Philippians 2:5–11*; Thurston and Ryan, *Philippians*, 80–92.

27. All Scripture quotations in this section are from Philippians 2:1–11 unless otherwise noted.

the Christ from all eternity because Jesus, who is the Christ, came to exist as man only in time. Who then is the "Christ Jesus" who is in the form of God and yet did not count this equality with God something to be grasped? The answer to this question is resolved in the very last declaration. Jesus Christ is to be declared Lord "to the glory of God the Father." If God is the eternal Father, he must have an eternal divine Son, and it is that divine Son who is in the form of God, equal in divine form (being) as the Father, who did not count his divine equality with his Father something to be grasped. The Son only became the Christ, then, in his not grasping his equal divinity to his Father, but rather in his coming to be in the form (*morphē*) of man, that is, for the Son of God to come to exist as man. He who is the Son of God existing as man is Jesus—the anointed Messiah.

Before proceeding to the second action, that of taking on the form of a servant, we must define more clearly what it means for Christ Jesus, the Father's Son, not to "grasp" (*harpagmos*). This word is never employed in the Greek Old Testament and is also rare in secular literature. Its root meaning is that of "robbery," which would not seem to apply in the present context. Scholars conclude that *harpagmos* connotes that someone does not take advantage of his or her position for selfish reasons and gain. Thus, Christ Jesus, who is divinely equal to the Father as the Father's Son, does not, then, take advantage of his divine status, selfishly clinging to his divine prerogatives. Instead, he "emptied himself, taking on the form of a servant, being born in the likeness of men." This, then, brings us to the second action which is in contrast to the first—that of "grasping."

Instead of selfishly grasping on to his divinity, the Son "emptied [*ekenōsen*] himself." What then is the nature of this "emptying?" Does it mean that the Son divested himself, either completely or in some lesser manner, of his divinity and, in so doing, came to exist as man? There have been in the past some theologians who have argued for such a position— what is known as Kenotic Christology.[28] However, such an interpretation is fallacious for at least two reasons. First, it is ontologically impossible for God to cease being God, either in his totality or in some lesser form. God as God cannot cease to be, for if he could cease to be, he would not have been God in the first place. Second, from a christological perspective, even if God could cease to be God or empty himself of some divine attributes, such as omnipotence and omniscience, so as to become man, it would no longer be truly God who is man. He would either have transformed himself into man and so ceased to be God, as a caterpillar becomes a butterfly, and, in so doing, ceases to be a caterpillar. Or he would have emptied

28. For a critique of Kenotic Christology, see my *Does God Change?*, 101–23.

himself of some of his divine attributes in becoming man, in which case he who is man would not be fully divine but some lesser variation of God. But such is contrary to the very biblical proclamation and the church's doctrinal tradition. The very nature of the Incarnation demands that it is truly *God* who truly *is* truly *man*.[29]

For the Son of God to "empty himself" consists then both in his not selfishly clinging to his divinity with its divine prerogatives, and in his simultaneous taking on the "form [*morphē*] of a servant." Such an understanding is in keeping with what Paul exhorts the Philippians to do. They are not to grasp, in selfish conceit, to seek their own interests, but instead to look "to the interests of others" (Phil 2:3–4). By taking on the form of a servant, the Son of God was not selfishly looking to his own divine interests, but, in love, seeking the good of others, that is, the salvation of humankind. The word "form" (*morphē*) is employed here as a metaphor, since a person's metaphysical nature or essence (what one is) is never one of being a servant. Yet, by immediately stating, "being found in the likeness [*homoiōmati*] of man," the term "form" or "nature" does now assume an ontological meaning, for it refers to being "born in the likeness of men." In becoming man, the Son assumes not simply the nature of man but, in coming to exist as man, he does so as a man who is a servant. Jesus' manhood is characterized by or stamped with the "form" of servanthood.[30] This twofold act, that of not "grasping" but rather of "emptying" himself in the taking on the form of a servant in coming to exist as man, is then the Son of God's primordial act of humility—the foundational humble act from which all of the subsequent humble acts flow. The hymn next narrates these subsequent humbling-acts.

Not only did the Son humble himself in becoming a servant-man, but also in "being found in human form he humbled himself and became obedient unto death, even death on a cross." The very nature of being a servant demands obedience, and so Jesus, the Father's Son, was humanly

---

29. The Council of Nicaea (AD 325) declared that the Son is one in being or consubstantial with the Father, and so as divine as the Father is divine, within the context of the Incarnation. While existing as man, the Son of God is truly and fully divine.

30. In casting Jesus in the form of a servant, the hymn is alluding to the Suffering Servant Songs within the Prophet Isaiah (see Isa 42:1–4; 49:1–6; 50:4–11; 52:13—53:12). Jesus as the Suffering-Servant-Son, through his obedient suffering on behalf of humankind's salvation, will be raised up to his Father into everlasting glory. The Philippian hymn, therefore, is in accord with what is enacted and declared within John's baptism. There Jesus assumes his saving commission by becoming the Suffering-Servant-Son and, in so doing, his Father declares: "This is my beloved Son, with whom I am well pleased" (Matt 3:13–17). Equally, this is also in accord with the Gospel of John wherein Jesus consistently declares that he is the Father's obedient Son, an obedience that leads to the salvific hour of his death and resurrection (see John 4:34; 5:30; 6:38; 12:27; 17:4).

obedient to his Father not only unto death but even unto death on the cross. There is no one who is more humble than the incarnate Son of God, for he not only did not selfishly grasp at his divinity and emptied himself in becoming man, but he also, as man, obediently humbled himself to the extreme—to the point of death upon a cross, the most humiliating manner of death ever conceived. Implied within this humble obedience is the sacrificial nature of Jesus' death—a death wherein he offered his holy and innocent life to his Father so as to obtain humankind's forgiveness for sin and so reconciliation with God.

What is professed here in the first part of the Philippian hymn conforms to Colossians and Ephesians. Colossians speaks of the fullness of God dwelling in Christ and "through him to reconcile to himself all things, whether on earth or in heaven, making peace through the blood of his cross" (Col 1:20). Similarly, Ephesians declares that in him (Jesus Christ) we have redemption through his blood, the forgiveness of our trespasses (Eph 1:7). As we will now see, Philippians, in accord with Colossians and Ephesians, also affirms that Jesus' redemptive death is the cause of his exaltation.

At this juncture, then, within the hymn we arrive at the most important word within the hymn—"therefore" (*dio*). Because of all that has gone before, because of all of the Son's acts of humility beginning with his incarnation and concluding with his humiliating death on the cross, God, his Father, "has highly exalted him and bestowed on him the name which is above every name." The Son's incarnation as man and the saving works that he has enacted as man have merited the Father's response to all that he has salvifically achieved—his pre-eminent exaltation. This exaltation resides in the Father raising Jesus gloriously from the dead. As in the Colossian and Ephesian hymns, Jesus is "the first-born from the dead" so that he might be pre-eminent in every way, and thus capable, as the risen Christ, of all things finding their unity in him (see Col 1:18; Eph 1:9–10). Moreover, within the Philippian hymn, this exaltation is certified and attested in the Father bestowing upon him a name that exceeds all names: the name of Jesus–YHWH-Saves. Ephesians declares the same: The Father "made him sit at his right hand in the heavenly places, far above all rule and authority and power and dominion, and above every name that is named, not only in this age but also in that which is to come" (Eph 1:20–21).

Therefore, "at the name of Jesus every knee should bow, in heaven and on earth and under the earth, and every tongue confess that Jesus Christ is Lord, to the glory of God the Father." This supreme exaltation of Jesus' name consists in his being proclaimed "Lord," and such glorying is, as in Colossians and Ephesians, cosmic in scope. Jesus is "Lord" of heaven and earth and under the earth; and, therefore, every knee throughout the entire universe is to bow before him and the tongue of every creature, no matter the manner of its existence, is to declare him to be such. Significantly, it is the *incarnate* Son of God, the man Jesus Christ, who is to be confessed as Lord. Thus, neither angels of whatever rank nor any founder of any other religion, is Lord. The Father has singularly bestowed upon Jesus alone such cosmic pre-eminence and earthly primacy. Moreover, to affirm and confess that Jesus Christ is the only Lord is to "the glory of God the Father," for such a proclamation is a confirmation and endorsement of the Father's righteous decree. All then who knowingly and willingly refuse to make such a confession are not simply offending Jesus but are, even more so, insulting his Father. Of course, at the end of time, when he comes in glory, every creature will, either in exuberant joy or in fearful terror, eternally confess and proclaim Jesus Christ to be Lord to the glory of God the Father. Again, what is professed in Philippians concurs with the Ephesians' declaration of the divine mystery that, in the fullness of time, all things, in heaven and on earth, would be united in him (see Eph 1:10). Likewise, in being the head of his body, the church, Jesus reconciles all things in himself (see Col 1:18, 20).

Moreover, what we find in the Philippian hymn, as in Colossians and Ephesians, is a clear, straightforward proclamation of how Jesus became Jesus–YHWH-Saves. The initiating act, the *sine qua non* act, is the Incarnation itself, for, in that humbling, incarnational act, the Son of God came to exist as the servant-man, Jesus. As the humble obedient servant, Jesus performed, in all humility, the saving will of his Father, and in so doing definitively became Jesus–YHWH-Saves. Precisely because Jesus became Jesus in enacting his Father's saving will, his Father raised him to glory and exalted his name, Jesus, to be the name that is above every other name. All of creation is to bow in adoration at the sound of his name and every creature within the entire cosmos is to profess that he, Jesus, is Lord, for he is YHWH-Saves. He alone is the author of a new heaven and a new earth; the one in whom, through whom, with whom, and for whom human beings come to be children of his Father through the indwelling of his Spirit.

Conclusion

By way of conclusion, I will not summarize what we have learned in examining Paul's three christological hymns—that should now be self-evident. Here, I wish to highlight four points contained within our study, points that I mentioned at the onset of this essay.

The first is that Jesus, as the Son of God incarnate, established, through his death and resurrection, a new order of salvation. Because of

Jesus' saving actions, it is now possible to have a new kind of relationship with the Father by being united to Christ in communion with the Holy Spirit. Such a relationship with the Father was not possible prior to Jesus' salvific actions. Second, only by being united to the risen Christ Jesus is one able to share in, and so reap the benefits of, his salvific works. These two truths—Jesus' saving actions as such and our ability to partake of them by living in Christ—establish Jesus as the universal Savior and definitive Lord, and thus, why he is pre-eminent, why Jesus holds primacy and why his name is above every other name.

Third, while *Dominus Iesus* accentuated the first point, Jesus' saving actions, it did not do justice to the second point—that Jesus is supreme, for only in communion with him is one united to his Father through the indwelling of the Holy Spirit. Jesus holds primacy of place as Savior and is the cosmic Lord of all because the Father eternally predestined that all would be united to him, he who is the Spirit-filled Christ. I hope that this essay demonstrates that this second truth is essential for fully grasping Jesus' singular primacy.

Lastly, in relation to the issue of the pluralism of religions and other religious founders, the three Pauline Hymns provide a resounding answer. They robustly profess, unreservedly teach, and ardently affirm that Jesus alone, and no other, holds singularity of place within the order of creation and within the order of redemption, for he alone, and no other, was willed by the Father to hold such supreme pre-eminence and primacy—honors that the Father himself bestowed upon him. Thus, Christianity, with its prefigurement within Judaism, are the only religions positively and un-equivocally willed by the Father, for Judaism prophetically anticipated Jesus, and he is the founder of Christianity. Actually, Jesus literally embodies in himself the entire Christian Gospel—the all-inclusive Good News. So may all creation, by the power of the Holy Spirit, declare that Jesus Christ is Lord, to the glory of God the Father. In becoming Lord, Jesus has become, and will be forever, Jesus–YHWH-Saves.

Bibliography

Brown, Raymond E. *An Introduction to the New Testament*. New York: Doubleday, 1997.
Congregation for the Doctrine of the Faith. *"Dominus Iesus": On the Unicity and Salvific Universality of Jesus Christ and the Church*. https://www.vatican.va/roman_curia/congregations/cfaith/documents/rc_con_cfaith_doc_20000806_dominus-iesus_en.html.
Fee, Gordon. *Pauline Christology: An Exegetical-Theological Study*. Peabody, MA: Hendrickson, 2007.

Francis, Pope. *A Document on Human Fraternity for World Peace and Living Together.* https://www.vatican.va/content/francesco/en/travels/2019/outside/documents/papa-francesco_20190204_documento-fratellanza-umana.html.

MacDonald, Margaret Y. *Colossians and Ephesians.* Sacra Pagina 17. Collegeville, MN: Liturgical, 2000.

Martin, Ralph P. *A Hymn of Christ: Philippians 2:5–11 in Recent Interpretation & in the Setting of Early Christian Worship.* Downers Grove, IL: InterVarsity, 1997.

Schnackenburg, Rudolf. *The Epistle to the Ephesians.* Edinburgh: T. & T. Clark, 1991.

Thurston, Bonnie B., and Judith Ryan. *Philippians and Philemon.* Sacra Pagina 10. Collegeville, MN: Liturgical, 2005.

Weinandy, Thomas G. *Does God Change? The Word's Becoming in the Incarnation.* Still River, MA: St. Bede's, 1985.

———. *The Father's Spirit of Sonship: Reconceiving the Trinity.* Edinburgh: T. & T. Clark, 1995.

———. *Jesus Becoming Jesus.* Vol. 1, *A Theological Interpretation of the Synoptic Gospels.* Washington, DC: Catholic University of America Press, 2018.

———. *Jesus Becoming Jesus.* Vol. 2, *A Theological Interpretation of the Gospel of John.* Washington, DC: Catholic University of America Press, 2018.

———. "The Will of God the Father: To Unite All Things in Christ." https://www.catholicworldreport.com/2019/06/02/pope-francis-the-uniqueness-of-christ-and-the-will-of-the-father/

Williamson, Peter S. *Ephesians.* Catholic Commentary on Sacred Scripture 3. Grand Rapids: Baker Academic, 2009.

Patrick J. Hartin

Bibliography of Scholarly Publications

LISTED BELOW ARE THE academic writings of Fr. Patrick Hartin, which span forty-five years. Throughout his career, Fr. Hartin has also written for publications devoted to high school and adult religious education and formation. This work has included high school textbooks in biblical studies—*In the Beginning Was the Word: Biblical Studies for Standard 8* (Johannesburg: Premier, 1975); and *The Word Endures for Ever: Biblical Studies for Standards 9 and 10* (Johannesburg: Premier, 1977)—as well as columns with advice for religious education teachers and essays aimed at adult religious formation. These have appeared in *Religious Education, The Wayside Messenger, Khulisa, The Southern Cross* (a South African Catholic newspaper), *The Trefoil, Lumen Christi,* and *Give Us This Day.* The enduring value of this work, with its pastoral themes, reflects Fr. Hartin's untiring commitment to the cause of biblical studies within the Catholic Church.

1976

"Gnosticism and the New Testament." *Theologia Evangelica* 9, 131–46.

1985

"A Community in Crisis: The Christology of the Johannine Community as a Point at Issue." *Neotestamentica* 19, 37–49.

1986

"*Anakephalaiōsthai ta panta en tō Christō* (Eph 1:10)." In *A South African Perspective on the New Testament: Essays by South African New Testament Scholars, Presented to Bruce Manning Metzger (Emeritus Professor Princeton University) during His Visit to South Africa,* edited by Patrick J. Hartin and Jacobus H. Petzer, 228–37. Leiden: Brill.

"Deconstruction and Theology." *Journal of Theology for Southern Africa* 54, 25–34.

A South African Perspective on the New Testament: Essays by South African New Testament Scholars, Presented to Bruce Manning Metzger (Emeritus Professor Princeton University) during His Visit to South Africa, edited by Patrick J. Hartin and Jacobus H. Petzer. Leiden: Brill.

1987

"The Angst of Waiting: A Deconstructive Reading of Luke 12:35–40." *Journal of Literary Studies* 3, 42–56.

"An Inquiry into the Character of Ethical Statements and Their Verification and Justification." *Koers: Bulletin for Christian Scholarship* 52, 310–35.

"New Testament Ethics: Some Trends in More Recent Research." *Journal of Theology for Southern Africa* 59, 35–41.

"The Pharisaic Roots of Jesus and the Early Church." *Neotestamentica* 21, 113–24.

1988

"Angst in the Household: A Deconstructive Reading of the Parable of the Supervising Servant (Lk 12:41–48)." *Neotestamentica* 22, 373–90.

"Apartheid and the Scriptures: The Contribution of Albert Geyser in This Polemic." *Journal of Theology for Southern Africa* 64, 20–33.

"Religious Instruction by the Churches." *Scriptura* 26, 1–7.

"Theology and Critical Rationalism: How Theology Faces the Challenge with a New Paradigm." In *Paradigms and Progress in Theology,* edited by Johann Mouton, 129–41. Pretoria: Humanities Science Research Council.

1989

"The Biblical Creation Accounts and Evolution: A Catholic Perspective." *Koers: Bulletin for Christian Scholarship* 54, 290–302.

"James and the Q Sermon on the Mount/Plain." *Society of Biblical Literature Seminar Papers* 28, 440–57.

1990

"Perspectives on the Death of Jesus: Religious or Political?" In *'n Vriend in ons Poorte: Studies obgedra aan Prof. Paul du Plessis*, edited by J. H. Coetzee et al., 94–111. Johannesburg: Rand Afrikaans University.

"The Role of Peter in the Fourth Gospel." *Neotestamentica* 24, 49–61.

1991

"A Community of the Forgiven Responding to the God of Forgiveness (Being a Serving Community)." In *Theological Reflections on the Pastoral Plan*, edited by Patrick J. Hartin et al., 204–24. Pietermaritzburg: Cluster.

"Criteria for Koinonia with God (1 John)." In *Teologie in Konteks: Feesbundel vir A. B. du Toit*, edited by J. H. Roberts et al., 515–32. Pretoria: Orion, Halfway House.

"Disseminating the Word: A Deconstructive Reading of Mark 4:1–9 and 4:13–20." In *Text and Interpretation: New Approaches to the Criticism of the New Testament*, edited by Patrick J. Hartin and Jacobus H. Petzer, 187–200. Leiden: Brill.

"Ecclesiastical Authority in Moral Matters with Special Reference to Sexual Ethics." *Grace and Truth* 10, 111–31.

James and the Q Sayings of Jesus. Journal for the Study of the New Testament, Supplement Series 47. Sheffield: Sheffield Academic. *See* 2015

"Jewish Christianity: Focus on Antioch in the First Century." *Scriptura* 36, 35–50.

"Methodological Principles in Interpreting the Relevance of the New Testament for a New South Africa." *Scriptura* 37, 1–16.

"'Remain in Me' (John 15:5): The Foundation of the Ethical and Its Consequences in the Farewell Discourses." *Neotestamentica* 25, 341–56.

"*Sensus Fidelium*: A Roman Catholic Reflection on Its Significance for Ecumenical Thought." *Journal of Ecumenical Studies* 28, 74–87.

Text and Interpretation: New Approaches to the Criticism of the New Testament, edited by Patrick J. Hartin and Jacobus H. Petzer. Leiden: Brill.

Theological Reflections on the Pastoral Plan, edited by Patrick J. Hartin et al. Pietermaritzburg: Cluster.

1992

Third World Challenges in the Teaching of Biblical Studies. Occasional Papers of the Institute for Antiquity and Christianity 25. Claremont, CA: Institute for Antiquity and Christianity, Claremont Graduate School.

"Towards a Christian Vision as the Basis for Ethical Decisions." *Scriptura* 42, 65–73.

1993

"'Come Now, You Rich, Weep and Wail . . .' (James 5:1–9)." *Journal of Theology for Southern Africa* 84, 57–63.

"The Religious Nature of First Century Galilee." *Neotestamentica* 27, 331–50.

"The Role of the Disciples in the Jesus Story Communicated by Mark." *Koers: Bulletin for Christian Scholarship* 58, 35–52.
"The Role of the Women Disciples in Mark's Narrative." *Theologia Evangelica* 26, 91–102.

1994

"Ethics and the New Testament: How Do We Get from There to Here?" In *The Relevance of Theology for the 1990s*, edited by Johann Mouton and Bernard C. Lategan, 511–25. HSRC Series on Methodology. Pretoria: Human Sciences Research Council.
"The Wisdom and Apocalyptic Layers of the Sayings Gospel Q: What Is Their Significance?" *Hervormde Teologiese Studies* 50, 556–82.
"'Yet Wisdom Is Justified by Her Children' (Q 7:35): A Rhetorical and Compositional Analysis of Divine Sophia in Q." In *Conflict and Invention: Literary, Rhetorical, and Social Studies on the Sayings Gospel Q*, edited by John S. Kloppenborg, 151–64. Valley Forge, PA: Trinity.

1996

"'Call to Be Perfect through Suffering' (James 1,2–4): The Concept of Perfection in the Epistle of James and the Sermon on the Mount." *Biblica* 77, 477–92.
"Evaluations and Responses to Q 4:9–13." In *Documenta Q: Reconstructions of Q through Two Centuries of Gospel Research: Excerpted, Sorted and Evaluated: Q 4:1–13,16: The Temptations of Jesus Nazara*, edited by Christoph Heil, passim. Leuven: Peeters.
Review of *Restoring the Diaspora: Discursive Structure and Purpose in the Epistle of James*, by Timothy B. Cargal. *Toronto Journal of Theology* 12, 96–98.
"'Who Is Wise and Understanding among You?' (James 3:13): An Analysis of Wisdom, Eschatology and Apocalypticism in the Epistle of James." *Society of Biblical Literature Seminar Papers* 35, 483–503. *See* 1997, 2005

1997

"Christian Ethics in a Pluralistic Society: Towards a Theology of Compromise." *Religion and Theology* 4, 21–34.
"The Poor in the Epistle of James and the Gospel of Thomas." *Hervormde Teologiese Studies* 53, 146–62.
"'Who Is Wise and Understanding among You?' (James 3:13): An Analysis of Wisdom, Eschatology and Apocalypticism in the Epistle of James." *Hervormde Teologiese Studies* 53, 969–99. *See* 1996, 2005

1998

"Disciples as Authorities within Matthew's Christian-Jewish Community." *Neotestamentica* 32, 389–404.

1999

Review of *Community of the Wise: The Letter of James,* by Robert W. Wall. *Review of Biblical Literature* (February). https://www.bookreviews.org/pdf/2351_1549.pdf.
"The Search for the True Self in the Gospel of Thomas, the Book of Thomas and the Hymn of the Pearl." *Hervormde Teologiese Studies* 55, 1001–21.
A Spirituality of Perfection: Faith in Action in the Letter of James. Collegeville, MN: Liturgical.

2000

"Apocryphal and Pseudepigraphical Sources in the New Testament." In *Dictionary of New Testament Background,* edited by Craig A. Evans and Stanley E. Porter, 69–71. Downers Grove, IL: InterVarsity.
"Poor" and "Wealth." In *Eerdmans Dictionary of the Bible,* edited by David Noel Freedman et al., 1070–71, 1371. Grand Rapids, MI: Eerdmans.
"The Woes against The Pharisees (Matthew 23,1–39): The Reception and Development of Q 11,39–52 within the Matthean Community." In *From Quest to Q: Festschrift James M. Robinson,* edited by Jon Ma. Asgeirsson et al., 265–83. Leuven: Peeters.

2003

A Commentary on the Letter of James. Sacra Pagina 14. Collegeville, MN: Liturgical.
See 2009

2004

James of Jerusalem: Heir to Jesus of Nazareth. Interfaces Series. Collegeville, MN: Liturgical.

2005

"'Who Is Wise and Understanding among You?' (James 3:13): An Analysis of Wisdom, Eschatology, and Apocalypticism in the Letter of James." In *Conflicted Boundaries in Wisdom and Apocalypticism,* edited by Benjamin G. Wright III and Lawrence M. Wills, 149–68. Society for Biblical Literature, Symposium Series 35. Atlanta, GA: Society of Biblical Literature. *See* 1996, 1997

2006

James, First Peter, Jude, Second Peter. New Collegeville Bible Commentary, New Testament 10. Collegeville, MN: Liturgical.

"James of Jerusalem in the Early Christian Church." *The Bible Today* 44, 273–78.

"The Letter of James: Its Vision, Ethics, and Ethos." In *Identity, Ethics, and Ethos in the New Testament*, edited by Jan G. Van der Watt, 445–71. Beihefte zur Zeitschrift für die neutestamentliche Wissenschaft und die Kunde der älteren Kirche 141. Berlin: de Gruyter.

"The Role and Significance of the Character of Thomas in the Acts of Thomas." In *Thomasine Traditions in Antiquity: The Social and Cultural World of the Gospel of Thomas*, edited by Jon Ma. Asgeirsson et al., 239–53. Nag Hammadi and Manichaean Studies 59. Leiden: Brill.

2007

"The Religious Context of the Letter of James." In *Jewish Christianity Reconsidered: Rethinking Ancient Groups and Texts*, edited by Matt Jackson-McCabe, 203–31. Minneapolis: Fortress.

Review of *Character Ethics and the New Testament: Moral Dimensions of Scripture*, edited by Robert Brawley. *Review of Biblical Literature* (September). https://www.bookreviews.org/pdf/5782_6102.pdf.

2008

"Ethics in the Letter of James, the Gospel of Matthew, and the Didache: Their Place in Early Christian Literature." In *Matthew, James, and Didache: Three Related Documents in Their Jewish and Christian Settings*, edited by Huub van de Sandt and Jürgen K. Zangenberg, 289–314. Atlanta, GA: Society of Biblical Literature.

Review of *Ephesians: Empowerment to Walk in Love for the Unity of All in Christ*," by John Paul Heil. *Catholic Biblical Quarterly* 70, 372–73.

Review of *Four Times Peter: Portrayals of Peter in the Four Gospels and at Philippi*, by Richard J. Cassidy. *Review of Biblical Literature* (March). https://www.bookreviews.org/pdf/5868_6426.pdf.

Review of *Not by Paul Alone: The Formation of the Catholic Epistle Collection and the Christian Canon*, by David R. Nienhuis. *Review of Biblical Literature* (November). https://www.bookreviews.org/pdf/6406_6905.pdf.

2009

Apollos: Paul's Partner or Rival? Paul's Social Network: Brothers and Sisters in Faith Series. Collegeville, MN: Liturgical.

A Commentary on the Letter of James. Sacra Pagina 14. Second edition revised and expanded. Collegeville, MN: The Liturgical. *See* 2003

"The General Letters." "The Letter of James." "The First Letter of Peter." "The Second Letter of Peter." "The Letter of Jude." In *The New Collegeville Bible Commentary: The New Testament*, edited by Daniel Durken, 767–806, 822–27. Collegeville, MN: Liturgical.

An Introduction to the Bible. With Robert Kugler. Grand Rapids: Eerdmans.

"James and the Jesus Tradition: Some Theological Reflections and Implications." In *The Catholic Epistles and Apostolic Tradition: A New Perspective on James to Jude*, edited by Karl-Wilhelm Niebuhr and Robert W. Wall, 55–70. Waco, TX: Baylor University Press.

Review of *Purity and Worldview in the Epistle of James*, by Darian Lockett. *The Expository Times* 120, 460.

Review of *A Synopsis of the Apocryphal Nativity and Infancy Narratives*, by James Keith Elliott. *Novum Testamentum* 51, 196–98.

"Two Sayings Gospels: The Gospel of Thomas and The Sayings Gospel Q." *The Bible Today* 47, 167–71.

2010

Review of *The Cradle, the Cross, and the Crown: An Introduction to the New Testament*, edited by Andreas J. Köstenberger et al. *Review of Biblical Literature* (August). https://www.bookreviews.org/pdf/7456_8139.pdf.

Review of *James: Zondervan Exegetical Commentary on the New Testament*, by Craig L. Blomberg and Mariam J. Kamell. *The Expository Times* 121, 254.

Review of *The Writings of the New Testament: An Interpretation*, by Luke Timothy Johnson. *Review of Biblical Literature* (August). https://www.bookreviews.org/pdf/7524_8209.pdf.

2011

Exploring the Spirituality of the Gospels. Collegeville, MN: Liturgical.

"Humility" and "Judgement." In *Dictionary of Ethics and Scripture*, edited by Joel B. Green, 389–90, 431–33. Grand Rapids: Baker Academic.

"James and Eschatology: Place and Function of Eschatology within a Letter to the 'Twelve Tribes in the Dispersion.'" In *Eschatology of the New Testament and Some Related Documents*, edited by Jan G. Van der Watt, 451–71. Wissenschaftliche Untersuchungen zum Neuen Testament 2, Reihe 315. Tübingen: Mohr Siebeck.

2014

"Wholeness in James and the Q Source." In *James, 1 & 2 Peter, and Early Jesus Traditions*, edited by Alicia J. Batten and John S. Kloppenborg, 35–57. London: Bloomsbury.

2015

"Faith-in-Action: An Ethic of 'Perfection.'" In *The Letter of James: The Christian Reflection Project: A Series in Faith and Ethics*, edited by Bob Kruschwitz, 20–28. Waco, TX: The Institute for Faith and Learning, Baylor University. https://www. baylor.edu/content/services/document.php/174970.pdf.

"Gospel of Thomas." In *Lexham Bible Dictionary*, edited by John D. Berry. Bellingham, WA: Lexham. https://app.logos.com/books/LLS%3ALBD/headwords/Gospel%20 of%20Thomas.

James and the "Q" Sayings of Jesus. Bloomsbury Academic Collections. London: Bloomsbury. *See* 1991

A Window into the Spirituality of Paul. Collegeville, MN: Liturgical.

2016

Exploring Biblical Kinship: Festschift in Honor of John J. Pilch, edited by Joan C. Campbell and Patrick J. Hartin. The Catholic Biblical Quarterly Monograph Series 55. Washington, DC: Catholic Biblical Association of America.

Review of *James Through the Centuries*, by David B. Gowler. *Catholic Biblical Quarterly* 78, 366–67.

2017

Review of *A Synopsis of the Apocryphal Nativity and Infancy Narratives: Second Edition, Revised and Expanded*, by James Keith Elliott. *Novum Testamentum* 59, 332–35.

2018

Review of *The Letter of James: Worship to Live By*, by John Paul Heil. *Review of Biblical Literature* (January). https://www.bookreviews.org/bookdetail.asp?TitleId=8948.

2021

"The General Letters." In *The Cambridge Companion to the New Testament*, edited by Patrick Gray, 290–312. Cambridge: Cambridge University Press.

"The Letter of James." In *The Jerome Biblical Commentary for the Twenty-First Century*, edited by John J. Collins et al. London: Bloomsbury. [forthcoming]